D0627271

Youth Leaving Foster Care

YOUTH LEAVING FOSTER CARE

A Developmental, Relationship-Based Approach to Practice

Wendy B. Smith

OXFORD

UNIVERSITY PRESS

Oxford University Press, Inc., publishes works that further
Oxford University's objective of excellence
in research, scholarship, and education.

Oxford   New York
Auckland   Cape Town   Dar es Salaam   Hong Kong   Karachi
Kuala Lumpur   Madrid   Melbourne   Mexico City   Nairobi
New Delhi   Shanghai   Taipei   Toronto

With offices in
Argentina   Austria   Brazil   Chile   Czech Republic   France   Greece
Guatemala   Hungary   Italy   Japan   Poland   Portugal   Singapore
South Korea   Switzerland   Thailand   Turkey   Ukraine   Vietnam

Published by Oxford University Press, Inc.
198 Madison Avenue, New York, New York 10016
www.oup.com

Oxford is a registered trademark of Oxford University Press

Smith, Wendy Benjamin, 1946- Youth leaving foster care : a developmental,
relationship-based approach to practice / Wendy B. Smith.
p. cm.
Includes bibliographical references and index.
ISBN 978-0-19-537559-6 (hardcover : alk. paper)
1. Foster children–Services for–United States. 2. Foster children—Psychology.
3. Foster children–Counseling of. 4. Foster children–Family relationships—United States.
5. Foster children—Deinstitutionalization—United States. 6. Ex-foster children—Social
conditions--United States . 7. Ex-foster children—Education—United States. 8. Foster
children—Government policy—United States. I. Title.
HV881.S66 2011
362.73'3—dc22
2010049034

---

1 3 5 7 9 8 6 4 2

Printed in the United States of America
on acid-free paper

For all children who have been in foster care

ACKNOWLEDGMENTS

The idea for this book took shape some years ago, when I developed a course on youth leaving foster care, and could not find a text on the subject. I had treated alumni of foster care in my psychotherapy practice, had helped to design a transitional living program informed by attachment theory, and had long been active in a nonprofit organization that assistsyouth who have been in care. Most of what I had read focused on a single perspective—policy, program, outcomes, or youth narratives—and theoretical frameworks were largely absent. My goal in writing this book was to integrate these interpenetrating, overlapping elements and to ground them in theory. I was fortunate to have my idea met with enthusiasm by many individuals, including Maura Roessner of Oxford University Press.

There are many people to thank for their contributions to this book. First, the young people who generously shared their time and their stories with me—many youth from California Youth Connection, and at greater length, "Robert," "Marie," "Ericka," "Summer," and "Jessica"—who provide the living heart of this book.

I would like to thank the students and faculty at the University of Southern California School of Social Work, whose questions and interest spurred me on. Faculty members who deserve special thanks for their encouragement are Michalle MorBarak, Ron Astor, Dorian Traube, Devon Brooks, Jacquelyn McCroskey, Dean Marilyn Flynn, and Vice Dean Paul Maiden. I am grateful to Catherine Portuges, whose insight and keen editorial eye greatly improved the book proposal, as did the responses of reviewers. Thanks to Elizabeth Calvin and Carol Biondi, who provided invaluable comments on the juvenile justice system; to Adam Boltuch, for the design and creation of the Foster Care Timeline; and to Karl Calhoun for his interest and questions. Thanks also to Priscilla Roth, Judith Schore, Laura Parsons, and Elizabeth Forer, who offered helpful comments on early chapters. Jacqueline Mondros's wholehearted support has been a sustaining presence. The insight and challenging questions of fellow members of the Center for the Study of Intersubjectivity contributed to the final version of the book.

Many dear friends, my sister Roberta, and our parents, Alfred and Selma Benjamin, cheered me on throughout.

A very special thank you is due to Catherine Conner, whose assistance has been a critical factor, first in putting the original course together, and then with research and manuscript preparation for the book. I am so grateful for her efficient, knowledgeable management of the logistics of this project, and for her serene intelligence.

I want to thank my extraordinarily patient children and grandchildren: Rebecca, Alex, Jake, Matt, Erica, Elizabeth, Jesse, Aniela, Henry, Nate, and Marlowe. The time taken from them has been substantial and their support unwavering. My deepest gratitude goes to my husband, Barry. Without his complete and unstinting belief in me, I'm not sure I could have written this book.

—Wendy Smith

CONTENTS

INTRODUCTION

Whatever affects one directly, affects all indirectly. I can never be what
I ought to be until you are what you ought to be. This is the interrelated
structure of reality.

—Martin Luther King, Jr.

Those who work with foster care alumni come from a wide range of backgrounds and perspectives: they may be staff in public or private child
welfare agencies, transitional living programs, group homes, residential
treatment settings, mental health or juvenile justice settings; school social
workers, college counselors, lawyers, or youth advocates; staff or volunteers in community organizations; or policy makers. The kinds of experience and knowledge that individuals carry into their work with these
young people are as diverse as the settings they represent. It is the
purpose of this book to integrate new research and thinking from varied
disciplines to provide a theoretical and practical foundation that will
enhance the efforts of all those who work to improve the lives of youth
who have been in care.

Specifically, I argue that development in childhood and adolescence,
attachment experiences and disruptions, and the impact of unresolved
trauma and loss on development and relationships are important and, thus
far, under-studied areas. The book proposes a biological-psychological-
social perspective that emphasizes the relational, experience-dependent
nature of development, attachment, and resiliency. It is increasingly recognized that all youth need at least one relationship with a caring and
committed adult, and attention to ensuring such a relationship is now
included in legislation and programs. However, as I hope to demonstrate,
the effectiveness of programs, services, and policies will benefit from a
more comprehensive understanding of the interacting biological, psychological, and social forces that have influenced and continue to influence
youth emerging from state care.

In September, 2008, there were 463,000 children in foster care in the
United States; 27,785 of them exited care at ages 18 to 20 (U.S. Department
of Health and Human Services, Administration for Children and Families,

Administration on Children, Youth, and Families, Children's Bureau, 2009). Compared to a total number of American children under eighteen estimated at 76,000,000 (roughly one-quarter of the entire population) (U.S. Census Bureau, 2010), youth in foster care do not constitute a large percentage of the population. Despite their relatively small numbers, they are a population that compels our attention and concern—because their struggles are considerable and because they have been in our care. We are their "corporate parents" (Courtney, 2009), sharing responsibility for them, and they are our children.

Younger children in care have been the subject of legislative and research interest for some time, but public attention did not focus on the problems of youth who turn eighteen and "age out" of care until the mid 1980s, when the Title IV-E Independent Living Program (ILP) was enacted to provide services to youth in care who are 16 to 18 and those recently discharged. Since then, as the data on poor outcomes for these youth accumulated, legislators increased funding to states and expanded the upper age limit of those served to 21. Currently, all fifty states and the District of Columbia receive Title IV-E Independent Living funds. The Fostering Connections to Success and Increasing Adoptions Act of 2008, passed unanimously by both houses of Congress, expands state options for keeping youth in care up to age 21 in certain circumstances, and there is some evidence from states where this has been the practice for a number of years that the outcomes of those who remain longer in care are improved (Courtney, Dworsky, & Peters, 2009; Dworsky, 2008).

In general, however, in the nearly fifteen years since passage of Title IV-E ILP, the hoped-for improvements in outcomes for foster care alumni have not materialized to any significant degree (Dworsky, 2008). Along many dimensions, youth emerging from care are doing poorly as a group when compared with their peers in the general population (Courtney et al., 2007; Courtney et al., 2009). They face challenges in multiple domains: housing, education, employment, incarceration, early parenthood, mental and physical health, and health access (Child Welfare League of America, 2005).

Outcomes are unlikely to get dramatically better in the absence of a deeper and more expanded understanding of the challenges facing these youth. The research literature has tended to emphasize the more easily quantifiable outcomes, but is gradually expanding to include interpersonal well-being, aspirations, satisfactions, and social supports (Pecora et al., 2010). Qualitative studies that attempt to explore the experiences of alumni of foster care in greater depth are beginning to appear (Samuels, 2008; Scannapieco, Connell-Carrick, & Painter, 2007), and hold the promise of greater insight into psychological sequelae that influence emotional and interpersonal adaptation in adult life.

A brief overview (Figure 1) of some key outcome indicators shows where current societal support still falls short. Longitudinal and snapshot studies of foster care alumni report that 18% to 36% of them have experienced homelessness since exiting care, and up to 35% have moved five or more times since discharge (Child Welfare League of America, 2005; Courtney et al., 2007; Courtney et al., 2009; Reilly, 2003). In California, children in foster care comprise less than 0.3% of the state's population, yet 40% of those living in homeless shelters are foster care alumni (Packard et al., 2008); in national studies, 39% of homeless subjects say they have a history of foster care placement (Park et al., 2004).

Educational outcomes are dismal: studies report a range of 25% to 50% of foster care alumni who have not completed high school, compared to 7% of peers in the general population, and only 20% to 30% have attended any college, compared to 53% to 60% of peers in the general population (Child Welfare League of America, 2005; Courtney et al., 2001; Courtney et al., 2007; Courtney et al., 2009; Packard et al., 2008; Reilly, 2003).

Employment and economic well-being indicators are no better. Four years after exit from care, fewer than half are currently employed, compared to 76% of their peers, who also earn about $1.00 more per hour (Courtney et al., 2007; Courtney et al., 2009). Mean earnings of foster care alumni remain well below the poverty threshold at two and three years after discharge from care. The situation is even worse for African American alumni, who earn significantly less than whites and have a decreased likelihood of employment (Dworsky, 2008). Female alumni are about four times as likely as the general population to receive public assistance (Packard et al., 2008), and 50% of youth who have been in care experience material hardship, with 25% reporting low or very low food security (Courtney et al., 2007).

Foster care alumni have significantly higher levels of criminal justice system involvement than peers. Four years after exit, 81% of males report having been arrested at least once since discharge, compared to 17% of their peers (Courtney et al., 2007; Courtney et al., 2009). In another study, 45% of foster care alumni report having had trouble with the law since leaving care; 41% have been in jail and 7% are in state prison (Reilly, 2003).

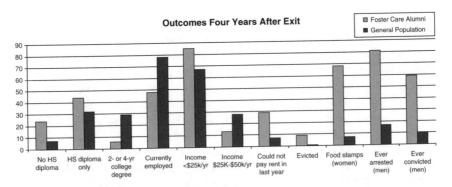

Figure 1 Outcomes Four Years After Exit. Illustration by Catherine Conner.

Female alumni have higher levels of criminal justice system involvement than male peers in the general population (Courtney, 2009; Courtney et al., 2009). In California, where the rate of imprisonment for the general population is 0.13%, it is 4% for foster care alumni (Packard et al., 2008).

In a large study, 71% of female alumni of foster care report having been pregnant by age 21, and repeat pregnancies are more often the rule than the exception. Half of the males had impregnated a female, compared with only 19% of peers in the general population. At 21, more than half of the women and nearly one-third of the men had at least one child; nearly all of the women and one-third of the men had their children living with them (Courtney et al., 2007). Keep in mind the poor economic status of many of these young people.

Obtaining affordable health care is a significant issue for half of all youth who have been in foster care; approximately one-fifth of them report not receiving medical or dental care when they need it. Alumni of foster care are less likely to have health insurance than their peers (57% vs. 78%), despite the fact that federal legislation now gives states the option to provide Medicaid to youth in care until they are 21 (Courtney et al., 2007; Courtney et al., 2009; Dworsky & Havlicek, 2008).

There is growing evidence that there is a greater incidence of physical impairments among children in foster care, and that they have mental health disorders in disproportionate numbers. In one study, 42% of foster care alumni were depressed in the year following discharge, compared to 27% of their peers (Anctil et al., 2007). A study of 17-year-olds in care reported that 37% met the criteria for a psychiatric diagnosis in the past year, and 61% met criteria for a lifetime disorder (Pecora et al., 2009). In a context of lack of health insurance or access to care, health and mental health problems are likely to go untreated or undertreated, and acute problems may become complicated or chronic.

Children of color are disproportionately represented in the foster care population (Figure 2): black children are 15.3% of the American child population and 31% of the foster care population; white children are 58.6% of the child population and 40% of the foster care population; Hispanic children are 18.3% of the child population and 20% of the foster care population; children of two or more races are 2.7% of the general population and 5% of the foster care population (U.S. Department of Health and Human Services, Administration for Children and Families, Administration on Children, Youth, and Families, Children's Bureau, 2009; U.S. Department of Health and Human Services, Health Resources and Services Administration, Maternal and Child Health Bureau, 2004). These children also frequently experience disparate and inequitable service provision while in the foster care system (Child Welfare League of America, 2005), and the fact that they face greater challenges than their white counterparts as they enter the adult world is neither surprising nor acceptable. There are higher rates of poverty, single-parenthood, and incarceration among black foster care alumni (Wertheimer, 2002).

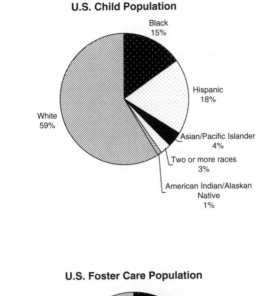

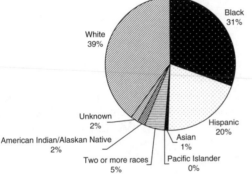

Figure 2 U.S. Child Population and U.S. Foster Care Population. Illustrations by Catherine Conner.

By age eighteen, children who have spent time in foster care are likely to have experienced abuse or neglect, family disruption, loss of family relationships, and to have spent an average of 6.1 years in care. More than one-third of them have had eight or more different placements (Pecora et al., 2010). Their struggles begin early in life and, for too many, continue into adulthood. Youth who "age out" of foster care—those who leave care because they have reached the age of 18 (or, in some states, 19, 20, or 21) rather than because they are reunified with their families or adopted— are particularly challenged because they face adulthood with few or no supports.

The transition to adulthood for the average young person in our society is different today than it was 50 or 100 years ago; today, 45% to 55% of young people 18 to 24 are living at home with one or both parents. They receive material assistance of approximately $38,000 from their parents between the ages of 18 and 34 (Courtney et al., 2007). Young people transitioning from foster care into adulthood face a dramatically different situation. For many of them, turning eighteen heralds a sudden falling away of the relational, financial, and social resources that could offer scaffolding and support.

The fact that outcomes among foster care alumni have not improved to a greater degree despite the increased funding and attention from policy makers and providers suggests that our understanding of how to help them more effectively is not yet sufficient to do the job. Part of what is at issue involves large-scale social and institutional changes. Poverty, institutional racism, and the child welfare and juvenile justice systems are fundamentally implicated in the entry of children into care and their status as they leave care. However, these matters are beyond the scope of this book, the focus of which is more squarely on the young people emerging from foster care.

Plan of the Book

The first section of the book, Chapters 1 and 2, sets the stage for a more comprehensive understanding of the context from which foster care alumni emerge. In Chapter 1, I present a brief history of the foster care system and legislation relevant to youth leaving care. The chapter includes discussions of parental incarceration, placement disposition, kinship foster care, and the continuing problem of overrepresentation of children of color in foster care. In Chapter 2, the theoretical frameworks of the book are introduced: the biopsychosocial perspective, dynamic nonlinear systems theory, development and developmental traumatology, attachment theory, ambiguous loss, and resiliency theory. An extended case example is used to illuminate the uses of theory in deepening our understanding of lived experience.

The second section of the book, Chapters 3 to 5, is devoted to child and adolescent development. Chapter 3 presents an overview of infant brain development and the stress response system, followed by a summary of recent research on the neurobiological impacts of trauma and maltreatment. In Chapter 4, I discuss attachment theory in early childhood, its implications for later development, and the effects of maltreatment on attachment systems. The chapter includes an illustrative case example. Chapter 5 explores adolescent development in the context of foster care, with special emphasis on identity development, and includes a third case example.

The third section, Chapters 6 through 9, focuses on mental health issues faced by many alumni of foster care. An introductory section provides context by discussing the use of *Diagnostic and Statistical Manual* diagnoses, mental health service use in the foster care population, evidence-based practice, and culturally sensitive practice. Each of the mental health chapters provides an overview of a particular mental health problem and currently supported intervention approaches, as well as developmental and attachment implications and impacts of maltreatment. Each mental health chapter concludes with treatment principles. Chapter 6 focuses on anxiety, trauma, and post-traumatic stress disorders; Chapter 7 focuses on mood disorders; Chapter 8 focuses on substance-abuse disorders; and Chapter 10 takes up delinquency as a mental health problem, and includes a detailed discussion of "crossover kids" and the juvenile justice system.

The fourth section, Chapters 10 through 12, explores issues and outcomes of youth who need special attention, developmental and other dimensions of the transition itself, and programs for transitioning youth. Chapter 10 examines issues affecting three groups of youth with special needs: youth with disabilities, LGBT youth, and pregnant and parenting youth. The chapter includes practice principles related to each of the three groups. Chapter 11 presents developments of emerging adulthood, including separation from foster care, decisions about education and career, and relationships with significant others. In this chapter, practice principles related to education, employment, and relationships are offered. Chapter 12 focuses on outcomes following exit from care, independent living services, and transitional living programs. The chapter provides key principles for developmentally informed, relationship-based practice.

The fifth and final section of the book is a chapter on current policy and research trends. Chapter 13 offers policy recommendations and suggestions for future research based on the theoretical frameworks of the book, and summarizes its central themes.

Youth Leaving Foster Care

PART I

SETTING THE STAGE

Part I is designed to orient the reader, practically and theoretically. Some readers will be knowledgeable about the foster care system, but for those who are not, Chapter 1 provides a historical overview and a summary of legislation affecting foster youth. Selected issues affecting foster care alumni are introduced, including kinship foster care, parental incarceration, and overrepresentation of youth of color in the foster care system. The foster care system is a part of the history of each youth who has been in care, and is essential to our comprehension of the whole individual.

Chapter 2 introduces the reader to the theoretical underpinnings of the book. The literature on children and youth in foster care has often lacked a solid theoretical foundation, focusing heavily on outcomes and programs instead. Many individuals who work with these young people may be only slightly or not at all familiar with the theories in this book; Chapter 2 provides a summary and discussion of the biopsychosocial perspective, dynamic nonlinear systems theory, the developmental perspective (including neurobiological development and developmental traumatology), attachment theory, grief and ambiguous loss theory, and resiliency theory. These perspectives will inform practice and program principles later in the book.

1

THE CHILD WELFARE SYSTEM
AS CONTEXT

Comprehension of the needs and experiences of young people leaving foster care begins with understanding the system from which they are emerging. The child welfare system comprises complex, overlapping, and interacting public and private entities at the federal, state, regional, and local levels. The vast array of programs and services is intended to be a safety net for the protection of neglected and abused children. A primary part of this system is foster care: out-of-home care provided to children because their parents have been determined to be unable or unwilling to care for them. Federal, state, and local governments spend over two billion dollars annually on foster care costs and services for foster children and their families (Foster, 2001). While a full explanation or description of the system is not possible here, Chapter 1 presents an overview of the legislation and changing philosophy of the federal system. Important issues that contribute to general and individual experiences in the foster care system, such as overrepresentation of children of color, parental incarceration, kinship care, and placement disposition, will also be discussed.

Historical Trends

In colonial times and the eighteenth century, attention and services were mainly directed to orphans and children who had been abandoned. Children were viewed as small adults who ought to be trained so that they could become productive workers. Before the establishment of orphanages in the eighteenth century, orphans were sometimes indentured to families whom they would live with and work for. They were fed, clothed, housed, and taught skills by their masters, some of whom

5

also provided education. The relationship was primarily an economic one and, for many years, affected children from all classes (Hacsi, 1995).

The 1800s saw an expansion of institutions for poor and delinquent children, usually segregated by religion or race. There were large numbers of children whose parents had died as a result of illness or war, and others who had been abandoned due to their parents' inability to care for them (Lindsey, 2004). The concept of childhood as an early version of adulthood was changing; children remained at home longer, and childhood was beginning to be seen as a separate, more innocent stage (Hacsi, 1995).

In just twenty years, between 1853 and 1874, both the New York Children's Aid Society and the New York Society for the Prevention of Cruelty were founded, reflecting an increasing awareness of the need of some children for protection (Figure 1.1). The latter agency assisted dependent children who were poor, children who were neglected, and juvenile offenders. They differed in respect to what brought them to the agency's attention, yet all were treated in the same way (Hacsi, 1995). The changing views of children led to greater interest in the idea of foster care, and the government became more involved in the welfare of children. The focus shifted from orphans to children whose mothers were considered unable to care for them (Lindsey, 1994; Lindsey, 2004).

In 1909, the White House held its first Conference on Dependent Children, putting forth the view that children should not be removed from their families for reasons of poverty alone. Three years later, Congress established the U.S. Children's Bureau (Ashby, 1997).

The child welfare institutions and interventions of the eighteenth and nineteenth centuries developed from a view that the state should enter in only if and when the resources of the family and kinship network fail, and when the government must step in, it should be in the most minimal and time-limited way. Within this perspective, the nature and level of interventions varied with social views of the time, from supportive services such as in-home counseling, to income assistance and concrete services, and finally, to substitute (out-of-home) care. Interventions were directed at the individual or family level, with little emphasis on the environmental or-social surround as part of the problem to be addressed (Lindsey, 1994; Lindsey, 2004).

Foster Care Legislation in the Twentieth Century

In 1935, Congress enacted Title IV of the Social Security Act, establishing Aid for Dependent Children (ADC). The legislation provided financial assistance to poor families; funding for services to assist families was not added until 1962 (Courtney et al., 2008). When families could not provide for their children, or if there was evidence of neglect or abuse, children

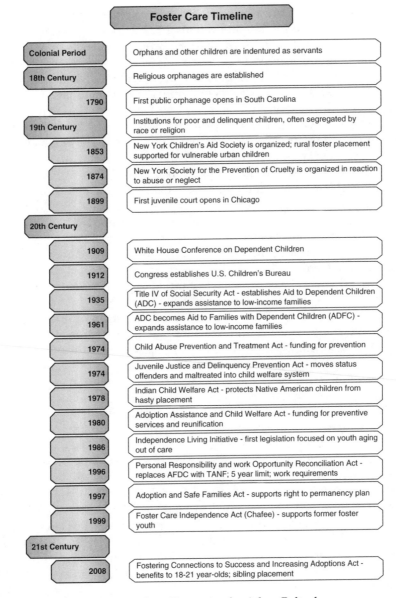

Foster Care Timeline

Colonial Period	Orphans and other children are indentured as servants
18th Century	Religious orphanages are established
1790	First public orphanage opens in South Carolina
19th Century	Institutions for poor and delinquent children, often segregated by race or religion
1853	New York Children's Aid Society is organized; rural foster placement supported for vulnerable urban children
1874	New York Society for the Prevention of Cruelty is organized in reaction to abuse or neglect
1899	First juvenile court opens in Chicago
20th Century	
1909	White House Conference on Dependent Children
1912	Congress establishes U.S. Children's Bureau
1935	Title IV of Social Security Act - establishes Aid to Dependent Children (ADC) - expands assistance to low-income families
1961	ADC becomes Aid to Families with Dependent Children (ADFC) - expands assistance to low-income families
1974	Child Abuse Prevention and Treatment Act - funding for prevention
1974	Juvenile Justice and Delinquency Prevention Act - moves status offenders and maltreated into child welfare system
1978	Indian Child Welfare Act - protects Native American children from hasty placement
1980	Adoiption Assistance and Child Welfare Act - funding for preventive services and reunification
1986	Independence Living Initiative - first legislation focused on youth aging out of care
1996	Personal Responsibility and work Opportunity Reconciliation Act - replaces AFDC with TANF; 5 year limit; work requirements
1997	Adoption and Safe Families Act - supports right to permanency plan
1999	Foster Care Independence Act (Chafee) - supports former foster youth
21st Century	
2008	Fostering Connections to Success and Increasing Adoptions Act - benefits to 18-21 year-olds; sibling placement

Figure 1.1 Foster Care Timeline. Illustration by Adam Boltuch.

entered the child welfare system. The number of dependent children in foster placement was fairly stable at 3.5 to 4.5 per 1000 during the 1940s and 1950s (Ashby, 1997). However, these numbers skyrocketed in the 1960s and 1970s, peaking in the late 1970s and early 1980s, as a result of several developments.

The first development was a heightened awareness of and interest in child abuse, marked by the publication of the work of C. Henry Kempe and colleagues on the "battered child syndrome" in 1962 (Kempe et al., 1985). In response to reports of much higher estimates of numbers of abused children than had previously been recorded, legislation was enacted to increase assistance to poor families with an emphasis on family rehabilitative social services. Congress passed the Child Abuse Prevention and Treatment Act (CAPTA) in 1974, providing financial assistance for prevention and treatment programs and, in the second development contributing to the exploding numbers of children in placement, mandating the reporting of suspected child abuse (Jones, 2006). Abuse was viewed as a family problem in which the interests of children were in conflict with those of parents, leading to interventions that separated children from parents (Schorr, 2000). The Juvenile Justice and Delinquency Prevention Act of 1974 prohibited placement of maltreated dependent children or status offenders in juvenile detention or correctional facilities, so these children, too, were coming into foster care. As the numbers climbed, the Indian Child Welfare Act of 1978 was enacted to protect Native American children from hasty placements (Allen & Bissell, 2004).

The crack epidemic of the early 1980s and the entry of drug-exposed infants into care was the third force (along with awareness of abuse and mandated reporting) behind the dramatic upsurge in foster placements (Johnson & Waldfogel, 2002). Children were staying in care longer, were poorer and more troubled. The growing number of children in placement and the increasing length and number of placements led to the passage of the Adoption Assistance and Child Welfare Act of 1980. The Act targeted preventive services and reunification of families through the strengthening of Title V Child Welfare Services and the creation of Title IV-E Foster Care and Adoption Assistance. It provided that "reasonable efforts" must be made to prevent placement, and that the least restrictive, most family-like setting must be employed (Allen & Bissell, 2004). Family preservation with short-term services designed to maintain children in their homes was the strategy employed to bring the numbers down, but later evaluations revealed disappointing social and economic outcomes. Child welfare agencies promoted case management, which often served as a substitute for, rather than an adjunct to, the counseling services that were needed (Schorr, 2000).

The legislation called for reasonable efforts to reunify families in which out-placement had occurred. Hearings to move children to permanent homes were to be held in a timely fashion. National attention to the effects on children of rising divorce rates in the 1970s resulted in more studies of childhood, and greater emphasis on the standard of "best interests of the child" when custody decisions were made. Lawmakers hoped this standard could be applied to foster children as well as children of divorced families. The 1980 Act deemphasized the rights of parents and focused instead on the well-being of children (Sanders, 2003).

Children still remained in care for long periods, however; agencies and courts could refuse to terminate parental rights, citing failure of the agency to show that reasonable efforts had been made to restore the family. Case reviews were often more a matter of paperwork production than meaningful evaluation of the family situation (Sanders, 2003).

As caseloads and regulations grew, social workers' jobs became routinized, with more paperwork and less time spent working with children in their homes. The U.S. Children's Bureau, which had required that child welfare agencies employ line workers with graduate degrees in social work, declined in influence, and this requirement was abandoned. Increasing unification of income maintenance and social services meant that income-maintenance workers could become child welfare workers. Further indication of the decreased skill and knowledge of staff working in child welfare is that, in 1958, 62% of child welfare workers had college degrees; by 1988, only 28% had them. During a period when the proportion of the general population with college degrees tripled, the proportion of agency staffs with college degrees dropped by more than half (Schorr, 2000). Just as the foster care population numbers and needs for skilled practitioners expanded, the staff available to provide services were less equipped to do so.

The Personal Responsibility and Work Opportunity Reconciliation Act (commonly known as "welfare reform") passed in 1996, eliminating Aid to Families with Dependent Children (AFDC), along with its concept of entitlement, and replacing it with Temporary Assistance for Needy Families (TANF). The problem for families in need of child welfare services is that the law makes it more difficult for high-risk families in poverty to maintain their children safely at home (McGowan & Walsh, 2000). The five-year lifetime limit on receipt of TANF funds, the strict work requirements on parents receiving these funds (especially for those with drug convictions), and the family-cap provision that denies benefits to children born into a family already receiving TANF together comprise a series of insurmountable obstacles to families needing economic supports as they try to ameliorate their situations and avoid removal of their children. Many states reduce the benefit levels of those who either do not work or do not meet other program requirements, making poor families even poorer. Increases in the poorest child population are associated with higher rates of maltreatment, and declines in welfare benefits are associated with higher rates of foster care (Paxson & Waldfogel, 2002).

In reaction to the worsening foster care picture and heightened social consciousness about the needs of children and the effects of damaging childhood experiences that evolved, the Adoption and Safe Families Act (ASFA) was passed in 1997. It focused on ensuring that children in care were guaranteed a plan for permanency. As did earlier legislation, the act emphasized child safety over keeping families together and provided financial incentives to states to promote permanency planning and adoption. Stricter guidelines for permanency planning were established, shortening the timeline for hearings to 12 months after entry into care rather than 18. Parental rights proceedings were to be initiated when a child had been in foster care for 15 out of the last 22 months, unless certain exceptions applied (Weinberg, 2007; Welte, 1997).

Snapshot of the Foster Care Population

The mean age of children in foster care is almost ten years, and the mean age of those entering care is eight years. Sixteen percent of the 273,000 who entered care in 2008 were less than one year old, and 25% entered at age fourteen or older. The average length of stay in care was just over 27 months, with 41% of stays lasting less than one year, 12% lasting three to four years, and 12% lasting five years or longer. Nearly half of the children in care in 2008 were placed in non-relative foster family homes; one quarter were in relative foster family homes; and the other quarter were in group homes, institutions, pre-adoptive homes, on trial home visits, in supervised independent living, or were runaways. Approximately half of the children were expected to reunify with their parent(s) or principal caretaker(s). Of those who exited care in 2008, over half reunified with parent(s) or caretaker(s), 8% were living with other relative(s), 19% were adopted, 7% were in guardianship, 10% emancipated, and 3% were transferred to another agency or were runaways (U.S. Department of Health and Human Services, Administration for Children and Families, Administration on Children, Youths, and Families, Children's Bureau, 2009 [hereafter, US DHHS, ACF, ACYF, CB]). (See Figure 2 in the introduction for the ethnicity of those in care during 2008.)

Kinship Foster Care

Placement with relatives has long been a part of the foster care system, but it increased in frequency during the late 1980s along with the rise in number of children entering care. Though recognized as a safety net, or even a permanency option, there had been no dedicated federal funding stream for kinship care until the Fostering Connections Act of 2008, which established the Kinship Navigator program to assist caretakers in locating and accessing resources, and the Kinship Guardianship Assistance Payment, which allows states to claim federal reimbursement (under Title IV-E) for a part of the cost of providing kinship guardianship assistance to children who leave foster care for placement with a relative who has chosen to become the child's legal guardian (Stoltzfus, 2008).

Currently, 24% of children in foster care are placed with relatives, 47% with non-relatives, and 20% in group homes or institutions (US DHHS,

ACF, ACYF, CB, 2009). Children who are more likely to be placed with relatives are African American or Native American, are two years old or older, have had no prior placement or known disability, and are those whose authority for placement was either court-ordered or a police protective hold (Beeman, Kim, & Bullerdick, 2000). Kinship care is thought to help children maintain emotional bonds with their birth parents and ties with their extended family, as well as to minimize disruption in their lives.

African American children make up the majority of those in kinship care and are nearly twice as likely as white children to be placed with relatives. While kinship care has historically been part of African American family life, some authors point out that those in kinship foster care have lower rates of reunification than those in non-kin care, and that this disproportionately affects African American children (Harris & Skyles, 2008; Schwartz, 2008). In addition, kinship caregivers receive little preparation for their new roles, are older, more economically disadvantaged, less well educated, and less likely to report being in good health (Holtan et al., 2005; U.S. Department of Health and Human Services, Administration for Children and Families, 2000).

Children in kinship care settings have dual connections to the caregiver (a grandparent who is also acting as a parent, for example) and may experience role ambiguity or confusion about behavioral expectations. One study found that 44% of children in kinship care indicated that they had to assume a caregiving role, in comparison with only 22% of children in non-relative foster care. At the same time, children in kinship care display greater continuity of connections, see their birth parents and siblings more frequently, and spend less time in care than those in non-relative placements (Holtan et al., 2005; Schwartz, 2008; Taussig, Clyman, & Landsverk, 2001; U.S. Department of Health and Human Services, Administration for Children and Families, 2000). In one study, the odds of feeling like a part of the family are three times higher for children placed with grandparents, aunts, or uncles than for those in non-relative homes; furthermore, the odds of remaining in the same home are higher the closer the degree of relatedness between child and caregiver (Testa, 2005). Adolescents in kinship care are more likely than those in non-relative care to expect to live with a relative after foster care or high school, and therefore may be less anxious about the future and face fewer challenges during the transition to adulthood (Iglehart, 1995).

Legislation Focused on Youth in Transition

The first piece of legislation to deal directly with emancipation from foster care was passed in 1986, as the public began to recognize that foster youth need additional help as they transition out of the state's care.

The Independent Living Initiative (Public Law 99-272) amended Title IV-E of the Social Security Act to provide federal funds to states to help youth aging out of foster care. This law funded independent living programs that included outreach, education and employment assistance, daily living skills, counseling, coordination of services, and a transitional independent living plan for each participating youth. While states could not use the funds for room and board, they could use them for supplemental services such as mentoring, training for foster parents, and youth advisory committees (Collins, 2001). Public Law 99-272 was reauthorized as part of the Omnibus Reconciliation Act of 1993 to provide more funding and flexibility in providing services to youth transitioning out of care, as well as to youth between 18 and 21 who have left foster care. Medicaid benefits were extended to these youths until the age of 21 (Allen & Bissell, 2004).

The Foster Care Independence Act (Public Law 106-169), enacted in 1999, permanently reauthorized the Independent Living Program, replacing it with the John H. Chafee Independent Living Program. This legislation doubled the funding level for support services for youth aging out of the system, and allow these funds to be used for housing as well as other services. The Chafee Act was a catalyst for broader policy reforms for transition-age youth (Allen & Bissell, 2004)).

The latest bill passed in support of youth in foster care is the Fostering Connections to Success and Increasing Adoptions Act of 2008, which represents a "fundamental reform" of policy in that the state's responsibility for youth in foster care no longer ends with their eighteenth birthday, but continues as they transition into adulthood (Courtney, 2009). The Act amends Title IV-E of the Social Security Act to give states the option to provide care and support to youth in foster care until the age of 21 if they are enrolled in school or vocational training, employed, or medically unable to work or attend school. Additional provisions in the Act relate to kinship guardianship, training for agencies and relative guardians, joint placement of siblings, tribal foster care, and adoption incentives (Children's Defense Fund, 2009). The Chafee Act and the Fostering Connections Act will be discussed in greater detail in Chapters 12 and 13.

Since the 1990s, the developmental needs of children, along with greater recognition of the impact of early losses and adverse experiences, are increasingly a focus of concern in child welfare agencies; at the same time, however, high caseloads and increased documentation requirements lead to decreased time for providing services to meet these needs, and to high staff turnover (Chipungu & Bent-Goodley, 2004). Young people who have spent time in foster placement may have received much less attention to developmental and psychological problems resulting from maltreatment and from experiences in foster care than they need.

The child welfare system is a product of society; it unavoidably reflects some of our society's ills in its structure and its operations. Social problems that have a direct relationship to youths' experiences in care arise from complex interactions among race, class, parental incarceration, and child welfare. The next sections of the chapter highlight these issues to further specify the contexts within which emancipating youth have grown up.

Children of Color in the Child Welfare System

African-American children continue to be overrepresented in the child welfare system. They comprise 15% of the child population in the United States, but they represent 32% of the children in substitute care in 2008 (Harris et al., 2009). White children were 59% of the child population in 2004, but only 40% of children in substitute care in 2008. Children of color constituted 41.4% of the child population in 2004; yet they are close to 59% of the children in care (US DHHS, ACF, ACYF, CB, 2009; US DHHS, Health Resources and Services Administration, Maternal and Child Health Bureau, 2004). Moreover, children of color are treated differently while in care, with fewer familial visits, fewer contacts with workers, fewer written case plans, fewer assessments, and longer stays in care (Ards et al., 2003; Chipungu & Bent-Goodley, 2004; Curtis & Denby, 2004; Harris et al., 2009; Texas Health and Human Services Commission & Department of Family and Protective Services, 2006 [hereafter, Texas HHSC & DFPS). They are less likely to be returned home to their families, less likely to be adopted, and are more likely to leave care without a permanent connection to a caring adult (McRoy, 2005).

Disproportional representation in child welfare has been identified for years and exists similarly in the juvenile justice system; the overlap between children in foster care and those in the juvenile justice system will be discussed in Chapter 9. Although black children were excluded from social welfare systems for families earlier in the history of child welfare, they are now disproportionately likely to receive services (Cahn, 2002). Hispanic children have more proportional representation: 18% of the child population in 2003 and 20% of the children in foster care in 2008 (US DHHS, Administration for Children and Families, 2006; US DHHS, Health Resources and Services Administration, Maternal and Child Health Bureau, 2004; US DHHS, ACF, ACYF, CB, 2009).

While poverty is often cited as a contributing (or even inextricably complicating) factor, Cahn, discussing Roberts' *Shattered Bonds*, states that, even when controlling for poverty, family structure, parental employment, and geographic location, black children are more likely to be labeled as abused, more likely to be placed in foster care, and more likely to have longer stays in care than white children. There is no evidence that the actual incidence of maltreatment differs significantly among black families (Cahn, 2002). Roberts makes the case that the system is not administered evenhandedly, but it is unclear whether this imbalance is due to racial animus, poverty, or other factors (Roberts, 2002).

Two important findings emerged from a study using recent data from Minnesota, which leads the nation in racial disproportionality in child maltreatment. First, when data are examined by counties, disproportional representation among substantiated and reported cases is less than when data are looked at in aggregate on the state level, leading the authors to conclude that aggregation bias may account for some of the disproportionality among substantiated cases. Second, however, they found racial disparities and disproportionality in how children of color are treated that cannot be fully explained by characteristics of victims, offenders, counties, reporters, or type of maltreatment (Ards et al., 2003).

Poverty as a Factor in Racial Disproportionality

Researchers disagree about whether the high rate of poverty among African-American households is responsible for the overrepresentation of African-American children in the foster care system. In 2007, 34% of African-American children lived in poverty, compared with 10% of white children (Fass & Cauthen, 2008). Black children have been the major victims of the dismantling of the welfare program mandated by the welfare reform legislation of 1996; there were drastic reductions in the number of poor children receiving assistance. Lindsey gives the example of the populous state of Illinois, where black children are nearly 75% of the TANF child population, but only one-fifth of the state's child population (Lindsey, 2004).

Receiving public assistance has a positive relationship with increased overrepresentation of African-American children in substitute care (Derezotes & Poetner, 2005). Rates of reported abuse and neglect are 22 times higher in families whose income is less than $15,000 than for those with incomes over $30,000 (Cahn, 2002). Neglect is concentrated in poor families, and the rate of substantiated abuse cases in one study was three times higher in high-poverty zip codes than in median-poverty zip codes (Roberts, 2002). It is not clear what accounts for this strong correlation, which may be a matter of differences in detection and reporting.

Poor families are more likely to come under scrutiny when they are under the supervision of social service or law enforcement agencies, and thus the detection and reporting factor may be higher for them. Some researchers point to the stresses that stem from poverty as possible contributing factors in child maltreatment, as well as the lack of resources to provide adequate food, shelter, and other necessities. Poor families may be overwhelmed by the struggle to meet basic needs; living in substandard housing with inadequate food and health care may result in chronic depression or feelings of despair, which, in turn, leave parents unable to provide appropriately for their children's emotional and developmental needs. Extreme stress can make some parents more aggressive toward their children (Roberts, 2002). Paxson and Waldfogel (2002) found that, holding income fixed, children of single mothers who work are at greater risk of maltreatment than those who do not. Their findings suggest that moving these mothers off welfare and into low-paying jobs will not benefit children, and could harm them (Paxson & Waldfogel, 2002).

Whether poverty is indirectly causal (increased detection, stresses associated with poverty) or directly causal (inability to provide food, clothing, shelter) of child neglect, the fact is that "inadequacy of income, *more than any factor*, constitutes the reason that children are removed" (Lindsey, 2004). Children may be left unattended or under-supervised in a dangerous neighborhood when parents go to work and cannot pay for child care. Parents' inability to find decent, affordable housing is often the reason why children remain in care (Roberts, 2002).

American children live in poverty at alarming levels: in 2007, 18% of American children were poor. Black children are disproportionately affected: 34% of black children were poor, compared with 10% of whites. Hispanic children, too, live in poverty in numbers higher than their percentage of the population. In 2007, 29% of them were living in poverty (Fass & Cauthen, 2008). Extreme poverty affected 15% of black children compared with 5% of white children (Roberts, 2002), and there has been a substantial increase in the number of black children living in extreme poverty. In addition, black children stay poor longer than white children (Lindsey, 2004). Poverty is directly and indirectly related to entry into foster care; black children are more often poor and disproportionately represented in the foster care population.

In a penetrating examination of the systemic problem of increased focus on child abuse, blurring of child abuse and neglect, and gradual shifting of focus away from the vast numbers of children living in extreme poverty and despair, Lindsey (2004) puts forward the case that the child welfare system has, in effect, lost its way. He suggests that the responsibility for protecting criminally abused children more rightly belongs with the police and the courts, thus freeing the child welfare system to provide an infrastructure of social programs that will protect the greater number of disadvantaged and impoverished children (Lindsey, 2004).

Race and Decision-Making

There is some evidence of differential treatment of families and children of color at many points within the child welfare system. First, families of color are more likely than Caucasians to be the subject of a child maltreatment report and may be more likely to have a report substantiated through investigation (Courtney et al., 1997). Race appears to influence which harms mandatory reporters label as abuse or neglect, with African-American families more likely to be reported than white families for equally severe injuries to children (Roberts, 2002). In the phase of disposition, or decision about placement made by court representatives, black children are only half as likely as white children to receive services in their own homes rather than being removed and placed in foster care (Roberts, 2003).

Lindsey looked at the decision-making process to ascertain its reliability and found that the system was unable to determine which children should be removed and which should be left in their homes. He concludes that this most fundamental decision of the child protection system is made in a "capricious and idiosyncratic" way, lacking "both reliability and validity in [the] . . . core decision-making process" (Lindsey, 2004). Placement rates vary widely from state to state, as do rates of substantiation of reports, with no readily identifiable reason (Roberts, 2002). Yet, despite the randomness of the process, the overrepresentation of black children holds constant, raising the question of the presence of racial bias in these determinations. The Department of Health and Human Services reported in 1999 that the majority of African-American children (56%) were placed in foster care, but the majority of white children (72%) received in-home services (Derezotes & Poetner, 2005). In Texas, a system-wide study concluded that "All of these interwoven features of risk, race, ethnicity, and poverty tend to be related to the case decision at the conclusion of the investigation" (Texas HHSC & DFPS, 2006).

Parental Incarceration

Conventional wisdom on the growth of child welfare caseloads in the 1980s and 1990s focuses on crack and HIV/AIDS as the main culprits. However, another important factor may be the greater number of women imprisoned and the longer sentences brought about by the Anti-Drug Abuse Act of 1986 (Swann & Sylvester, 2006). The number of incarcerated parents more than doubled between 1986 and 1997, and the number of children with a parent in prison rose dramatically (from 600,000 in 1986 to more than 1.3 million in 1997) (Johnson & Waldfogel, 2002). The number of women incarcerated for drug offenses during this period rose by a whopping 888%, and the number of mothers in state and federal prisons more than tripled (Swann & Sylvester, 2006).

Children of incarcerated mothers are more likely to be displaced from the home than those of incarcerated fathers, and more likely to enter the child welfare system. It is estimated that 10% to 14% of children with incarcerated mothers end up in foster care, but when fathers are incarcerated, children most often live with their mothers or stepmothers. Between 1986 and 1997, children with incarcerated parents became an increasingly large share of the non-relative foster care population and of children who live with grandparents. Parents who were incarcerated during 1997 were a more troubled population than those incarcerated in 1986, with more histories of abuse, previous arrest, parental incarceration, and regular drug use; therefore, their children may have been at risk long before their most recent incarceration (Johnson & Waldfogel, 2002).

Parental incarceration interacts with foster care in other ways as well. The Adoption and Safe Families Act created tension between what parents must do to get their children back and what incarcerated parents are able to do. ASFA requires the state to petition for termination of parental rights when a child has been in care for 15 of the most recent 22 months, yet the average time served by parents is 80 months in state prison and 103 months in federal prison (Swann & Sylvester, 2006). Communication between mothers and caseworkers is often limited, with 66% of mothers reporting that they did not receive a copy of their child's case plan. In addition, 80% of protective service agencies had no specific policies or guidelines for placing children whose mothers had been arrested (Johnson & Waldfogel, 2002). Sentences that are, on average, longer than the 22 months at issue in termination of parental rights, and the often limited or nonexistent communications between agencies and incarcerated mothers, put these mothers at high risk of losing their children.

Youth Leaving Care

Youth who have been in foster care have been socialized and affected by the child welfare system as a whole, and by their specific placement(s). The experience of the government as "parent" becomes part of the youth's internal world, as well as an external reality. The age at entry into foster care, along with the number and length of stays, play important roles in the overall status of youth leaving care. Forty-three percent of children are five years or younger when first placed; 19% are between six and ten; 25% are between the ages of 11 and 15; another 12% are between 16 and 18. In 2008, 53% of those exiting care had been in care for a year or more (US DHHS, ACF, ACYF, CB, 2009).

The developmental stage and status of the individual child interacts with her or his age of entry and time in care. Normative developmental tasks and changes are influenced by events in the family and in placement, including the number and nature of the placement experiences. Placement instability is known to be an important factor in later outcomes (Pecora et al., 2006), but it has most often been studied in quantitative terms, which shed little light on the ways children move through the system. In much of the literature, placement moves are conceived of only as events, when they are also processes, the effects of which continue to unfold over time (Unrau, 2007). Youth remember multiple foster care moves as experiences of profound loss, with lasting negative impact. Moves often take place with no preparation and no opportunity to grieve the separation and losses (Unrau, Seita, & Putney, 2008).

Not enough is known about the variation in placement types and the services provided, nor about the pathways or patterns that may exist in placement changes (James, Landsverk, & Slymen, 2004) and how particular placement types or services may affect children (Pecora, 2007; Wulczyn, Kogan, & Harden, 2003). Placement changes occurring during the first year in care are associated with later placement instability, whereas children who stabilize early experience fewer placement moves and fewer stays in residential care settings. Higher levels of behavior problems are found to both predict and result from multiple placement changes, potentially leading to even more instability (James, Landswerk, & Slymen, 2004).

Older children in care are likely to have experienced more disruption and trauma in their families of origin and also while in care. In one study, 66% of a sample of emancipated youth reported having experienced neglect, 57% reported one or more incidents of physical abuse prior to placement, and 31% reported a history of sexual abuse; 76% of this sample reported at least one form of child maltreatment. When asked if they had experienced neglect or abuse while in the child welfare system, 33% responded that they had, with 13% of these youth reporting physical assault by a caregiver (Courtney et al., 2001). In another study, most of the sample of 252 youth had entered care in their early teens, stayed several years, had numerous placements, and experienced some form of group care (psychiatric hospital, group home, or residential treatment center) (McMillen & Tucker, 1999). Many of these youth have special needs as a result of neglect and abuse, including mental health or medical problems, pregnancy or parenting-related problems, substance abuse, educational deficits, or developmental needs (Leathers & Testa, 2006). These needs may not have been addressed in a meaningful way during placement, or services may have been disrupted by emancipation, which itself can lead to the loss of relationships and community.

Services to aid the transition out of care have received greater attention since passage of the Foster Care Independence Act of 1999 and the Fostering Connections to Success and Increasing Adoptions Act of 2008; however, the scope and quality of these services vary greatly. Fewer than one-third of states have exercised the option to extend Medicaid to age 21. High rates of staff turnover, limited involvement of foster parents, lack of coordination of services, lack of youth employment opportunities and scarcity of housing, and transportation problems present barriers to adequate preparation for the transition (Massinga & Pecora, 2004).

In addition to a history of maltreatment, youth emerging from the foster care system may very well have lived in poverty, had a single parent, experienced discrimination or a dangerous neighborhood, and been exposed to adults using drugs or engaging in violence. The many losses inherent in a removal from home and foster care can be described as "ambiguous losses," those with no clear boundaries, endings, or societally recognized rituals for grieving the loss (Samuels, 2009). By the time they reach their eighteenth birthdays, children in care may have lost one or both parents, siblings, friends, and extended family members. They may have been displaced multiple times, having to build and possibly lose one relationship after another. Numerous entries into and exits from schools may have brought attendant losses of friendships and teachers. There may have been multiple neighborhoods, communities, and cultures entered and left because of changes in placements. It is against this backdrop of instability and months or years in the state's care that foster care alumni begin their tentative journey toward adulthood. Our journey as those who seek to assist them begins here as well. Keeping in mind the foster care system and its influential role in the lives of foster youth, we now turn to the theoretical perspectives that will provide insight and direction in our work to improve policies, programs, and interventions.

2

THEORETICAL PERSPECTIVES

It is the theory that decides what can be observed.

—Albert Einstein (1879–1955)

Much of the literature and most of the research on foster youth is atheo-retical, yet theories help us make sense of experience and can guide us in choosing how and when to intervene effectively. Theories and observations shape each other: we attend to the data whose importance is suggested by our (consciously or unconsciously held) theories; what we see then refutes, supports, or elaborates those theories. The perspectives introduced in this chapter—the biopyschosocial model, dynamic systems theory, the developmental perspective, attachment theory, grief and resiliency theories—offer important insights into the challenges faced by foster care alumni and will help us to be more effective in our attempts to support them in their transition to adulthood. The case of Robert will serve as illustration throughout the chapter. Each of the perspectives could itself occupy a chapter (or a book); only aspects that are useful to the purpose of this book will be addressed.

> *Robert, a 24-year-old Mexican American, is earning a master's degree in psychology. He finds it difficult to empathize with some of the clients at the outpatient clinic where he is an intern. Robert chose this graduate program because it is located in his hometown, enabling him to search for the mother he hasn't seen in over ten years.*
>
> *Robert was twelve years old, and his brother eleven, when their schizophrenic mother left home one day, never to return. Her previous disappearances had always ended after a few days. This time, the days stretched on, and the boys couldn't manage by scrounging food from garbage cans. They entered the foster care system, where they remained until they were 18.*
>
> *Robert's father had abandoned the family when Robert's mother was 15 and pregnant with his younger brother. She managed, barely, to maintain the family in a low-income neighborhood. Over the next ten years, the symptoms of her advancing mental illness intruded into their lives, interrupting her jobs, causing strange behaviors. She could be physically abusive, burning Robert with an iron on one occasion, or locking the children out of the home for hours on others.*

Her mental illness hung between her and her children like a curtain, precluding emotional closeness and comfort.

Sometimes she failed to notice or attend to her children's health problems. Robert had to call 911 when he was ten to get medical attention for an injured knee that had gone untreated for a year. A month-long detention in foster care followed that call, but the children were returned to their mother and remained with her until her disappearance two years later.

Robert remembers a series of foster homes as well as a stay in a group home. Placement experiences were lonely at best and traumatic at worst. He was introduced to drug- and sex-related behaviors at an early age. His participation in these activities gave rise to mixed feelings of belonging and alienation. These experiences were sometimes frightening, but also offered relief from emotional pain.

Robert saw his mother very rarely; his brother was placed elsewhere and, over the years of separation, they grew estranged. There were desperate times, and Robert attempted suicide at 16. While his relationships were superficial and opportunistic by necessity, he was helped by a number of therapists.

Robert was bright and saw education as a possible way forward: during high school, he concluded that a full scholarship somewhere would offer him the best way to avoid homelessness. Despite the prejudice and discrimination he experienced related to his ethnicity, he could see that being bilingual and a person of color were also strengths that could help him. Robert set himself determinedly on a course toward a college degree. Maintaining attendance at a good high school even as his placements shifted required two-hour bus rides each day. He achieved his goal, attending a good college with full scholarship. Therapist mentors encouraged him to go to graduate school.

Robert's path has been lonely to a degree that is hard for most of us to fully comprehend. He is confused about relationships, and doubts his ability to love or be loved. He often feels suspicious of the motives of others. Robert is highly anxious; sometimes his thoughts are scattered and confused. Intense rage toward others, especially those who have had an easier life, rises up unpredictably. He worries about the heritability of his mother's mental illness and the likelihood of his becoming ill. He is in transit, with no real home base, either physically or emotionally.

Robert was determined to find and make contact with his mother; he enlisted a private detective whom he persuaded to donate his services. Robert himself combed the streets in the neighborhoods where she had been seen for many nights, questioning homeless people five days a week for months. Shortly before the conclusion of his internship, he found her, living on the street, in her own mental world. He spoke with her, but she did not know him.

Biopsychosocial Perspective

The biopsychosocial perspective rests on a multi-systemic framework that recognizes the interdependence of systems within the individual and those in the individual's larger environment. The biopsychosocial model was originally introduced by George Engel in the field of medicine to account for biological, psychological, and social factors that have an impact on the progression of and recovery from illness and disease (Lakhan, 2006). It aims to incorporate these dimensions of human experience into a model that is both comprehensive and succinct.

The *biological* dimension includes neurological, physiological, genetic, temperamental, and health factors or characteristics. Contemporary models of development are "moving toward brain-mind-body conceptualizations" (Schore, A. 2003). The *psychological* refers to inner constructs (defined variously, depending on other theories employed), including conscious and unconscious phenomena, thoughts, attitudes, affects (which also have a biological substrate), identities, and culture as experienced by the individual. The *social* includes external systems with which the individual interacts, those that impinge upon or otherwise influence the individual. The "social" in the biopsychosocial model might also be thought of as "the environment."

Closely related is the person-in-environment model, which further articulates the dynamic aspect of the relationship between the person and his or her environment(s) as the continuous, mutually affecting interaction of the individual and the surround. This attention to reciprocal relationships, familiar in the social sciences, is increasingly making its way into biomedical research, where the interaction between genetic factors and environments is deepening our understanding of the complex etiology of medical and psychiatric disorders, and of neurobiological development, to be discussed in Chapter 3 (McCutcheon, 2006).

> *The application of a biopsychosocial lens to Robert allows us to consider his health (childhood injuries, childhood hernia that went untreated for three years, poor nutrition, small stature that may be constitutional, but may also have been affected by limited care and nutrition in early years), his high intelligence and resiliency, and his family history of schizophrenia. Psychological factors include sequelae of abuse, neglect, and abandonment, which are evident in his problematic attachment patterns and struggles with anxiety and depression. We can include his fortitude (resiliency has both biological and psychological aspects) and determination, and his compromised sense of efficacy and identity. Social dimensions are the worlds of Robert's neighborhoods and the institutions of his childhood and adolescence, including the foster care system, and the college and graduate school environments. A critical factor in any description of Robert's psychosocial systems is the aloneness with which he navigates them. Relationships are often transitory, as they have been throughout much of his life, so that there are new losses as well as old ones that, in turn, increase his wariness.*

Dynamic Nonlinear Systems Theory

Dynamic nonlinear systems theory is based on Bertalanffy's general systems theory and suggests that every living organism is an open system that maintains itself in continuous inflow and outflow, exchanging matter with the environment in which it is embedded (Lin, 2002). Individual parts of systems are viewed as complex and variable, with connections between them varying in degree of looseness. How tightly or loosely coupled parts of systems are will determine the rapidity and nature with which a change in one affects the other. In enmeshed families, for example, the slightest change in one person reverberates quickly and intensely throughout the family system. In a more detached family system, the depression or illness of one member might have less immediate or powerful effects on another.

Development of the system is seen as evolutionary—that is, it changes and stabilizes over time in response to internal and external forces (Miley, O'Melia, & DuBois, 2004). This perspective, closely related to an eco-systems perspective, assumes that there is an ongoing interaction whereby the *environment* (widely and broadly defined) affects the individual and the *individual* affects the environment in a continuous reciprocal interchange. Human interpersonal relationships are sometimes described as the most complex natural system known (Fogel, 2000).

> Robert's family is a system within which the family members are subsystems. The family itself is embedded in the larger environment of a low-income neighborhood in a complex urban center. Robert (and his ability to develop optimally) is continuously affected by the changes in his mother's mental state and physical behaviors. Robert's mother is affected by her interactions with him and with others on the street, or with the social service agency. As her children grow and interactions become more complicated or challenging, she may be less able to manage with limited internal and economic resources. Her rejecting or indifferent behaviors may increase. The boys may have various responses to these changes in their mother: they may become less or more aggressive, less or more withdrawn, and their behaviors in school or in the neighborhood may become more problematic.

Nonlinear dynamic systems theory builds on systems theory by adding the three principles of *complexity*, *continuity in time*, and *dynamic stability*. *Complexity* refers to the way in which many interacting parts work together to produce a coherent pattern under particular conditions. In this view, there is no such thing as unicausality (a single cause of an event or outcome) (Thelen, 2005), and the environmental surround is always a part of a person's behavior, including social, cultural, and physical factors.

> No single factor of Robert's early life can account for his behavior at a single point in time; rather, it was the interplay of internal and external systems that produced, for example, his call to 911 or his decision to go to college.

The second principle, *continuity in time*, suggests that the state of a system at any given time depends on its previous states and is the starting point for future states (Thelen, 2005). Another way of saying this is that each moment is a product of all preceding experience, and all future moments are built on the present moment. Each of us is precisely who we are at any given moment because of every single thing that has happened to us up to this moment. The implication of this is that all interventions have the potential to make a difference to what comes after.

> *Robert's state at the moment of high school graduation would reflect the fear, mistrust, and isolation of his previous experiences, as well as everything he had learned, culturally, socially, physically, and cognitively. He would begin the next chapter of life in a state of greater inner disorganization and less confidence and hope than someone who had experienced more continuous caring from the environment up to that point. This state would be the starting point for succeeding states. An encouraging or attentive teacher or social worker could then move him toward or into a more optimistic state.*

Dynamic stability, the third principle of dynamic systems theory, states that some behaviors are so constrained by human structure and social systems that they are highly stable patterns, but only for a time. An example is crawling, an available solution that babies discover when they do not yet have the balance and strength for walking, but want to get to something they cannot reach. Each child gets to it in his or her own way and develops a unique pattern, which will be stable and useful for a period. As the baby shifts to a new mode made possible because of further development or inputs, that stability is lost (Thelen, 2005). Dynamic stability reflects the ongoing mutually shaping interaction of the person and the surround. This principle again suggests the plasticity and responsiveness (adaptability) of the individual as well as the potential of new experience or developmental capabilities to have impact on a person and on relationships.

> *In the group home, Robert learned to use and deal drugs and to engage in unemotional sex, evolving a temporary pattern that was responsive to the demands of his environment. His behaviors, in turn, elicited attention from others who exploited him for their own purposes, making his social world feel even more threatening to him. When his academic success provided a different context and self-definition, other behavior patterns and experiences of self could develop.*

The interaction between experience and maturation is dynamic: our experiences, along with our biological growth, provide opportunities to develop different aspects of ourselves. Living forms (including human beings) combine stability of structure with fluidity of change; preceding change, they become more and more unstable until they reach a point of instability (disorganization) from which they reorganize to attain new, more complex forms of organization (Kozlowska & Hanney, 2002). This has implications for all transitional moments in life, including the transition from foster care.

Experiences of maltreatment and foster placement interact with maturational processes, allowing or encouraging some aspects of the child to develop, and inhibiting or discouraging others. It may be that potential but less-developed aspects of the person require shifts in the surrounding systems (social or otherwise) in order to emerge more fully. The transitional years are an opportunity for new self-development if the programmatic and relational environment can shift in the right directions to promote it.

Dynamic systems theory helps us understand the mechanisms and outcomes (whether adaptive or maladaptive) of change processes. Small differences in any part of a system can generate large changes. *For example, if one of the youth in a group home had encouraged Robert to join a school interest club, his involvement in high-risk activities might have been limited or curtailed.* Similar actions may produce very different results in different children, because of their constitutional givens and because of the lives that have brought them to the present moment.

Developmental Perspective

A developmental perspective takes account of the child's movement from infancy through childhood, adolescence, and early adulthood. The biopsychosocial model outlined above can help us understand how the human mind undergoes normal maturation and developmental change over these years. Mental development arises from the transactions among biological, social, and psychological stimuli (Gemelli, 1996). Biological stimuli include those from within the infant's body, including the brain, and those from the surface of the infant's body. The developing central nervous system gives rise to new motor abilities, and there are maturational advances in body growth and control over sphincters. Psychological stimuli emanate from within the infant's innate (temperamental) and representational inner worlds. The social environment (other people) is a steady source of stimuli, as well as being the medium through which the nature and amount of stimuli is determined or controlled.

As development proceeds, the infant/child undergoes changes in its structures and the processes they perform in response to all that is occurring internally and externally (Gemelli, 1996). These changes in structures and processes may be thought of broadly as changes in organization of behavior over time. The organization of behaviors with regard to context reveals meaningful individual differences, which we may think of as aspects of personality or the self. Central aspects of individual organization originate in the organization of early primary relationships (Sroufe et al., 2005). The initial surround of youth in the foster care system must be conceived of as an integral part of their organization of behaviors.

Similarly, the new surround at the exit from care will present opportunities for new organization.

New technological and theoretical advances in research on the neurobiology of the developing brain have greatly expanded the understanding of infant development. Through the recently developed techniques of functional neuroimaging (positron emission tomography, or PET scans) and functional magnetic image resonance imaging (fMRI), the brain's functioning can be imaged and observed in a variety of conditions (Applegate & Shapiro, 2005). These tools can show us how the brain reacts to experience, and which areas in the brain may be affected or implicated in these responses. Brain responses to caregiver behaviors can be mapped. The relationship-dependent nature of infant development is outlined below and discussed more fully in Chapter 3.

The infant in utero is a part of the mother-infant system, which, up to birth, is physiologically one system. Variations of the smallest degree (mother's change in temperature, blood pressure, or heart rate, for example) occur simultaneously to mother and fetus. When the baby emerges into the outside world, there are new environmental demands with which the baby interacts, resulting in new and more complex forms of patterning within the infant system and also the mother-infant system. Outcomes (in this case, how the brain and the baby develop) depend on initial conditions and on subsequent ones (Sroufe et al., 2005).

> The infant Robert was born to an adolescent mother whose mental illness may have already been making an appearance. She was an immigrant, isolated from her family of origin. She may have received little or no prenatal care, and her own nutrition may have been poor. Robert's needs during infancy may have been overwhelming to his teenaged mother. Her second pregnancy, during his first year of life, further complicated a mother-infant system that had been abandoned by the father, and that may not have been well-regulated or comfortably functioning at the outset.

Many authors point to the complex nature of the relationship between context and brain development, describing the brain as an organ of adaptation that builds its structures through interactions with others, in the interface between experience and genetics (Cozolino, 2006a). Applegate and Shapiro state that "it is an open, nonlinear dynamic system whose adaptive development and self-organization depend on attuned interactions with caregivers" (Applegate & Shapiro, 2005). More specifically, Schore and Schore suggest that the dyadic interaction between the newborn and the mother regulates the baby's (physiological) homeostasis (J. Schore & Schore, 2008). In other words, what goes on between caregiver and infant is continuously affecting and shaping the biological equilibrium and stability of the infant.

Biological forms develop through a process of increasing differentiation and increasing subordination or hierarchization of parts, so that parts and functions become both more defined and more ordered. The developing brain exemplifies this process: at the beginning there is an overproduction of neurons, then some are pruned (or fall away), and others become interconnected to create systems (Sroufe et al., 2005). New circumstances and conditions affect these pruning and connecting processes, causing some potential developments to be curtailed and others optimized in response to the specific environment.

It is within the early dyadic relationship with a caregiver that the infant brain matures and is shaped. Attachment communications between caregiver and infant are critical to the development of structural right-brain neurobiological systems, which are centrally involved in the processing of emotion, the modulation of stress, self-regulation, and the origins of the sense of self (J. Schore & Schore, 2008).

Early Adverse Experience and Developmental Traumatology

There is a growing body of research into the effects of early adverse experience on subsequent development and health. The ACE (Adverse Childhood Experiences) Study, which posed the question of whether and how childhood experiences affect adult health decades later, found that 1) adverse childhood experiences are vastly more common than is generally acknowledged or recognized, and 2) these experiences have a powerful relationship to adult health fifty years later. The study demonstrated that the higher the number of adverse early experiences, the greater the likelihood of developing a variety of physical and emotional illnesses (Fellitti, 2002).

Children who enter foster care are known to have had adverse childhood experiences, whether maltreatment; exposure to violence; or the loss of a family member to death, incarceration, or abandonment. As we will see in subsequent chapters, events and relationships associated with placement may constitute further adverse experiences. A neglected child may be placed in multiple homes and attend multiple schools, with repeated losses of relationships and stability; maltreatment may occur in a foster placement. The ACE Study shows us the impact of trauma on health and well-being, but traumatic experience also dynamically interacts with developmental tasks and phases in the biological, psychological, and social realms.

Developmental traumatology is the systematic investigation of the psychiatric and psychobiological impact of chronic interpersonal violence on the developing child. This model brings together knowledge from developmental psychopathology, neuroscience, and stress and trauma research. Several basic assumptions underlie the model. It assumes that there are an infinite number of stressors, but finite ways the brain and body can respond. The stressor of a dysfunctional and traumatized interpersonal relationship complicates or interferes with the child's ability to form relationships. Maltreatment in childhood is more detrimental than in adulthood because it can cause delays in or deficits to developmental achievements in behavioral, cognitive, and emotional regulation (De Bellis, 2001).

De Bellis points out that the biological stress system responses of the child are based on the nature of the stressor, the frequency or chronicity of the stressor, individual differences (genetic vulnerability, for example) in biological stress systems' regulation and responses, and, finally, the individual's ability to either maintain homeostasis (return to the state of equilibrium) or to permanently change in response to the stressor (De Bellis, 2001). The symptoms of post-traumatic stress disorder (PTSD) are common responses to severe stressors. When trauma occurs during development, chronic PTSD symptoms are often the first step on a trajectory to more severe symptoms and compromised functioning, eventually increasing the intergenerational transmission of abuse or neglect.

Numerous researchers find that adverse childhood events are risk factors for many common psychiatric conditions, including depressive and anxiety disorders, suicidality, and personality disorders. In addition, childhood abuse may complicate treatment: medication treatment–resistant patients reported significantly greater levels of childhood emotional abuse than treatment-responsive patients, for instance (Chapman, Dube, & Anda, 2007).

In the optimal child-caregiving surround system, the ongoing interaction creates a positive dynamic whereby each party affects the other in ways that contribute to a sense of well-being and to growth. The child needs food or holding or stimulation, the caregiver provides it, the child's state improves or develops, the caregiver is gratified and her confidence and good feeling grow, leading her to further attune to her child. In a dysfunctional or abusive environment, the organization of infant behaviors is responsive to a malignant circumstance. Survival requires an adaptation strategy, even on the biological level.

> When Robert was small, his mother's mental illness created a disorganized environment, physically and emotionally. He organized in response to this unpredictable situation, drawing back and becoming guarded. His withdrawal may have been experienced by her as a rejection, increasing her suspiciousness and leading to further withdrawal.

When an infant's cries evoke a shaking or a slap, he or she learns not to signal distress, and important needs may go unattended. Very young infants who are frightened by an angry caregiver may avert their gaze or simply freeze in an attempt to draw as little notice as possible; once crawling or walking has developed, they may back away. This type of behavior may prevent an escalation of physical violence, but it also thwarts or delays the unconstrained development of livelier potentials in the infant. In a situation of neglect, the infant may attempt more and more drastically to compel the attention of the preoccupied (depressed or substance-affected or mentally ill) parent, resorting to self-destructive or other-destructive behaviors. The parent may withdraw further or become angry, and the cycle intensifies.

The inner adaptation in such situations may be even more problematic, leading to depression, despair, self-hatred, overwhelming rage, and chaotic or frightening representations. Behaviors and inner expectations that may serve to protect the child in an abusive situation can be extremely problematic in a more benign environment, such as a new foster home or a classroom situation. The sense of trust, autonomy, and initiative that develop in early childhood in response to a positive environment will be correspondingly influenced by a dangerous or threatening environment (Erikson, 1968). The effects of traumatic childhood experience continue to be felt in middle childhood and adolescence, which will be discussed in Chapters 4 and 5.

Attachment Theory

Attachment theory will be presented in detail in Chapter 4; however, it may be helpful for the reader to know why the theory appears as a thread in this book. Attachment theory is useful in further delineating the child–caregiver(s) system of early life and its relationship to development and interpersonal behavior in childhood, adolescence, and adulthood. Its emphasis on the importance of human relationships can inform our understanding of the experience of placement and leaving care and provide direction in program and policy design.

In the fields of psychology, psychoanalysis, social work, psychiatry, and counseling, early attachments are increasingly recognized as an important motivating force driving behavior. The recognition that relationships constitute "a fundamental and necessary building block in the evolution of the contemporary human brain" (Cozolino, 2006b) points to the need to examine and understand the nature of early relationships.

Briefly, the theory suggests that the intimate emotional bonds between people are a basic component of human nature, meant to insure protection and survival, and are as necessary as the drives for food and sex. A corollary and related need is exploration of the environment. With a "secure base" (the attachment figure), children feel safe enough to explore their worlds; as they do so, internal aspects of development progress, along with the capacity to relate to others and to the larger world. It is this interdependent nexus of relationship and exploration opportunities that provides a strong foundation for development of children's potentials. The early experiences in attachment are what children take forward as templates of expectations for future relationships with people and things (Bowlby, 1988).

Trauma and attachment implicate similar neurological systems; physiological responses to trauma may be related to responses to attachment stress (Bolen, 2000). The removal of a child from the attachment figure, even in the context of an ambivalent attachment, may be traumatic in its disruptive power and may compound the stress response. As mentioned earlier, the effects of extreme stress on the developing child can lead to PTSD, as well as to many other symptoms.

Despite a current trend in favor of attachment theory, some raise questions about certain of its key assumptions, and readers may wish to know what the evidence says about these. Bolen reviews the research and presents the current state of the evidence (Bolen, 2000). The question of whether attachment has a physiological base has not yet been resolved by research. A controversial assumption of attachment theory is that attachment is universal and crosses cultures. Studies show that it can be considered universal in that some kind of attachment behaviors are observed between attachment figures and children across cultures, but that there are important cross-cultural differences in the distribution of attachment patterns. Different cultures may show greater or smaller numbers of secure or insecure attachments.

Studies of intergenerational transmission of attachment patterns suggest that parents' inner working models of their own early experience do influence their responses to their child's signals, thus influencing the child's attachment pattern (Bolen, 2000). Research indicates that the qualities of both the attachment figure and those of the child are equally important, that they are in continuous interaction, and that transmission is a dynamic property. The research on the stability, predictability, and dynamic nature of attachment reveals consistent support for all of these characteristics (Bolen, 2000).

Ambiguous Loss, Disenfranchised Grief

Grief is thought to be a byproduct of maintaining the attachment bond; the separation distress that ensues when the attachment figure is absent is the prototype of the grief reaction (Archer, 2001). Stage theories of grief are widely accepted, and usually articulate four or five stages involving shock or denial, yearning or searching, anger, despair or depression, and acceptance or reorganization (Maciejewski et al., 2007). Children need to mourn their losses, or they are at risk for distorted or delayed grief reactions that may be set off with great intensity by a subsequent loss (Crenshaw, 2006–2007). Children in foster care sustain repeated losses: of family members (due to death, mental illness, or incarceration, for example) and of their family itself, when they are removed and placed. Subsequent losses often follow as one placement succeeds another.

More particularly, children in care experience ambiguous losses, those that remain unclear and where closure is not possible. In these situations, someone may be physically absent but psychologically present ("leaving without good-bye") or psychologically absent while physically present ("goodbye without leaving"). The child must live with the paradox of absence and presence (Boss, 2007).

> *During childhood, Robert experienced both with his mother. She might be terrifyingly physically present, but was psychologically in a mental and emotional space far from her young son, unable to provide love and protection. When he entered the foster care system and "lost" her, she remained a painful psychological presence in his mind, so much so that he organized his young adult life around the attempt to locate and reconnect with her.*

The grief of children in care may not be acknowledged by others, sometimes because those around them are busy constructing a new situation for them and are more preoccupied with safety and logistics, or because the children are thought to be too young to comprehend their losses, or because they are being removed from a bad situation. The losses they feel may simply be unrecognized. Significant losses in which the loss is not recognized or the griever is not recognized as a griever (because of age or mental status, for example) lead to disenfranchised grief. Disenfranchised grief, by its very nature, exacerbates grief by precluding social support and solace (Doka, 1999).

Resiliency Theory

Resilience is variously defined as good outcomes in spite of serious threats to adaptation or development (Masten, 2001), the phenomenon of overcoming stress or adversity (Rutter, 1999), and the capacity of dynamic systems to withstand or recover from significant disturbances (Masten, 2007). The concept of resilience draws from and links together the constructs described earlier (the biopsychosocial perspective, dynamic systems theory, developmental theory, attachment theory). Increasingly, studies of resilience recognize the biopsychosocial nature of these processes and, therefore, draw on many disciplines (counseling and social psychology, neurobiology, family systems) (Luthar & Brown, 2007).

Resiliency researchers point out that resilience to stress is multi-determined and contextual (Haglund et al., 2007; Luthar & Brown, 2007; Masten, 2001). There has been controversy about how to define and operationalize the concept, but there is now wide agreement that it is a dynamic process, rather than a static trait or characteristic (Luthar & Brown, 2007; Masten, 2007). Resilience cannot be considered apart from risks and protective factors in both the person and the environment. Risk and protective factors emanate from the inner world of the child (low self-esteem, unresolved trauma, for example), from the inner worlds of significant others, and from outer worlds and systems that impinge on the child (Schofield & Beek, 2005).

The importance of early caregiving environments is supported by powerful evidence in the literature. The brain responds to environmental inputs such that harsh early environments lead to decreases in neural networks and brain size, whereas beneficial early interventions result in enrichment of the networks among neurons and increase brain size (Luthar & Brown, 2007). Physical changes in the brain can have implications for the vulnerability to psychopathology later on due to increased or decreased capacity to manage stressful circumstances. Masten points out that adversity may wreak its most lasting and devastating damage to development through its effects on developing adaptive systems; that is, during early life (Masten, 2007); and Luthar and Brown state unequivocally that "the single most deleterious environmental risk is sustained presence of abuse and neglect; conversely, loving relationships have high protective potential" (Luthar & Brown, 2007).

> *The risk factors for the infant Robert are his arrival into a world in which his mother is distressed from his earliest days: She is an adolescent herself, an immigrant far from her family, immediately pregnant (and subject to the hormonal shifts of his postpartum weeks, then quickly to those of her next pregnancy), abandoned by the children's father, and without resources. Protective factors exist within Robert in the form of his physiological fortitude, potential for high IQ, and capacity to adapt. His mother's ability to be loving is inconsistent at best. During Robert's early and middle childhood, his world requires that he mediate his own childhood needs himself, which he somehow manages to do, an illustration of the dynamic nature of resiliency.*

Some researchers have reported on the phenomenon of "stress inoculation" (Haglund et al., 2007) or "steeling" (Rutter, 1999), whereby exposure at a young age to milder or more manageable forms of stress appears to aid in building a resilient neurobiological or psychological profile. It is also true that children may have resilience in relation to some stressors, but not others.

> *Robert's mother becomes increasingly erratic as her illness worsens; he is subjected to physical abuse and neglect. Episodes of abandonment occur. Robert focuses on getting enough food, looking out for his brother as best he can, and getting through school. He learns he can survive extremely frightening circumstances and loneliness in foster care. He is able to elicit and mobilize interest and encouragement from teachers and therapists.*

Multiple risk factors in combination are associated with increased risk of multiple problems; the cumulative effect often involves a synergistic interaction among risk factors. Similarly with protective factors, there may be little effect from any one variable and a greater impact from a combination of variables (Rutter, 1999). The dynamic interaction between genetic factors, environmental risks (or protections), and the child's prior experiences is constantly evolving and subject to influence by new variables.

Sensitivity to environmental risk may be influenced by genetic factors and by prior experience. Chronic psychosocial adversity may make children more sensitive to acute stressors, but, as mentioned earlier, it may also have a steeling effect. Genetic factors such as IQ and temperament may play a role in sensitivity to psychosocial risk (Rutter, 1999).

Resilience research demonstrates that the impact of adversity can be reduced through positive interpersonal processes and coping strategies that lead to success and enhanced self-esteem. Positive experiences that directly counter or compensate for a risk factor can "neutralize" or counterbalance the negative impact of an earlier experience (Rutter, 1999). New positive experiences can have a "turning point" effect, neurobiologically and psychosocially (Glicken, 2004; Haglund et al., 2007; Masten, 2001; Rutter, 1999).

Another important aspect of resilience is the individual's cognitive processing style. How the person views negative experiences and how this is incorporated into the sense of self is likely to play a part in allowing the individual to move forward in a positive way. Human beings are continually interpreting and adapting to changes in their environments. The meanings we ascribe to changes in our environments have an influence on our subsequent actions, which then have impact on the other systems with which we come into contact (McGuire, 2005).

> *Robert has been able to use his mental abilities to focus on getting through school. Only recently is he sure enough that he will survive that he can begin to reflect on his early experience; indeed, there is much he cannot remember as yet, due to its overwhelming nature. His depression, anxiety, deep confusion about how to relate to others, and impulsiveness in attempting to establish intimacy are the external manifestations of the chronic childhood trauma that he experienced. The academic and interpersonal positive turning-point experiences, as well as a few friendships from high school and college, helped him stay on a constructive life course, enlarging his sense of a self that can be successful. Robert's sense of a self that can be loved, however, is less fully developed at present.*

Summary

The young people leaving foster care who are at the heart of this book have, in all likelihood, traveled a bumpy road from conception and birth to an early or middle childhood marked by loss, family disruption, maltreatment, and other kinds of trauma. They have moved into one or multiple placement experiences, which themselves may have offered further loss or trauma, and finally to their eighteenth birthdays and into the world beyond foster care. Our understanding of their physiological, cognitive, emotional, and social development from their earliest days, including early and subsequent attachment experiences, will be crucial to our work with them.

The environmental surround, of which the foster care system is a critical part, will likewise be important to our work. The foster care, educational, and other social systems are dynamic, changing in response to legislative, political, and social contexts, and are susceptible to being changed by our actions. The multiple cultural contexts—of the family of origin, the foster family (families), the group home, the larger majority culture, the mainstream culture of biological families—must all be considered and must inform our practice and our programs. As we think about what youth leaving foster care need from us, we must also think about how they have responded to the adversity in their lives, what strengths they carry within, and how to build upon those strengths. The theories summarized in this chapter provide an organizing framework that can guide our thinking and our work.

PART **II**

DEVELOPMENT

Part II takes the reader on the developmental journey from infancy through adolescence. As outlined in Chapter 2, the application of a developmental perspective is central to more effective support for foster care alumni because it allows us to consider the young person in terms of what has occurred (or failed to occur) up to the point of transition. Such a perspective is made possible with a thorough understanding of the nature and timing of normal development, along with knowledge of how adverse childhood experiences such as maltreatment and entry into foster care can interact with developmental tasks and milestones. (Presentation of emerging adult development, the years from late adolescence through the mid-twenties, appears in Chapter 11 and provides a foundation for the discussion of program and practice elements for youth leaving care.)

Chapter 3 begins with a description of the brain: its structure, regions, and development. The impact of trauma on brain development is discussed. The body's stress-response system is explicated, with attention to how childhood maltreatment interacts with the infant's ability to manage stress. The chapter helps the reader understand the importance of affect regulation to learning and to the later development of psychopathology.

Chapter 4 focuses on the development and nature of attachments and the ways in which childhood trauma, maltreatment, and disruption of attachments can affect the growing child. The chapter presents the basics of attachment theory and attachment classifications, including those found most frequently among children with a history of maltreatment. Problems of early attachment play a crucial role in subsequent relationships, with foster parents, group-home staff, teachers, and clinicians—and therefore powerfully influence placement stability, school readiness, and school performance. Program and practice models that are informed by an understanding of early attachment problems are likely to be more successful because they account for difficulties in moving successfully into relationships and maintaining them.

Chapter 5 presents biological, psychological, and social developmental tasks of adolescence, from a normative standpoint, and for adolescents in foster care. The development of a sense of identity, including ethnic and sexual identity, is discussed, with attention to the impact of maltreatment and foster care experience. Chapter 5 takes us through the years of development up to the age of transition, and gives us a foundation for understanding the mental health problems that will be the subject of Part III.

3

NEUROBIOLOGY AND DEVELOPMENT

Nearly all young people who remain in foster care until the age of emancipation have experienced extreme forms of adverse early experience in addition to repeated separations from biological and other caregivers. The traumatic events that led to or accompanied removal from their families of origin have left their marks, influencing subsequent development and relationships. In this chapter, we start at the beginning, examining infant brain development and the stress-response system. A summary of recent research captures advances in knowledge of the neurobiological impact of trauma in infancy and its role in the development of risk for psychopathology in childhood, adolescence, and adulthood. Memory and affect regulation will be discussed, as well as fluid cognition, an increasingly studied dimension of intelligence sometimes called the *working memory* (Blair, 2006).

Development occurs in a psychosocial context; as described in Chapter 2, context and child exist in a reciprocally interacting and mutually shaping dynamic system. Empirical evidence shows that, while both environmental influences and genetic influences are strong and pervasive, either one alone is rarely determinative in causation of psychiatric disorder (Rutter, 2002), or in optimal developmental outcomes. The examination of infant development that follows is offered to illuminate how, from the first moments of life, everything that happens, inside and outside, makes a difference to the growing child.

The Brain: Structures and Functions

The concept of a complex, nonlinear dynamic system can be applied to the brain itself: it is continuously developing and changing as it interacts with a changing environment. To appreciate the vulnerability of the developing brain to environmental influences, particularly traumatic events, it is necessary to have a basic understanding of the brain. In a relatively undifferentiated state at birth, the brain becomes an increasingly complex system as later-evolving structures are added to the early-appearing primitive parts during the first year of life (Cozolino, 2006a). The specific capacities of each person's brain are determined by both genetic information and experiential stimuli (Siegel, 2003). Experience (presence of positive or negative stimuli) has differential effects depending on genetic potentials and on timing relative to the developmental process. Early-occurring child abuse or neglect, or trauma that occurs in utero, for example, can exert an influence on brain development.

The brain is made up of tri-partite cells called neurons. They are comprised of various proteins, made of amino acids from the foods we eat. The three parts of the neuron are the cell body, the axon, and the dendrite. The cell body contains the proteins that have been assembled based on instructions contained in each cell's DNA (genes). The axon is a fiber that extends out from the cell body. It will eventually become covered with myelin, a fatty white substance that serves as an insulator and enhances the axon's firing efficiency. A neuron is said to "fire" when it sends a signal to another neuron, generating an electrical impulse. Each cell has a number of dendrites: elaborate, branching appendages that interconnect with dendrites of other neurons (Cozolino, 2006a; De Bellis, 2005). The axon of one neuron links with the dendrite of another; each dendrite can accept multiple axon terminals. Every individual has billions of neurons, each with up to 10,000 connections to other neurons.

At the beginning of life, more neurons are produced than are necessary. In response to experience (stimuli or the lack thereof), some are pruned (fall away), and others interconnect into systems, and then into larger systems of systems. This process leads to differentiation and refinement, building on previously existing structures. If early fetal brain damage occurs as a result of trauma or malnourishment during pregnancy, it can have long-lasting effects (Sroufe et al., 2005).

At the juncture of connection between the axon of one neuron with the dendrite of another, there is a tiny gap called a synapse, over which chemical molecules known as neurotransmitters pass from one neuron to another. Neurotransmitters may be of the excitatory type, those that stimulate increased neuronal activity, or the inhibitory type, those that slow activity. The "firing rate" refers to the transmission of energy and information; the "base firing rate" (regular intervals) for any individual can be powerfully affected by stimuli as the infant responds to external and internal events.

The activation of neural firing patterns in response to stimuli (experience) can lead to the turning on of genes, and then to a cascade of biochemical changes in the neural cell that eventually enables proteins to be produced (Siegel, 2003). In this way, experience can activate genes, leading to protein production and changing the very structure of the brain.

Regions of the Brain

The brainstem is the region of the brain that develops first. Areas of the brainstem, also referred to as the lower structures, comprise the inner core of the brain deep within the skull. The brainstem receives information from perceptions and from the body and mediates basic elements of energy flow, including arousal, alertness, temperature, respiration, and heart rate (Applegate & Shapiro, 2005; Cozolino, 2006a). The midbrain is at the upper end of the brainstem and is associated with vision, hearing, eye movement, and body movement.

The Limbic System

The regions of the brain that are most critical in work with young people emerging from foster care are the limbic structures and the cerebral cortex (Figure 3.1). These areas of the brain are most central to the processing and regulation of emotion, to thinking and planning, and to coping with stress. The specific impacts of early adverse experience on these brain functions are discussed later in the chapter.

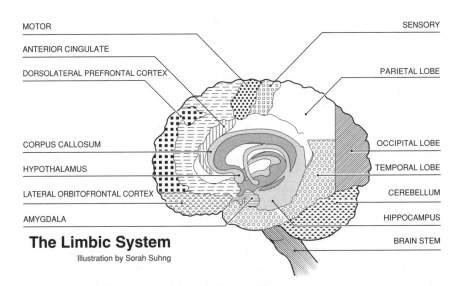

Figure 3.1 The Limbic System. Illustration by Sorah Suhng.

The limbic system, which includes the orbitofrontal cortex, the amygdala, and the anterior cingulate regions, is thought to play a central role in the coordination of the upper and lower brain. It mediates emotion, motivation, learning, and goal-directed activity. The limbic structures are involved in the integration of a wide range of mental processes, including the appraisal of meaning, social cognition, and the regulation of emotion. The amygdala is implicated in the processing of fear, sadness, anger, and in the perception of such states in others, as in facial emotional recognition (Siegel, 2003). In fact, the limbic system is thought to be responsible for much of the integration and self-regulation of all of the brain structures (Applegate & Shapiro, 2005).

The limbic system houses the medial temporal lobe, including the hippocampus, which plays a central role in consciously accessible forms of memory. The limbic and lower regions also house the hypothalamus and pituitary glands, which are responsible for physiological homeostasis or bodily equilibrium, established by way of neuroendocrine activity (neuronal firing and hormonal release).

The Orbitofrontal Cortex

The cerebral cortex organizes sensory, motor, and conscious experiences, as well as learned interactions with the world. The growth of the cortex is experience-dependent, whereas the growth of the brainstem relies on the inborn genetic template (Cozolino, 2006b). We are born with the blueprint for our brainstem, but the way our cortex develops depends upon what our early lives are like. The cerebral cortex, or neocortex, is the most evolved part of the brain, with a number of lobes that mediate distinct functions. The orbitofrontal cortex (OFC) is located in the frontal lobe, where reasoning and associational processes reside. It is of greatest interest to us because of its location, its involvement in some critical functions, and its experience-dependent, experience-susceptible nature.

The OFC is "one synapse away" from all three major regions of the brain; it integrates the cortex, limbic structures, and brain stem into a functional whole (Siegel, 2003). It is involved in regulation of the autonomic nervous system, controlling such things as heart rate, respiration, and the intestines. A part of the autonomic nervous system is the sympathetic nervous system, which functions to activate the system in response to threat or other motivations. The parasympathetic nervous system is involved in conservation of bodily energy, immunological functions, and repair of damaged systems (Cozolino, 2006a).

The OFC is believed to be central to processing behavioral expression and the regulation of emotion, response flexibility, and the creation of self-awareness and autobiographical memory (Siegel, 2003). Since it is interconnected with other limbic areas, it acts as the "association cortex" (Applegate & Shapiro, 2005). Neurons that fire specifically in response to the emotional expression of faces are contained within the OFC.

The dorsolateral prefrontal cortex (DLPFC) is also involved in emotion processing and the maintenance of information in the presence of distracting stimuli. It is thought to be involved in response inhibition and may therefore be important for impulse control (Lee & Hoaken, 2007).

Mirror Neurons

Mirror neurons are nerve cells in areas of the brain involved in planning and carrying out movement, first discovered in studies of macaques in the early 1990s. They were named "mirror neurons" because they fire when an animal acts and also when it simply watches another animal performing the same action. These neurons may play an important role when we monitor what goes on around us and in inferring the intentions of others. Some studies show that mirror neurons are involved in interpreting the facial expressions and actions of others (Society for Neuroscience, 2008). Mirror neurons are active during the early critical periods of brain development described below; it makes sense to assume that they play a central part in the important learning about human relations, behavior, and the self that occurs during these early years. On the symbolic level, the capacity to understand another person's internal world may be related to activation of shared representation through mirror neurons (Gabbard, 2005). When significant others in the infant's world engage in abusive or frightening behavior, or are unresponsive during these critical developmental periods, the internalized representations of these experiences begin to shape what is known about how people relate to one another.

Right and Left Hemispheres

Most of the brain is split into left and right hemispheres, connected with bands of tissue called the *corpus callosum* and the *anterior commissures*; these tissues transfer information between the two sides of the brain and help to integrate functions of the two hemispheres. The right hemisphere is dominant in its growth during the first three years of life and is dominant for nonverbal and tonal aspects of language, facial expression of affect, perception of emotion, and regulation of the autonomic nervous system and the body state. It is thought by some researchers that the early-maturing right hemisphere is involved in the coherent sense of self, connecting the individual to emotionally salient experiences and memories (Schore & Schore, 2008).

The left side of the brain develops later than the right and is characterized by linearity and logic. The left side processes language in a linguistic fashion, responding to grammar, words, and patterns (Applegate & Shapiro, 2005; Siegel, 2003). These left-side capacities must connect with the subjective emotional self-experience stored in the right side in order to have an autobiographical sense of self (Siegel, 2003). It is the corpus callosum that provides neural integration of hemispheres, allowing us to function mentally and physically. As we will see later in the chapter, trauma may impair the growth of the corpus callosum, thus interfering with the hemispheric integration needed for a coherent sense of self and life events.

Sensitive Periods

In the early stages of development, there is heightened sensitivity to certain environmental stimuli. During the first eighteen to thirty-six months, when the brain has the highest number of synapses (before a great deal of pruning has occurred), learning is easier (Cellini, 2004), and, in general, there is "exuberant neural growth" (Cozolino, 2006b). Different regions of the brain have different critical periods: the sensitive period for the orbitofrontal cortex is from six to twelve months, with a major maturational surge at ten to twelve months. At this time, the infant needs exciting, highly pleasurable face-to-face interactions with the caregiver. High states of positive arousal, such as those in games of peek-a-boo, activate the baby's sympathetic nervous system and lead to a rush of biological processes in which noradrenaline and endorphins are released in the brain (Applegate & Shapiro, 2005; Cozolino, 2006b). Conversely, prolonged states of negative arousal activate stress hormones (to be discussed later in the chapter).

The first three years are critical growth periods for right and left hemispheres and the corpus callosum. Early-occurring abuse and neglect have been shown to reduce the size of the corpus callosum, which, in turn, is associated with diminished communication between the two hemispheres (Teicher et al., 2003). The majority of brain development occurs in the first five years; however, development of brain structures and synaptic pruning continue throughout middle childhood and adolescence. Structural changes improve brain functioning by selectively pruning away unused synapses and improving the conductance of electrical signals among active neurons. Patterns of connectivity among neural systems are dependent on use (Lee & Hoaken, 2007); the stimuli present in the environment influence which systems are used more and less frequently, and the brain develops accordingly.

Memory

Memory, both conscious and unconscious, may best be thought of as sets of firing patterns in neural networks; the increased probability of firing a similar pattern is how the network "remembers" (Applegate & Shapiro, 2005). Information we have been exposed to in the past is organized into a neural representation, which is then activated in the present. We have two kinds of memory systems: explicit or declarative, and implicit or non-declarative memory.

Explicit memory, which includes factual information or semantic memory and episodic or autobiographical memory, develops around age two because it depends on the maturation of the hippocampal area of the limbic system. The explicit memory system is built to remember things (objects, people, places, information), event details, and contextual aspects of experience. The hippocampus and OFC work together to combine time features, language, and ascription of meaning to events (Applegate & Shapiro, 2005; Kaplow et al., 2006).

The implicit memory system, on the other hand, is present from birth and mediated by the amygdala. It is rapid, unconscious, and tightly connected to body response systems to help individuals survive in the face of threats. Implicit memory is organized to give the emotional valence of events without the details of the context (Kaplow et al., 2006). The infant perceives the environment and recalls it in behavioral, sensory, and emotional ways which are not consciously remembered, but which exert powerful influence (Applegate & Shapiro, 2005).

Usually, the two memory systems are highly coordinated, but in conditions of extreme stress or trauma, they can become uncoupled so that sensory and affective elements become dissociated from coherent semantic memory (Kaplow et al., 2006). That is, a person might feel powerful emotions without understanding why. Children who have experienced maltreatment may be at the mercy of strong feelings connected to early frightening events which they cannot consciously recall or understand.

Early Life Stress (ELS)

ELS is the type of stress experienced when a child is confronted with a situation that is appraised as personally threatening and for which adequate coping resources are unavailable (Heim, Meinlschmidt, & Nemeroff, 2003). Abuse, neglect, parental absence or loss, family violence, and parental rejection during childhood are experiences that overwhelm a child's developing psychobiological resources. Research on how these experiences affect brain function and development has burgeoned in the past decade as a result of the advances in brain imaging, leading to interdisciplinary approaches such as developmental psychopathology, developmental neurobiology, and developmental traumatology (see, for example, Blair, 2006; De Bellis, 2001; and Penza, Heim, & Nemeroff, 2003). These approaches integrate neuroscience, development, and psychology to provide a deeper understanding than we have previously had of just how adverse experience in the early years can continue to affect a person throughout life in the absence of intervention, and how intervention can, in fact, improve the long-term outcomes of maltreated children.

The Brain's Response to Stress

Stress can be mild, moderate, or severe, and can be episodic or chronic. While stress is an inevitable part of life, and at some levels can promote both neural growth and adaptive capacity, severe or prolonged stress in early life can have far-reaching developmental consequences. Discussion of the impact of abuse, neglect, and parental loss follows this overview of the stress-response system.

Both the prefrontal cortex and the limbic system play central roles in fear conditioning and stress responsivity. The OFC helps regulate affect and autonomic activity and plays a part in extracting emotional content from environmental stimuli. The dorsolateral prefrontal cortex is thought to be involved in emotion processing, necessary for encoding of information in the working (short-term) memory and for maintenance of information in the presence of distracting stimuli. The DLPFC helps with impulse control in response to stress (Lee & Hoaken, 2007).

In the limbic system, the hippocampus has a role in memory formation and retrieval and is thought to act in response to signals from the amygdala. The hypothalamus regulates the autonomic nervous system through hormonal production and release (Lee & Hoaken, 2007).

The Hypothalamic/Pituitary/Adrenal Axis (HPA)

The HPA axis is the center of stress and immunicologic response in mammals (McCutcheon, 2006) (Figure 3.2). When stressful events occur, two systems are activated to assist the organism in adapting to the changing environmental demand: the sympathetic division of the autonomic nervous system and the HPA axis. The sympathoadrenal activation results in increased release of epinephrine (adrenaline) and norepinephrine (noradrenaline) and shifts in blood flow to certain organs, all reflecting an alarm reaction to enable optimal coping with the perceived threat. When the HPA axis is activated, the hypothalamus synthesizes and releases corticotrophin-releasing factor (CRF). CRF is the neurotransmitter (chemical messenger) believed to coordinate stress-response elements into a coordinated coping reaction (Heim et al., 2003). Release of CRF in turn signals release of adrenocorticotropin hormone from the pituitary gland, which stimulates production and release of cortisol from the adrenal cortex (McCutcheon, 2006). Cortisol, often called the "stress hormone," affects metabolism, the immune system, and the brain. Physiological and behavioral changes occur, such as suppression of food intake, alteration of sleep patterns, and fight or flight responses (Heim et al., 2003).

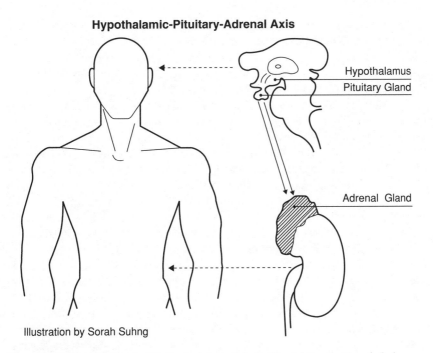

Hypothalamic-Pituitary-Adrenal Axis

Hypothalamus
Pituitary Gland

Adrenal Gland

Illustration by Sorah Suhng

Figure 3.2 Hypothalamic-Pituitary-Adrenal Axis. Illustration by Sorah Suhng.

The Neurobiological Effects of Early Trauma

Individuals differ in their reactivity to stress; however, in all individuals the physiological stress-response system described above is set in motion in response to situations perceived to be threatening. Trauma induces increased adrenaline levels and over-excitation of the limbic system (Cellini, 2004), whereby CRF is released, the HPA axis is activated, and an increased release of cortisol takes place, affecting behavior and the brain itself. Cortisol mobilizes and replenishes energy stores, and its release contributes to increased arousal, vigilance, and inhibition of growth. It has a role in the formation, processing, and retrieval of memories, especially fearful memories. Studies have found that cortisol levels are dysregulated in mood and anxiety disorders and in PTSD (Haglund et al., 2007).

Exposure to early life stress modifies the sensitivity and response bias of the stress-response system (Rick & Douglas, 2007). Studies of adult women who were abused as children, in comparison with those who were not, show a robust association of early life stress with HPA axis abnormalities among women with major depression or PTSD, as well as among younger girls living with ongoing abuse (McCutcheon, 2006; Penza et al., 2003). In other words, the effects of early childhood abuse on the stress-response system continue to be identifiable, even among women with comparable current psychiatric disorders and among girls who are currently victims of abuse. Some researchers suggest that many of the nation's leading health and social problems have common origins in the enduring neurodevelopmental consequences of abuse and related aversive experiences during childhood, and that understanding this will aid in the prevention and remediation of these problems (Anda et al., 2006).

The nature of the changes in the brain will depend on the timing of the event(s) relative to the age of the child, frequency or chronicity of the stressor, the nature of the event(s), and genetic characteristics of the child's biological stress system (McCutcheon, 2006; Rick & Douglas, 2007, Rutter, 2002). Where emotionally stimulating experiences (such as the pleasurable face-to-face contact between infant and caregiver) generate brain growth, prolonged stress can result in neuron loss or atrophy. Abuse, neglect, understimulation, and prolonged shame reduce levels of endorphins and dopamine and increase stress hormones and noradrenaline (Cozolino, 2006b). This biochemically less desirable state may be repeatedly reproduced by chronic abuse. As described earlier, neural patterns are use-dependent; in cases of chronic abuse, the neural pathways or patterns that are strengthened are those that prepare a child to cope with an environment of deprivation and strife, at the expense of those that could enhance his or her ability to function in a positive environment (Cellini, 2004; Teicher et al., 2003). Foster care alumni with histories of chronic abuse may have found themselves, in one placement after another, unable to make use of the best efforts of concerned caregivers because they have learned at the neural level to remain on alert.

Neglect is the type of maltreatment most frequently reported to child protective service agencies, with referrals rising continuously over the past decade (English et al., 2005). Neglect has been variously defined and includes a complex array of caregiving failures or deficiencies, the most fundamental of which is the failure to meet basic needs of physical safety, shelter, food, adequate supervision, and a relationship with a caregiver. Legally, the standard is omissions resulting in imminent risk or observable harm, but developmentally, lack of sensory stimulation, comfort, and emotional security may result in harm as well (English et al., 2005).

In conceptualizing the traumatic effects of neglect, De Bellis suggests that the dysfunctional parent–child interpersonal relationship in the form of neglect is a chronic stressor that may influence the development of biological stress-system responses, leading to adverse brain, cognitive, and psychological development. Further, he proposes that neglect is likely perceived and processed through the senses as intense anxiety, generating response in neurotransmitter systems (including serotonin), the neuroendocrine system, and the immune system. Maltreated children show alterations in the development of the HPA axis, as well as higher levels of norepinephrine and free cortisol (De Bellis, 2005). Increased levels of CRF and cortisol lead to suppression of the immune system; it is commonly understood that people who are stressed are at greater risk for the development of illness and infections.

Stressful experience during the first years of life and the resulting elevated levels of stress hormones can accelerate neuronal atrophy or loss, delay myelination (formation of the protective sheath that encases axons and increases connectivity), cause abnormalities in developmentally appropriate pruning, and inhibit neurogenesis (De Bellis, 2005). In severe, early, and chronic abuse, studies have found reductions in overall brain size, impairments in the development of the corpus callosum (the tissues that provide neural integration for right and left hemispheres), and reductions in the size of the hippocampus. It is thought that these may be due to the neurotoxicity of excessive stress-hormone secretion (Siegel, 2003).

Cognitive and psychological functions may be affected by early adverse experience. A large body of research demonstrates heritability for general intelligence, but also considerable environmental influence on intelligence, particularly early in the life span (Blair, 2006). *Fluid intelligence* involves the effortful maintenance of information needed for goal-directed behavior and is sometimes also called executive function or working memory. More susceptible to environmental influence than what is called general intelligence (Blair, 2006), fluid intelligence is clearly important to success in school and in life. Fluid cognitive processes are mediated in the prefrontal cortex; they influence and are influenced by emotional and autonomic responses to stimuli, including traumatic stimuli. Because they interact with and are part of the limbic system, dysfunction in one component of the system is likely to lead to difficulty in the self-regulation, not only of behavior and emotion, but also of cognition (Blair, 2006). Fear takes precedence over everything else, including schoolwork; it is not surprising that maltreated children and adolescents may exhibit both behavioral and academic problems.

The alterations in brain chemistry, structure, and function evoked by the stress of maltreatment create problems in the two self-regulatory domains of attention and information-processing. Reduced capacity and heightened demand in the brain areas responsible for these functions can compromise the ability to focus attention and categorize information. The child's attention and memory encoding are focused on detecting threats rather than becoming oriented in response to neutral stimuli. There may be impairments in conscious recognition, interpretation, reflective memory, and decision-making (Ford, 2005).

Information-processing during the first two years involves the developing capacity for narrative knowledge and autobiographical self-awareness. The child moves from a "proto self," processing wordless knowledge of its psychophysiological experience, to a "core self," with an observing/acting "me" (Parvizi & Damasio, 2001). There is a continually changing neural mapping of the self (body) state as it interacts with the external environment. Experiences of abuse or of parental love during the "wordless knowledge" phase are incorporated on a physical and emotional level and become a part of the developing self. By age two, the core self emerges based on psychological capacities that are enabled by the further development of the amygdala, hippocampus, prefrontal cortex, and somatosensory cortices (Parvizi & Damasio, 2001; Ford, 2005).

In the third year, the child is able to mentally represent the self and other selves in organized chronological narratives that have continuity over time, allowing him or her to reflect without acting. Also, the three- to four-year-old can integrate past with present and anticipate future events based on retrieved representations, including, of course, representations of trauma. Abused children are much more attuned to recognition of angry faces and have difficulty disengaging their attention from them. Abused children with PTSD may also have deficits in selective or sustained attention, hypothesis testing, problem solving, and short-term memory (Ford, 2005).

Studies suggest that intellectual ability, as reflected by IQ score, may be affected by child maltreatment. Findings have led researchers to hypothesize that smaller intracranial volumes may be associated with permanent neuronal loss leading to lower IQ (De Bellis, 2001). Others suggest that neglect interferes with effective development of the prefrontal cortical regions and thus, poorly developed executive functions may result in inattention, inability to focus, and poor academic achievement (De Bellis, 2005).

Risk and Resilience

Resilience is a process and not a set of factors or traits; it is a capacity that is developed rather than possessed (Noam & Hermann, 2002). Both the susceptibility to risk and the capacity to overcome adverse or stressful experience are affected, if not determined, by each individual's unique combination of constitutional givens, the nature of the stressor(s), and the characteristics of the environment. Genetic factors have an impact through their role in influencing the susceptibility to environmental risk, though variations in sensitivity to risk may also derive from children's prior experiences. Rutter points out that chronic psychosocial adversity may make children more sensitive or vulnerable to the experience of acute stressors and that temperament may play a part in sensitivity to psychosocial risk (Rutter, 1999). Each individual responds in a specific way to traumatic experience, based on the particular genes, experience, and environment of that individual. While most often we think about resilience as a psychological phenomenon, it is not separable from neurobiology; our ability to overcome or rebound from adversity is embedded in our neural and hormonal circuitry.

In a discussion of the psychobiological mechanisms of resilience, Haglund et al. (2007) suggest that individuals who experience unmanageable stress in childhood may be more vulnerable to future stressors than those not exposed and, more specifically, that there may be a critical period in the first weeks of life when traumatic experiences are particularly disruptive to the development of the neural circuitry involved in the stress-response system. On the other hand, exposure at a young age to milder, manageable forms of stress appears to aid in building a resilient neurobiological profile (Haglund et al., 2007). Rutter refers to this as the "steeling" effect of overcoming adversity (Rutter, 1999).

On the neurohormonal level, the important factor is the corticotropin-releasing hormone (CRH) released from the hypothalamus in response to stress, which then activates the HPA axis and the release of cortisol. Resilient individuals appear to have the capacity to effectively regulate CRH levels. Individuals with mood and anxiety disorders and PTSD, however, have dysregulated levels of cortisol, which mobilizes and replenishes energy stores, increases arousal, and plays a role in information-processing and retrieval of memories (Haglund et al., 2007).

Exposure to childhood adversity is associated with alterations in the reward circuits in the brain, causing decreased responses to reward-predicting cues (Dillon et al., 2009). A dysfunctional reward system (including dysregulated serotonin and/or dopamine levels in the brain) may help to explain the difficulties maltreated children have with taking in and responding to positive interpersonal experiences in foster care. However, the plasticity of the reward system and its ability to respond to changing environmental circumstances can also play an important part in developing increased resilience (Haglund et al., 2007).

Affect Regulation

The ability to maintain or moderate emotional arousal, such that an optimal level of engagement with the environment is possible, is present in rudimentary form at birth but must then be refined and elaborated in subsequent months (Applegate & Shapiro, 2005; Cicchetti & Valentino, 2006). It evolves as a function of the child's internal characteristics and external experiences occurring in the context of the early caregiving interactions. The development of affect regulation is a dynamic process influenced by biological factors such as central nervous system functioning, development of neurotransmitter systems, and the caregiver's response to and tolerance of affect (Cicchetti & Valentino, 2006). The infant learns to identify and manage emotions by way of what she or he feels inside and the environmental response to those feelings. When the infant is distressed, the HPA axis is activated. If the caregiver responds with soothing, arousal is diminished and the infant can return to sleeping, feeding, and attending to a now more manageable environment. If there is no response or if there is a threatening response, arousal is heightened, and the infant's system may become overwhelmed.

The gradual development of the neural systems involved in affect regulation requires protection from intense, prolonged, and overwhelming affect states. Emotionally stimulating experiences generate brain growth; dysregulated affect and chronic stress can result in neuron loss through the cortical-limbic circuits. Ideally, repeated experiences of moving from regulation to dysregulation and back to a regulated state are stored in neural networks of sensory, motor, and emotional memory. They become encoded as implicit (unconscious) memories that then help the infant restore regulation in future moments (Cozolino, 2006b). Repeated experiences of fearful, dysregulated states with no soothing or rescue are also stored in implicit memory, to be reactivated in future situations that suggest danger to the child.

Studies of maltreated children have shown deviations in emotion expression, emotion recognition, and emotional behavioral reactivity (Cicchetti & Valentino, 2006; Sullivan et al., 2008). Infants as young as three months who had been severely physically abused showed greater rates (than non-maltreated infants) of fearfulness, sadness, and anger. Maltreated children showed less accurate recognition of emotions, with a hypersensitivity to detection of anger; they were more likely to overextend the "anger" label to ambiguous, non-anger contexts (Cicchetti & Valentino, 2006; Sullivan et al., 2008). When a child's attention is focused on perceived threats, there is less attention available for other matters, including more positive aspects of the environment. Learning is affected, as well as social information processing.

In a paper on the relationship between physical abuse and aggressive behavior problems, Teisl and Cicchetti (2008) point out that distortions in social information processing are frequently seen in physically abused children. These children more often attribute hostile attribution to others, access more aggressive behavioral responses, and view aggression more favorably than children who have not been harmed (Teisl & Cichetti, 2008, p. 3). The authors suggest that emotion regulation is also a factor in the development of externalizing behavior problems among physically abused children. They note that the type of maltreatment experience affects behavioral outcomes; children who experienced forms of maltreatment other than physical abuse may engage in different defensive reactions, such as fearful avoidance, rather than aggressive responses (Teisl & Cicchetti, 2008).

Development of Psychopathology

While conceptual models of development differ, there is widespread agreement that behavior and experiences in childhood are relevant to mental disorder in adulthood, and that there is environmental mediation of the risk for psychopathology. Higher rates of aggressive disorders, post-traumatic stress disorder and other anxiety disorders, and depressive disorders have all been reported in adults who were maltreated as children (De Bellis, 2001; McCutcheon, 2006; Penza et al., 2003; Plomin et al., 2001; Rutter, 2002; Rutter, 2008). The dynamic nature of the relationship of the developing maltreated child with his or her specific environmental surround is at play in the emergence and development of psychopathology.

The earlier discussion of the effects of trauma on cognitive and emotional self-regulatory brain regions and capacities shows how a foundation for future developmental problems can be established early in life. Infants who are sensitized in the first three to six months to anger or violence begin at a disadvantage with regard to prospects for inner security and resilience. Unresolved trauma, chronic fear, and neglect can lead to hypervigilance for threat, inability to regulate strong emotions, unregulated hostility, and attention and social information processing problems. Animal and human adult studies show that severe stress and PTSD are associated with alterations in biological stress systems and brain function; it is probable that many of the acute and chronic psychiatric symptoms associated with maltreatment arise in conjunction with alterations of biological stress systems (De Bellis, 2001).

Some effects of maltreatment, such as deficient development of abstract cognitive abilities, including empathy and perspective taking, may become more evident during adolescence. There is more exposure to risky activities and more opportunity to engage in aggressive behaviors. The hormonal changes associated with puberty generate intense emotions; when the capacity for affect regulation is already compromised, the adolescent may be more vulnerable to behavioral acting-out, including the use of drugs and alcohol, suicidality, or antisocial acts.

In later chapters, we will explore some of the serious mental health problems that can result from adverse early experience, along with current models of intervention. Fundamental to understanding these psychiatric disorders is knowledge of the impact of attachment and placement experiences on development during childhood and adolescence, particularly as they are layered upon trauma or loss occurring in childhood. We next turn to an examination of early attachment.

4

THE IMPORTANCE OF
EARLY ATTACHMENTS

This chapter provides an introduction to the basics of attachment theory, first proposed by John Bowlby in 1958. His innovative theory, which drew on evolutionary biology, animal studies, developmental psychology, cognitive science, and systems theory, is now widely recognized in social science and mental health fields as critical to the understanding of development and interpersonal relationships. He proposed that children engage in "attachment behaviors" designed to increase their proximity to the "attachment figure" (usually the mother) by alerting her to the child's need for interactions (Cassidy, 1999). The manifestation of attachment behaviors and patterns varies across cultures, but the construct of attachment itself has universal application (Bolen, 2000; Bolen, 2002). It is the attachment relationship which helps the very young child tolerate states of arousal, sustain investment in the outside world, and manage emotions in developmentally appropriate ways. For children in foster care whose primary relationships have been disrupted by adverse events during childhood, including removal from their families and entry into the foster care system, attachment theory has profound and poignant relevance.

This chapter explicates the theory and introduces the four primary attachment classifications as they appear in the general population. The effects of childhood maltreatment on attachment are examined, as well as how these effects are manifested in the context of entry into foster care.

Attachment Theory

Infant survival and development depend on an adequate caregiver. Attention to adverse effects of inadequate caregiving environments such as high mortality rate, poor growth, and delayed development began to make an appearance in the literature in the 1950s, and Bowlby concluded in the 1970s that the caregiver relationship was as vital to mental health as nutrients were to physical health (Zeanah, Mammen, & Lieberman, 1993). Using an ethological, evolutionary perspective, he suggested that attachment behaviors are biologically based. The child's cries and vocalizations draw the attachment figure near to provide the infant with protection from predators (or other dangers) and to teach the infant how to survive in a given environment (Cassidy, 1999).

Attachment is dyadic and reciprocal: the attachment behaviors of the infant/child elicit the caregiving behaviors of the attachment figure (Bolen, 2002). The caregiving behaviors of the attachment figure, in turn, influence the ways in which attachment needs will be expressed. The particular nature and quality of the attachment relationship are largely determined by the qualities of the caregiving environment, yet infants become attached whether or not their physiological needs are adequately met. Attachment experiences have consequences for the later development of a variety of skills and capacities, including social competence, active problem-solving, mastery motivation, the capacity for empathy, the ability to form and maintain friendships, and the ability to rely on other adults when necessary (Cassidy, 1999).

Attachment behaviors are designed to bring the caregiver closer and to heighten the attentiveness of the caregiver so that he or she can provide a safe haven in times of stress or danger. Two conditions of danger were noted by Bowlby as central to activating the attachment system: first, environmental or internal changes that threaten survival, and, second, conditions heralding separation from the attachment figure, even in the absence of threats from the environment (Main & Hesse, 1992); as, for example, when the parent is unavailable psychologically or physically. Either of these conditions is likely to activate attachment behaviors.

> Marie, a 25-year-old African American, is the second youngest of four siblings, with older half-siblings on both sides. At the time of Marie's birth, her mother had a ten-year-old son from a previous relationship, and three- and five-year-old daughters. Both Marie's parents were crack addicts, high or seeking drugs. Her situation exemplifies the conditions of danger that would activate her attachment system. Her parents' drug addiction—being under the influence or engaged in obtaining drugs—prevented them from responding with adequate caregiving behaviors, and the responses they could provide were likely to have been minimal and inconsistent.

In addition to the function of protection, the attachment figure serves as a secure base from which the infant can explore novel environments. The exploratory system, necessary for learning about the environment, is unlikely to come into play when danger is present and the attachment system is activated. As will be seen in the description of the attachment classifications, optimal development depends on the availability of both these functions (protection and a secure base) in the caregiver. On the neurobiological level, the caregiving relationship as mediated by the attachment figure is an important regulator of emotion and arousal. The caregiver/infant dyad comprises a system that operates to provide bio-behavioral regulation during stress and security in moving out and beyond the dyad.

> Marie was born with crack and PCP in her system, affecting her biological state from conception. When she was two years old, her mother gave birth to her youngest child. One year later, her mother was sexually assaulted and stabbed to death. Marie's first three years were spent with a mother who was high or seeking drugs, then pregnant, then tending to an infant, then completely absent. The time most central to development of regulatory capacities within the caregiving environment was spent essentially alone, and Marie had no help managing the devastating loss of her mother. Later in childhood, when she again experienced losses, of her pastor and her grandfather, her grief was overwhelming, and she tried to end her life.
>
> Marie's eventual aggression and difficulty controlling her impulses can be understood to arise out of the absence of an emotion-regulating attachment experience early in life. When she felt threatened, hurt, or fearful, she had minimal ability to tolerate or manage those feelings.

Internal Working Model

Bowlby borrowed from psychoanalytic thinking in his emphasis on the importance of representation in interpersonal relationships. Like Freud, Klein, and Winnicott, Bowlby believed that experiences in the external world are in some way reproduced or reflected in the internal world of thought and feeling, there to be employed for predictive and coping purposes in the outer world (Bretherton & Munholland, 1999).

Internal working models are the inner representations of the attachment experiences: the interaction with the attachment figure, the sense (model) of that person, the sense (model) of the self. These models include the perceived or expected availability of the caregiver, the kind of response the infant expects, and the sense of self as lovable and worthwhile or not. Although longitudinal studies have found evidence for the developmental continuity of internal working models, these models appear to be susceptible to revision and updating in response to developmental changes and the dynamic interactions of current circumstances (Fairchild, 2006). Internal working models in turn have a shaping effect on perception, behavior, and experience.

> Following the murder of her mother, Marie's family moved to an apartment, where six children slept in one bed until they were evicted and became homeless. For a time the family lived in their car, eating from trash containers and using park washrooms. Sometimes the children had to urinate in the open if park bathrooms were closed. Marie found this frightening and humiliating.

When the family's homelessness was reported, Marie's father spent a short time in jail, and the children stayed with a relative. Soon after his return, four-year-old Marie witnessed an altercation in which her father was pushed off a balcony and lay in the street, covered in blood. He told her to call 911; his arm and leg were broken. This incident remains a haunting and traumatic memory.

Marie has other bitter memories of her father. At age three, she fell off a bike and hurt her lip. Her father soothed it with ice, but as she lay next to him recovering, he touched her sexually. In the next year while still with her relatives, the sexual touching was repeated during visits with her father.

Internal representations of Marie's parents were problematic at best, as neither could be relied upon to comfort or to provide safety. Her internal sense of self as a lovable individual deserving of care could neither develop fully nor be sustained in a context of fear, maltreatment, and abandonment. Her father rests in her mind as a man brutal not only to her, but to her mother, whom she believes he may have murdered. Her subsequent relationships are marked by layers of mistrust that cover her deep longing for safety and love.

Attachment Classifications

Infants can display subtle behaviors that are responsive to the caregiver from the earliest weeks, but it is only during the last quarter of the first year that infant behavioral (motor) activity reaches a more easily observable threshold. In the first three months of life, the infant is capable of limited discrimination of the attachment figure, primarily through hearing (recognition of caregiver's voice) and smell. From three to six months, there is increased capacity for discriminating social and visual responsiveness, and from about eight months to three years, the child is able to actively seek proximity and contact (Zeanah et al., 1993).

Mary Ainsworth studied the behaviors of 12-month-olds to arrive at classifications of what appeared to be fairly distinct patterns. Using a procedure called "The Ainsworth Strange Situation," in which infants are observed in the presence and absence of their caregiver and upon reunion, she identified three categories of attachment: secure (Group B), insecure-avoidant (Group A), and insecure-ambivalent (Group C) (Ainsworth et al., 1978). A fourth category, disorganized/disoriented (Group D), was later identified by Main and Solomon (Main & Solomon, 1986) and is now also widely used, despite disagreement about whether it accurately describes the attachment phenomena it purports to capture. Attachment classifications are relationship-specific; an infant may be securely attached to one parent, for example, and insecurely attached to the other.

The validation of the attachment classification system has been "an ongoing priority" because the process requires matching a particular case to a multidimensional template or prototype. Unlike research in which events can be tallied and coded, attachment research requires extensive training for researchers to establish a minimum reliability standard in matching cases to a template. Given this requisite training, within-laboratory agreement for trained coders tends to be very high and is relatively high even across laboratories (Solomon & George, 1999). Each of the categories is discussed below, with a review of current research on disorganized attachment.

Group B: Secure

Security, defined as the state of being untroubled about the availability of the attachment figure, cannot be directly observed, but must be inferred from observable behaviors (Solomon & George, 1999). This attachment pattern is the most common, found in 55% to 65% of normative populations (Goldberg, Muir, & Kerr, 1995). Secure infants use their caregivers as a secure base for exploration. They explore freely when the attachment figure is present, checking her whereabouts and reactions from time to time, and curtailing exploration in her absence. They are distressed to some degree when she is gone, but are happy to see her when she returns and are then able to resume play. If they have been at the more distressed end of the range of reaction to absence, they seek contact with the caregiver upon reunion and are comforted by it.

Secure attachment can be described as feeling sure that the attachment figure will be there when needed and will be comforting, whether physiologically or psychologically. The representation of the other is as caring and responsive, and the representation of the self is as deserving of response and care. The representation of the relationship is one in which there is freedom to explore an interesting world and there will be help if danger threatens. The child can alternate between attachment behavior (proximity-seeking) and exploratory behavior, depending upon the availability of the attachment figure and the "strangeness" of a situation (Main & Solomon, 1986). The securely attached child associates dyadic interaction with positive feelings.

Group A: Insecure-Avoidant

In this pattern, found in 20% to 25% of normative populations, the infant shows minimal interest in the caregiver, explores busily on his or her own, and does not check in with the caregiver as the child with a secure attachment pattern does. The child is not terribly distressed at separation from the caregiver and either ignores or avoids the caregiver on reunion (Goldberg et al., 1995).

The internal representations of the avoidantly attached child are bleaker: the model of the caregiver is tinged with negative expectations, and the self is a devalued self. These children have learned not to turn to the caregiver for help or for comfort, but, rather, to do things on their own. The internal model of dyadic interaction is one in which there is little positive to be gained; rather, interaction is to be feared or avoided. The infant focuses instead on "independent" exploration of the environment.

Group C: Insecure-Resistant (also called Insecure-Ambivalent or Anxious)

These children, 10% to 15% of the normative population, experience the greatest degree of distress at separation and have difficulty settling down in the caregiver's absence (Goldberg et al., 1995). Preoccupation with the caregiver interferes with their ability to explore freely. Upon reunion with the caregiver, these children both seek and resist contact and may appear angry or passive.

The internal models of the ambivalently attached child are infused with anxiety and uncertainty about the availability of the caregiver. The intermittently or selectively responsive caregiver is simultaneously an object of longing and a source of frustration and disappointment. Self-representations have a corresponding uncertainty: am I lovable, deserving of attention and care, or are my needs annoying and forgettable? Dyadic interaction is fraught with the possibility of comfort and closeness, interrupted by indifference, unresponsiveness, abandonment. The child's heightened display of emotionality and dependence around separation serves to draw the attention of the caregiver (Main & Solomon, 1986).

Following the fight in which Marie's father was injured, the children were removed from his care. A cousin took them in. "She beat us every day," Marie told me. When she was five, her father died of an aneurysm, possibly from the fall a year earlier. The younger children remained with their abusive relative, except Marie, who "finally got the courage to hit her back," and ran away at age 11. At this point, she entered the foster care system and was placed in a foster home with her older sister. She was ejected from that home after fights in which she struck both her sister and her foster mother.

Over the next six months, Marie had five different placements that she remembers, though there may have been more. "I'd shut down and then I'd blow up and get kicked out." She was sent to group homes and a probation placement; she was medicated and placed in psychiatric facilities. When her pastor died, she jumped in front of a moving car and, as a result, Marie was put in restraints and kept under observation for 14 days.

In one of her last group homes, despite heavy medication and feelings of hopelessness, Marie connected with a staff member who "stuck by me and calmed me down." But then her grandfather died, and her frantic, despairing state resulted in medication that sedated her most of the time. Marie pulled her hair out and soothed herself by rocking in her bed. She wet her bed until she was 15. She was violent with staff and with residents.

Marie's pattern of attachment is an example of the insecure-ambivalent or anxious classification: despite many hurtful experiences, she continued to attempt to form attachments, with her pastor, her grandfather, and a few staff members. Her extreme anxiety is reflected in bed-wetting and hair-pulling. She was filled with rage and acted out against others, but also against her own body. Yet she maintained enough hope to respond to those who showed her care and concern. When asked if she had positive memories of her mother, she told me "She rocked me to sleep sometimes." This act (and possibly others like it not remembered at the explicit level, but encoded in implicit memory) may have been internalized in loving representations, existing alongside fearful, isolated, and disappointing ones, and allowing Marie to believe in the possibility of love.

The wary, but hopeful expectancy of an anxious attachment can allow a maltreated child or adolescent to attempt connection with a foster parent or a social worker. We can see that any new relationship has potential for both new growth and for new disappointment.

Group D: Insecure-Disorganized/Disoriented

Based on close review of videotaped strange situation behavior of infants who were not classifiable into the three previously described patterns, Main and Solomon identified a fourth pattern of behavior (Main & Solomon, 1986). This pattern, found in only 15% to 20% of normative populations (Goldberg et al., 1995; Main & Hesse, 1992) was found in *80% to 82%* of maltreated infants (Main & Hesse, 1992; Lyons-Ruth & Jacobvitz, 1999). As with all the attachment classifications, the pattern is specific to the dyad, and an infant who is disorganized with one parent or caregiver is not necessarily disorganized with a second. In one sample, almost all of the infants were disorganized only in the presence of one parent (Main & Solomon, 1986).

The children in Groups B, A, and C have strategies for managing their environments: the securely attached child uses the attachment figure as a secure base from which to explore; the avoidantly attached child emphasizes exploration and avoids contact; and the ambivalently attached child clings desperately to the attachment figure. The disorganized/disoriented child appears to have no coherent strategy at all. Contradictory or mutually inhibiting behaviors are most obvious during the reunion episodes of the strange situation procedure. The infant can neither approach nor avoid the attachment figure (Bernier & Meins, 2008). Behaviors seem to be out of the usual sequence, such as showing extreme distress on separation and backing away upon reunion; greeting the caregiver brightly, then turning away and showing strong avoidance; holding arms up to the caregiver, then moving away with a dazed expression. These contradictory behaviors suggest that avoidant and contact-seeking impulses are present simultaneously.

Attachment behavior is activated by perceived threat or danger in the (internal or external) environment or separation from the caregiver. Secure, avoidant, and ambivalent infants deal with these dangers by checking in with the caregiver, focusing away from the danger onto exploration, or clinging to the caregiver. Main suggests that neither consistent, low levels of rejection by the caregiver nor unpredictable responsiveness is likely in itself to lead to disorganized attachment. Rather, disorganized, disoriented behavior could be expected if the infant has been alarmed, not just by the external situation, but by a parent who behaves in a frightening or frightened manner (Main, 1995). Such situations put the infant into a state of "fright without solution" (Bernier & Meins, 2008). Fear of the parent activates the attachment system and the infant feels compelled to seek proximity, yet proximity increases the infant's fear, leading to simultaneous approach and retreat (Lyons-Ruth & Jacobvitz, 1999).

Bernier and Meins conclude that there are convincing links between maternal frightening behaviors and disorganized attachment, as well as between maternal distance (failure to greet upon reunion, for instance) and infant disorganized attachment. A second robust predictor is an unresolved state of mind in the parent relative to her own early traumatic experience. The authors attempt to clarify the mediating pathway between the parent's behavior and the resulting disorganized attachment. They propose a "threshold approach" in which certain child-centered characteristics set the threshold of vulnerability or resilience to forming disorganized attachment. Insensitive or disturbing parent practices then breach the threshold. Social-environmental risk factors can also alter the threshold level by inducing atypical parenting (Bernier & Meins, 2008). For example, a parent with a traumatic history who experiences unemployment and lack of a social support network has a colicky, hard-to-soothe child. The parent is frightened, angry, and overwhelmed, and becomes physically abusive; or, the parent has a substance-abuse problem and, while high or in search of drugs, ignores the needs of the child.

> When Marie's bike accident frightened her, she turned to her father. He both soothed and abused her, creating just such a situation of proximity leading to increased fear. Repeated interaction of this kind could easily lead to disorganized attachment, but this did not happen in Marie's case, perhaps because she had been able to hold on to some positive experiences with her mother.

Crittenden's *dynamic-maturational perspective* suggests, to the contrary, that disorganized children do have strategies that are adaptive, changing over time, circumstance, and developmental maturation to provide optimal safety. Her emphasis is on the power of danger to instigate mental activity; sensory stimuli initiate simultaneous but different processing pathways. The infant must "decide" whether to continue processing or take immediate protective actions. If danger is felt to exceed a certain threshold of intensity, behavior is initiated and processing is suspended (Crittenden, 1999; Crittenden, 2001). In other words, if the baby feels frightened enough, she or he begins to do something that communicates distress. As noted earlier, when an infant signals distress, the caregiver may respond by soothing or comforting, may act to increase the infant's distress, or may be unpredictably and inconsistently sensitive to the infant. In the latter two conditions, the infant inhibits displays of negative affects to prevent punitive outcomes or learns to express feelings at increasingly low thresholds of arousal in order to increase the caregiver's attentiveness at an earlier point.

Crittenden encourages us to question whether there is a contingent relation between display of the "disorganized" behaviors and the interpersonal context. If there is a contingent relation, she sees the behavior as organized. If the contingent relation increases the safety or comfort of the child, then the organization can be considered adaptive. She suggests that "disorganization" should be considered a provisional category which may reflect children's disorganization or reflect the investigator's inability to discern the organization at the time of coding. The dynamic-maturational perspective takes account of changing circumstances and developmental changes (Crittenden, 1999).

> *Marie's attachment behavior serves as an illustration of Crittenden's model: acting out in placement might appear disorganized and incoherent, yet there may have been strategic aspects to it. If she felt striking out protected her, or brought the proximity of someone who might help her, it may have been a more organized attachment strategy than it appeared.*

The internal working models of children with Type D attachments are likely to reflect frightening aspects of the attachment figure, as well as of the interactions with that person. The sense of self may incorporate frightening and frightened aspects in a confused and disorganized constellation. If there is another attachment figure to whom the child has a more benign or positive attachment, the effects of the representations of the disorganized attachment may be mitigated to some degree, and the self-representation might be more mixed. A foster parent can offer an opportunity for positive attachment experiences and development of representations that are more loving and lovable.

Attachment and Neurobiology

Chapter 3 described in detail the neurobiology of infancy and early childhood, taking note of the caregiver-mediated social environment as both context of and a powerful influence on development. More specifically, the caregiving environment, operating through the attachment relationship, shapes the maturation of the infant's right brain. When the caregiver is reliably and sensitively able to respond to the infant's signals, these experiences imprint the maturing central nervous limbic system that processes and regulates social-emotional stimuli and the autonomic nervous system that generates somatic aspects of emotion (A. Schore, 2003). This imprinting is the neurobiological aspect of the internal working model, informing and elaborating the developing representations. The early-maturing right hemisphere is also involved in the development of a coherent sense of self (or the inner working model of the self) because of its role in connecting emotionally salient experiences and memories (J. Schore & Schore, 2008).

In insecure or disorganized attachment, these same affective communications function in a distorted way, inducing or increasing arousal levels without providing interactive soothing or repair. Face-to-face interactions with the primary caregiver (whether soothing, frightening, or indifferent) influence gene expression and the biopsychosocial processes related to affect regulation, attachment, and subjective and intersubjective experiences (Corbin, 2007). When the infant's distressed states last for a long period, increased cortisol levels lead to enduring hyperarousal and, eventually, to dissociation or disengagement (A. Schore, 2003). Just as the repair and harmony of the secure attachment shape emotional and physiological expectations, so, too, do negative attachment experiences. The resulting representations of self and other may be characterized by hyperarousal at one end and numbness at the other.

> *Marie's behavior provides an example: she described herself as "shutting down" and then "blowing up." She would withdraw into herself as a coping strategy, trying to manage a difficult feeling or situation. She would cease communicating with others. Then someone else would do or say something that seemed threatening, setting off her chronically overactivated stress-response system, and she would "blow," lashing out verbally or physically.*

Child Maltreatment and Attachment

The attachments of abused and neglected children who are removed from home are shaped by the experiences of maltreatment and disruption. It is well documented that maltreatment is associated with negative effects on both children and adults (Finzi et al., 2001; Manly et al., 2001). The type of maltreatment and the developmental timing of its occurrence affect the nature and magnitude of effect. Some studies point to higher rates of avoidant attachment for abused children and higher rates of ambivalent attachment for neglected children (Baer & Martinez, 2006; Finzi et al., 2001). McWey found that 86% of the maltreatedchildren she studied, whether neglected or abused, displayed avoidant attachment (McWey, 2004). Some researchers report that as many as 80% to 82% of maltreated children have disorganized attachments (Lyons-Ruth & Jacobvitz, 1999; Main & Hesse, 1992).

Emotional abuse is the most difficult type of abuse to capture, but may be an underlying component of all maltreatment (Baer & Martinez, 2006). Verbal aggression has received little attention as a specific form of abuse, but is associated with higher risk for development of psychopathology and may have lasting consequences. A study of effects of exposure to verbal aggression found that the combination of exposure to verbal aggression and domestic violence had effects as great as familial sexual abuse or exposure to three kinds of abuse (physical, sexual, and emotional)

(Teicher et al., 2006). In one study, 64% of children experienced multiple subtypes of abuse (Manly et al., 2001).

Child maltreatment occurs in a context of dynamic interplay among characteristics of the child, the family, and the environment. The child's developmental status is continuously evolving, with new capacities coming online and altering perceptions and responses to stimuli. The timing, severity, type, and frequency of maltreatment, along with the characteristics of the perpetrator, all play a part in the effects on the child's ongoing and future attachments and development.

Problematic early attachment has many implications, and because many foster care alumni have had disrupted or dysfunctional early attachments, their continued development and functioning as adolescents and young adults can be negatively affected. Early disorganized attachment is often the first step in developmental pathways that can lead to increased vulnerability to later psychopathology. There is some evidence that it is linked to borderline disorders, complex PTSD, and dissociative disorders (Liotti, 2004). Physically abused children have been described as lacking empathy for the distress of peers and as showing more verbal and physical aggression, while neglected infants are easily victimized, more anxious, and more dependent (Finzi et al., 2001).

Children with disorganized attachment have experienced a frightened or frightening caregiver who has unresolved traumas of his or her own. When these unresolved traumatic memories surface in the mind of a parent while responding to attachment needs of the child, the suffering linked to these memories activates the parent's attachment system (rather than only the caregiving system). Strong emotions of fear or anger are aroused in the parent, whose attempts to soothe the child may be interrupted with abrupt manifestations of alarm or anger, frightening the child. The child initiates defensive behavior of avoiding or distracting, the parent distances further or becomes further enraged, and there is no solution or soothing (Liotti, 2004).

It is easy to see how the inner representations that result from these experiences follow the child into new relationships. As Sroufe and Fleeson put it, "The whole relationship resides in each individual" (Sroufe & Fleeson, 1986). When the child enters out-of-home care, for example, his existing expectations will powerfully affect his perception of the foster parent's behavior toward him. He may see danger where there is none and engage in distancing or attention-getting behaviors that have negative effects on his reception in the new family.

Along with the psychosocial context and quality of the attachment relationship from which a child is being removed, the timing of the separation and the quality of the substitute care during the separation will play important roles in the child's ability to form additional healthy attachments. Separation from a caregiver in the context of family discord is traumatic and may have greater effects than even the death of a parent (Corbin, 2007). If the separation occurs during the first few months of life and is followed by good quality of care, it may not ultimately have a deleterious effect on social or emotional functioning. Separations occurring between six months and three years will be more problematic, due to attachment issues and to limited language abilities to understand and cope with the experience. Negatively tinged internal working models have had more time to develop and take hold. Children older than three to four years who are placed for the first time are more likely to be able to use language to help them cope, but here, too, the nature of the early attachment, the reasons for the disruption, and the separation itself will have an impact on the child's ability to benefit from the new situation (Committee on Early Childhood, Adoption, and Dependent Care, American Academy of Pediatrics, 2000; Dozier et al., 2002).

Development in Early Childhood

The attachment relationship is the critical context within which the infant develops during the first year. This relationship optimally provides three protective factors to the baby: the learning of empathy; the control and balance of feelings, especially destructive ones; and the development of cognitive capacities. In times of distress, the infant signals to mother to draw her close, and the mother's caregiving soothes and calms the baby's nervous system. Physiological equilibrium is restored, and both baby and mother relax. This pattern, occurring repeatedly, leads to a balanced, goal-directed partnership, imprinting on the infant brain and forming the template (internal working model) for anticipated behavior. With repeated experiences of misattunement, the structural and chemical processes that could have supported feelings of relief and connection are instead set to handle erratic and stressful responses. Infants who are abused or who are left alone to cry in states of arousal may be flooded by fear or rage. By the age of 10 to 12 months, these patterns are internalized at the body (hormonal) level and representationally; the infant can store memory, even if the caregiver is not there. Indeed, infants perceive and are able to remember very explicit details in ways that are later lost to us (Kaplow et al., 2006).

In the first year, the caregiver's function is mainly nurture; in the second year, the caregiver must begin to socialize the infant by providing guidance and discipline, helping the child develop inhibitory mechanisms. If these experiences are excessively harsh, prolonged shame or fear experiences can ensue, and the child's ability to connect intimately can be damaged. This is especially the case if the first year's task of attunement has not been achieved. Early unregulated humiliation may lead to severe emotional disorders; aggression is underregulated, and the capacity for empathy fails to develop fully.

The preschool years, ages two through five, are a period of rapid advances in locomotor, cognitive, affective, perceptual, and language capacities. The second and third years are the time of primacy for language and gender identity. At about age two the brain is sufficiently mature to allow the child to learn and speak a language, but environmental stimuli must be available to release the biological disposition.

The ability to learn hinges on a child's freedom to direct her or his attention away from internal needs and basic survival. The interrelatedness of the biological, psychological, and social aspects of development are apparent in school readiness. Unregulated aggression and overactivation of the stress-response system interfere with the development of academic and social skills. A warm, nurturing relationship is the foundation for self-esteem, efficacy, self-control, and relatedness, fundamental contributors to school readiness. Attachment classification is predictive of school success (Venet et al., 2008). In the classroom and on the schoolyard, a problematic internal working model gives rise to interactions with teachers and peers that replicate aspects of the home situation.

Another important developmental task of early childhood is the mastery of impulses, also acquired in the context of the caregiver relationship. Optimally, toddlers learn to delay gratification, comply with requests, postpone action, and behave in socially acceptable ways. The developing rudimentary sense of time helps with impulse control, as does whatever sense of trust in caregivers has developed. Language and fantasy can be useful tools in managing impulses. The development of symbolic imagery allows the creation of imaginary situations in which disturbing problems can be expressed and controlled.

It is increasingly possible for the child to behave in a goal-directed way in order to achieve intended outcomes. Ideally, the sense of self as an originator of action and someone who can have an effect on the world is now underway. There are developments in social, communicative, cognitive, and motor skills, though the pace and sequence of developments vary a great deal.

Gender identity and an ethnic aspect of the self-representation begin to emerge during the preschool years. Both of these building blocks of the sense of self are taken in from the environmental surround, as mediated through significant others. The caregiver's feelings about herself and about the baby's bodily self are transmitted through sensory contact in early weeks and months, and the child internalizes a sense of gendered and ethnic self over time. For children (and parents) of color, the task of developing a healthy self-representation is complicated by living in a mainstream culture that offers devalued or negative messages.

Child Maltreatment and Early Development

The biological status of a child under age three is fragile, so an assault on a child at this age has greater impact than at any other age. The most critical issue at this age is physical survival; 78% of maltreatment fatalities occur in this age group (US DHHS, ACF, ACYF, CB, 2008). The rapid, sequenced biological maturation of a young child means that an assault (severe nutritional neglect or a blow to the head, for example) may cause irreparable harm to the developing brain.

Injuries to the brain from hitting and shaking can result in damage to intelligence, seizures, motor problems, language problems, weight loss, inability to fight infections, and hearing loss. Sustained poor physical growth can also result. Early and prolonged maltreatment can seriously compromise the child's capacity to resolve subsequent developmental challenges competently. Chronically maltreated children also suffer from the disruption to goal-corrected partnerships with their caregivers, which, in turn, impairs optimal development of relations with others (Manly et al., 2001)

Research has shown that children who experience maltreatment during their first five years exhibit significantly more externalizing behavioral symptoms, including aggression, and have lower ego resilience (Manly et al., 2001). These are the more readily observable and quantifiable indications of internal processes that are more complex. Early childhood is the period during which the child develops a conscience or sense of right and wrong. Children's theories of morality during these years may be based on magical thinking, with the self at the center of causation. For example, when a child is physically neglected by a substance-abusing parent, he or she may think this is the result of having broken a toy or crying and making the parent mad.

Children are cognitively able to understand that other people have their own private mental states and motivations at about age four. The ability to take the other person's perspective becomes increasingly possible. The capacity for empathy develops more fully when the environment is benign and does not require serious defensive operations (avoidance, dissociation, aggression) to cope. In a dangerous or frightening situation, the child is forced to locate the "badness" either in himself or in the caregiver; his options are to feel like a bad person or to live in a bad world. For most young children, it is untenable to live in a world in which those closest are to be feared. They manage by turning away from the caregiver (avoidant attachment), complying with or clinging to the caregiver while turning on themselves (ambivalent attachment), or some combination of the two (disorganized attachment).

Development and Foster Care

Entry into foster care is associated with risk for high rates of psychological and behavioral problems (Goldsmith, Oppenheim, & Wanlass, 2004). Multiple interacting factors are involved: chronic poverty, disrupted and dysfunctional family situations, child maltreatment, and foster placement. It is not possible to isolate the contributions of each of these factors, but it is important to note the impact of placement on child development.

Children who have been placed due to neglect or abuse may be relieved by the protection of the foster family, yet they may simultaneously begin to experience intense grief over the loss of their primary attachment figure. The average stay in care is 27 months (US DHHS, ACF, ACYF, CB, 2009), and the child may be torn between longing for a return to her or his parent and forming a new attachment to the foster parent (Goldsmith et al., 2004). Children who have developed avoidant attachment patterns might not turn to the new caregiver for much-needed comfort, creating distance or problems for themselves and their relationship with the foster family. The caregiver feels helpless and rejected, and the child feels alone, fears another loss, and behaves badly in order to control the timing of the next rejection or failure of placement.

Children with significant behavior problems are likely to remain in care for longer periods and are at risk for multiple placements (Lawrence, Carlson, & Egeland, 2006). Placement instability is the characteristic most associated with negative outcomes for youth in out-of-home care two to five years after emancipation (Harden, 2004; Penzerro & Lein, 1995). Thus it can be seen that a malignant cycle develops: severe maltreatment gives rise to insecure attachment and entry into care; once in care, the child's attachment style, which was adaptive in the maltreating environment, gives rise to behaviors that prevent positive attachment experience in the new home, leading to alternative placement; the child experiences further rejection and the problematic attachment behaviors continue or worsen; further unsuccessful placements ensue, along with more serious behavioral expressions.

The impact of placement varies with age and developmental status of the child. If placement occurs during infancy, the separation disrupts the biopsychological regulation of the baby, which must be reestablished in the foster care situation. As we have seen, the early development of neuroendocrine system regulation is dependent on the caregiver's stable presence (Dozier et al., 2002). If the new caregiver is not nurturing, regulatory systems and the attachment system will be disrupted and at risk. On the other hand, a new surround that is attuned and responsive can help to reset the biopsychological rhythm, establishing a more promising foundation for future development.

In the preschool period, the typical (non-foster) child is using her or his more integrated sense of self to respond to challenges and has increased ability to regulate behaviors and emotions. For the toddler in foster care, there may be a more fragmented sense of self and family, with deficits in inhibitory control. He or she may have dysregulated cortisol levels, making it hard to respond appropriately to even moderately stressful everyday challenges. He or she may have developed behaviors that were adaptive to dealing with a maltreating family, but are disappointing or alienating to a new caregiver and lead to decreased nurturance (Dozier et al., 2002).

In middle childhood, a key developmental task for children is to learn to control their behavior, both in the classroom and in social situations. Children who have problematic attachments and traumatic histories are unlikely to be as successful as their non-maltreated peers in managing their impulses and behavior. Their negative expectations with regard to how others will treat them also contribute to difficulties in class and on the schoolyard; maltreated children with insecure attachments are likely to interpret even ambiguous behaviors as hostile.

> *Marie's middle childhood was spent in the care of her physically abusive cousin, who used the children she had taken in as small servants in her home. These experiences offered Marie no opportunities to develop positive attachments or self-representations, and served to underscore her self-doubts and anger. At age 11, she was unable to control her rage any longer and lashed out at her cousin.*

At adolescence, the risky behaviors associated with problems in inhibitory control can be more dangerous: substance use, sex, and antisocial acts may put these adolescents in harm's way. Foster care placement instability increases with children's ages, and the uncertainty about where home is going to be can make it even harder for children to make good choices about what risks to take (Dozier et al., 2002). The following chapter examines the issues for adolescents in greater detail.

When children are moved into foster care, the primary motivation of child welfare workers is to provide safety and protection to the children as quickly as possible. By the time children reach the foster care system, there have been failures of nurture from the family system, as well as larger failures from the environmental surround and from whatever efforts may have already been made by the child welfare system. Much that should have happened to insure healthy development has not occurred; much that is potentially damaging to the body, mind, and spirit of these children has happened. They carry forward the influence and the scars of these experiences. However, at the time of placement, it is not the internal world of the child that is the first priority of the system. The integration and meaning-making that is occurring inside the child, with whatever developmental tools are then available, is a lonely and isolated process. In the case of multiple placements, this process happens again and again. For the most fortunate of foster children, there are foster parents, group home staff members, and social workers with whom they are able to make successful and constructive connections that help them make sense of their experiences. For many of the youth aging out of care, there has been no such reparative relationship.

5

ADOLESCENT DEVELOPMENT IN FOSTER CARE

Adolescence is a time of significant change in every domain of experience: biological, psychological, social. It has been said that adolescence begins in biology and ends in culture (Smetana, Campione-Barr, & Metzger, 2006); while the biological changes of puberty are universal, the timing and meaning of these changes are experienced through the sociocultural medium. The roles and expectations involved in transitioning from childhood through adolescence to adulthood are culturally and contextually determined, as are the kinds of possible identities available to a given individual. Similarly, the balance between independence and interdependence, or connectedness with others, is weighted more in one direction than the other in different cultures.

In this chapter, we explore dimensions of adolescent development in the context of maltreatment and out-of-home care, using the biopsychosocial perspective, the concept of mutual, dynamic person-environment influence, and the continuing importance of attachment to increase our understanding of the young person moving toward adulthood.

Biological Changes of Adolescence

Puberty, the umbrella name for the complex processes of sexual development and accelerated growth, is usually underway long before the external manifestations are evident (Collins & Steinberg, 2006) and leads to massive hormonal changes, changes in body size and structure, an increase in sex drive, and changes in cognitive functioning (Rutter, 2006). Gonadal, or sex, hormones are released, and the adrenal system matures; the affective changes often associated with adolescence may be more closely linked to levels of adrenal hormones than gonadal hormones (Collins & Steinberg, 2006).

Secondary sex characteristics (breast development, appearance of pubic hair, enlargement of testicles and penis) appear only after the hormonal changes have begun, yet these physical changes are the ones that often have the greatest impact on a teen's sense of self and the reactions of others to that self. If puberty occurs in a non-normative time frame (for the culture), early development for girls and late development for boys can cause problems. Self-concept and self-image are shaped by the immediate peer environment, and they influence social interactions and the development of peer relationships. There is strong evidence that the impact of pubertal maturation on adolescent psychosocial development is more likely to be interpersonally mediated than to result from the direct action of hormonal change on mood or emotional functioning (Collins & Steinberg, 2006).

Brain Development in Adolescence

Some brain areas in the prefrontal and parietal cortices continue to develop into adolescence, with recent studies indicating that the time when the brain actually reaches maturity may be much later than adolescence (Blakemore & Choudhury, 2006). At the same time that children are growing more rapidly and beginning to develop sexually at younger ages, some higher cognitive-executive functions mature only gradually across adolescence, independently of the timing of puberty. This mismatch has been likened to "starting engines with an unskilled driver" (C. Nelson et al., 2002).

The sensory and motor regions of the brain become fully myelinated during the first few years of life, but axons in the frontal cortex continue to be myelinated during adolescence. Increased myelination results in an increase in the speed with which neural information is transmitted, leading to greater capacity for judgment and information-processing. Synaptic density reaches its peak in most areas of the brain much earlier, followed by experience-dependent pruning; in the prefrontal cortex, however, proliferation in synapses occurs in childhood and then again at puberty, followed by further pruning and reorganization (Blakemore & Choudhury, 2006). Improved connectivity between regions of the prefrontal cortex and several areas of the limbic system also occurs during adolescence (Collins & Steinberg, 2006), allowing increased communication between cognition and affect.

Cognitive capacities develop further during adolescence, including the capacity for abstract and multidimensional thought, self-reflection and self-awareness, and future-time perspective (Davis & Vander Stoep, 1997). These capacities work in conjunction with brain development as the social information processing network (SIPN), which encompasses detection (of information), affect (reactions to stimuli), and cognition/regulation (perceptions about others, management of responses, generation of goal-directed behavior) (C. Nelson et al., 2002). While there is no evidence that the detection processes undergo change during adolescence, the other two parts of the SIPN do. Affectively, puberty and the release of gonadal hormones affect the neurotransmitters and alter responsiveness to social stimuli, including sexual behavior and social bonding. The cognitive and regulatory processes change more slowly as a result of myelination and pruning, gradually permitting greater inhibitory control (C. Nelson et al., 2002).

Despite rapid and considerable changes related to a growing and now-sexual body, development of the capacity to make reasoned decisions (judgment) and to more thoughtfully contain impulses is slower in coming. For the young person approaching exit from foster care, there are simultaneously greater anxieties and fewer supports. Ordinarily, the teen's social network changes from being more family-oriented to being more peer-oriented, and the social reorientation of this period can be stressful in itself. For youth in care, not only are the buffering effects of family absent, but family has often been a cause of stress and dislocation. The "emancipation" from foster care can be a time of heightened sensitivity to negative interpersonal events, with little cushion for the young person, sometimes leading to mood disorders or anxiety disorders, both known to rise dramatically during adolescence (E. Nelson et al., 2004).

Central Developmental Tasks of Adolescence

Puberty is biological (and universal), but adolescence is variously defined and marked in different cultures. In industrialized societies, it is rare to have formal rites of passage; more often, the transition to adulthood is marked by changes in legal status, such as being able to drive, drink, vote, or be discharged from care. These legal changes cast little light on the psychological transitions required to achieve adulthood.

Most theorists agree that central issues of adolescence in the United States revolve around identity and independence, though the capacity for interdependence as an equally important development is currently receiving greater attention (Collins & Steinberg, 2006). The young person who has successfully transitioned to adulthood has a sense of self that incorporates sexual and ethnic aspects; continuity between past and present self-experiences; a personal philosophy or set of beliefs; positive expectations for the future; educational and occupational choices; life goals; and the ability to have meaningful relationships of both a social and intimate nature. These developments are fluid; changes in circumstance and context interact powerfully with the young person's current self to produce further changes in any or all of these aspects of self. Past experience, consciously or unconsciously held, and particularly in the areas of attachment and trauma, continues to exert a shaping influence on current experience and the emerging adult sense of self.

> *Summer, a Caucasian woman now in her early thirties and recently married, described a terrifying childhood spent hovering fearfully at the periphery of the violence of her alcoholic father. Her mother, herself a victim of incest, fled from her husband's beatings and infidelity when Summer was three years old. Two weeks later, her father brought home a new woman and her two children, introducing them as "your new mommy, sister, and brother." The couple were drinking buddies who engaged in brawls and beatings several times a week: "They would beat each other up, there would be blood, my dad would pass out." His new wife, Karen, beat Summer's older sister and then kicked her out of the home a year later when she was ten; she went to live with their mother. Summer then became a target for abuse.*
>
> *The family lived on an isolated farm in a western state; Summer often couldn't get to school, or arrived in tattered, dirty clothes. She had no friends. Her father frequently drove drunk with the petrified children in the car; there were accidents and arrests. Police took the children to their grandparents, but Karen intimidated them, sometimes physically assaulting them, and took the children home. Summer recalls many interviews by police and social workers in which she insisted everything was fine. She longed to tell the truth, but Karen threatened her: "I'll kill your mother, your father, and beat you to death."*
>
> *Summer was removed a few times, and recalls carrying a black plastic bag full of her belongings as police took her to strangers' homes. There were brief stays in foster homes and with families from the church. When Summer was ten, her mother took her to another state to live with her. By then, Summer's older sister had attempted suicide, survived, and had been emancipated at age 16.*
>
> *At the age of ten, Summer has already experienced a lifetime of chaos and trauma, in which she rarely knows what will happen next, where she might find herself, and with whom. Her circumstances and context are so fluid and unreliable that she will be hard-pressed to develop an internal sense of self that is solid. As we will see later in this chapter, the foundation on which she will need to build her identity is fraught with doubt, uncertainty, fear, and mistrust.*

Identity Development

Many theories of adolescent development draw on Erikson's psychosocial stage model, in which predictable changes in personality development over the life span result in part from a series of psychosocial crises determined by biological, psychological, and sociocultural forces. The individual resolution of each stage depends upon the development of basic ego strengths, which are then successively integrated into the personality and contribute to subsequent stages (Crawford et al., 2004).

The crisis of adolescence is the conflict between identity consolidation and identity diffusion. The optimal outcome, in Erikson's terms is, "a feeling of being at home in one's body, a sense of 'knowing where one is going,' and an inner assuredness of anticipated recognition from those who count" (Erikson, 1968). An unsuccessful resolution, on the other hand, is characterized by a diffuse sense of identity, confusion about social roles, uncertainty about internal states and feelings, and difficulty with occupational and educational goals (Crawford et al., 2004).

In the bestpossible scenario, the adolescent engages in a process of search and eventual commitment. Some authors propose four categories of ego identity statuses: *achieved identity*, characterized by an exploration and a resulting commitment; *moratorium*, in which there is ongoing search but no commitment; *foreclosed identity*, commitment with no exploration; and *identity diffusion*, where there is neither ongoing search nor commitment (Roberts et al., 1999).

Identity development occurs over time and in context: family, extended family, social network, school, neighborhood, community, and the larger institutional and sociocultural surround cannot be divorced from the emerging sense of self. All aspects of the environment are themselves located in particular historical, political, economic, and geographical contexts, which also have shaping effects. For youth in foster care, the child welfare system and the specific out-of-home settings in which the child has been placed are parts of the shaping environment.

Identity and Foster Care

Kools interviewed youth aged 15 to 19, all of whom had been in foster care two years or more. She found that long-term care has a negative impact on the central processes of their identity development. Kools proposes two processes of identity development that are particular to youth in care: devaluation of the self by others, and self-protection. Devaluation of the self, she suggests, arises from the underlying institutional structure of the group-home model and a diminished and stereotypical view of the foster child. The institutional structure is characterized by excessive restrictiveness, lack of consideration and respect, a focus on pathology, and discontinuity of caregiving (Kools, 1999).

The negative view of the child in care is of someone abnormal or damaged, psychologically impaired, or delinquent. In addition, these children are frequently in the position of being asked intrusive, intensely personal questions about their families and past experiences. Kools points out that all of these conditions lead to devaluation, which is manifested in depersonalization (the person is not treated like a specific individual) and stigmatization (social shame) (Kools, 1997).

The child in care may adopt a stigmatized self-definition, leading to low self-esteem, low self-confidence, and difficulty believing in a positive future. Low self-esteem has been found to be characteristic of children in care, with multiple placements found to be detrimental to self-esteem (Lyman & Bird, 1996). Due to the difficulty of exploration imposed by institutional constraints and the negative self-view, the adolescent in care may move prematurely into a *foreclosed identity* that has been defined for—rather than by—the adolescent.

Children in care develop defenses to cope with the devaluation of foster care status and day-to-day experiences. Some defenses may have been instituted even earlier in life to cope with abuse or traumatic loss. These coping strategies and defenses are meant to protect the vulnerable self, yet they may also have deleterious effects on relationships and potential interpersonal supports. Self-protective strategies include hiding one's status as a child in care, minimizing the perceived impact of that status, distancing oneself from others in order to hide one's status and to avoid investing in relationships, and keeping relationships superficial to avoid future loss or hurt (Kools, 1999). The conditions of foster care promote these processes, even though they may have had their genesis in the pre-placement history of the child. The young person in care, thus defended, has a façade of competence and independence that may further serve to keep needed support at a distance. Responsive interactions and strong bonds are thought to facilitate adaptation during the transitions of adolescence (Collins & Steinberg, 2006), but these are often not available to youth in care, and the potential comforts of current or future close relationships are denied. The youth may feel (even more) unlovable and unable to withstand additional disappointments.

Sexual-Identity Development

An important part of identity is the sense of oneself as a sexual being, including both gender and sexual orientation. Gender identity is the sense of oneself as male or female, including feelings about one's behavioral self-presentation and expression as male or female. Research suggests that gender identity occurs by 27 to 30 months, if not earlier (Ruble, Martin, & Berenbaum, 2006). The response of the primary caretaker(s) to a child's maleness or femaleness plays a crucial role in the child's eventual sense of sexual self.

Transgender youth, those who experience their gender identity as different from their birth gender, usually develop awareness of this lack of fit later, around puberty, but sometimes it happens earlier in childhood. Family and others have most often reacted negatively, and school attendance may have been traumatic. In one study, youth reported confusion about sexual orientation and gender identity until they identified as transgender. Their awareness of their sexual orientation usually developed either between ages four and nine or between ages 13 and 15, as they experienced attraction to others of the same sex (Grossman & D'Augelli, 2006).

The adolescent is adjusting to a sexually maturing body, managing sexual desires, forming sexual attitudes and values, experimenting with sexual behaviors, and integrating all these dimensions into his or her sense of self (Collins & Steinberg, 2006). Sexual abuse during childhood or adolescence can profoundly affect the sense of self and feelings about sex itself. Frequently identified outcomes of childhood sexual abuse are either a heightened or a diminished sexuality. Heightened sexuality is manifested by early age of voluntary coitus, more partners, early pregnancy, sexual preoccupation, and using sex as a means of achieving nonsexual goals. Diminished sexuality appears as fear of sex, sexual avoidance, sexual aversion, low sexual arousal, and sexual anxiety (Simon & Feiring, 2008).

> *At age 11, Summer went to live with her mother, her second husband, and his 17-year-old son. The family was staying in a small cabin; over Summer's protests, her mother left her to share a room with the 17-year-old. During the first night, he molested her. Her mother took her and left, after sustaining a beating by her husband, but the months following were not much better for Summer. Her mother was with a different man every night and may have been prostituting herself. Before a year went by, she declared that she was unable to care for Summer. She dropped her off at her grandparents', saying it was only for the summer, but she did not return. Summer's father showed up drunk and tried to kidnap her, despite a police restraining order.*
>
> *Summer's introduction to sexuality was violent and exploitive; there was no caring or tenderness in it. She witnessed her mother's self-exploitation during the very time when her own nascent sense of sexual self was tenuous. Her experience of adult relationships throughout her young life was characterized by violence, abuse, rage, and fear. An intense and long-lasting romantic attachment in which she was repeatedly betrayed and lied to became a central focus of her emotional life as an emerging adult.*

As can be seen in Summer's example, the impact of sexual abuse is moderated by the developmental stage when the abuse occurs. The strongest effects are found in those who were adolescents at the time of abuse discovery, giving support to the idea that adolescence is a time of greater vulnerability for the development of sexual problems in response to child sexual abuse. For non-abused youth, views about the functions of sex and its relationship to intimacy are rooted in experiences and representations of nonsexual intimate relationships (Simon & Feiring, 2008).

Sexual orientation, one's sexuality-related predispositions or attractions, is part of sexual identity. Sexual identity is the way we define ourselves in terms of attractions, thoughts, fantasies, and lifestyle (Auslander, Rosenthal, & Blythe, 2005). Because there are often many and serious conflicts with regard to sexual orientation and sexual behavior, the road to a sexual identity that feels both consonant with the self and accepted by the social, familial, and cultural surround may be a rough one.

The development of sexual identity unfolds over time and is determined by both internal and contextual factors. The individual's genetic endowments interact with opportunities, constraints, and other features of the environment. The origins of sexual orientation have been the subject of great debate, with some researchers suggesting that social factors have greater importance and others using hormonal, genetic, and brain-structural evidence to support a biological basis (Ruble et al., 2006). While there are similarities in models of homosexual and hetero-sexual identity development, there are also differences, as discussed in the models presented here.

Homosexual Identity Development

Children develop their perceptions of themselves as homosexual over time; the ages at which homosexual events are encountered and the stages with which these events are associated vary widely. Troiden (1988) and others propose stage models, usually ending with commitment to and integration of a homosexual identity. In these models, the first stage, occurring prior to puberty, is *sensitization*. The child perceives that she or he is different from same-sex peers, often due mainly to different pre-ferred activities or interests, and has feelings of marginality. Only a small percentage of children, however, see themselves as sexually different before age 12 (Troiden, 1988).

Identity confusion occurs during middle to late adolescence. The young person ponders the possibility of being gay and may feel confused by his or her lack of arousal toward opposite sex members and arousal toward same-sex peers. The sense of difference takes on a sexual quality. Social stigma and the need for secrecy, social isolation, ignorance, and misinfor-mation about homosexuality can all make powerful contributions to the young person's confused sense of self. Chapter 10 includes a more detailed discussion of responses to sexual-identity confusion.

Sometime during middle to late adolescence, the young person begins to identify as gay during the stage of *identity assumption*. He or she estab-lishes gay relationships and shares his or her homosexual identity with a select group of people (Auslander et al., 2005). The meanings that are attached to the homosexual label begin to transform in a more favorable direction, though the young person must still develop strategies to cope with social stigma in the larger social surround (Troiden, 1988).

In late adolescence or early adulthood, the individual reaches the stage of *identity commitment*, which includes internal and behavioral dimen-sions. Internally, there is an integration of same-sex sexuality and emo-tionality, along with a view of the homosexual identity as a valid and satisfying one. Externally, the individual enjoys same-sex love relation-ships and is able to disclose homosexuality to heterosexual audiences so that secrecy and "passing" can be discarded (Troiden, 1988).

Recent theorists take a social constructionist view, in which identity formation (including sexual identity) is a continual, two-way interactive process between the individual and the social environment, wherein sex-ual identity is maintained through social interaction (Alderson, 2003; Horowitz & Newcomb, 2001). While there is empirical support for the sequencing of milestone events in sexual-identity development, stage models fail to account for the large number of sexual-minority males who do not use sexual behavior to arrive at gay identity (Horowitz & Newcomb, 2001). Ecological, narrative, and social-constructionist views look at desire, behavior, and identity as three constructs related to sexual identity. Each can be considered separately, releasing homosexuality from being considered solely as a sexual preference and allowing a conception of identity that is broader and more dynamic.

In one study, 9% of women and 10% of men reported some aspects of same-gender sexuality, some with same-gender desire only, and some with desire and behavior only. Of the individuals who reported some aspects of same-gender sexuality, 15% of women and 24% of men had desire, behavior, and identity (Horowitz & Newcomb, 2001). Stage models ignore sociohistorical contexts, assume an endpoint to sexual-identity development, and do not fully capture the fluidity and varied quality of young people's experience (Alderson, 2003). Narrative models give greater recognition to the salience of context, including cohort, geographical location, and sociohistorical context (Cohler & Hammack, 2007).

The journey toward a minority sexual identity for any young person may have involved rejection by family, a reduction of social supports, and experiences of discrimination or harassment (Williams et al., 2005). For children in foster care, it may have been part of a traumatic family experience and may be associated not only with rejection and loss, but with violence. If minority sexual identity has resulted in running away or life on the street, it may lead to identity foreclosure in the sense of being defined (negatively) by a sexual dimension of identity that is devalued by others. In addition, the young person may believe that other aspects of the self are less salient to others and, therefore, to herself or himself.

Heterosexual Identity Development

Models of identity development for majority groups (whites, heterosexuals) are less prominent than those for nondominant groups, perhaps because individuals who are oppressed must pay more attention to these processes in order to buttress their well-being in a less receptive environment. However, the successful integration of sexual identity is equally important for the developing heterosexual adolescent. Here again, prevailing models emphasize stages or phases, although heterosexual identity is also a product of a continuous two-way interaction between the young person and the social environment.

Hoffman (2004) describes five "statuses" of heterosexual identity development, the first of which is *unexplored commitment to a heterosexual identity*. As with identity foreclosure, the youth has taken on a sexual identity with no exploration of its meaning or fit, or of alternative identities or experiences. The second status is *active exploration*, in which the youth engages in external or behavioral exploration, and also in an internal trying on of fantasies and thoughts. Third is *diffusion*, similar to exploration, but often resulting from a crisis and lacking the goal-directed intentionality of exploration. *Deepening and commitment* is the fourth status, sometimes preceded by active exploration, but sometimes evolving gradually without exploration. Finally, *synthesis* describes the sense of integration and congruence among dimensions of individual identity, individual sexual identity, and group membership identities (Hoffman, 2004). The development of heterosexual identity may be complicated by childhood sexual abuse or other trauma, but most often does not have to be achieved against a backdrop of stigma and devaluation.

Adolescent Ethnic Identity Development

Ethnic identity, like identity itself, is a multidimensional construct with many definitions. Most researchers agree that it is based on the social realms (cultural, familial, communal, broader sociopolitical environment) in which individuals interact (Pizarro & Vera, 2001; Yeh & Hwang, 2000). Ethnic identity is variously described as a cognitive, information-processing framework within which one perceives and defines situations, events, and other people (Yeh & Hwang, 2000); a sense of psychological connection within a group of people with a common history traceable to a common place of origin (Bennett, 2006; Branch, 2001); or as overlapping or synonymous with racial identity (Buckley & Carter, 2005; Sellers et al., 2003).

The body self is inevitably an ethnic or racial self (in the same way that it is an anatomically male or female self); consciousness of one's ethnic nature is to a great extent experience-dependent. The child comes to know how his primary world is experiencing him, and this awareness has a determining impact on his sense of his physical being: Is it a good thing in this particular family or world to be male or female, to be light-skinned or dark? This early sense of ethnic self is the beginning of an ethnic identity that will be elaborated in adolescence and young adulthood.

Models of Ethnic Identity Development

Ethnic identity development, the process of ascribing meaning to one's membership in an ethnic group, appears to be more challenging and more salient for members of ethnic minority groups than for members of the majority, perhaps because minority adolescents are faced with identification with less powerful groups (Pizarro & Vera, 2001; French et al., 2006). A review of studies of ethnic identity development and self-esteem reveals three primary theoretical perspectives underlying the research in this area: (1) *social identity theory*, which emphasizes identification with a particular ethnic group as most central; (2) *ego identity perspective*, which emphasizes individual exploration of values, goals, and beliefs as the basis of identity achievement; and (3) the *acculturation perspective*, which suggests that ethnic identity changes as a function of acculturation processes, with bicultural identity seen as the healthiest outcome (Umana-Taylor, Diversi, & Fine, 2002).

Most theorists agree that ethnic identity development progresses from a state of conscious unawareness through exploration to an achieved or incorporated ethnic identity; however, they differ on the terminology and specifics of the stages or statuses of their models (Branch, 2001; French et al., 2006; Quintana, 2007). Some suggest that ethnic categorization happens during childhood, as the child learns that he or she shares certain cultural attributes with others, and that other groups share different distinct cultural attributes (Pizarro & Vera, 2001). Ethnic constancy, or the understanding that one's ethnic categorization is unchangeable, occurs between eight and ten years of age (Rotheram-Borus et al., 1998). These are the beginnings of awareness of ethnicity as an aspect of the self. At this point, the child may see her or his ethnicity as a fact, but the process of incorporating it as a meaningful dimension of sense of self or identity is only just beginning.

Phinney posits three stages for adolescents of all ethnic groups: unexamined ethnic identity, ethnic identity search, and achieved identity (French et al., 2006). Cross suggests a five-stage model for (adult) African Americans: pre-encounter, when the individual believes race does not matter; encounter, involving some kind of eye-opening experience; immersion-emersion into black culture; internalization, during which the individual develops pride in identity as a black person; and internalization-commitment, in which the individual tries to advance the status of African Americans and eliminate racism in society (French et al., 2006; Buckley & Carter, 2005). Stages are neither linear nor static, and these authors point out that individuals move through and back into statuses. Experiences of discrimination often lead to awakening and exploration, beginning the process of developing a more defined ethnic identity.

Personal identity is connected to group reference identity, and it is important for stigmatized groups to develop a positive orientation toward their racial-ethnic group. When individuals have high regard and positive feelings toward their ethnic group, they demonstrate higher self-esteem in later life; in addition, ethnic regard moderates the relationship between daily (nonracial) stress and the level of well-being on the next day (Quintana, 2007). Youth of color need not only positive group orientation, but also resources to buffer them against racial discrimination, such as awareness and preparation for discrimination.

A study of self-esteem among a large sample of adolescents from different ethnicities found that the self-esteem of biracial youth is significantly lower than that of black youth, but significantly higher than that of Asian youth. Biracial youth report significantly higher levels of ethnic identity than white youth, but lower levels of ethnic identity than black, Latino, and Asian youth. A significant positive relationship between ethnic identity and self-esteem was found across all groups. These findings support the idea that ethnic identity is more salient for youth of color than for white youth, and that it is more complex for biracial than monoracial youth (Bracey, Bamaca, & Umana-Taylor, 2004; Roberts et al., 1999). Discrimination, racism, and the sense of otherness demand greater engagement with the ethnic dimensions of identity from youth of color.

Ethnic identity, strongly influenced by both social context and external factors, incorporates a cultural-ethnic notion of the self. Western cultures conceive of a self that is independent, a "distinct and decontextualized entity containing dispositional attributes," while some other cultures see the self more in relation to others (Yeh & Hwang, 2000). Until as recently as the Fostering Connections Act of 2008, this Western view of the self has been embedded in the policies governing transition from care in the United States. Young people exist within and in relation to their current (and past) environmental surrounds. The sense of self is in constant relation to the immediate caregiving context as well as the larger society. Nowhere is this clearer than in the case of ethnic and sexual aspects of the developing self.

Earlier in the chapter, we looked at Erikson's psychosocial stages of ego identity: diffused, foreclosed, in a state of moratorium, or achieved. The ethnic dimension of identity is sometimes described along very similar lines (Branch, 2001; French et al., 2006). The discussion of ethnic and sexual identities is to some degree a misleading reification of these dimensions, as the relationship of sexual, ethnic, and other aspects of identity is complex, interpenetrating, and dynamic and can never be truly disentangled. The sense of self across all dimensions is emergent and somewhat fluid during adolescence; during young adulthood, the more enduring aspects of self become further consolidated.

Attachment in Adolescence

The biological, cognitive, and emotional changes of adolescence give rise to changes in adolescent attachment relationships. Developments in abstract reasoning and the increased ability to differentiate oneself from others allow the adolescent to see relationships differently, one from another, and from hypothetical ideals. In the normative population, this occurs against the backdrop of (and with the help of) parents, who simultaneously adapt their attachment strategies to the changing needs, demands, and capabilities of the young person. The exploratory part of the attachment system is highly activated during adolescence, but still depends on the secure base (enduring relationship) as a safety net for the young person to move out into the world with greater autonomy. The conceptual difference between attachment needs of infancy and those of adolescents is the shift from a secure physical base to one that is cognitive and emotional (Bettmann & Jasperson, 2010). If we employ Crittenden's dynamic maturational model of attachment as designed to protect the self from danger—shifting to new perceptions and strategies as new capacities for detection, assessment, reflection, and behavior come online—we can appreciate how changing abilities and contexts have transformative potentials for adolescent attachment patterns (Crittenden, 2000).

> *When Summer was 11, an aunt and uncle came to her rescue, bringing her to Los Angeles to live with them. She felt clean and safe for the first time, but her father's visitation rights meant she had to stay with him twice a year. Drunken beatings continued at Christmas and during the summers, until Summer was in the 10th grade and refused to stay with him.*
>
> *Summer's aunt and uncle were the first adults in her life to offer stability, reliability, and protection—in short, a secure base that could provide a foundation for adolescent development. At the same time, the attachment experiences that shaped her early life remained in her internal world: parents who frightened and hurt her, who disappeared or reappeared unpredictably according to their needs and never to hers, parents who failed to protect her from abuse by others. Summer could not allow herself to feel very much, because so much of what lay beneath the surface was painful beyond bearing. She coped by shutting down her affective life as much as possible. In her internal representation of herself in relation to others, she could expect little, and she felt herself to be without value. She had trouble accepting her aunt and uncle's love or rules; they had trouble accepting her acting-out behavior. As happens with many children in foster care, the love offered by substitute caregivers is at odds with the internalized schemas, and is not easily taken in and digested. In Summer's case, her relatives were committed to her despite the relationship and behavior difficulties. They became her legal guardians and provided a predictable and safe surround.*

Adolescence is a time of developmental discontinuity; for those leaving the foster care system, there is also an abrupt and complete change in context, including, for youth who do not enter a transitional living program, the loss of a caregiving surround. In ordinary circumstances, an adolescent would be negotiating a changing relationship with parents. For youth in foster care, this process has long since been interrupted or aborted. Early experiences of danger and attachment strategies designed to meet it may still be powerfully at work. Furthermore, the loss of the foster family or group home staff to whom the young person has become attached during placement may evoke self-protective strategies that interfere with developing new relationships during the transitional period.

Research on adult survivors of child abuse finds greater psychopathology to be associated with insecure attachment patterns characterized by a negative sense of self (as unworthy of love) and a negative sense of the other (as unresponsive and unloving) (McLewin & Muller, 2006). Negative expectations cause individuals to either avoid relationships or to be anxious and preoccupied about them, often interfering with the establishment or maintenance of positive new relationships. The potential buffering effects of supportive relationships are then unavailable, leading to further isolation, unstable relationships, and losses.

One study of adolescents leaving care finds that 80% of youth surveyed exhibit two distinct profiles (Keller, Cusick, & Courney, 2007). The first, *distressed and disconnected*, represents the youth most likely to experience difficulties. These youth have had multiple placements, including in non-family settings, and have run away on one or more occasions. They have experienced more abuse and violence and have a higher prevalence of mental health and substance-abuse diagnoses. They are more socially isolated, with less social support. The second group is *competent and connected*, likely to continue with the steady progress they appear to be making. They have had placement changes and have often been placed with kin. They feel close to at least one person and are likely to be enrolled in school (Keller et al., 2007).

There are two additional profiles: *struggling but staying*, experiencing some problem behaviors and grade retention, but more likely to be receptive to intervention than the first group; and *hindered and homebound*, at 5%, the smallest and most atypical group. Though many of these youth have had only one placement, often with kin, and are connected to relatives and neighborhoods, they have high rates of grade retention, the lowest reading scores, a higher rate of parenthood, and are considered ill-prepared for the transition to adulthood. While most youth in kinship care exhibit fewer problem behaviors than those in non-relative care, the youth in this group may suffer from variation in caregiver encouragement to pursue education and work experience (Keller et al., 2007). Implicit in the descriptions of all four groups is the element of attachment to one or more dependable others. The youth who seem poised to embark more successfully on the transition feel connected to someone; the majority of the most vulnerable are those who are emotionally and socially isolated.

Peer relationships acquire heightened importance during adolescence as sources of intimacy, feedback about social behavior, social influence and information, and attachment relationships and lifelong partners (Allen & Land, 1999). In late adolescence, long-term relationships can be formed in which peers serve as attachment figures. Such relationships can provide opportunities for healing and growth, but they may also serve as arenas for the reenactment of disappointing or hurtful early attachment experiences. Young people who have little confidence in their ability to solve problems or manage painful affects may be overwhelmed by the affects generated in relationships, even those on the less intimate level of workplace relationships.

Research suggests links between adolescents' attachment patterns and psychosocial functioning in many spheres (Allen & Land, 1999). For example, preoccupied strategies (negative view of self, positive view of other) are associated with depression. Dismissing strategies (positive view of self, negative view of other) are found to be related to externalizing problems such as substance abuse and conduct disorders. In the sexual arena, secure attachment is associated with having first intercourse at a later rather than an earlier age, and with fewer sexual partners and greater use of contraception (Allen & Land, 1999). Such findings suggest the profound and various ways in which the nature of self- and other-representation arising out of early attachment experiences can affect the developing person.

The fact that development continues to be experience-dependent also tells us that changes in the environmental resources and opportunities surrounding a young person can lead to positive adaptations in attachment strategies and representations over time. Although maltreatment is associated with lower developmental achievement along Erikson's psychosocial stages, perceived social support is related to higher levels of developmental achievement and appears to mediate the relation between maltreatment and development (Pepin & Banyard, 2006).

Maltreatment and Risky Behavior

Poverty and low socioeconomic status place adolescents at risk for taking risky actions (delinquency, substance abuse, carrying a weapon, for example) and non-actions (failure to use contraception, get healthcare when needed) (Harris, Duncan, & Boisjoly, 2002). Adverse childhood experience increases the vulnerability to risky behavior, as does minority status. In a recent study that examined the effects of race on the relationship between hopelessness and risk behaviors of adolescents living in high-poverty, inner-city neighborhoods, researchers report that risky behaviors and hopelessness are generally high, with some racial differences, but that minority status within a given neighborhood is a more significant predictor of risky behavior than race itself. Members of a minority group within a social environment are more adversely affected (by negative socioeconomic circumstances) than when they live in environments with others similar to themselves (Bolland et al., 2007). These findings have relevance to minority status in other contexts, suggesting that risk of hopelessness and high-risk behaviors may be elevated for sexual-minority youth who exist in majority-heterosexual environments, and beyond this, for foster care alumni, who are a minority in the normative population.

Many researchers have looked at the effects of abuse on a variety of negative outcomes, such as anxiety, depression, suicidal behavior, substance abuse, risky sexual behaviors, delinquency, and increased victimization. Maltreatment has been tied to poor social controls, poor emotional regulation, and acquisition of deviant values, all of which play a part in high-risk behavior (Chapple, Tyler, & Bersani, 2005). Neglect increases the risk of victimization, because lack of monitoring exposes youth to potential offenders and because youth who feel uncared for are more likely to engage in risky behaviors (Tyler, Johnson, & Brownridge, 2008). Childhood sexual abuse also affects victimization and sexual risk behavior during adolescence (Johnson, Rew, & Sternglanz, 2006; Tubman et al., 2004; Tyler & Johnson, 2006), and is a predictor of adolescent suicidality (Salzinger et al., 2007). Victim reaction to sexual abuse is manifested in both psychological and social functioning in the sexual and interpersonal realms, including unprotected sex, delinquent or criminal behavior, prostitution or promiscuity, and inappropriate sexual behavior (Johnson et al., 2006).

> *Summer spent middle and high school "ditching school, doing drugs, sleeping around." She didn't care about the consequences: "Since my parents were fuck-ups and didn't care about me, then why should I care about myself? Alcohol was more important to my dad than I was to him." When friends offered a new drug, Summer took it. She went to raves and parties where drugs were in plentiful supply. She found herself sneaking alcohol from her aunt and uncle's liquor cabinet, then hiding it by adding water to the bottles. Ironically, she recalled doing the very same thing as a child in an attempt to minimize her parents' consumption of alcohol.*
>
> *The risky behavior that Summer engaged in can be seen as a consequence of her devalued sense of self and her lack of meaning to her parents (and therefore to the larger world). The relief from unbearable feelings that drugs and alcohol provided, and the transitory sense of fitting in with other kids, were additional motivators in Summer's acting-out behaviors.*

Independence and Interdependence

Independence is seen as a desired outcome of adolescent development in our society. Personal agency and self-definition are valued over interpersonal competence and social connectedness (Collins & Steinberg, 2006), which are de-emphasized in popular conceptions of successful young adulthood. Independence includes emotional, behavioral, and philosophical dimensions; the young person should feel independent, be capable of decision-making and self-governance, and have his or her own world view. In some cultures, however, independence is valued differently, with greater emphasis on interpersonal connectedness. In the United States, adolescent psychosocial development revolves around gradual individuation and separation from the parent(s), with the adolescent learning to do things more and more independently from the parent's ways, desires, or beliefs. Increased capacity for reflection and abstract reasoning, along with the press of sexual maturation, and the greater emphasis on peer relationships, propel and enable these changes.

> *As we reflect on Summer's passage through adolescence, we can see that the chaotic nature of her life up until puberty precluded a gradual exploration and consolidation of identity. It is only during adolescence that her immediate caregiving surround held constant (and safe) long enough for her to be able to develop the kinds of mastery (of impulses, affects, investments in school and activities) that children in more optimal situations have managed much earlier.*

When childhood is focused on survival and recovery from immediate frights and assaults, other kinds of development take a more circuitous path or are delayed. With no positive attachment context out of which to derive a sense of oneself as lovable and capable, these developments are temporarily sidetracked at best, and derailed at worst.

Youth leaving foster care experience the same psychological, cognitive, and sexual maturational processes as youth in the general population, but their circumstances lead to sudden separation from the authority figures in their lives. The shift from dependency to independence is dramatically compressed, sometimes into a single day following high school graduation, or the eighteenth birthday. Opportunities for the practice of decision-making and other life skills may have been limited or nonexistent in the placement experience and the relationships that have been sustaining over the previous months or years may not survive emancipation to provide support in the beginning months or years of young adulthood.

Connection with others, including peers, which is so often disrupted when a youth leaves foster care, is not only a component of self-perceptions of general competence (Collins & Steinberg, 2006), but a source of emotional and instrumental support. Most young people in the general population receive these kinds of supports from parents or relatives as they move into young adulthood, and the confidence and freedom to turn to family members for help adds to their sense of hope for themselves and for their future significant relationships. Adolescents in transition to adulthood are vulnerable to the benefits of opportunities and the dangers of isolation; it is a moment when intervention and support can make a great difference to optimal development, and lack thereof can mean the foreclosing of potentials.

> In the final semester of her senior year at high school, when friends were getting accepted to colleges, Summer realized that she hadn't applied because she didn't see herself as someone with a future. Then, she thought, "I don't want to be a loser or be like my parents." She enrolled in community college. The interruption of the cycle of trauma, displacement, and broken attachments and the new environmental surround of stability and connection allowed her to imagine a different future for herself.

The biological, psychological, and social systems of adolescents are undergoing profound simultaneous change. On the biological level, the body is transforming, physically and sexually, and the executive functions of the brain are reaching greater maturity. Psychologically, youth are beginning to think about who they are and can be, what opportunities and roles might be available to them. In the social dimension, the family, neighborhood, community, and culture they live in will have powerful influence on their developing identities, the peers and role models they may have, and the paths they take into adulthood. For many foster care alumni, the (often painful) past has been shaped by maltreatment, instability, and loneliness, leaving them vulnerable to self-doubt, risky behavior, and bleak views of the future. The threshold of adulthood is a moment at which sustained support and encouragement can make a transformative difference.

PART **III**

MENTAL HEALTH

Emotional problems are developmental outcomes, arising from successive transactions between the child and the environment. "Disturbance is the outgrowth of patterns of maladaptation interacting with ongoing challenging circumstances in the absence of adequate support" (Sroufe et al., 2005b). The traumatic family histories and accumulated losses of many youth in foster care result in increased risk for mental health problems (Pecora et al., 2009; Pecora, 2010). Research on emotional, behavioral, and substance-abuse disorders among youth in care support this conclusion, finding, for example, 61% of 17-year-olds with at least one lifetime mental health disorder, 25% of older adolescents with clinically significant internalizing symptoms, and 28% with significant externalizing symptoms, all significantly higher rates than among peers in the general population (Pecora, 2010). Youth exiting foster care do not leave their psychological problems behind them, and these problems can both complicate and be complicated by the changed circumstances of leaving care. Indeed, among foster care alumni, studies find high rates for some diagnoses, the most prevalent of which is PTSD (Pecora et al., 2010).

In previous chapters, we looked at contextual features of the foster care experience and at developmental aspects of childhood and adolescence. Because so many adolescents arrive at the age of emancipation with mental health problems, these will be part of our work with them, on individual and programmatic levels. The chapters in this section consider in detail only some of the emotional and behavioral disorders that foster care alumni carry with them, as it is beyond the scope of this book to examine all of the potentially relevant mental health problems. Each of the four chapters provides an overview of a problem area (anxiety disorders, mood disorders, substance-abuse disorders, and delinquency as a mental health problem) and currently supported intervention approaches, as well as developmental and attachment implications and the role of childhood maltreatment. This introduction to Part III presents general mental health considerations that apply across all of the mental health chapters.

The Diagnostic and Statistical Manual of Mental Disorders (DSM)

The following chapters employ DSM-IV diagnoses as identifiers and organizational vehicles, but the reader should bear in mind that these diagnoses are simply ways of categorizing symptoms and behaviors. The DSM enables communication among professionals and can provide directions for treatment. The Manual has major limitations for purposes of understanding mental heath problems. First, with the exception of noting age of onset of symptoms, it gives little attention to development and the transformations that may occur as children (or adolescents) grow. Second, it stops at the descriptive level; consideration of underlying conditions, meanings, and functions of behavior is not a part of the DSM structure. The adaptive and maladaptive value of any single dimension of a child's functioning or behavior cannot be understood in the absence of the larger context of the current environment and the child's development over time (Davies & Cicchetti, 2004). The DSM conceives of the individual as a one-person system who contains (or fails to contain) the problem. (Some limited attention is given to contextual factors in the multiaxial system.)

Assessment of psychological or psychiatric problems should always incorporate strengths, individual and contextual, as well as vulnerabilities and symptoms. Symptomatic behavior is an expression of both past and present difficulties; this behavior continues to affect and be affected by the current environment and by ongoing developmental changes. Cultural background is a consideration in assessing any psychiatric disorder, as there are cultural differences in symptom expression and meaning, as well as in coping behaviors. Foster care alumni often have complex attachment- and trauma-related disturbances that are not well captured in the present classifications of mental disorders (Tarren-Sweeney, 2008).

Comorbidity

This term is borrowed from medicine, where it denotes the existence of one or more diseases in addition to the one that is the primary diagnosis. In the mental health field, it is commonly used to indicate that the client's symptoms meet the criteria for two or more diagnoses. Some practitioners believe that the need for comorbid diagnoses might result from the fact that existing psychiatric diagnostic categories are inadequate to describe the variability and complexity of psychological problems. DSM diagnoses cannot reflect either underlying issues or the moment-to-moment effects of the dynamic relationship of the client (and his or her disorder) to the contextual surround. Comorbid or dual diagnoses carry the same limitations, but may be useful in pointing the way to appropriate interventions.

Developmental Considerations

Childhood and adolescence are marked by rapid physical and emotional development; it is during these periods (more than any other times) when the highest levels of problem behaviors are seen (Wolfe & Mash, 2006). In the general population, there is a marked rise in criminal behavior during adolescence, attempted suicide rates peak in late adolescence, female preponderance of depression appears for the first time, and overt schizophrenic psychoses become progressively more frequent during the teen years (Rutter, 2006). One study of a national sample of transition-age youth found a steady rise in psychiatric diagnoses from age 15 (22%) to age 21 (40%) to age 26 (48%). The same study found that 11 years was the median age of onset for anxiety and impulse-control disorders, and 20 years was the median age of onset for substance abuse (Pottick et al., 2008).

Against this backdrop of graduating risk of psychiatric disorder and criminal behavior over the teen and young adult years for all individuals, the situation of children in foster care, exposed to considerably more lifetime stress, acquires greater urgency. With the compelling evidence from many studies that early life stress constitutes a major risk factor for the development and persistence of mental disorders, a shorthand formula might be: genetics (which includes biological and temperamental factors) + early life stress (which includes familial and environmental factors) + ongoing stress = individual stress-responsiveness and manifestation of psychiatric disturbance (Heim & Nemeroff, 2001).

Problems in attachment have been implicated as causal contributors to, predictors of, and manifestations of psychopathology. Insecure and disorganized attachment patterns have been shown to be associated with higher levels of depression, anxiety, and substance abuse and with elevated risk for personality disorders (Bifulco et al., 2006; Westen et al., 2006). Psychopathology is associated with profound insecurities in one's state of mind regarding attachment experiences (Wallis & Steele, 2001). Impairments in interpersonal relationships are central to understanding the effects of child abuse on mental health outcomes; research indicates that individuals with good relationship experiences across different domains during childhood and adolescence are particularly likely to demonstrate resilience (Collishaw et al., 2007). However, disrupted and disturbed attachments are often at the forefront of the adverse experiences of children in foster care, preceding their entry into care and continuing during placement.

Mental Health Service Use

The high rate of mental health disorders and utilization of mental health services among foster care populations is widely reported (Dworsky & Courtney, 2009; McMillen et al., 2004; Shin, 2005). This is not surprising in view of the significant association of all types of child maltreatment with elevated risk for psychiatric disorders (Chapman, Dube, & Anda, 2007; Schneider, Baumrind, & Kimerling, 2007; Tiet et al., 2001).

While in care, a high percentage of youth with mental health disorders receive treatment, although some studies suggest that their needs are often not addressed (Dworsky & Courtney, 2009). A review of the literature reported that one-half of youth in care use mental health services, and that those with a history of maltreatment are 23 times more likely to use mental health services, probably because of court-mandated mental health screening (Shin, 2005). The inclusion of court orders and child protection mandates makes it difficult to know how much of reported service utilization reflects deliberate help-seeking by adolescents (Unrau & Grinnell, 2005). Also, many youth are moved directly into the most invasive and stigmatizing types of services (inpatient and residential programs) without first receiving outpatient services (McMillen et al., 2004).

Substantial racial disparities are found in service use. African American children are the largest racial group in care, yet the rate of mental health service use is lower than for comparable white children (Kerker & Dore, 2006). Since youth in care share common enabling characteristics for gaining access to healthcare, disparities may reflect bias; some professionals may view emotional and behavioral problems in mental health terms for white youth, but not for youth of color. The large number of youth of color receiving residential services may also reflect the shortage of foster families willing to take older African American youth (McMillen et al., 2004).

Most research suggests that there is a severe drop-off in service use following exit from the system, sometimes due to discontinuation of Medicaid and sometimes initiated by youth who wish to stop taking medications or receiving other treatment (McMillen et al., 2004; McMillen & Raghavan, 2009). Youth interviewed about their experiences of mental health services emphasize the importance of communication, helpfulness, consistency, and support, while also reporting negative experiences regarding medication concerns (Lee et al., 2006). Continuity of treatment is important during transitional periods when other supports shift suddenly, yet often treatment ends abruptly with changes in living situation, leaving the emotionally disturbed young person both untreated and more alone. As we look at the specific mental health problems in the chapters ahead, continuity, consistency, and relationship will be critical dimensions in choice of interventions.

Evidence-Based Practice and Psychotherapy with Youth Leaving Care

Initially developed in the field of medicine, the evidence-based practice model is now being applied in a broad range of human-service systems, including mental and behavioral health care, social work, and criminal justice (Hunsley, 2007). Soydan (2006) defines evidence-based practice as an integration of the best scientific evidence with the practitioner's professional skills, and the values, traditions, and needs of the client in a specific context. There is debate about what constitutes the best scientific evidence as well as about how best to implement evidence-based practice (Hunsley, 2007; Westen, Novotny, & Thompson-Brenner, 2004).

Mental health, unlike clinical medicine, is informed by a variety of disciplines and research paradigms; the nature of reality and causation may be understood differently by those with a constructionist or interpretive approach to knowledge and research (McGuire, 2005). Variation among individuals, both clients and practitioners, as well as among circumstances and contexts, cannot be fully accounted for in some types of research designs, but should be a factor in evidence-informed clinical decisions.

Studies of "empirically supported relationships" focus on people rather than disorders, and particularly on the role of the therapist, the client, and the interactions between them (Messer, 2004). This type of research, though less advanced than research designs employing randomized control trials, for example, may be more helpful in designing treatments and programs for youth leaving care, who have complex, traumatic histories and may especially need help with relationship issues. Research in the area of emotion-regulation suggests that an increased focus on emotion in child psychotherapy may be beneficial (Southam-Gerow & Kendall, 2002). A recent meta-analytic review of studies of the efficacy and effectiveness of psychodynamic psychotherapy provides solid support for the effects of psychotherapy, with overall effect size greater than for medication. Distinctive features of psychodynamic techniques, such as focus on affect, identification of recurring themes and patterns, focus on interpersonal relations, and focus on the therapy relationship, were found to be instrumental aspects of cognitive behavior therapies as well. Perhaps most important, a recurring finding was that benefits of psychodynamic psychotherapy not only endure, but increase with time, in contrast to benefits of non-psychodynamic empirically supported therapies, which tend to decay over time for depression and generalized anxiety (Shedler, 2010).

Ethnicity and Culturally Sensitive Practice

Over half of the children in foster care in 2008 were of color, as will be the youth who age out of care in any given year (US DHHS, ACF, ACYF, CB, 2009). Yet the literature that provides the evidence for evidence-supported treatments (ESTs) is drawn preponderantly from non-minority populations, and groups such as Asian Americans and American Indians or Native Alaskans are almost completely absent. However, there are some studies of the effectiveness of evidence-based treatments with Latino and African American children and adolescents, and these suggest that ESTs are also effective for them (Miranda et al., 2005). Research on cultural adaptations of existing ESTs—culturally supported treatments, or CSTs— is only just beginning. A cultural adaptation is defined as any modification to an evidence-based treatment that involves changes in the approach to service delivery, nature of therapeutic relationship, or components of treatment itself to accommodate the cultural beliefs, attitudes, and behaviors of the target population (Whaley & Davis, 2007). One author points out that existing ESTs are actually CSTs for a specific ethnic group, European Americans, and that we cannot simply export something designed for one culture to another (Hall, 2001).

Symptom expression and diagnosis may be influenced by the culture of the client and by the culture of the mental health professional. For example, prevalence studies of psychiatric disorders in treated populations of African Americans suggest that blacks with affective disorders are often misdiagnosed as schizophrenic, due either to clinician bias (failure to adhere to strict diagnostic criteria) or differences in cultural expression of symptoms (high scores on scale of distrust are more predictive of diagnosis of depression for blacks than for whites). Mild paranoia may be susceptible to sociocultural influences and related to depression, and a moderate level of paranoia may be associated with both depressive and psychotic disorders (Whaley, 1997). African American youth, who make up 31% of the foster care population (US DHHS, ACF, ACYF, CB, 2009) and who may have experienced institutional racism and discrimination, may leave care with considerable mistrust based on these experiences. If, in addition, they suffer from depression, the clinician who lacks cultural sensitivity or knowledge of the system may draw the wrong diagnostic conclusions.

Youth of color exiting care with mental health problems may be reluctant to seek help for a number of reasons. Some barriers may be system-related, such as restrictions or discontinuities of services, or lack of coverage (Kerker & Dore, 2006). Young people may have negative feelings related to treatments received in care that were imposed upon them by the courts or schools. Cultural beliefs can and do influence help-seeking behavior. Ethnic and cultural groups differ on what is perceived to be a mental health problem, as well as on social norms for what behaviors are considered undesirable, deviant, or of concern. In some cultures, it is believed that the best way to deal with problems is to avoid thinking about them. Help-seeking is most likely to occur when a problem is seen as undesirable and unlikely to go away on its own (Cauce et al., 2002).

Culture is an important shaper of the concept of self; whereas mainstream psychotherapies may reflect majority cultural values that emphasize uniqueness and independence, Latino youth, who are 20% of the foster care population (US DHHS, ACF, ACYF, CB, 2009) may have an ideal self that is more collectivistic and emphasizes social bonds and communal goals. Treatment frameworks must be amenable to adaptations that are congruent with the cultural values of the individual youth, focusing on social and cultural contexts as well as internal realities (Comas-Diaz, 2006).

As we look at the current treatments for mental health problems in the next few chapters, the individual client must remain central in our considerations. Every treatment, psychosocial or pharmacological, must take account of all of the features—biological, intrapsychic, social, cultural, and contextual—of the particular young person. Interdependence, spirituality, and discrimination more often characterize ethnic minority cultures than the majority culture; the clinician (and the interventions) will be more effective if they are sensitive to these dimensions of a client's experience. At the same time, the literature contains some unsupported biases about what kinds of treatment groups of individuals will accept. For example, there is a persistent sentiment against the use of psychodynamically informed treatment with Latinos, despite the lack of rigorous data supporting this stance (Gelman, 2004).

Another controversial issue is whether, when, and how to initiate a discussion of race and ethnicity in psychotherapy, especially when there is a racial or ethnic difference between client and therapist (Cardemil & Battle, 2003). The early discussion of race by therapists is recommended in the literature, yet, in focus groups, a number of participants said it would make them suspicious about the therapist's possibly racist attitudes (Thompson, Bazile, & Akbar, 2004). For many young people who may themselves be reluctant to initiate a conversation about race, however, it may be a relief when the therapist is open to including this aspect of internal, external, and therapeutic reality. It may strengthen the therapeutic alliance, reducing the likelihood of premature termination, and it may help the therapist gain greater knowledge of the client's cultural strengths, resources, or conflicts.

As we turn to specific mental health problems, I caution the reader to keep in mind the dynamic nature of the young person's relationship with her or his now radically changing environment, of which the assessing and treating clinician is an interacting part. How development has proceeded for the particular youth, what trauma he or she may have sustained, in what circumstances, and with what impacts on development, are all dimensions of the adaptation or maladaptation represented by the presenting symptoms. Change is possible at any point, though it is easier before a pathway has become entrenched. The strategy for intervention must be to identify and alter factors that maintain the person on a maladaptive pathway, or to identify interventions that would encourage a return to a more constructive pathway (Sroufe et al., 2005a).

General Practice Principles

1. Treat the individual rather than the disorder.
2. Choose treatment based on symptoms, strengths, vulnerabilities, culture, history, developmental status, current situation/environment and its resources, available treatments, and evidence of effectiveness.
3. Make gender, ethnicity, and culture important considerations in assessment and treatment.
4. Address trauma- and attachment-related issues along biological, psychological, and social dimensions.
5. Attend to the relational aspects of assessment and treatment. Offer services in a context of authenticity, reliability, and willingness to recognize ways in which you are continuously interacting with the client and his or her world.

6

ANXIETY, TRAUMA, AND
POST-TRAUMATIC STRESS DISORDERS

Anxiety disorders involve disturbances in the capacity to regulate anxious states, and result from complex interactions among biological, genetic, familial, temperamental, developmental, and environmental factors. Anxiety disorders are the most commonly diagnosed disorders in both adult and adolescent populations, including child welfare populations, with a prevalence rate between 9% and 20% (Emslie, 2008; Garland et al., 2001; Kendall, Hedtke, & Aschenbrand, 2006b; Lemstra et al., 2008). Among older adolescents about to exit care, PTSD was the most common diagnosis, and occurred at rates above those seen in the general population (Keller, Salazar, & Courtney, 2010). The reported prevalence rate of PTSD among children exposed to abuse ranges from 21% to 55%, possibly due to different definitions of PTSD and abuse (Linning & Kearney, 2004; Stovall-McClough & Cloitre, 2006; Wolfe & Mash, 2006). In this chapter, we will focus on the anxiety disorders and interpersonal trauma, beginning with a discussion of the nature of anxiety, theories about etiology, and risk and protective factors. The specific disorders are then described, followed by assessment, intervention, and key treatment principles.

Anxiety

Anxiety or fearfulness in the face of an actual or imagined threat is universal, but for most individuals, it is adaptive and situational and passes when the threat is removed. Over the course of development, the content of fears and anxieties shifts from concrete external things to things that are more internalized and abstract. Infants fear strangers, loud noises, and unexpected objects; young children fear separation from their parents, animals, the dark, kidnappers, robbers, ghosts, and monsters; older children fear bodily injury, death, and failure; prepubescent children and adolescents have fears related to social comparisons, physical appearance, personal conduct, and tests (Dadds & Barrett, 2001). The boundary between normal and pathological anxiety is determined by subjective discomfort, frequency and duration of anxiety symptoms, and the degree to which functioning is impaired. In addition to internal distress, anxiety disorders have psychosocial implications in domains such as peer relationships, school performance, and social competence.

Anxious children show attentional biases toward threatening stimuli (Kendall, Hedtke, & Aschenbrand, 2006b), interfering with important developmental tasks such as successful peer interaction and schoolwork. A shy individual who has experienced child abuse may selectively attend to threatening aspects of any environment, attributing threat in neutral situations and overestimating the likelihood of negative events. The child's physiological stress response system is called into action, often when there is no real threat, possibly leading to the development of the avoidance behaviors or emotional distress of any one of a number of anxiety disorders. The anxious child in a foster care placement overreacts to perceived threats, often inviting negative response from the environment, leading to another placement and attendant losses.

Theoretical Perspectives

Until fairly recently, the dominant theories about the etiology of anxiety disorders have been behavioral or learning approaches that emphasize conscious cognitive processes, or psychodynamic approaches that emphasize unconscious affective processes (Epstein, 1994; Mineka & Zinbarg, 2006). Learning theories hypothesize the contribution of conditioning events, which can be direct (abuse, witnessing violent acts), vicarious (seeing another person's fearful behavior around an aversive stimulus), or instructional (hearing from another that stimuli are fear-inducing) (McClure & Pine, 2006). Psychodynamic theory is based on Freud's original idea that pathological anxiety results when overwhelmingly painful memories, impulses, or thoughts fail to remain repressed. The unbearable repressed material breaks into consciousness, but in a disguised form, such as an obsession or a panic attack (Maxmen & Ward, 1995).

In the last two decades, advances in neuroscience have led to greater appreciation of the biological dimensions of anxiety, including genetic vulnerabilities to the development of anxiety disorders, complex interactions between brain activity and stressful events, and also potential therapeutic implications. Animal studies show that the amygdala, in conjunction with the prefrontal cortex, thalamus, and hippocampus, plays a central role in acquiring and expressing fear responses (Garakani, Mathew,

& Charney, 2006; MacMillan et al., 2009). Recall from Chapter 3 that the HPA axis activates and coordinates the body's stress response system, based on information received from the amygdala and hippocampus (as well as from the autonomic nervous system). In other words, experiences that are frightening (trauma, abuse) are mediated through these brain areas and systems. There is increasing evidence that childhood maltreatment can lead to neuroendocrine dysregulation, causing either increased cortisol production or blunted cortisol response (Shea et al., 2004). Adults with PTSD, for example, who experienced childhood maltreatment tend to have elevated cortisol response to social and cognitive stressors, and maltreated children with anxiety disorders tend to have elevated basal cortisol. The repeated experience of arousal and anxiety generated by the effects of maltreatment on HPA function is likely to have negative implications for mental health going forward (Tarullo & Gunnar, 2006). Anxiety, or the avoidance of anxiety-generating cues, can become a way of life on biological, psychological, and social levels.

A comprehensive view of anxiety disorders, like other psychological problems, should incorporate aspects of the three perspectives described (learning theory, psychodynamic theory, neuroscience) as well as developmental timing and status, early and current life stressors and losses, and relational dimensions.

> *Both Robert and Marie, for example, suffered from anxiety symptoms related to early physical and sexual abuse, disrupted attachments, compromised capacity for self-regulation, and repeated losses of home during childhood and adolescence. Marie experienced the additional trauma of witnessing the violent accident in which her father was thrown from a balcony into the street. When subsequent stressful events occurred and dysregulating anxiety ensued, neither child had a consistent attachment figure to provide soothing and regulation. Marie attempted to manage by means of hair-pulling, lashing out, or retreating into her own world; Robert turned to drugs and alcohol to calm his overactivated system.*

Risk and Protective Factors

Compelling evidence suggests that early life stress, such as that experienced before, during, and after entry into foster care, is a major risk factor for the development and persistence of mental disorders; this backdrop should always be kept in mind as we consider more specific factors (Heim & Nemeroff, 2001). It is important to draw a distinction between *risk* factors and *vulnerability* factors. Risk factors are significantly correlated with the appearance of symptoms but are not necessarily causally related, and vulnerability factors are more strongly causally related to the development of symptoms (Elwood et al., 2009). Vulnerabilities interact with a stressor to lead to the development of symptoms (Elwood & Williams, 2007). Exposure to traumatic events, for example, is a risk factor for the development of PTSD; however, not all those exposed develop the disorder. Emotional dysregulation, anxiety sensitivity, and attentional bias toward threat stimuli, on the other hand, are affective and cognitive vulnerabilities that could interact with trauma exposure to increase the likelihood of developing symptoms (Elwood et al., 2009; Kendall, Hedtke, & Aschenbrand, 2006b)

Individual-Level Vulnerability Factors

Genetic predisposition to anxiety disorders appears to aggregate within families; youth whose parents have anxiety or mood disorders seem to have greater likelihood of developing one of these disorders (Kendall, Hedtke, & Aschenbrand, 2006b; Maxmen & Ward, 1995). Studies show that high levels of what is called "negative affect" (fear, anxiety, hostility, scorn, disgust) and low levels of ability to employ self-regulative processes are consistently related to the development of anxiety disorders (Kendall, Hedtke, & Aschenbrand, 2006b). Behavioral inhibition—the tendency to approach new situations with more restraint, avoidance, and distress than other children do—is also thought to be a predisposing factor to social and other anxiety disorders (Ginsburg, Riddle, & Davies, 2006; Kendall, Hedtke, & Aschenbrand, 2006b; McClure & Pine, 2006; Warren et al., 1997). Problems in regulation at the neurobiological level and the negative interpretations of ambiguous stimuli that often result from maltreatment are additional physiological and psychological vulnerabilities.

Female gender is associated with higher rates of PTSD, and females are more likely than males to experience child sexual abuse. Higher risk of exposure to potentially traumatic events does not appear to fully explain the higher rates of PTSD in females; when male and female victims of sexual assault or abuse are compared with one another, females show more PTSD than male peers. It is unclear how sex acts as a vulnerability or resilience factor (Tolin & Foa, 2006).

Family-Level Factors

Parenting styles that are overly controlling, rejecting, critical, or reinforcing of anxious behavior have been found to be associated to anxiety disorders, whereas families in which there is greater cohesion and warmth seem to be a protective factor (McClure & Pine, 2006; Warren et al., 1997). In a study of the relationship between attachment and anxiety disorder, a specific link was found between insecure anxious attachment (Type C) and anxiety disorders assessed 16 years later, though temperamental characteristics were not captured in the study (Warren et al., 1997). Separation distress and anxiety are paramount during early and middle childhood; if removal from home or change in placement occurs abruptly during these years, and there are individual vulnerabilities, it is easy to see how a separation anxiety disorder might develop. A history of childhood abuse elevates the risk of PTSD (and other mental health disorders) sevenfold, although many individuals who have been abused do not develop any disorder (Collishaw et al., 2007). Risk factors include severe, lengthy, and varied abuse; being female; and having more than one perpetrator (Linning & Kearney, 2004; Shea et al., 2004).

A longitudinal study of young adults who had anxiety disorders in adolescence found higher rates among those who come from socially disadvantaged families that are characterized by parental change, severe punishment, sexual abuse, parental alcohol problems, and poor parent–child attachment (Woodward & Fergusson, 2001). Research supports the presence of strong links between family dysfunction and anxiousness in children, and suggests that emotional abuse is as strongly associated with anxiety as physical abuse (Dadds & Barrett, 2001; Pagani et al., 2008; Schneider, Baumrind, & Kimerling, 2007). Resilience to negative effects of child abuse is related to good relationship experiences across different domains and across childhood, adolescence, and adulthood (Collishaw et al., 2007).

Peer Factors

Peer relationships and experiences are more influential in the development of social anxiety than in other anxiety disorders. From middle childhood through adolescence, school performance and socially oriented concerns are more paramount. Poor peer relationships, characterized by negative, aversive, or exclusionary experiences, can lead to avoidance of social interactions (Kendall, Hedtke, & Aschenbrand, 2006b). The development of coping skills and the ability to shift away from negative internal states may be critical to the management of social anxiety and the prevention of a social anxiety disorder (McClure & Pine, 2006).

Neighborhood and Community Factors

Youth with low socioeconomic status are approximately two and a half times more likely to suffer from depressed mood or anxiety than those with higher socioeconomic status (Lemstra et al., 2008). Living in violent environments has been shown to be linked to a variety of mental health disorders for children and adolescents, including anxiety disorders, and PTSD in particular (Stein et al., 2001). Family violence may have been the reason for a child's entry into the child welfare system, but many children in foster care continue to have high levels of violence exposure even after removal from their families of origin. Subsequent exposure to violence may occur at school, in other community settings, as a result of continuing contact with the biological family, or in foster homes. Being the victim of violence is the strongest predictor of developing stress symptoms, but additional or other violence exposure can significantly affect a child's level of symptoms (Stein et al., 2001). Children with high levels of exposure and inadequate social support have the highest level of intrusive thoughts about violence, and those with high levels of intrusive thoughts and inadequate social support have the highest level of internalizing symptoms (Kliewer et al., 1998).

Although research on these disorders among youth of color is only beginning to emerge, anxiety disorders are found to be common among youth of different nationalities (Safrenet al., 2000). Research to date suggests that African Americans do not differ from Caucasians in the prevalence, severity, or manifestation of PTSD despite greater exposure to certain types of trauma (Hood & Carter, 2008). A recent study of older adolescents in the child welfare system finds that in general, African American youth and those in kinship foster care are less likely to have mental health and substance-use problems (Lee et al., 2006). In another study, race/ethnicity is significant for social phobia, but not significant when considering other mental health outcomes among African American and white foster care alumni (Harris et al., 2010; Lee et al., 2006).

The Anxiety Disorders

The central feature of the nine anxiety disorders identified in the DSM is intense fear or worry associated with emotional distress and avoidance behaviors. Each disorder is associated with a specific set of symptoms that, along with the degree of impairment or distress and the duration of the symptoms, form the basis for diagnosis. In every case, we want to understand the circumstances, function, and meaning of the onset and maintenance of the disorder for the specific young person.

Separation anxiety disorder (SAD) is the only anxiety disorder classified as one that is first diagnosed in childhood; the others may begin in childhood, adolescence, or adulthood. SAD has an onset before age 18 and involves excessive anxiety about being apart from primary caregivers or attachment figures, fearing loss or harm to the self or the other. *Generalized anxiety disorder* (GAD) involves excessive, uncontrollable worry about events or daily activities. *Social phobia* (SoP) revolves around social or performance situations in which the individual may be observed or evaluated by others, or those in which he or she is exposed to unfamiliar people. Specific phobias are defined by the objects or events a person fears to the point of having to avoid situations in which those objects or events might be encountered. *Obsessive compulsive disorder* (OCD) is characterized by mental or physical activities that an individual feels driven to perform repeatedly every day for at least an hour (compulsions) and/or by intrusive recurrent thoughts or images that are unwelcome and distressing (obsessions). *Panic disorder* (PD) involves recurrent attacks of intense fear or anxiety when no real danger is present. These attacks are cognitively or physically highly distressing. *Post-traumatic stress disorder* (PTSD) and *acute stress disorder* (ASD) are characterized by significant symptoms following the witnessing or experiencing of a traumatic or life-threatening event and will be discussed in greater detail later in this chapter (American Psychiatric Association, 2000).

Large epidemiological studies of anxiety disorders in adults have consistently shown ages of onset in childhood and adolescence. Specific subtypes have different peak periods of onset, with SAD and phobias peaking in middle childhood, GAD typically peaking in late childhood, and SoP and PD peaking in adolescence. These authors note gender differences in rates of particular disorders: SAD is more common in girls, and some studies show higher rates of SoP in girls. Panic attacks are relatively equal in males and females, though males' panic symptoms are more severe. Finally, the studies reviewed showed no differences in rates of phobias and GAD (Kendall, Hedtke, & Aschenbrand, 2006b).

The few studies of racial/ethnic differences in anxiety symptoms among adolescents report mixed findings. Some describe variability in symptoms, with Caucasian youth showing lowest levels of fear, Hispanic youth reporting more somatic symptoms and higher rates of SAD, and African Americans reporting higher levels of anxiety symptoms. Other studies do not find group differences (Kingery, 2007; McLaughlin, Hilt, & Nolen-Hoeksema, 2007). Research examining whether Latino youth are socialized to believe that somatic anxiety symptoms carry negative consequences and are to be avoided suggests that caregivers and clinicians need to be alert to the possibility of hidden or unavowed anxiety (Varela et al., 2007). To date, the literature examining anxiety disorders among youth of color is limited, and researchers point out that youth of color are more likely to experience certain psychosocial stressors, including poverty. Rates of anxiety disorders are higher among those with low socioeconomic status; the effects of stress and socioeconomic status on mental health need to be disentangled to provide a clearer picture (Safren et al., 2000).

Interpersonal Trauma

Traumatic experience occurs in many forms: threats to life or bodily integrity; child-maltreatment of a physical, sexual, or psychological nature; the witnessing of serious harm to another, and so on. Children or adolescents thus exposed are affected neurobiologically (discussed in detail in Chapter 3) and psychologically. The explosion of research and discovery in the neurobiological and cognitive-behavioral literature has led to dominance of the medical model in conceptualizing the trauma experience, sometimes resulting in neglect of the essence of the experience for the individual involved (Wrenn, 2003). The effects of trauma on the sense of self, others, and the world are as critical to future adaptation or maladaptation as the effects on the neurobiological stress-response system. Complex trauma results in losses of core capacities for self-regulation *and* interpersonal relatedness (Cook et al., 2005).

Early-life trauma occurs within the caregiving environment, most often as a consequence of disturbance or disruption in the attachment relationship(s) and, in the case of children in foster care, followed by disruption of that environment. Severe disruptions of attachment lead to increased susceptibility to stress, inability to regulate emotions or arousal without assistance, and altered help-seeking, at both extremes (Cook et al., 2005). Youth may have difficulty managing internal states and external behaviors, compartmentalizing the painful feelings and memories that threaten to overwhelm them.

Children exhibit a wide range of PTSD symptoms that differ according to type of stressor, developmental stage, cognitive ability at the time of trauma, level of family functioning, and the number of secondary adversities encountered after the trauma (Lipschitz, Rasmusson, & Southwick, 1998). When the trauma is child abuse, the form and duration of abuse and the relationship with the perpetrator play a role in the child's response. Severity of maltreatment and depth of betrayal of trust will be important factors in the development of psychopathology.

PTSD and Complex PTSD

The core symptoms of PTSD are intrusion, avoidance, and arousal. Intrusion is also called re-experiencing (of the trauma) and is manifested in intrusive thoughts, nightmares, or for children, in repetitive play. Avoidance behaviors include purposeful efforts to avoid trauma cues, inability to remember elements of the trauma, social detachment, and numbing. Arousal phenomena include difficulty sleeping, hypervigilance, and psychosomatic symptoms (Brown, 2005). Other symptoms include impaired affect and social relationships, self-destructive behavior (including self-mutilation), impulsivity, dissociation, feelings of ineffectiveness and shame, hostility, and beliefs about the permanency of damage (Linning & Kearney, 2004).

Empirical evidence supports the relationship between trauma and dissociation—the disruption in the usually integrated functions of consciousness, such as memory, identity, and the perception of the environment (Draijer & Langeland, 1999). Dissociation is a powerful defensive process in which some part of a person's experience is segregated from conscious awareness. Adult survivors of childhood sexual abuse often report "watching" the abuse take place, as if from outside their bodies. The affective aspect of the experience has been separated from the cognitive; this is felt to be necessary to surviving the experience. Dissociation can also occur in the opposite direction (affects are vividly present, but without cognitive memory), or in a more global inability to remember the trauma. More frequent sexual abuse is associated with higher levels of dissociation (Draijer & Langeland, 1999), and a subset of severely and chronically abused individuals have amnesia not just for the trauma, but for whole periods of their lives (Chu et al., 1999).

PTSD as a diagnosis does not capture the developmental effects of childhood trauma, such as the complex disruptions of affect regulation, disturbed attachment patterns, loss of autonomous strivings, altered schemas of the world, self-hatred and self-blame, or chronic feelings of ineffectiveness. Many forms of interpersonal trauma do not meet the DSM-IV criteria for a traumatic event, but are traumatic nonetheless. There may be a need for a new diagnosis of "developmental traumatic disorder." This diagnosis would be organized around the dysregulation triggered by traumatic reminders and the anticipatory organization of behavior to prevent the recurrence of trauma effects (van der Kolk, 1996).

The relational context and sequelae of childhood trauma are likewise not reflected in the PTSD diagnosis. Distrust of others and the anxious apprehension embodied in insecure attachment and PTSD interfere with satisfying personal relationships (Muller, Sicoli, & Lemieux, 2000). Complex PTSD is a new diagnosis developed to account for the interpersonal aspects of both the traumatic stressor and the trauma response. It integrates disorders of affect regulation, dissociation, somatization, and altered perceptions of the self and others. A study of the degree of overlap between PTSD and borderline personality disorder (BPD) in sexually abused women found that all of the women with a history of childhood sexual abuse met the criteria for both disorders. In another study, more than half of all BPD patients had histories of severe physical or sexual abuse starting before age six (van der Kolk, 1996). Complex PTSD combines Axis I (PTSD) and Axis II (BPD) symptoms, rather than necessitating comorbid diagnoses of both disorders (McLean & Gallop, 2003).

A third proposed new diagnostic category is "disorder of extreme stress not otherwise specified" (DESNOS). DESNOS refers to a condition arising from exposure to multiple traumas or high levels of chronic stress. It is thought to more fully capture the effects of trauma on a range of core psychological functions, such as dysregulation of affects and impulses, disorders of attention and consciousness, distorted interpersonal relationships, distortions of systems of meaning, and somatization of external stress manifesting as disease or physical disorders (van der Kolk, 1996; Wheeler, 2007).

Assessment and Diagnosis

Anxiety Disorders

Anxiety disorders are often misdiagnosed or overlooked, despite high rates of prevalence, in large part because anxiety is experienced by most people in stressful situations. The fundamental process in all anxiety disorders is anxious apprehension, a future-oriented mood state in which the individual prepares to cope with upcoming negative events. This state of anxious apprehension is accompanied by high levels of negative affect, chronic overarousal, and a strong sense of uncontrollability, sometimes eventuating in avoidance behaviors (Fong & Silien, 1999).

The exploration of presenting symptoms of anxiety should begin with detailed inquiry about what the person is experiencing cognitively, affectively, and behaviorally. It is important to determine the content of the anxiety as well as the context in which it arose or continues to arise. A critical question is whether the fear or anxiety is in response to a real and current threat, a past trauma, or a threat that is more imagined than actual. In view of the likelihood of trauma both previous to and subsequent to entry into care for foster care alumni, the exploration of trauma exposure must be sensitive and thorough. Another way to think about the painful internal affective states of anxiety disorders is to consider and ask about Freud's four basic danger situations: loss of a significant other (abandonment, anger, anxiety, depression, or guilt); loss of love (rejection, rage, anxiety, depression, guilt, feelings of being unworthy and unlovable); loss of bodily integrity (fears of mutilation); and loss of affirmation by one's own conscience (guilt, anxiety, shame) (PDM Task Force, 2006).

Assessment must be sensitive to cultural variations of the expression of anxiety, which may lead to greater emphasis on somatic or cognitive symptoms. Asian cultures, for example, discourage expression of emotional problems in favor of somatic complaints (Dhooper & Moore, 2001). Similarly, coping behaviors in reaction to loss or trauma may be culturally determined, with dissociation being more or less acceptable in a given culture (Paniagua, 1998).

If the youth reports panic attacks, the clinician should determine whether they are cued (as in SoP, specific phobias, and PTSD) or uncued (as in PD). Alumni of foster care may have been thrust into painful, socially embarrassing situations at a new placement or school that are connected to the onset of panic attacks. If panic attacks are not present, the diagnosis is more likely GAD, OCD, PTSD, or ASD. To make these further distinctions, the clinician should ask about avoidance behaviors, intrusive thoughts, and repetitive or compulsive behaviors. Medical conditions, medications, and substance use can exacerbate anxiety, so a medical and substance use history is an important part of the initial assessment.

PTSD (or Complex PTSD or DESNOS)

The strong association between PTSD and poor psychosocial and health functioning among adolescents with foster care experience underscores the importance of accurate assessment (Garakani et al., 2006; Mueser & Taub, 2008; Shea et al., 2004). Although a frightening event or stressor (or trauma of a chronic nature such as child abuse) is at the heart of this diagnosis, not all those exposed to trauma will develop the disorder. The core symptoms of PTSD are high levels of anxiety, arousal, avoidance, and re-experiencing (intrusion) and dissociation symptoms that are not associated with other anxiety disorders (McClure & Pine, 2006). Youth who have experienced childhood abuse, or complex trauma, may show impairment in a number of domains. Many will have insecure attachments, difficulty in knowing how or what they feel, impaired capacity to self-regulate and self-soothe, lack of control or overcontrol of impulses and behavior. Cognitive capacities may have been affected, resulting in difficulties in problem-solving or inability to pay attention in the classroom (Cook et al., 2005). The young person may have a sense of helplessness and vulnerability or a devalued and negative sense of self.

Assessment for PTSD must include a sensitive inquiry into past trauma, which the young person may or may not be able to address at the first point of contact. To ensure that the diagnosis is not overlooked, a brief trauma history should be included in all evaluations for anxiety (Sher, 2004). Because the aftereffects of psychic trauma (an inevitable concomitant of child abuse) can be both far-reaching and subtle, the assessment must also be wide-ranging. The presenting symptoms might not be arousal, avoidance or re-experiencing, but, rather, substance abuse or problematic relationships or self-destructive behaviors. Exploration for traumatic stressors and for symptoms in the core areas will ultimately determine if there is a stress disorder.

Interpersonal violence and exploitation in childhood can have a highly negative impact on the victim's capacity to develop and maintain relationships (Pearlman & Courtois, 2005). Harm arising from within primary attachments intrudes on both the ability to trust and the developing sense of self as lovable. It is not surprising that the consequent internal models of the self and other will be characterized by doubt and mistrust, possibly leading to social alienation and limiting social sources of support and nurture. The adolescent who has been maltreated may appear guarded, defensively flat, or, at the other extreme, indiscriminately intimate and revealing.

Dissociation and somatization may also be prominent manifestations of unresolved traumatic experience. Physical problems with no identifiable medical cause, eating disorders, substance abuse, and self-mutilation may be the indication or communication of trauma which cannot yet be admitted into conscious awareness; these more concrete behaviors may contain and help manage unbearable thoughts or affects.

Treatment

This section outlines empirically supported psychosocial and medical treatments for anxiety and stress disorders, as well as some specific considerations with regard to youth leaving care. From a dynamic systems perspective, which takes into account both attachment and neurobiological phenomena, treatment cannot be considered apart from either context or relationship. The therapeutic alliance is a condition of the treatment situation; the degree to which it is emphasized or employed will vary with the type of intervention, but the relationship of client to provider is an always-present dimension with great potential to advance or impede the treatment. Because youth in care have often experienced betrayal, abandonment, or unreliability in previous relationships, this dimension of treatment will be critical. Some research suggests that the early alliance is particularly predictive, and that attrition from therapy can be predicted with measures of the quality of the early relationship (Creed & Kendall, 2005).

The preponderance of research on treatment for anxiety disorders focuses on cognitive-behavioral and psychopharmacological therapies, in part because these types of interventions lend themselves more readily to measurement, quantification, and standardization in the form of manuals. Studies indicate that SAD, SoP, and GAD respond to similar psychosocial and pharmacological treatments, and that treatments shown to be effective are generally consistent in theoretical rationale (the cognitive behavioral model or the serotonin hypothesis) (Velting, Setzer, & Albano, 2004). A synthesis of systematic reviews of cognitive behavioral therapy (CBT) reported that the best evidence for the potential of CBT in adolescents is in the treatment of GAD, OCD, and PTSD (Munoz-Solomando, Kendall, & Whittington, 2008). Another study, which evaluated 32 methodologically rigorous studies, found that individual and group CBT were probably efficacious for treatment of phobic and anxiety disorders in children and adolescents (Silverman, Pina, & Viswesvaran, 2008). On the other hand, a review of five independent meta-analyses found that the benefits of non-psychodynamic empirically supported therapies tend to decay over time for generalized anxiety, while the benefits for psychodynamic psychotherapies not only endure, but increase with time (Shedler, 2010).

Cognitive Behavioral Therapy

CBT is based on social learning principles and aims to interrupt the conditioned responses that maintain problematic anxiety, using psychoeducation, somatic management, exposure, modeling, and cognitive restructuring (Dadds & Barrett, 2001; Velting et al., 2004). Psychoeducation includes explaining the three aspects of anxiety to be addressed in treatment: physiological reactions, cognitive elements, and behavioral reactions. Clients whose anxiety causes insomnia are taught deep breathing and progressive muscle relaxation to help with letting go enough to fall asleep at night.

Exposure, a key element, brings the individual into contact with the feared stimuli, usually in a systematic, graduated, controlled way. This is done through images, through simulations, or in vivo. The individual gains control over the feared stimuli and the reactions to it. The second key element is *cognitive restructuring* wherein the client learns to identify anxiety-provoking thoughts and to then challenge them with coping-focused thinking and action plans. The negative "self-talk" that increases anxiety is identified, and clients are taught to "say" different, more positive statements to themselves. Cognitive restructuring also includes altering the amount of attention paid to threatening versus nonaversive stimuli (Dadds & Barrett, 2001; Velting et al., 2004).

CBT for anxious adolescents should include content about maturational change and should take into account the biological, psychological, and social dimensions of adolescent development. CBT may be especially well suited to adolescents because of cognitive developments in abstract reasoning and problem-solving, but motivation and rapport-building within the therapeutic relationship will be critical factors (Kendall, Hedtke, & Aschenbrand, 2006b).

Pharmacological Treatment

Pharmacotherapy is based on biological theories that anxiety results from dysregulation in specific neuronal pathways in the central nervous system, leading to alterations in neurotransmitter levels and receptor activity. Pharmacotherapy with selective serotonin reuptake inhibitors (SSRIs) alters the neuronal uptake pump for serotonin, causing an increase in the level of serotonin in the pathways to the central nervous system, thereby promoting better regulation (Keeton & Ginsburg, 2008).

Medication is rarely used as the sole treatment for anxiety disorders with children and adolescents and is typically one part of a treatment program in more serious cases (Dadds & Barrett, 2001). There is growing consensus among researchers concerning the potential efficacy of SSRIs in the treatment of childhood and adolescent anxiety disorders (Birmaher et al., 2003; Pine, 2002), with poor results and sedating effects for benzodiazepines, ambiguous findings for tricyclic antidepressants, and little data on Buspirone (Kendall, Hedtke, & Aschenbrand, 2006b; Rosenberg, 2003). A review of controlled studies of SSRIs supports their use in acute and long-term treatment of OCD in children (Compton, Kratochvil, & March, 2007). SSRIs have been found to be safe and efficacious for treatment of GAD, SoP, SAD, and PD in children and adolescents (Compton et al., 2007; Kendall, Hedtke, & Aschenbrand, 2006b; Pine, 2002).

Researchers found that age, gender, ethnicity, intellectual level, and intensity of adverse events did not affect the results. Outcomes were not better if the dosage was higher, and those who did not respond to SSRI treatment did not become responsive if the dose was increased (Research Units on Pediatric Psychopharmacology Anxiety Study Group, 2003). The Federal Drug Administration reviewed the safety of antidepressants in child and adolescent trials in depression, anxiety, and ADHD, finding a modest but significant increase in the relative risk for suicidality; these findings led to the "black box" warning now required in the sale of these drugs (Compton et al., 2007).

Children in foster care have higher levels of mental health disorders than their peers, but receive psychotropic medication at disproportionate levels relative to their peers (Zima et al., 1999). Concomitant psychotropic medication is frequent for youth in care, with approximately half of those receiving it in therapeutic foster care or group homes taking multiple medications (Breland-Noble et al., 2004; Zito et al., 2008). Youth leaving care may have had negative experiences with medication, as in the example of Marie, and may therefore be reluctant to consider this type of treatment, even when anxiety symptoms are distressing.

Combined Treatment: CBT and SSRIs

While CBT and pharmacotherapy are efficacious interventions for over 50% of children and adolescents with SoP, GAD, and SAD, a substantial number of these (between 20%–45%) receive less-than-optimal gains (Keeton & Ginsburg, 2008). Some researchers suggest that effectiveness can be optimized by using both treatments, either sequentially or in tandem (Dadds & Barrett, 2001; Keeton & Ginsburg, 2008; Kendall, Hedtke, & Aschenbrand, 2006a). SSRIs can be used early on to alleviate distressing symptoms and to instill hope and motivation to undergo CBT, though there is some risk that if symptoms are reduced, the client will be less motivated to learn and apply the skills taught in CBT. A thorough assessment, positive therapeutic alliance, and sensitivity to the youth's history of treatment while in care will help to individualize the treatment plan and its sequencing.

Supportive Expressive Treatment

Many authors point to the need to understand how and why a disorder developed for the particular person rather than looking only at symptomatology. Young people who suffer from anxiety, and especially those who have been traumatized, need a climate of safety in order to undergo any kind of treatment. Creating and ensuring an atmosphere of safety, competence, and predictability is the first step in any successful therapy.

Supportive expressive therapy aims to understand anxiety symptoms in the context of interpersonal conflicts. The treatment is focused on the client's relationship patterns in past and current relationships, including the therapeutic one (Crits-Christoph et al., 2004). The individual resolves anxieties associated with these conflicts and is helped to find new ways of expressing and coping with emotions. The shattering disruptions to attachment relationships that accompany child maltreatment and entry into care follow the young person into the treatment situation, along with the anxious, dysregulated state. Treatment for traumatized, anxious youth leaving care should address the need for developing greater ability to self-regulate painful affective states and impulses (Racusin et al., 2005).

Psychodynamic therapies provide opportunities for the unfolding of traumatic memories within an emotionally safe and regulating environment. Individuals who have developed an inner working model of insecure attachment and associated relational behaviors need a treatment that addresses developmental and relational difficulties in addition to PTSD or anxiety symptoms. Relational forms of therapy are increasingly focused on the challenges in treating traumatized individuals, including dissociative processes and borderline-type relationship patterns. The therapeutic relationship is both the catalyst and the setting for the client's relational history to be played out and examined (Pearlman & Courtois, 2005).

For clients with unmanageable anxiety, a course of SSRIs might also be part of an expressive therapy treatment plan. Anxiety symptoms may be intruding into the client's daily life to the degree that the ability to work or attend school is compromised. The client may be unable to sleep at night and may be too anxious to engage in therapy. SSRI treatment may enable a return to better day-to-day functioning so that the underlying causes of the anxiety can be addressed. Medication may also be an important adjunct during times when traumatic memories and events being addressed in therapy engender renewed anxiety symptoms or sleep disturbance.

Key Treatment Principles

1. Explore in detail symptoms, recent events, trauma history, substance use, and self-harming behavior.
2. Regard symptoms as adaptations or maladaptations to specific environments, past or present.
3. Regard somatic symptoms as possible expressions of anxiety or post-traumatic stress.
4. Consider cultural aspects of anxiety symptom expression and coping strategies.
5. Ascertain developmental status at the time of trauma and currently.
6. Make treatment choices in light of past treatment experiences, individual strengths, vulnerabilities, and current circumstances and supports.
7. Focus on quality of therapeutic relationship, safety, resolution of past trauma and disrupted attachment, and opportunities to develop capacity for self-regulation.

7

MOOD DISORDERS AND SELF-HARM

The prevalence of depressive disorders during adolescence has increased in recent years, and rates are now roughly comparable to those in the adult population, with up to a 25% prevalence in the general population by the end of adolescence (Kessler, Avenevoli, & Merikangas, 2001; Rudolph, Hammen, & Daley, 2006). Major depressive disorder has a strong association with maltreatment, especially among girls (MacMillan et al., 2009); more than 25% of transition-age foster care alumni scored in the clinical range for major depression, a rate almost three times as high as the rate found in the general population of those 18 and older (Southerland, Casanueva, & Ringeisen, 2009). Childhood maltreatment makes an adolescent or an adult three to four times more likely to become depressed or suicidal (Brown et al., 1999) and has been found to be a powerful initiating condition for self-injurious outcomes (Yates, 2009). This chapter will examine the depressive disorders, beginning with a discussion of the nature of depression, theoretical perspectives, and a review of risk and protective factors. The depressive disorders are described, as well as suicidal and self-harming behaviors. The chapter concludes with sections on assessment and treatment, and key treatment principles.

Depression

Mood disorders involve dysregulation of affect at the physiological level and disturbances in the cognitive and socioemotional spheres; in all these dimensions, there are continuing reciprocal problematic effects. For example, the young person experiences a loss of pleasure in activities (anhedonia), cannot sleep, and feels apathetic. Failure to engage in daily activities may give rise to feelings of worthlessness or guilt, leading the young person to isolate him- or herself. Left to his or her own harsh internal representations, the depression deepens, possibly leading to self-injury or suicidal thoughts.

Depression in adolescence is sometimes characterized by irritability rather than sadness. Problems or changes in sleep, appetite, and activity level often accompany the depressed mood. The young person may feel unloved and unlovable, helpless, and misunderstood. Somatic symptoms such as lack of energy, bodily pains, frequent illnesses, and insomnia contribute to the negative feelings about self and life. Relationships with others are also negatively affected and may be marked by greater aggression, clinginess, or withdrawal. Substance use or high-risk sexual behaviors may seem to offer escape or relief from painful affects. Because adolescents are thought of as being prone to mood swings, irritability, and sadness, depressive symptoms are often overlooked or untreated. The transition to adulthood entails life decisions that greatly impact long-term adjustment in the areas of education, career, relationships, and family; depression at this time can compromise one's ability to make good choices (Gutman & Sameroff, 2004). The demands of this life stage can put maltreated youth in an especially vulnerable position as they face not only the challenges of leaving care and entering adulthood, but also the lack of family support at a critical time (Southerland et al., 2009).

Developmental tasks of early and middle childhood, such as the capacity for affect regulation and differentiation, the ability to modulate attention and arousal, and the development of a secure attachment relationship, may have been poorly resolved in the context of a dysfunctional family, leaving the child vulnerable to depression in adolescence. Parental maltreatment or loss compromise optimal development and consolidation of these capacities, resulting in a negative and pessimistic sense of the self and the world, a mindset that is associated with depression.

Jessica, a 32-year-old Latina who is both a mother and a lawyer, entered foster care at birth when her mother's paranoid schizophrenia led to an involuntary hospitalization. During childhood Jessica entered and left care repeatedly; her mother's psychosis was a constant, yet she was frequently released from two- and three- day holds with medication she didn't use. Jessica's father was incarcerated, and the plan was for family preservation, but Jessica lived in terror of her mother's delusions, which increasingly focused on her daughter. Jessica was grateful for foster care, as she feared an escalation of the violence her mother directed at her. During fourth and fifth grades, her mother's suspicions that Jessica was "in the FBI or the CIA" spiked, until late one night when Jessica was 12, her mother woke her, screaming, and threw her out of the house.

Jessica lived on the street in San Francisco where she met other runaways who introduced her to a man who became her pimp. He had many young girls working for him, prostituting and selling crack. Jessica felt safer with him and in this situation than she had ever felt in her life, and felt "good" about earning money and contributing to her own support. One night, she and another girl were pistol-whipped and robbed of the night's earnings; she knew could not return to her pimp without her money. She phoned her social worker, who placed her in a group home. Jessica worried that she'd be returned to her mother, not knowing that she was hospitalized. Other youth in the home advised her to act out aggressively so she wouldn't be sent home, with the result that she was heavily medicated and moved to a Level 14 group home. Multiple psychiatrists gave her diagnoses, including anxiety disorder, attachment disorder, adjustment disorder, and PTSD, but depression was the diagnosis she received most consistently. Medications were prescribed, with frequent changes and in different combinations. She was given Prozac, Paxil, Zoloft, Risperdol, and lithium. When staff thought she was too aggressive, or needed to "relax," they gave her nonprescription Benadryl. She gained 100 pounds in eight months.

Jessica's view of her own situation at the time was that she was sad, anxious, deeply lonely, and hopeless about life. She had never experienced happiness, only "stress, trauma, and drama." She saw little reason to live and tried to kill herself many times, resulting in involuntary holds in psychiatric hospitals. "When I think about why I wanted to die or act out, it really had to do with the fact that I knew no one loved me or cared if I lived, which was my external reality. Seems like 'lonely stressed child with no family in foster care' would have been a more accurate diagnosis than anything DSM could manufacture."

Jessica's example captures perfectly the symptomatic behaviors and picture of a depressed adolescent: sadness, irritability, eating and sleeping problems, aggression, feeling hopeless and unloved. Her example also powerfully demonstrates the complex contextual contributors, and the influence of early maltreatment, attachment to a frightening and frightened mother, and absence of any positive attachment opportunities.

Theoretical Perspectives

Theories of adolescent depression include genetic and biological models emphasizing heritable biological vulnerabilities and neurobiological processes, cognitive models emphasizing negative belief systems, behavioral and interpersonal models emphasizing aversive experiences or interactions with others, family models based on psychodynamic and attachment issues, and socioenvironmental models that emphasize the impact of the environment on depression onset and exacerbation. A more integrative model points to the complex interplay among all of these factors and developmental challenges facing the individual young person (Rudolph et al., 2006).

A dynamic social-neuroscience perspective proposes that there are developmental variations in brain processes that are shaped by environmental inputs, and that mood disorders reflect core deficits in emotional adaptation (Miller, 2007). Heredity (genetics) and early experience are critical determinants, laying the foundation upon which maturational events have their influence, potentially triggering a depressive episode. Whether exposure to early stress leads to the development of depression is thought to be determined by genetic susceptibilities, frequency and nature of the stressors, gender, developmental timing, and presence or absence of social supports (Andersen & Teicher, 2008; Kaufman et al., 2004). As described in Chapter 3, trauma and maltreatment can have profound effects on the development of brain structures that are critical to management of affect.

Aaron Beck, who formulated the cognitive theory of depression, proposes a combined model, incorporating his original ideas with advances in neurobiology. This newer model suggests that cognitive vulnerability arising from early adverse events fosters negative attitudes and biases about the self in the form of schemas that are later activated when other adverse events impinge on that cognitive vulnerability. Beck now adds the genetic vulnerability of brain differences, specifically in the serotonin transporter, which cause individuals to experience higher levels of depressive affect or cortisol response in the presence of a life stressor. In short: stress leads to a distorted cognitive appraisal by which the event and/or its meaning is exaggerated, engaging the stress-response system. The limbic system activity is dominant over prefrontal activity (affect is dysregulated; executive functions take a back seat) and results in depressive symptoms (Beck, 2008).

Attachment theory also proposes an interplay of neurobiology and psychology, but places more emphasis on the affective and relational aspects than on the cognitive ones. Inner representations of a devalued self and an indifferent, hurtful, or fear-inducing other are central to depressive outcomes. Both models attend to the influence of early interpersonal experience in setting the psychophysiological stage for future development of depression.

Risk and Protective Factors

As these theories suggest, the risks and vulnerabilities associated with adolescent depression constitute a complex and interacting web of individual, familial, and environmental factors. Genetic inheritance and makeup, specifically the presence of a particular variation of a serotonin transporter gene promoter (the short allele rather than the long one), when combined with a history of maltreatment, has been linked to risk for depression (Kaufman et al., 2004). However, the presence of social supports moderates these risks, indicating pathways for intervention and toward resilience even for children whose genes and early adverse experiences put them at risk.

Some research suggests that children are four to seven times more likely to be depressed if they have a history of abuse or family violence (Kaplan et al., 1998; Reinherz et al., 2003; Tarren-Sweeney, 2008; Wise et al., 2001). Sexual abuse is the most potent factor in predicting depression (Brown et al., 1999; Buzi, Weinman, & Smith, 2007). Severe stress early in life can alter the biology of the stress-response system, leading to psychopathology characterized by attachment difficulties, trauma-related anxiety, inattention and hyperactivity, and depression.

We can speculate that Jessica's stress-response system was severely dysregulated; in order to protect herself as a child, she had to remain on high alert at all times. Frequent removal to new people and environments would have been preceded by frightening experiences; the return home was full of foreboding and was preceded by loss of the relative safety of the foster home.

The hormonal, socioemotional, and environmental changes of adolescence can create additional stressful life events (aging out of care, unplanned pregnancy), which further alter risks for depression; in turn, depressive symptoms can alter risks for future negative life events (Patton et al., 2003). The breakup of a romantic relationship may set the stage for developing a major depressive disorder for the first time in adolescence; in one study, almost half of the first onsets were preceded by a breakup in the previous year (Monroe et al., 1999). Early or late puberty for girls, low self-esteem, feelings of worthlessness, physical illness, and poor school performance are also considered risk factors (P. Lewinsohn, Rohde, & Seeley, 1998).

Unresolved loss or grief is a critical risk factor. Losses that are unrecognized or disenfranchised are unlikely to elicit social support and solace (Doka, 1999). Jessica's loss of her father to incarceration, for example, was never addressed, nor the loss of her childhood itself. When children are removed from home or moved from one foster placement to another, there may be successive unresolved losses. Response to loss can follow a variety of trajectories—normal grief, chronic grief, improvement during bereavement, resilience, chronic depression—depending on genetic strengths or vulnerabilities, internal resources, and supports available in the new environment (Maciejewski et al., 2007).

The Mood Disorders

Depression is more than sadness and more constant than normal grief or mourning. While some of the particulars of specific disorders differ, those who are depressed feel despair, hopelessness, and self-hatred that interfere with their usual functioning in work, school, or relationships (PDM Task Force, 2006).

Major Depressive Disorder (MDD) and Dysthmic Disorder (DD)

The diagnostic criterion for MDD is the presence of one or more major depressive episodes during which symptoms such as depressed mood, loss of interest or pleasure in usual activities, neglect of personal care, and problems eating or sleeping have been present for at least two weeks. DD in children or adolescents is characterized by chronic symptoms that are not disabling, but have been present more days than not for a period of at least one year. Such symptoms include low energy, low self-esteem, problems with eating or sleeping, feelings of hopelessness, and poor concentration. The classification of MDD and DD as two separate entities has been questioned as a large-scale study revealed that children with either condition alone could not be differentiated on clinical features (Rudolph et al., 2006).

MDD is the most common depressive disorder in adolescents, who are likely to have their first episodes at about age 15. For girls, the first episode may occur at menarche (Hauenstein, 2003; Reinherz et al., 2003). Prevalence estimates vary from 20% to 28% for youth aged 15 to 19 (Richardson et al., 2003; Rohde et al., 2006). Whereas prepubescent girls and boys do not differ in rates, a dramatic shift occurs sometime between ages 11 and 14, and by age 15, girls are twice as likely to have experienced a major depressive episode (Cyranowski et al., 2000). Researchers have suggested a number of contributing influences: hormonal changes, social roles and affiliative concerns, stress and coping processes, and interactions among these (Rudolph et al., 2006).

Of the relatively few studies of ethnic and cultural differences, one large-scale study reported comparable rates of MDD among nine ethnic groups, except for higher rates among those of Mexican descent (Rudolph et al., 2006). Other community-based studies suggest that youth of color are at least as likely as white youth to have a depressive disorder or symptoms of one, although youth of color are less likely to have received antidepressant medication or professional help (Richardson et al., 2003; Zito et al., 2008).

The duration of MDD is reported to range from two to 250 weeks, with a mean duration of about 26 weeks, and a median duration of eight weeks (Lewinsohn et al., 1994; Rudolph et al., 2006). Longer duration and recurrence are predicted by the characteristics of the first episode: age of onset, duration, receiving treatment, severity of symptoms, and suicidal behavior (P. M. Lewinsohn et al., 1994). Treating early and shortening the length of the first episode are important, not only in alleviating debilitating symptoms, but in building resilience and a better long-term outcome.

Bipolar Disorder

Bipolar disorder (BD), also known as manic-depressive illness, is characterized by mood swings from depression to mania. The criteria for the depressive end of the bipolar continuum are the same as those for MDD, but the individual also experiences manic states. Once rarely diagnosed in childhood or adolescence, BD is now said to be much more common in children than was previously thought. In one study of adults with BD, 50% to 66% reported an onset prior to age 18, and 15% to 28% reported onset prior to age 13 (Miklowitz & Chang, 2008). Others estimate that up to one-third of children with depression may be suffering from the onset of bipolar disorder, and one-third of those diagnosed with ADHD may actually be suffering from emerging bipolar disorder (Wilkinson, Taylor, & Holt, 2002). Mania in children and adolescents may be characterized by irritability and outbursts of rage rather than euphoria, and thus may be undiagnosed. Studies of adults with bipolar depression have found that a high percentage experienced childhood trauma, and that those with childhood adversities had a longer delay from the onset of illness to first psychopharmacological treatment for mania or depression (Leverich & Post, 2006).

Bipolar disorders are further classified according to the presence of full manic episodes along with MDD (Bipolar I) or, in Bipolar II disorders, a history of at least one major depressive episode and the existence or presence of hypomanic episodes, which are less severe than manic episodes. In cases where mood fluctuations are present, but not severe enough to be considered bipolar, the diagnosis is cyclothymic disorder (PDM Task Force, 2006).

BD often begins with milder mood symptoms, the most frequently occurring of which is depression. Those at highest risk are children whose first-degree relatives had or have bipolar disorder; offspring of bipolar parents are at four times greater risk for development of a mood disorder (Miklowitz & Chang, 2008). For children in care whose family medical history is unavailable, assessment and diagnosis are more difficult.

Suicidality

Suicidality is the term for phenomena ranging from suicidal thoughts (ideation), to suicide attempts, to completed suicide. In the general population, suicide is the third leading cause of death among 15- to –24-year-olds; attempts are rare before adolescence, but then increase rapidly (Goldston, Daniel, & Arnold, 2006; Wilcox, Storr, & Breslau, 2009). Eighty to ninety percent of adolescents who attempt suicide have a diagnosable disorder, and the odds of completing suicide are 27 times greater among teens with a mood disorder versus those with another diagnosis or no diagnosis (Esposito & Clum, 2003).

Foster Care and Suicide

Youth involved with the child welfare and juvenile justice systems have adverse early life experiences that place them at very high risk for suicide; a recent study in Canada found that the risk of suicide for these youth was five times that of the general adolescent population (Dore, Aseltine, Franks & Schults, 2006). A large-scale study of suicide attempts among former child welfare clients in Sweden demonstrated "striking excess risks" (four to five times that in the general population) for hospitalization for suicide attempts (Vinnerljung, Hjern, & Lindblad, 2006). Trauma involving assaultive violence and child sexual abuse has been found to predict suicidal behavior (Aglan, Kerfoot, & Pickles, 2008; Wilcox et al., 2009).

> *Jessica, Robert, and Marie all attempted suicide during adolescence. Jessica had been beaten and terrorized by her mother, as well as sexually abused by a psychotic uncle; Robert had been physically abused by his mother; and Marie had been sexually abused by her father and physically abused by her cousin.*

Among adolescent girls, recent changes in residence are associated with greater risk of suicide, suggesting additional risks for youth in foster care who may face multiple placements during the teen years (Haynie, South, & Bose, 2006). Jessica and Marie's suicide attempts, which occurred in a context of losses and placement failures, illustrate how the accumulation of unresolved losses can contribute to a sense of hopelessness.

Ethnicity, Gender, and Suicide

In a review of 40 years of research on cultural aspects of suicide, results were equivocal, with some studies reporting no or small differences, some reporting higher ideation or behavior among one group, and others reporting a higher degree of suicidal behavior in another group (Colucci & Martin, 2007). Some research points to an elevated rate of suicide among American Indians relative to that of all other ethnicities, whose rates are clustered more closely together; these authors state that socioeconomic status may be an important factor in the differences they report among ethnic groups (Goldston et al., 2006). Other authors note that the array of psychosocial strains faced by black and white adolescents differs. Blacks experience a greater number of status strains, but for females of both ethnicities, the feeling that one's parent does not care about one greatly increases the risk of suicidal behavior (Watt & Sharp, 2002).

> *Here again, the examples of Robert, Marie, and Jessica are illustrative: the absence of maternal care due to mental illness and drug addiction played an important part in the despair that led to self-harm. All three young people experienced hopelessness and a sense of not mattering enough to someone central in their lives. It is unclear what role ethnicity played in their suicidal behavior.*

The ratio of male to female suicide deaths rises dramatically over time: for 10- to14-year-olds, the ratio is 3.8 to 1; for 15- to 19-year-olds, it is 4.7 to 1; and for 20- to 24-year-olds, it is 6.7 to 1. The gender difference goes in the opposite direction for suicide attempts, however, with girls making first attempts more frequently than boys from age 12 through late adolescence, and differences dissipating in young adulthood (Goldston et al., 2006).

Sexual Orientation as a Risk Factor

Sexual orientation appears to be an important risk factor for suicidal behavior among adolescents. As discussed in Chapter 5, adolescence is typically the time of exploration and beginning consolidation of one's adult sexual identity. Compared with their heterosexual peers, lesbian, gay, and bisexual youth report elevated rates of both suicidal ideation and attempted suicide (Silenzio et al., 2007). Estimates of life-threatening behaviors and completed suicide do not yet exist for transgendered youth, but since research indicates that transgendered youth experience victimization from their peers, negative parental reaction to their gender expression, and family violence that is similar to their LGB counterparts', it is reasonable to assume that their vulnerability to suicidal thoughts and behavior is similar. Among one group of transgendered youth, one-fourth reported having attempted suicide; three-quarters of these youth related their first attempt to their transgender identity (Grossman & D'Augelli, 2007).

Nonsuicidal Self-Injury (NSSI)

Nonsuicidal self-injury is another manifestation of deliberate self-harm; up to 79% of those who self-injure report a childhood history of abuse or neglect (Yates, 2009). NSSI includes skin cutting, burning, interfering with wound healing, punching objects or oneself, and inserting objects under the skin (Lloyd-Richardson, 2008). Frequency rates in nonclinical populations range from 5.1% to more than 40% of adolescents and young adults; self-injuring adolescents, however, are more likely to be diagnosed with MDD and dysthymia than those who do not self-injure (Lloyd-Richardson, 2008).

Self-injury usually first appears between the ages of 14 and 24 and may involve more than one method (Klonsky & Muehlenkamp, 2007). Studies of racial differences report mixed findings, with some showing similar rates across ethnicities and others showing that NSSI is more common among white youth (Lloyd-Richardson, 2008). While female gender is associated with greater likelihood of engaging in deliberate self-harm, there are no gender differences in types of self-harm (Jacobson et al., 2008).

Childhood sexual abuse, physical neglect, and emotional abuse are strongly associated with NSSI in the literature (Glassman et al., 2007; Yates, 2009). Self-harm is counterintuitive; most children seek to protect themselves from harm in any way available, instinctively drawing back from fire or sharp instruments. The internalized negative representations of a defective self and dangerous others that may result from maltreatment, however, can lead children toward self-injury. Children with no positive relational resources may use their bodies for self-punishment or for self-soothing and definition (Yates, 2009). Maltreatment experiences influence the developing affect-regulation and stress-response systems of the child at the same time that cognitive schemas relating to a devalued and unloved self are forming. When painful or stressful events occur during adolescence, the young person resurrects a familiar sensation, but now she or he can be in control of the timing, nature, and amount of pain. The infliction of physical and bounded pain can provide distraction from and a self-defined focus for what might otherwise be unmanageable feelings.

> *Jessica described that she was "a cutter" in foster care, but said that she felt it was more of a way to relieve her stress than a way to harm herself.*

Affect regulation is the most commonly identified reason for engaging in self-injury, but some self-injurers use it to end the experience of dissociation or depersonalization often associated with trauma. Self-injury is a strong predictor of suicidal ideation and behavior, and is sometimes used to avoid suicidal behavior (Hukkanen, Sourander, & Bergroth, 2003). There are also interpersonal functions, such as manipulating others, asserting one's autonomy in relation to others, and seeking help from others (Klonsky & Muehlenkamp, 2007).

Assessment

Assessment for depression should be an ongoing process that constitutes and offers interventions at the same time as learning about the specific nature of the individual's distress. Assessment is the first opportunity to offer hope, a new relationship with a caring adult, and management of the current crisis. The clinician must be alert to ethnic and cultural factors that may be influencing the presentation or interpretation of depressive symptoms and somatic complaints (AACAP, 1998). The young person's relationship and attachment history will be important components of the assessment, and will provide clues to potential obstacles to the early building of a therapeutic alliance.

The coexistence of personality disorders, anxiety disorders, and externalizing disorders with depressive disorders is common. Early-onset depressive disorders are associated with elevated levels of addictive substance use among adolescents (Sihvola et al., 2008), suggesting that screening for substance use should be part of assessment.

While sometimes difficult (or impossible) to obtain for foster youth, family history is valuable, as there is a strong genetic component in depression. Current and past functioning in a variety of spheres, and marked changes in mood, behavior, or functioning should be explored in detail. Because of the suspected under-diagnosis of bipolar disorder in adolescents, the American Academy of Child and Adolescent Psychiatry currently recommends screening for bipolar disorder as a minimum standard of practice, using the DSM-IV criteria to make the differential diagnosis (AACAP, 2007).

Suicide Risk Assessment

A suicide risk assessment is a first step, as the young person may need monitoring and supervision if it is determined that the criteria for suicide risk are met. There are well-known signs and predictors of high risk for suicide. The most ominous signs are probably the best known: talking repeatedly about one's own death, talking of reunions with lost important persons, and giving away prized possessions.

A person who manifests four or five of the following should be treated as high-risk: family history of suicide; history of previous attempts; a formulated and specific plan; recent loss of a parent through death, divorce, or separation; family history of relational instability or domestic violence; struggles regarding sexual identity; preoccupation with the anniversary of a particularly traumatic loss; psychosis; history of drug or alcohol abuse; serious depression; a history of unsuccessful medical treatment or a recent physical trauma; living alone and socially isolated; recent hospitalization for depression; radical shifts in characteristic behaviors or mood; pervasive feelings of hopelessness or helplessness; preoccupation with earlier abuse. These are primary risk factors for youth suicide, and they are also factors that characterize the histories of families and youth involved in the child welfare and juvenile justice systems (Dore et al, 2006).

The exploration entailed in risk assessment can also be seen as an intervention that helps the young person define the problem and envision alternative solutions at the same time as ascertaining what degree of support or protection may currently be available.

The phrase "cry for help" refers to behaviors or gestures that elicit or are meant to elicit a response, such as self-mutilation, suicide threats, "practice runs," or non-lethal overdoses. All should be taken seriously as warning signals that merit attention and response. Almost all suicidal persons provide clues or cries for help, some of which more easily recognized than others. No individual is 100% suicidal; there is always some ambivalence on which the sensitive practitioner can begin to build in the assessment phase.

In addition to risk for suicide, adolescent depression is associated with substance abuse and risky sexual behaviors (Domalanta et al., 2003). The assessment should include a risk behavior history. One of the powerful predictors of adolescent sexual risk behavior is a history of sexual abuse, which itself is often an underlying factor in the onset of depression (DiClemente et al., 2001). We begin to see how early trauma gives rise to problematic and negative self and other representations which contribute to depression and to risk-taking that constitutes self-harm, as, for example, when a young girl contracts a sexually transmitted disease or becomes pregnant.

Treatment

This section begins with interventions for suicidal and self-injuring youth; the immediate risks of harm require that these impulses be addressed immediately. Discussion of psychopharmacological and psychosocial treatments for dysthymia, major depression, and bipolar disorders concludes the section.

Interventions with Suicidal and Self-Harming Youth

The risk assessment should lead to a decision about whether the young person can be treated as an outpatient or needs a period of hospitalization to ensure safety from self-destructive impulses. The treatments discussed here are primarily outpatient treatments, though some pharmacological treatment may begin during an acute hospitalization.

There have been relatively few empirical studies of psychosocial interventions with suicidal and self-injuring youth, but that is not to say that such interventions are not occurring at a substantial rate. They include cognitive behavioral therapy, social problem–solving therapy, multisystemic family therapy, dialectical behavior therapy, and motivational-educational intervention, in both group and individual modalities. The studies that do exist have not reached definitive conclusions about the efficacy of any of these treatments in reducing suicidal ideation or behavior, and most outcome studies have focused on treatment of the primary diagnosis, which is often a depressive disorder (Goldston et al., 2006).

In a review of research on psychosocial treatment of youth suicide, Macgowan reports that only two interventions are probably efficacious, and both of these are short-term interventions involving family members. For youth leaving care, this is an unlikely scenario. The author does suggest that a number of interventions were promising in reducing indirect markers of suicidality, and that CBT and problem-solving were included in many of the treatments that were effective. Developmental group therapy (which takes into account developmental issues of adolescence and young adulthood) was significantly superior to the comparison group in reducing self-harm (Macgowan, 2004).

The American Academy of Child and Adolescent Psychiatry and others found support for the effectiveness of CBT, interpersonal therapy (IPT), dialectical behavior therapy (DBT), psychodynamic therapies, skills-based therapy, and supportive relationship–treatment in treating suicidal behaviors and NSSI (Donaldson, Spirito, & Esposito-Smythers, 2005; Klonsky & Muehlenkamp, 2007; Nock, Teper, & Hollander, 2007).

The choice of therapy depends on the assessment of the individual, as well as on the clinician's understanding of the underlying dynamics of self-harming behavior. Adolescent suicidal behavior is often reactive to interpersonal conflict, for example, and IPT focuses on the individual's history of and difficulties with relationships, losses in childhood, role transitions of adolescence, and the effects of poor social skills on relationship maintenance. DBT includes more emphasis on emotional regulation, helping the adolescent to increase tolerance for distress and use both emotional and rational input in making decisions. Psychodynamic therapies, less tested to date, focus on relationships and the interpersonal as well as intrapsychic conflicts that might lie beneath or set off suicidal thinking and impulses (AACAP, 2000).

Pharmacological treatments will be discussed more fully below, but it is important here to note the controversy about use of SSRIs with depressed adolescents who may be suicidal. As mentioned in Chapter 6, studies of suicide risk during antidepressant treatment found a significantly higher risk of suicidal behavior among adolescents treated with newer antidepressants than with a placebo, leading to the FDA's "black box" warning. Another study two years later found that the risk of serious attempts among adolescents was four times as high as in adults (Simon et al., 2006). A large-scale study in Britain found the balance of risks and benefits of SSRIs among young people unfavorable for sertraline (Zoloft), citalopram (Celexa), and escitalopram (Lexapro), with limited evidence in support of fluvoxamine (Luvox). Fluoxetine (Prozac) was the only drug found to have a favorable risk–benefit ratio and only in one of ten patients. On the basis of these findings, the Committee on Safety of Medicines in the United Kingdom advised that most SSRIs should not be used in people under 18, and that psychotherapy should be used as a first-line treatment when possible (Ramchandani, 2004).

Working with a suicidal young person requires attentiveness, support, availability, and the instilling of hope. The ambivalence about whether to live or die, whether one is a good or bad person, whether one is worthy of love or not—these doubts provide the opening for a caring and consistent practitioner to enter into a relationship that may be the lifeline for a young person otherwise at the mercy of his or her worst feelings. "No-suicide contracts" cannot be relied upon except with individuals deemed to be low-risk, and, in any case, never in the absence of a more comprehensive treatment plan.

Treatments for Depressive Disorders in Adolescents and Young Adults

Treatment should ideally be offered in the least restrictive setting that is safe for that particular person. Pharmacological treatment is often required for individuals suffering from MDD or BD, but these young people will also need psychosocial treatments to help them with the interpersonal aspects of the psychiatric problem and with their ongoing functioning in a psychosocial context. A meta-analysis of studies on treatment of child and adolescent depression concluded that, while several psychosocial interventions produced moderate to large treatment gains, the vast majority of pharmacological interventions were not effective in treating depressed children and adolescents (Michael & Crowley, 2002). Neurobiological and physiological development are still very much under way during adolescence and early adulthood; for this reason, the use of psychotropic (or indeed any) medications demands careful consideration of potential risks as well as benefits. It is too early in the history of psychotropic medications to know about all possible long-term effects, including effects on the developing brain and body. Unfortunately, adolescent patients often receive their first antidepressant prescription from a general practitioner, who is unlikely to have expertise in diagnosis or treatment of psychiatric disorders (Sewitch et al., 2005).

If a pharmacological intervention is necessary, this part of the treatment should be managed by a psychiatrist, while the therapy can be provided by a social worker, psychologist, or counselor. Psychotherapy is a useful initial acute treatment for mild to moderate depression (dysthymia), whereas bipolar depression and major depression with severe symptoms that prevent psychotherapy will require medication in the acute phase and possibly beyond (AACAP, 1998). The American Academy of Child and Adolescent Psychiatry practice parameters recommend limiting antidepressants to adolescents with the most severe disorders, but they are used far more commonly than would be expected on the basis of these recommendations (Olfson et al., 2003)

Medication will vary with diagnosis: as stated above, antidepressant treatment for major depression should avoid use of all SSRIs except fluoxetine. When the diagnosis is bipolar disorder, medications might be limited to a mood stabilizer, such as lithium, divalproate (Depakote), or carbamazine (Tegretol); or to an antipsychotic, such as olanzapine (Zyprexa), risperidone (Risperdal), or quetiapine (Seroquel). Evidence-based data regarding treatment of young people with BD is still limited, and drug efficacy trials showed inconclusive results for lithium's efficacy in the acute treatment of manic or hypomanic episodes in youth. Similarly, studies of mood-stabilizing treatment were not conclusive (Consoli et al., 2007).

A cross-ethnic study of adolescent bipolar patients showed that African American youth are treated with antipsychotic drugs during the maintenance phase of treatment significantly longer than Caucasians, though mood-stabilizer treatment is comparable. A significantly higher percentage of African American patients are diagnosed with psychotic features than are Caucasians, but it is not clear whether true ethnic differences in expression of the illness exists or if this is differential clinician emphasis on psychotic symptoms (Patel et al., 2005). Other research suggests more generally that disparities in access to and quality of health care for ethnic and racial minority populations remain a critical issue in mental health care, and that ethnicity and race have an effect on access to depression treatment that is independent of poverty, education, and insurance coverage.

Some disparities may result from barriers to effective communication between mismatched patients and providers, particularly for African Americans (Alegria et al., 2008).

Another cautionary note comes from a study of the use of multiple psychotropic medications among adolescents aging out of foster care. The risk of aggressive psychopharmacology is high among children in the child welfare system, 40% to 60% of whom are reported to meet criteria for at least one DSM-IV disorder (Raghavan & McMillen, 2008). Further, children in the system may be more likely to be prescribed multiple concurrent psychotropic medications. A previous study found half of all adolescents in high service intensity and congregate care taking multiple psychotropics, sometimes as many as four different medications. A more recent study found 23% receiving two or more psychotropics (compared with 14% in the national estimate) and a small fraction taking up to five (Raghavan & McMillen, 2008). Among youth in foster care, the diagnostic group most associated with receiving three or more medications is depression (Zito et al., 2008). Both Marie and Jessica described being heavily and multiply dosed with medications, disturbing examples of too-ready administration of multiple medications with young people still in the midst of development.

Most available evidence for psychosocial treatment of depression in young people supports cognitive behavioral therapy and interpersonal therapy, with a smaller amount of evidence in support of social problem-solving therapy (Chambliss & Ollendick, 2001; Rohde et al., 2004; Rohde et al., 2006; Shirk et al., 2008). The Treatment for Adolescents with Depression Study (TADS) found a combination of CBT and fluoxetine superior to either CBT or fluoxetine alone in achieving remission when outcome is measured at 12 to 18 weeks. By week 36, estimated remission is more than double the rate at 12 weeks, and, by then, rates converge no matter which treatment is given. The authors conclude that nine months of treatment is helpful in maintaining remission (Kennard et al., 2008; Kennard et al., 2009).

Depressed adolescents appear to do well in group-based cognitive behavioral therapy approaches such as the Adolescent Coping with Depression course (CWD-A), an intervention that includes a problem-solving component and a developmental group-therapy approach that focuses on relational and role issues specific to the adolescent transition (Macgowan, 2004; Rohde et al., 2006). Group interventions make sense from a developmental standpoint, as this is a period when the attitudes of peers have increased importance and influence.

Some young people need the safety and privacy of individual therapy and may be too emotionally fragile to tolerate the give-and-take of a group situation. The relationship with the therapist is important even in group treatment, but the salience of that relationship for a given individual will vary. Foster care alumni who have not had the benefit of safety or support in a relationship with an adult may require a period of individual therapy before a group intervention can be considered. A meta-analysis of studies on relationship variables in adolescent therapy showed that the therapeutic relationship is related to outcome across diverse types and modes of treatment, and is a "hardy nonspecific factor in therapy" (Shirk & Karver, 2003).

As noted, abuse in childhood is strongly associated with depression in adolescence; the resolution of early dysfunctional or disrupted attachments and traumatic experience may require longer-term individual therapy. Psychodynamic therapy is designed to help people explore the sources of depression, focusing on how life events and past relationships are negatively affecting current functioning. A recent study of individual psychodynamic therapy with a focus on relationships, life stresses, and dysfunctional attachments found that nearly 75% of cases (of both dysthymia and MDD) were no longer clinically depressed after therapy (Trowell et al., 2007). Psychodynamic psychotherapy seems to affect both internalizing and externalizing symptoms, reduce comorbidity, and possibly be responsible for less frequent use of mental health services during long-term follow-up (Muratori et al., 2003).

The capacity for affect regulation is compromised in depressive disorders, and the adolescent is at the mercy of distressing emotions. Many treatment programs emphasize problem-solving by changing dysfunctional thinking habits, or even encourage the avoidance of painful feelings, but do not help the young person learn to understand and better regulate emotions (Southam-Gerow & Kendall, 2002). Therapy should offer opportunities to develop greater ability to manage emotions, including deep sadness or intense anger. The therapeutic relationship provides both an arena and a vehicle for facing and surviving what may have previously been unmanageable feelings.

> Jessica did not feel helped by either the individual or the group therapy she experienced while in care; however, she finally had a good therapeutic experience after discharge, when she was in the Job Corps. She described the therapist as "more like a practical mom, who was interested in my having a good and happy adult life."

For adolescents like Jessica, who have been deeply traumatized by the primary attachment relationship, building the therapeutic relationship will take time, patience, and commitment on the part of the therapist.

With the exception of single-episode major depression, most depressive disorders are recurrent, though the rate of recurrence varies widely. Adolescents who suffer from depression need help with interpersonal difficulties, affect regulation, and problem-solving even when the acute symptoms of depression have lifted. Those who have been or are at risk for suicidal thinking or behaviors and those taking medication for major depression or bipolar disorders will particularly need ongoing monitoring and support. For depressed adolescents, the challenges associated with leaving care—greater autonomy, potential isolation and lack of support, and new roles in a changed social environment—can be especially difficult.

Key Treatment Principles

1. Assessment for depressive disorders should be an ongoing process, due to the recurrent nature of these disorders and the potential threat to life.
2. When possible, obtain a family history and trauma history.
3. Assess the risk for suicide and other self-harming behaviors, including substance abuse and risky sexual behavior.
4. Be alert to cultural expressions of and attitudes toward depressive symptoms and help-seeking for depression.
5. Make treatment choices based on differential diagnosis of depressive disorders along with strengths and vulnerabilities of the individual.
6. Exercise caution in the use of antidepressant medication for depressed and suicidal young people.
7. Incorporate opportunities for learning emotion-regulation.
8. Provide for continuity of care for depressed adolescents in transition.
9. Consider whether negative internal representations require individual rather than group therapy and long-term rather than short-term treatment.

8

SUBSTANCE ABUSE

Chapter 8 presents the problem of alcohol and substance abuse. Substance-use disorders have consistently been found to be higher among youth in the child welfare system than among their peers in the general population, with studies reporting ranges from 11% to 35%, compared to 9.35% in the general population (Narendorf & McMillen, 2010). In one recent study, 40% of older adolescents in care reported using alcohol, 36% reported using marijuana, and 25% had used both in the previous six months (Thompson & Auslander, 2007). National surveys tell us that the periods of greatest risk for substance-use initiation are during early adolescence and the transition to adulthood (Chung, 2008). Because the transition years are a time of heightened risk, and because substance-use disorders in adolescence predict adversity in adulthood (Brown & Abrantes, 2006), it is critical to identify factors which may increase risk. Youth who are transitioning out of foster care may be particularly vulnerable because of their histories of maltreatment and the move to independent living without the support of a family (Narendorf & McMillen, 2010).

This chapter begins with an overview of the problem, followed by a summary of prevailing theoretical perspectives and risk and protective factors, with particular attention to child maltreatment. Substance-use disorders, co-occurring disorders, and substances of abuse are described. The chapter concludes with a section on assessment and treatment, with key treatment principles.

Adolescent Substance Abuse

Substances of abuse are used to produce a change in one's affective state or consciousness, and it is not hard to understand the appeal of drugs and alcohol for young people with histories of trauma or maltreatment.

Almost all of these substances can lead to psychological dependence, and some of them to physical dependence as well (Brown & Abrantes, 2006). Substance involvement ranges from experimental use to emerging substance-related problems to substance-use disorders (Chung, 2008). Most adolescents who experiment with drugs or alcohol do not progress to adult substance-dependence (Feldstein & Miller, 2006), but adolescents may be more susceptible than adults to the development of dependence syndromes (Muck et al., 2001). There is considerable research on adult substance abuse and treatment; the recognition of important differences between adolescents and adults with regard to the nature, course, and functions of substance use and treatment considerations is a fairly recent phenomenon.

Theoretical Perspectives

Substance-abuse treatment models are often based on theoretical assumptions about the nature of addiction or alcoholism. Those most common to contemporary treatment approaches are summarized in this section. The first of these is *conditioning theory*, which defines addiction as an operantly conditioned response whose tendency becomes stronger as a function of the quality, number, and size of reinforcements that follow each drug ingestion. Reinforcers are the euphoria produced by the drug, social variables, and elimination of withdrawal sickness; cessation occurs when punishers become more immediate (Thombs, 1994).

Social learning theory focuses on the positive social, personal, and physiological expectations that result from observing the effects of substance use on others, especially influential others. Closely related is the *theory of planned behavior*, emphasizing learned attitudes about self-efficacy, expectations about personal consequences, and the value placed on those consequences. These attitudes then affect intentions to engage in substance use and influence actual behaviors. Both of these theories rely heavily on cognitive processes (Brown & Abrantes, 2006; Thombs, 1994).

The disease model undergirds Alcoholics Anonymous's 12-Step and related approaches. It positions addiction as a chronic and progressive primary disease, rather than as a problem that results from other conditions. The disease model is widespread, but it is not well supported by empirical data and ignores environmental forces and the role of learning.

Psychoanalytic formulations suggest that addiction is an outward manifestation of psychological problems such as ego deficits, difficulties with affect regulation, and disturbed attachments. The clarification of the meaning and psychological functions of use is considered a pathway to changing the behavior. Treatment is directed at both the addiction and the underlying problem (Thombs, 1994).

Maturation theory proposes that deviations in somatic and neurological maturation, along with stressful, adverse environments, predispose children to affect-regulation and oppositional behaviors that may ultimately lead to conduct and substance problems. The genetic and environmental interactions that result in increased risk for substance-abuse disorders are thought to begin at conception, in this view (Brown & Abrantes, 2006).

The domain model broadens the frame to include biological, intrapsychic, interpersonal, and sociocultural domains, and recognizes the ongoing influence of all of these systems (Brook, Brook, & Pahl, 2006; Brown & Abrantes, 2006). A developmental model emphasizes more particularly the psychosocial domains of personality characteristics, previous drug use, parental characteristics and drug use, relationships with family members, and features of the environment. As in psychoanalytic approaches, pathways to adolescent drug use and abuse are seen to have their origins in childhood, and longitudinal studies bear this out (Brook et al., 2006).

Risk and Protective Factors

Risk factors for substance abuse have been identified in all of the psychosocial dimensions: biological/genetic; personal characteristics, including ethnicity; family; peers; and environmental stress. Authors of a national study state that their finding of greatest importance was of the increased risk posed by physical or sexual abuse and by observed violence (Kilpatrick et al., 2000). The relationship of maltreatment to adolescent substance abuse will be discussed in a separate section below.

Individual Factors

Personality factors that predict more frequent drug use include unconventionality, sensation-seeking, rebelliousness, impulsivity, antisocial patterns, aggressivity, low school achievement, and problems with emotional regulation and control. Early temperamental dispositions, such as aggression and externalizing behaviors, are predictive of substance abuse, though these early risk factors can be modified by the presence of protective factors, such as parental warmth, conventionality, and positive attachment (Brook et al., 2006; Brown & Abrantes, 2006). Conduct disorder in early adolescence has been shown to predict early substance use and use in later life (Gibbons et al., 2007).

Neurobiological Risk Factors A growing body of evidence suggests that the neurobiological pathways and abnormalities present in anxiety and mood disorders are also involved in addiction (Brady & Sinha, 2005; Chambers, Taylor, & Potenza, 2003). The influences of maltreatment on the biological stress-response system (detailed in Chapter 3) may be contributory to enhanced risk of adolescent and adult substance-use disorders (SUDs) (De Bellis, 2002). The dysregulation of reward systems and the alterations of the HPA axis that are present in psychiatric disorders appear to be involved in addictive disorders as well. Epidemiological studies report that individuals with major depression are more likely to develop substance-use disorders, and those with SUDs are at greater risk of major depression than their peers. Similarly, the lifetime prevalence of SUDs in populations with PTSD is far higher than in the general population (Brady & Sinha, 2005).

Adolescent brain development involves changes that are characterized by greater motivational drives toward novel experiences; at the same time, the executive functions that increase decision-making ability and inhibitory control are not yet fully on board. These conditions, combined with changes resulting from early life stress, may predispose young people to risky behaviors, including experimentation with drugs (Anda et al., 2006; Chambers et al., 2003). The specific effects of alcohol or other substances on the stress-response system or the reward centers may contribute to increased use, and may subsequently cause further alterations to brain development (Anda et al., 2006).

Family Factors

The lack of a positive mutual attachment is a critical risk factor (Brook et al., 2006). Parental drug or alcohol use increases adolescents' risk, genetically (children of alcoholics, for example, have a three- to four-fold risk for developing alcoholism) and by modeling drug use (Brook et al., 2006; Brown & Abrantes, 2006; Brown et al., 2008). Expectations of positive effects from drug use play a mediating role between a family history of substance problems and substance involvement in offspring (Brown & Abrantes, 2006). Attachment problems and family substance abuse are likely to be present for many youth in foster care.

Peer Factors

The influence of peers increases during adolescence and affects substance use in direct and indirect ways. Unconventional adolescents tend to select deviant peers who influence attitudes and behavior via modeling; risk-taking increases in the presence of peers (Brook et al., 2006; Brown & Abrantes, 2006; Brown et al., 2008). Studies have found that peer influence is most important in the initiation and maintenance of drug use (but not drug abuse) and that the affiliation with like-minded friends can encourage resistance to change processes (Brook et al., 2006; Brown et al., 2008).

Environmental Factors

Ethnicity and socioeconomic factors can function as both protective and risk factors. A strong sense of ethnic identity and some cultural practices serve as protective factors, whereas marginalization, poverty, and limited access to education can result in further risks. A national study found reduced risk of substance abuse or dependence for African Americans, but not for Hispanics or Native Americans, relative to Caucasians, after controlling for victimization effects (Kilpatrick et al., 2000).

African Americans have lower rates of substance abuse, yet early experiences of racial discrimination have an impact on subsequent substance use. In a large-scale study of health in African American families, adolescents diagnosed with conduct disorders experienced more racial discrimination than those who did not have the diagnosis, and the diagnosed adolescents who experienced the greatest amount of discrimination were more likely to report using substances than any other group in the study. As there is evidence to suggest that African American adults have greater difficulties associated with their substance use than do white adults with similar use, increased substance use by African American adolescents is of concern (Gibbons et al., 2007).

Rates of substance abuse have historically been higher for adolescent males; however, the gender gap in adolescent substance use has narrowed, and recent national survey data show little difference in rates of past-year substance-abuse disorder prevalence by gender. Although gender is associated with differences in underlying problems, substance-use behaviors, co-occurring disorders, and treatment outcomes, its role as a direct risk or protective factor is diminishing (Brook et al., 2006; Brown & Abrantes, 2006; Chung, 2008; Weiss, Kung, & Pearson, 2003).

Childhood Maltreatment as a Risk Factor

Large national surveys of adult populations find a positive association between adverse childhood experiences and lifetime alcohol dependence, as well as initiation of drinking before age 15. The risk of alcohol dependence increases as the number of adverse events increases, and maltreatment during early childhood is associated with both early alcohol use and heavy episodic drinking (Hamburger, Leeb, & Swahn, 2008; Pilowsky, Keyes, & Hasin, 2009; Rothman et al., 2008). Adolescents with alcohol use disorders (AUDs) are six to 12 times more likely to have a history of physical abuse and 18 to 20 times more likely to have a history of sexual abuse than community controls (Perepletchikova, Krystal, & Kaufman, 2008).

Childhood sexual abuse is associated with age of initiation of injection-drug use, and drug use is associated with both sexual and physical abuse in childhood (Ompad et al., 2005; Vaddiparti et al., 2006). In one study, substance-abuse patients with histories of physical or sexual abuse had more severe interpersonal problems, higher rates of comorbid psychiatric disorders, and poorer functioning at entry into treatment and at follow-up than those without abuse histories (Rosen et al., 2002). A history of sexual abuse was the most powerful predictor of mental health problems, including drug abuse, among homeless youth and young adults in Los Angeles (Unger et al., 1997).

Substance-using adolescents show much higher rates of trauma exposure compared to non-using teens; estimates from treatment populations range from 55.5% to 90%, including interpersonal violence, sexual abuse, and physical abuse. Rates of sexual abuse among girls are nearly three times higher than those for boys (Hawke, Albert, & Ford, 2008).

The experiences of maltreated or traumatized children and adolescents leave them with over- or underactive stress-response systems, compromised capacity for regulation of overwhelming affects, fragmented or distorted views of the self and others, and disturbed attachment relationships. Substance use may offer immediate relief to unmanageable anxiety or depression and escape from trauma-related thoughts and memories. It may serve to temporarily calm the overheated stress-response system or to animate and buoy up a flattened sense of self. At the same time, use of drugs and alcohol increases other risks: delinquent behavior, exposure to violence associated with obtaining or using drugs, and high-risk sexual behaviors (Fishman, 2008).

Youth whose maltreatment resulted in foster placement were found to have experimented more with alcohol and drugs, at an earlier age, and to report more current use than youth who were not maltreated. Those who had been physically abused were more likely to engage in delinquent behavior, and those who suffered neglect had higher rates of substance use (Taussig, 2002). Another study of older youth in foster care found that nearly half had used illicit substances (compared to 26% of U.S. high school seniors), and that more than one-third met criteria for a substance-use disorder (Vaughn et al., 2007). Abuse and neglect experienced in childhood create extreme risk because they are the outcomes and manifestations of other risk factors (lack of positive mutual attachment, poverty, parental substance abuse) and because their occurrence interferes with the helpful influence of protective factors (parental warmth, conventionality, positive attachment).

> *Robert and Summer, described earlier, provide examples of the interaction of a number of risk factors. Robert was neglected and physically abused, lacked a secure attachment, was poor, experienced discrimination and marginalization, and did not experience the protective value of a positive ethnic identity. He was exposed to deviant peers who introduced him to substance use, and he developed expectations of physiological and affective relief. Summer witnessed domestic violence, was sexually abused, had an alcoholic father, and insecure and disrupted attachments. She, too, was introduced to substance use by peers at an early age. Both experienced placement instability and developed a sense of psychological aloneness, which increased the risk that substance-using behaviors would be maintained.*

Substance-Use Disorders

Most substances of abuse can lead to psychological dependence—the subjective feeling of needing the substance to function adequately—and some to physical dependence as well. Physical dependence refers to the body's adaptation to the presence of the substance such that it develops tolerance, or the need for more of the substance to achieve an effect previously attained at a lower dose. Physical dependence leads to withdrawal, adverse physiological symptoms thatdevelop when use of the substance stops abruptly (Brown & Abrantes, 2006).

Substance-use disorders are classified in the DSM as "substance dependence" or "substance abuse" (American Psychiatric Association, 2000). Either diagnosis requires that substance-related problems must have occurred repeatedly during a 12-month period, with significant distress or impairment in functioning. Substance abuse is a pattern of substance use that continues despite persistent or recurring problems at work, school, or home, and substance use in physically dangerous situations. Substance dependence involves repeated use that results in tolerance, withdrawal, and compulsive drug-taking behavior. The individual continues to use despite serious psychological, physiological, and interpersonal consequences; daily living comes to revolve around acquisition and use of substances. Physiological dependence, as evidenced by tolerance and withdrawal, may or may not be present.

These criteria were developed on the basis of adult populations and do not take developmental differences into account. Withdrawal symptoms are common among substance-abusing adolescents, but physiological dependence is less prevalent than among adults. Because the cognitive and affective features of withdrawal are more prominent than physiological ones in adolescents, the determination of dependence among adolescents requires us to look beyond physiological symptoms (Brown & Abrantes, 2006). Adolescents developing alcohol-use disorders tend to have a more rapid transition from use to dependence than do adults, and symptoms of tolerance and impaired control tend to occur early in the course of involvement (Clark, 2004). The term "diagnostic orphans" is used by a number of authors to capture the discrepancy between the adult-based criteria for diagnosis and the reality that many adolescents are symptomatic and have multiple substance-related problems, but do not meet criteria for either abuse or dependence (Chung, 2008; Winters, Stinchfield, & Bukstein, 2008).

Co-occurring Disorders

There is increasing agreement that co-occurring disorders are the norm, rather than the exception, for substance-abusing adolescents (Bender, Springer, & Kim, 2006; Hawkins, 2009). Among those with a current SUD or entering treatment, studies report a range of 62% to 90% of co-occurring psychiatric disorders (Hawkins, 2009). Because childhood maltreatment and exposure to other adverse events early in life are risk factors for substance abuse and for other psychiatric disorders, foster youth are at high risk for co-occurring disorders.

Dually diagnosed adolescents tend to have an earlier onset of substance use and to use more frequently and more chronically that those with SUDs alone (Bender et al., 2006). High rates of comorbidity are a result of shared risk factors, such as genetic predisposition or vulnerability, family history, individual personality variables, environmental factors, and traumatic events (Feldstein & Miller, 2006; Hawkins, 2009). Many dually diagnosed adolescents have experienced early significant loss or other adverse childhood experiences. Mental health problems (ADHD, CD, anxiety and depressive disorders) often precede substance abuse among youth, leaving them more vulnerable to developing an SUD as they reach adolescence.

Disruptive behavior disorders are the most commonly occurring comorbid disorders, and conduct disorder is the most common of these (Whitmore & Riggs, 2006). In one sample, ten times as many adolescents with conduct disorder showed SUDs as those without conduct disorder, and three times as many of those with ADHD had comorbid SUDs as those without ADHD (Feldstein & Miller, 2006). Traumatic experience has an impact on the stress-response and affect-regulation systems, which, in turn, influence impulsivity and decision-making. Survivors of maltreatment may be drawn to both substance use and other high-risk behaviors; in a sample of adjudicated delinquents, for example, youth with SUDs and externalizing disorders had higher levels of criminality and substance use than those with only SUDs (Feldstein & Miller, 2006).

Associations have been found between childhood physical or sexual abuse, PTSD, and subsequent SUD in adolescence and young adulthood (Anda et al., 2006; Cohen et al., 2003; De Bellis, 2002). Prevalence rates of PTSD and related symptoms are at least double among substance users seeking treatment, with some variation in numbers across studies, and considerable variation in symptoms. Adolescents who suffer from comorbid PTSD and SUD exhibit poor psychosocial functioning, high substance-abuse relapse rates, and severe PTSD symptoms (Hawke et al., 2008). An SUD can complicate PTSD symptoms when the substances used increase or depress the body's arousal level; trauma memories can be affected by the use of substances that alter information processing (Ford & Russo, 2006).

Depressive disorders occur in about 5% to 10% of school-age children and adolescents without SUD, but rates rise to 15% to 30% in adolescents with SUD (Whitmore & Riggs, 2006). The association between alcohol abuse and depression has been shown to exist both during adolescence and in the transition to adulthood, with significant association for boys, but not for girls, once sociodemographics and parental mental health are considered (Wu et al., 2007).

Depression and impulsivity can give rise to both substance abuse and other types of self-harm, including suicidal behavior. Substance abuse can lead to developmental failures, such as school difficulties and problems with peers, which then lead to suicidal behavior. The rates of SUDs among adolescents who die by suicide range from 27% to 50% across studies, a dramatically higher rate than that which is found in community samples (Goldston et al., 2008). In the Adverse Childhood Experience Study, a life-time history of suicide attempts was associated with emotional, physical, and sexual abuse (Fellitti, 2002), demonstrating again the dynamic inter-action of early experience, possible genetic contribution, adolescent devel-opment, and current circumstance (substance-use opportunities, available supports, other risk factors).

Substances of abuse

Alcohol

The substance most frequently used by adolescents is alcohol, which acts as a central nervous system depressant. First use occurs typically by mid-adolescence, with consumption changing dramatically from ages 12 to 18, rising from 38.9% to 51.7% of eighth graders, to 71.9% to 80.3% of twelfth graders having tried it (Clark, 2004; Johnston et al., 2009; Tyler, Stone, & Bersani, 2006). Binge drinking (five or more drinks in one episode) is reported by over 30% of twelfth graders in any two-week period (Clark, 2004). The age of first use has been found to be a risk factor for the onset of substance-use problems (Brown & Abrantes, 2006). Puberty appears to usher in a high-risk life phase. A study of the association between puber-tal development and early adolescent substance use found that puberty itself, rather than age per se, shows the strongest and clearest association with early adolescent use and abuse (Patton et al., 2004).

Alcohol use disorders during adolescence can affect the developing brain. As noted in earlier chapters, the prefrontal cortex and hippocampal areas of the brain are actively developing during adolescence; adolescents and young adults with adolescent-onset alcohol use disorders (AODs) have been found to have significantly smaller left and right hippocampal volumes. Adolescents with AODs tend to binge-drink, and because the hippocampus may be particularly susceptible to the effects of alcohol, this pattern may negatively affect hippocampal development (De Bellis et al., 2000).

Nicotine

The prevalence of nicotine use among youth in substance-abuse programs ranges from 60% to 84%. Health-related problems associated with nicotine use can begin as early as adolescence, and adolescents experience nicotine tolerance and withdrawal (Brown & Abrantes, 2006). Like alcohol, nico-tine is often the first drug used by young adolescents and is sometimes described as a "gateway" drug because it is thought to begin a developmental sequence of involvement with substance use, leading to marijuana and, eventually, more serious illicit drugs (Hasin, Hatzenbuehler, & Waxman, 2006). Smoking causes release of dopamine in the primary reward system of the brain, and this is thought to account for the addictive properties of nicotine (Anda et al., 2006).

Marijuana

Marijuana (cannabis) is usually thought of as having low addictive potential, but its increasing potency over the past 25 years has changed this. There are significant health risks associated with chronic use of marijuana, such as lung damage, decreased sperm production, blocked ovulation, antimotivational syndrome, and deterioration of neurocognitive functioning (Brown & Abrantes, 2006; Windle & Wiesner, 2004). Cannabis has acute effects on attention, memory recovery, and visual-motor coordination; the more lasting impairments are subtle and harder to document (Verdejo-Garcia et al., 2004). Lifetime rates of marijuana use rise from 26% among eighth graders to 49% among twelfth graders. Chronic heavy users have the highest delinquency rates, the most stressful life events, the lowest GPAs, and the highest percentage of drug-using friends (Windle & Wiesner, 2004). However, even those with minimal but chronic use have lower rates of college graduation and higher rates of deviancy and substance-use problems compared to abstaining youth (Tucker et al., 2005).

Stimulants

Adolescent use of stimulants, including amphetamines, cocaine, crack, and MDMA ("Ecstasy"), rose through the 1990s, but has had a slow steady decline since 2000. Still, the fact that 10% to 13% of twelfth graders have used amphetamines and 7.2% of twelfth graders have used cocaine is reason for concern (Johnston et al., 2009).

Amphetamines activate the dopamine system. Addiction can occur quickly, as repeated use reduces the brain's ability to manufacture dopamine, leading to increased cravings (Hohman, Oliver, & Wright, 2004). Methamphetamine is relatively inexpensive, easily available, and its effects can last for hours. Chronic use and higher doses can cause irritability, aggression, anxiety, depression, confusion, paranoia, delusions, hallucinations, seizures, and cardiac arrest (Brown & Abrantes, 2006; Rawson et al., 2005).

Opiates

The opiates (heroin, morphine, opium, codeine, Oxycodone, Percodan, Darvon, Demerol) have analgesic (painkilling) effects and depress most bodily functions. Use of heroin among adolescents rose rapidly in the 1990s, and has been gradually declining for the past nine years, with the exception of non-injected heroin use among eighth graders (Johnston et al., 2009). Most users are white and male; 43% of admitted patients initiated their opioid use before age 20 (Fiellin, 2008). About 30% of those who smoke heroin will graduate to injection use (Schwartz, 1998).

Like amphetamine, opiates activate the dopamine system. Heroin is believed to have the highest potential to produce rapidly developing dependence and addiction of any of the common opiate analgesics, quickly entering the brain and reducing the anticipatory anxiety associated with emotional or physical pain. The average price of heroin has decreased and the purity has increased, making it at once more available and more powerful (Schwartz, 1998). The intense euphoria produced by heroin, along with its pain-numbing properties, make it a compelling drug for young people suffering from depression, anxiety, and traumatic stress disorders.

Chronic use of opiates or amphetamine can result in cognitive deficits such as reduced ability to sustain attention and to think ahead; loss of the cognitive flexibility required to perceive, process, and respond to situations in different ways; difficulty making decisions; and impairments to memory and learning. Some of these problems may affect an individual's ability to engage in and remain in treatment (Ersche & Sahakian, 2007).

Inhalants

Another class of drugs with high availability and low cost and, therefore, common among younger adolescents is the inhalants. Inhalants include industrial and household compounds, such as glue, aerosol sprays, paint thinner, nail polish remover, and gasoline, which can be sniffed from soaked rags. While the effects are relatively short-lived, inhalants can cause serious damage to the kidney, liver, heart, and nervous system, as well as adversely affecting cognitive functions (Brown & Abrantes, 2006). In 2008, the estimated prevalence of inhalant use was 12.8% among tenth graders and 15.7% among eighth graders (Johnston et al., 2009).

Sedatives

Sedatives, like alcohol, are central nervous system depressants. These include barbiturates (Amytal, Nembutal, Seconal, Phenobarbitol) and benzodiazepines or tranquilizers (Ativan, Halcion, Librium, Valium, Xanax, Rohypnol). They are prescription drugs that are also available on the street. About twice as many adolescents report having obtained these drugs from a friend or relative as having bought them from a drug dealer or a stranger. Close to 9% of twelfth graders report using tranquilizers, and 8.5% of twelfth graders report using sedatives (Johnston et al., 2009). Adolescents who abuse sedatives or tranquilizers may well be suffering from undiagnosed anxiety and sleep problems.

Assessment

The substance-abuse/dependence assessment is designed to ascertain the existence and extent of the substance-related problem(s) and to identify the kind of treatment that is likely to be most effective for this specific individual. The individual conducting the assessment (and the one providing treatment) should be trained in adolescent development, co-occurring mental disorders, substance abuse, and addiction (Brannigan et al., 2004).

There are two types of assessment instruments: screening and comprehensive measures. Screening flags the presence of a substance-use problem; comprehensive assessment explores in greater depth the nature and extent of the problem, as well as other problems that may be present. Because substance-abusing adolescents so frequently suffer from other mental health problems, screening should include, not only substance involvement, but also history of childhood abuse, exposure to trauma, depression, high-risk behaviors, and suicidal behaviors (Brown & Abrantes, 2006; Cohen et al., 2003; Perepletchikova et al., 2008; Winters et al., 2008).

There are several well-validated substance-abuse screening instruments for adolescents, such as the Personal Experience Screening Questionnaire (PESQ), the Drug Use Screening Inventory–Revised (DUSI-R), and the Problem Oriented Screening Instrument for Teenagers (POSIT). These are self-report questionnaires and will be limited by an individual's comfort with self-disclosure and honesty in reporting (Brown & Abrantes, 2006). No single screening or assessment tool is regarded as the "gold standard," and the cultural fit of the tool for the specific client is important (Hawke et al., 2008; Perepletchikova et al., 2008).

Clinical Interview

A clinical interview covering the same ground can also serve as the initial screening method and can evolve naturally into a more in-depth exploration. The Adolescent Diagnostic Interview (ADI) is a structured interview that assesses DSM-IV criteria for SUDs as well as functioning in a number of domains, and there are other such instruments (Brown & Abrantes, 2006). As important as the particular instrument used is the clinician's ability to create an atmosphere in which optimal disclosure can occur while ensuring that the important domains and criteria are explored. The clinician should inquire in detail about the onset of drug use, frequency and quantity of use, and duration of use for each specific substance. Other domains for a comprehensive assessment include symptoms of co-occurring disorders, family history of substance-use or psychiatric disorders, parent–child relationship, childhood abuse, exposure to trauma, placement history including ages and circumstances, social functioning (peer drug-use or delinquency, school problems, relationship problems).

Treatment Planning

Treatment planning should include exploration and clarification of the client's goals and motivation for treatment. The assessment process should help both clinician and client identify the desired areas for change: quantity and frequency of drug use, related deviant behaviors, school behaviors, interpersonal functioning, and any co-occurring disorders (Winters et al., 2008). While research on adolescent motivation is in its early stages, available data suggests that adolescents seem less motivated than adults to seek or stay in treatment and are less internally motivated for treatment than adults. They often enter treatment as a result of external influences such as the court's order, and treatment that is court-mandated appears to be of little value (Battjes et al., 2003; Breda & Heflinger, 2007).

The American Society of Addiction Medicine has developed a guideline for matching patient to treatment that proposes six categories with treatment implications. These categories include level of intoxication and potential for withdrawal (which may call for inpatient or more intensive services); medical conditions; emotional, behavioral, and cognitive aspects (high levels of impairment in any of these areas will rule out or rule in some treatment approaches); readiness to change (motivation); relapse potential (need for monitoring); and the recovery environment (safety, aftercare, supervision, and supports) (Fishman, 2008). These criteria for placement were originally developed for adult patients, but they can help organize assessment data for adolescents.

Treatment Research

In the past thirty years, there has been increased attention to development and validation of treatments for substance abuse and, more recently, studies of treatment outcomes and effectiveness for adolescent substance-abusers. The predominant focus has been on cognitive behavioral therapy; a recent meta-review of 34 rigorous studies of a variety of drugs found consistent evidence of benefit from a variety of interventions, with highest effect sizes for contingency management, relapse prevention, and other CBT approaches (Dutra et al., 2008). Limited studies focusing on adolescent treatment suggest that the evidence is, as yet, insufficient to make recommendations for treatment models, but that there are some practices that appear to be important, such as maximizing treatment completion, including aftercare; providing comprehensive services, including family therapy; and facilitating or engendering peer and parent support (Muck et al., 2001; Waldron & Turner, 2008). Other studies point to the need for community-based adolescent programs, increased programs in facilities that serve adjudicated adolescents, and psychological services that address childhood abuse (Rounds-Bryant, Kristiansen, & Hubbard, 1999).

A substantial number of treatment programs exclude adolescents as a matter of policy, and many others integrate adolescents into their adult programs, but do not offer adolescent-specific or -only programs (Knudsen, 2009). Yet the national Drug Abuse Treatment Outcome Studies for Adolescents (DATOS-A) recognizes the need for distinctive treatment approaches for adolescents (Grella, 2006). Traditional models of treatment outcomes do not reflect the developmental differences in contextual risks, neurocognitive development, motivational distinctions, and developmentally related resources for success. As youth in foster care transition to independent living, opportunities to escalate their substance use increase, and the environmental scaffolding to support efforts to stop or reduce substance use may not be present (Brown et al., 2008). Multimodal interventions are needed to address the developmental and psychosocial circumstances of adolescents and young adults (Brannigan et al., 2004; Brown et al., 2008; Perepletchikova et al., 2008).

Gender

Gender is an important dimension to consider in treatment planning for adolescents with SUDs. Gender differences are found in the age of onset of substance-abuse disorders, the utilization of treatment, and in treatment outcomes (Grella, 2006; Heflinger, Chatman, & Saunders, 2006; Weiss et al., 2003). Substance-abusing girls are more likely to have internalizing symptoms, a history of sexual abuse, a history of suicide attempts, and higher rates of alcohol dependence than boys. Boys are more likely to have been physically abused, engage in illegal activity, and have involvement in the criminal justice system (Grella, 2006).

Among adolescents who receive Medicaid (youth in care and other low-income youth), males are more likely to receive substance-abuse treatment services than females, while the disparity exists in the opposite direction among the general population. Black male adolescents in the Medicaid population receive services at a lower rate and an older age than white males, whereas in the general population, white and black males are treated at essentially equivalent rates (Heflinger et al., 2006). Most drug-abuse treatment programs have been developed by (typically white) males for males, and fail to meet the practical and emotional needs of women, particularly those who might be pregnant, post-partum, or primary caretakers of their children. Few programs have gender-sensitive or gender-specific services, yet women tend to stay in treatment programs longer if they are women-only (Weiss et al., 2003).

Treatment Models

Substance-abuse treatment for adolescents should be matched to the needs of the specific individual in his or her psychosocial, developmental, and cultural context. Individual or group therapy, offered in a variety of settings from acute inpatient to residential to outpatient, should be chosen on the basis of those individual needs; instead, the matching that does occur often takes place "up front" when it is decided that an individual should enter a program of already bundled services that the agency, organization, or hospital offers (Fishman, 2008). The young person may need services other than substance-abuse treatment, but these may not be part of the program. The most important variables predicting successful treatment response in adolescent substance-use disorders are the specific therapeutic components provided and the training and experience of the providers (Cohen et al., 2003). Many highly regarded programs do not adequately address components such as standardized assessment instruments, attention to gender and cultural competence, engaging and retaining youth, and scientific evaluation of outcomes (Brannigan et al., 2004).

Individual treatment can be effective in strengthening protective factors in the personality domain, such as commitment to traditional values and academic achievement, responsibility, self-esteem, and conventionality. Group treatments, often selected for adolescent populations, capitalize on the influential role of prosocial peers, which can heighten the effect of other protective factors. Changing interpersonal relationships and interactions within the group can lead to improved self-regulation and psychosocial functioning (Brook et al., 2006), and these, in turn, may lessen the adolescent's dependence on drugs.

Most treatment approaches fall into four broad categories: 12-Step programs, family therapy, motivational enhancement interventions, and cognitive behavioral therapies. Elements of more than one approach may be combined in a particular program, along with new emphases on relationship and attachment dimensions, which may be incorporated into existing programs. The use and study of pharmacological interventions with adolescents is in its infancy (Perepletchikova et al., 2008).

Twelve-Step Models

These mutual-help programs are the most familiar, due to the long history of groups like Alcoholics Anonymous (AA) and Narcotics Anonymous (NA). The 12-Step approach is predicated on the disease model described earlier in the chapter and is organized around the "addict's" acceptance of the incurable and progressive nature of the disease and the necessity for abstinence to keep the problem in remission. The great majority of adolescent drug and alcohol treatment programs incorporate a 12-step component, with evidence suggesting that attendance appears to influence positive outcomes by enhancing motivation for abstinence and use of abstinence-focused coping strategies (Brown & Ramo, 2006). Benefits of the approach are the availability of cost-free meetings that anyone may attend, and a nonjudgmental attitude toward addiction. For some adolescents, however, the fit may not be ideal, as both addiction severity and motivation for abstinence may be lower than among adult members. Adolescents are significantly younger than the majority of other members and may also have discomfort with the spiritual or religious emphasis (Slesnick, Kaminer, & Kelly, 2008). Those who attend meetings at least once per week have higher rates of abstinence than those who do not; interestingly, a history of abuse in childhood is associated with greater attendance and involvement (Schneider, Burnette, & Timko, 2008). While available data suggest that adolescent AA/NA participants have better outcomes than non-participants, there is no evidence, as yet, to indicate which subgroups might benefit more or less from 12-step groups (Slesnick et al., 2008).

Family Interventions

Family interventions are often an effective component of adolescent substance-abuse treatment programs, and the efficacy and effectiveness of family therapy models is widely reported in the literature (Carroll & Onken, 2005; Feldstein & Miller, 2006; Slesnick et al., 2008), but they are not an option for youth leaving foster care. Several models have received empirical support, but they are rarely compared with one another, and there is no evidence to suggest that one type is actually superior to another (Feldstein & Miller, 2006; Perepletchikova et al., 2008; Slesnick et al., 2008; Thompson & Auslander, 2007).

Motivational Interviewing (MI) and Harm Reduction

MI and motivational enhancement therapy (MET), based on principles of motivational psychology, are intended to enhance an individual's intrinsic desire and motivation for change. MI is client-centered, emphasizing self-responsibility, and fits well with the adolescent need for autonomy (Masterman & Kelly, 2003). Five strategies are employed: expression of empathy, development of discrepancies (to puncture denial about having a problem), avoidance of arguments, "rolling with" resistance, and supporting self-efficacy. MI helps youth to recognize the seriousness of the problem, the ways in which substance use or abuse disrupts their lives, and that treatment is necessary to making changes. Though there is strong support for MI with adult alcohol users, the findings are mixed with adolescent substance users (Carroll & Onken, 2005; Perepletchikova et al., 2008).

Harm reduction conceptualizes abstinence as the "ultimate risk reduction goal," but recognizes that the goal of reduction of use-related harms is often more realistic than abstinence, especially for high-risk adolescents (Masterman & Kelly, 2003). When clients are ambivalent about or resistant to change, harm reduction can provide an opportunity to continue to build rapport. The approach supports any steps in the right direction and defines therapeutic progress in degrees rather than success or failure in achieving total abstinence (Logan & Marlatt, 2010).

Cognitive Behavioral Therapies

CBTs (discussed in Chapters 6 and 7) integrate strategies from classical conditioning, operant conditioning, and social learning perspectives, viewing substance use as learned behavior that is initiated and maintained by features of the environmental context. Treatment centers on recognizing the cues and contributors to the behavior so that, by substituting different environments or responses to the familiar ones, new or different behaviors can be learned (Brown & Abrantes, 2006; Carroll & Onken, 2005; Slesnick et al., 2008). CBT approaches include development of skills that can be used to foster abstinence, and have been demonstrated to be effective with alcohol-use disorders and drug-using populations (Carroll & Onken, 2005).

Integrated Treatment for Co-occurring Disorders

Substance abuse and dependence arise from the complex interaction of internal, external, and contextual factors and cannot be successfully understood or treated apart from the specifics of individuals and their circumstances. As noted earlier, the majority of substance-abusing adolescents have another psychiatric disorder and, very often, a history of childhood abuse. Co-occurring mental health and substance-use disorders should be conceptualized as problems with common developmental etiologies and trajectories; both should be regarded as primary and as needing treatment. Integrated care includes screening, assessment, treatment planning, treatment delivery, and continuing care (Hawkins, 2009).

A review of effectiveness of treatments for dually diagnosed adolescents found common threads and suggested guidelines that are consistent with the developmental, dynamic-systems perspective of this book. Assessment should be multi-pronged, strategies should enhance engagement and retention, and flexible plans should include the client's voice and should address both disorders concurrently. The treatment should be developmentally and culturally sensitive, ecologically grounded, and systems-oriented. The domains of problem-solving, decision-making, affect regulation, impulse control, and peer and family relations should be addressed. Treatment should be goal-directed, here-and-now–focused, and strengths-based. Finally, interventions should aim to produce sustainable changes over the course of treatment (Bender et al., 2006).

A number of effective and promising outpatient integrated treatment models overlap in framework, clinical strategies, and techniques. CBT is combined with motivational enhancement to promote rapid therapeutic connection, develop motivation to change, and increase coping skills to handle high-risk situations. "Seeking Safety" is a model that combines CBT with the discussion of interpersonal topics, flexibly customized to meet individual needs (Hawkins, 2009).

The goals of therapy for PTSD and SUD are complementary in some ways: replacing impulsive reactions with reflective reality-based decisions, developing skills to modulate intense and diminished states of bodily and emotional activation, and developing the ability to access long-term memory to formulate and follow through with organized choices. Treatment for abuse-related PTSD requires attention to basic self-regulatory deficits, and those same deficits are often what cause adolescents to turn to substance use (Ford & Russo, 2006). Trauma-focused CBT has been widely studied, and its effectiveness in treating victims of child maltreatment is well known, so despite the dearth of studies on the efficacy of trauma-focused interventions with substance-using adolescents, it is considered a promising treatment (Hawke et al., 2008). In one study, women with trauma histories and SUDs responded well to trauma-enhanced substance-abuse treatment, remaining longer in treatment and demonstrating better six-month outcomes (Amaro et al., 2007).

TARGET (Trauma Adaptive Recovery Group Education and Therapy), available as a manual for practitioners, is a group and individual therapy that provides education about the biological and behavioral underpinnings of PTSD and SUD, and gives guidance in applying information- and emotion-processing and self-regulation techniques. It has an experiential component in which an autobiographical narrative is developed that incorporates, but does not focus on, trauma and substance use. The treatment aims to help the client learn how to prepare for and productively process current trauma reminders and "reset" the body's stress-response system to current life circumstances. The therapeutic alliance plays an important role in repair of disorganized forms of attachment. TARGET is designed to complement, rather than compete with or replace all other SUD modalities (Ford & Russo, 2006).

No suicide-prevention programs have been developed specifically for substance-abusing youth, results from controlled psychosocial treatment studies for adolescents with suicidal behavior are inconsistent, and there has been little work focused on integrated approaches for these two problems (Goldston et al., 2008). However, given that a history of sexual and physical abuse is so often associated with suicidal and self-harming behaviors, the treatment approaches for co-occurring SUD and PTSD may be very useful for suicidal adolescents and young adults.

Culture and Ethnicity in Treatment

Many programs operate from a Eurocentric perspective and approach with no integration of different cultural practices or values. Programs that give little or no attention to cultural variables may be ineffective because they ignore important service needs of ethnic-minority individuals (Castro & Alarcon, 2002). For example, among African American youth, effects of social marginalization and discrimination may require an approach that is explicitly empowering and focused on Afrocentric values such as spirituality and collective unity (Moore, Madison-Colmore, & Moore, 2003). The TARGET intervention described above has been culturally and linguistically adapted for diverse client populations in recognition of the importance of the power of cultural influence in either enhancing or impeding the success of treatment. Guided self-change, a brief skills-oriented motivational intervention that can be used with individuals or groups, has been culturally adapted for use with Latino and African American youth (Tubman et al., 2002).

Relationship and Substance-Abuse Treatment

Pre-treatment motivation and post-treatment outcomes are strongly associated with a better therapeutic relationship between client and counselor (Joe, Simpson, & Broome, 1998; Joe et al., 2001). Engaging the client is critical to substance-abuse treatment; it is the relationship that provides the atmosphere within which rapid change is possible (Miller, 2000). Building motivation is the first task of treatment for most adolescents, and the relationship with the treatment provider is a determinant of whether even that first phase will go forward. Rapport with the clinician depends on the client's perception that the clinician is easy to talk to, warm, caring, honest, sincere, and "not in denial about problems" (Joe et al., 2001). The opportunity to develop a trusting therapeutic alliance is especially important for substance-abusing survivors of abuse, and studies have found that where, ordinarily, abuse survivors showed less significant positive treatment outcomes than non-abused patients, these differences were minimized among those who had more frequent treatment contacts (Rosen et al., 2002).

Successful substance-abuse treatment has two essential goals: reducing or eliminating the abuse of drugs or alcohol, and resolving emotional, behavioral, and mental health problems that are associated, either in a causal or a secondary way, with the substance abuse. Unmanageable emotions resulting from trauma and disrupted attachments are frequently determinants of substance use and related behaviors; a therapeutic relationship can provide the supportive foundation (or, in attachment terms, the secure base) upon which to safely relinquish the stimulating or numbing effects of drugs in favor of exploring the underlying feelings and increasing one's capacity for tolerating and regulating painful emotions.

Aftercare

Many adolescents vacillate between periods of recovery and periods of use and drug-related problems in the year following their first treatment episode, with use in up to 24% of them becoming worse in the six months after treatment (Brown et al., 1994; Kaminer, 2002). Research suggests that aftercare or post-treatment monitoring and recovery support services are promising interventions for enhancing relapse prevention for adolescent substance-abusers (Kaminer & Napolitano, 2004). Stepped down or lower-intensity aftercare programs can both initiate and sustain reductions in substance use or support continued abstinence (Kaminer, 2002). One such program calls for individual brief therapeutic phone contacts as a reliable and cost-effective way of providing clinical aftercare, especially where transportation is an issue (Kaminer & Napolitano, 2004).

A young person recovering from substance abuse will need help in constructing a new sense of self without the refuge of using drugs when anxiety or conflicts arise. Youth emerging from foster care (or the probation system) will be doubly challenged by the loss of institutional supports and surroundings and what may have felt like support from peer drug cultures or the drugs themselves.

Key Treatment Principles

1. Comprehensive assessment should include detailed inquiry about substance use, family and trauma history, client goals and motivation for treatment, and screening for co-occurring mental health problems.
2. Assess need for detoxification, residential, or outpatient treatment.
3. Give consideration to gender and cultural dimensions of substance use and treatment needs.
4. Build a therapeutic alliance during assessment to enhance motivation, and attend to relationship aspects as a critical component of the treatment plan.
5. Attend to increasing the client's capacity for affect regulation and impulse control.
6. Reduce environmental risks and build protective factors, such as prosocial involvements and activities.
7. Treat the client, not just the substance-related behavior. Attend to psychological and interpersonal needs underlying or accompanying substance use.
8. Institute an aftercare plan for contact and/or continuing treatment after sobriety or reduction in use has been achieved.

9

MENTAL HEALTH DIMENSIONS
OF DELINQUENCY

We should have a law creating a Juvenile Psychopathic Institute for Juvenile
Offenders, Mental Defectives, and etc. Many of these Juvenile Offenders need
the services of a good physician more than they do those of the jailor
   —Dr. William MacDonald, 1912 (Thomas, Stubbe, & Pearson, 1999)

In this chapter, we will consider aspects of *juvenile delinquency*—behavior
that is in violation of the law and compels the attention of the juvenile
justice system. Antisocial behavior by children and adolescents is perceived by society as either criminal (bad) or symptomatic of emotional
difficulties (mad) (Rawal et al., 2004) and treated accordingly. Unlike
other mental health problems, antisocial behavior cannot be considered
apart from its institutional contexts because it often elicits a law enforcement response, or a social service response, or both. This chapter is therefore divided into two sections, the first of which examines the nature of
conduct problems, theories about etiology, and a review of risk and
protective factors. A discussion of conduct disorders and co-occurring
mental health problems follows, and the first part of the chapter concludes
with assessment, intervention, and key treatment principles. The second
section presents an overview of the intersection of juvenile justice,
child welfare, and mental health systems, pointing up the pervasive problem of structural or institutional racism at important decision points,
and it concludes with some specific principles related to work with crossover kids.

The Problem of Delinquency

Aggression and Delinquency

Aggression and anger are universal and inescapable dimensions of human
existence. Anger prepares the body physiologically and psychologically

to initiate self-protective and instrumental activity (Dodge, Coie, & Lynam, 2006). When aggression becomes an inappropriate or overly dominant strategy, however, patterns of antisocial behavior can result and evolve into delinquency. Delinquent behaviors violate societal and legal norms and range from status violations and oppositional acts to physically aggressive and destructive acts. All forms of antisocial behavior have in common that they are experienced as aversive, disruptive, or unpleasant by those who are victims or who are close to the antisocial youth (Dishion & Patterson, 2006).

Aggression and other antisocial behaviors can be considered along various dimensions: whether they are overt (direct confrontation) or covert (behaviors that usually occur without adult awareness), whether they have a high or low degree of destructiveness, and whether they are reactive or proactive (bullying, for example) (Dodge et al., 2006; McMahon & Kotler, 2006). Violent offending and serious crimes are at the highest degree of destructiveness, severely harming others or property. Relational aggression involves manipulation of relationships and is more frequent among girls; it may be either overt or covert and is emotionally rather than physically harmful (McMahon & Kotler, 2006). Behaviors may involve excluding peers from group activities, withdrawing affection, and threatening to tell lies or rumors about another child to cause emotional harm. Relational aggression is less understood, but seems to be motivated by the aggressor's need for dominance and control (Herrenkohl et al., 2009).

The association between delinquent behavior and depression is well established both among incarcerated adolescents and in the general population for both sexes (Ritakallio et al., 2005). Violent behavior can function in several ways to maintain psychological equilibrium. It may serve to maintain a sense of self-cohesiveness and aliveness, to get rid of anxiety or helplessness by thrusting these feelings onto the victim, or to promote a sense of toughness and invulnerability that is preferable to depression or seems to be required by one's peer culture or neighborhood context (Pleasants, 2007; Snyder & Rogers, 2002). The meaning and function of violence for a given young person are often entirely overlooked by the juvenile justice and child welfare systems, which seek to contain or punish the behavior.

Theoretical Perspectives

Aggressive and violent behavior is a product of the person-in-environment system. A review of 39 empirical studies of biosocial interactions in the areas of genetics, psychophysiology, neurology, hormones, and environmental factors suggests that we are only just beginning to understand the complex interactions that give rise to antisocial behavior (Raine, 2002). Most perspectives on delinquency and aggressive or violent behavior incorporate factors such as biological risks; early life experiences and developmental achievements; social context (family, neighborhood, community, socioeconomic status); adolescent experiences; and immediate situational events and relationships. Overlapping theories that dominate much of the research and intervention literature are *general strain theory*, *self-control theory*, *coercion theory*, and *social control theory*. Each of these employs attachment as an important construct, either explicitly or as an underlying factor.

General strain theory identifies three types of strains that can lead to negative emotions and then to delinquent behavior. These are the failure to achieve positively valued goals, the loss or removal of positively valued goals, and the presence of disturbing stimuli. If the source of the strain is removed, or the individual learns to cope with the strain adaptively, delinquency may decrease or stop (Cernkovich, Lanctot, & Giordano, 2008).

Self-control theory, which has gained moderate support among researchers, posits that individuals who experience poor parenting are likely to have low self-control as a result of their parents' ineffective emotional bonding with them. Parents' deficient monitoring reduces the likelihood that they will notice and respond to deviant behavior, and the child fails to develop adequate self-control. Instead, the child's impulsivity predominates, along with a preference for risky behaviors that bring immediate rewards, and the risk for delinquency is increased (Higgins & Ricketts, 2005).

> *Ericka was the fourth of her crack-addicted mother's five children by different fathers and the second of her father's three children. When Ericka was two years old, her aunt got high while babysitting the children and fell asleep. Ericka and her maternal siblings left the house, looking for food. They wandered down the street to the donut shop to beg for something to eat. Someone called DCFS, and Ericka and her siblings were placed in foster care. Ericka lived with her paternal grandmother and three cousins who had two children of their own. When she was 14, her grandmother's boyfriend's drug business led to a police raid, and Ericka and the other children in the home were removed. Ericka lived briefly with different relatives, although it is not clear if this was by her choice or supervised by DCFS. None of these temporary arrangements worked out, and Ericka ran away, hoping she could join her sister at the group home where she was placed. She had no plan beyond being close to someone with whom she felt more connected.*
>
> *Ericka's first two years of life had taken place in a context of neglect occasioned by drug addiction and poverty, with little monitoring of her or her siblings. The opportunities for the kind of bonding that enables optimal development of sense of self and self-control were minimal. Later during childhood, she shared her grandmother with five other children, exposed to additional deviant drug-related activities and instability.*

Coercion theory, based on attachment theory, suggests that a child with an insecure attachment engages in disruptive behaviors to maximize parental attention. The parent expresses disapproval or administers a consequence, the child increases the disruptive behavior, and the parent accommodates in order to stop the behavior, which does then stop. The child learns that escalation of disruptive behavior will achieve desired goals, rather than learning to control her or his behavior and delay gratification in the service of parental approval. Thus begins a coercive patterning of behavior and expectation, which may be brought to school and become more extreme. Bullying other children at school illustrates the use of disruption and coercion to achieve immediate ends. In this model, the child fails to internalize parental or community standards and a concomitant desire to conform or behave well; instead, extrinsic motivation, aiming to maximize rewards and minimize punishment, develops. The enhanced sense of self-control that is associated with intrinsic motivation fails to emerge (Fonagy et al., 1997).

Social control theory further extends the conception of the role of attachment in developing internalized morality or self-control from the interpersonal to the institutional. Weakness in the individual's bonds to both prosocial others and social institutions is seen as critical to the development of delinquency. The key constructs are social capital (the bonds of commitment, trust, and obligation that arise from attachment and facilitate the exchange of resources) and social control (greater compliance and commitment from youth that result from having greater social capital). Investments of love and care by parents instill in children a sense of attachment and commitment, interpersonally and to society. A sense of obligation and connection helps provide control of the universal pre-socialized propensity to deviate from social norms, and the lack of such connection increases the risk for delinquency (Higgins & Ricketts, 2005; Ryan & Testa, 2005).

> *Ericka was a runaway, and DCFS picked her up. Three unhappy and unsuccessful non-kin foster placements followed. ("I was bad and talked back and lashed out.") Like many children who have been in foster care, Ericka located the "badness" in herself to a great degree, and the several group home placements that followed did nothing to make her feel better about herself. Her sense of herself as "bad" was underway, yet her ability to object to problematic circumstances and assertions of needing to be in better and different places revealed her capacity for resilience and her awareness that aspects of the other (outside world) were "bad," too.*
>
> *She fought with a girl at one school, was expelled from another school for having pepper spray, ran away frequently, and was sent to one group home after another. The investment of love and care needed to promote her connection to social institutions was insufficient at best. During a stay at a residential facility, Ericka and a friend were trying on sunglasses at a swap meet; as they strolled through the aisles, a security guard picked them up, assuming they were shoplifting. Ericka became a crossover kid at this point, adjudicated in juvenile court as delinquent; she received probation.*
>
> *She was in and out of schools, sometimes because of altercations, sometimes because her placement changed, finally arriving at a continuation school for*

probation-supervised youth. She had little interest in or connection to school. On an evening out, she and a girlfriend went with some boys to one of their homes; Ericka was raped within earshot of her friend and of others in the house. Her friend refused to testify, and the case was dropped. Ericka recalls being traumatized, receiving some counseling, and staying out of school for several months. Additional truancies and runaways (AWOLs) from placements followed. The night before a court appearance, she learned a staff member at her group home planned to recommend detention for her; she and another resident locked the staff member out of the facility. She was sent to a juvenile detention center the following morning. Two probation-supervised group homes followed. She could find no reason to stay at any of these, and her pattern of running away continued: "I wanted to see my family." Ericka's grandmother and a beloved cousin died just before her eighteenth birthday. Three months later, she was pregnant.

Empathy, which develops out of the early caregiving relationship, not only protects against aggressive impulses toward others, but also forms the basis for the feelings of concern about the welfare of others. Attachment theory suggests that when the early caregiving environment is characterized by maltreatment, internal representations of the significant other(s) may be hostile and overwhelmingly powerful, rather than benign and concerned. The child whose neurobiological stress-response system is too frequently in overdrive may have little capacity to reflect, understand, and make good decisions in the face of seemingly threatening or ambiguous circumstances.

As Ericka described her childhood and adolescence to me, there had been little opportunity for her to make an emotional connection to a caring adult figure. Her grandmother took her in and was deeply missed when she died, yet she was not presented as someone who could help during the years when Ericka was on the run. There was sporadic and unpredictable contact with both her mother, still addicted and now homeless, and her father, incarcerated for drug-related activities. Poignantly, a boy she saw every six months at their court appearances was mentioned as the friend who was a consistent figure in her life. Numerous changes in placements and schools precluded the possibility of making enduring connections to adults, peers, or academic aspirations.

For children and adolescents whose stress-response systems and ability to self-regulate have been compromised, it may only be possible to achieve a sense of mastery and control through physical experiences or actions that take the place of experiencing anger over neglect, rejection, or abuse (Fonagy et al., 1997).

When the press of emotion was great, when Ericka felt lonely or frightened or angry, running away offered immediate relief and distraction. In the absence of external or internal sources of coping and support, her available strategies were fight or flight. The effects of these maladaptive (but, for her, necessary) strategies added to the instability of her living and educational experiences;

*she was increasingly thrust back on her own inadequate resources. With the
exception of brief counseling following the rape, Ericka reached young adulthood
through her own determination, with little help from the child welfare, juvenile
justice, or mental health systems.*

Risks and Protective Factors

Risk and protective factors associated with delinquency exist at individual, family, school, peer group, and community levels. At the individual
level, the temperament and gender of the child may function as risks or as
protections; for example, a male child with a difficult temperament who is
slow to adapt, intensely reactive, irritable, and negative is more likely to
develop conduct problems than is an easygoing child of either gender
(Dodge et al., 2006). Evidence suggests that boys who have hyperactivity,
restlessness, trouble concentrating, and are described as aggressive during middle childhood are at greater risk of later violent behavior. Research
results for girls are less consistent (Hawkins et al., 2000).

Neurobiological Risk Factors

Prenatal, perinatal, and birth complications can compromise development in ways that contribute to risk for later antisocial behavior, especially in combination with other risk factors, such as maternal rejection or
family disadvantage. One study found a twelve-fold increase in recidivis-
tic violent offending through age 26 in offspring whose mothers smoked
and who were born into single-parent families (Dodge et al., 2006). On the
other hand, another study found that a stable home environment served
as a protective factor against the effects of prenatal trauma (Hawkins
et al., 2000).

Head injuries during infancy, either from accidents or physical abuse,
can cause multiple microscopic lesions throughout the brain, damaging
areas responsible for executive function, abstract thinking, and regulation
of emotion and behavior. Researchers speculate that frontal lobe injury is
a primary cause of sociopathy or cold-blooded criminal behavior.
Temporal lobe injuries are associated with "episodic dyscontrol," in which
violent behavior erupts, is unpatterned, and occurs without provocation.
Retrospective studies on juvenile and older death row inmates show that
a high percentage have a history of serious head injury (Karr-Morse &
Wiley, 1997).

As described in Chapter 3, child abuse can cause alterations to the
stress-response system that can interfere with threat assessment, leading
to aggressive responses in neutral situations. The interaction of the biological, memorial, and current-cue factors results in an emotional and cognitive appraisal and a response strategy that excludes both judgment and
inhibition of aggressive impulses. The physical structure and chemical

profile of the brain may be adversely altered from prolonged stress or injury during the first three years, although these effects can be greatly offset by the presence of a nurturing and responsive caregiver (Karr-Morse & Wiley, 1997). For many youth in the foster care system, however, maltreatment in childhood is followed by traumatic separation from parent(s) and placement instability, so that the negative sequelae of abuse and a problematic attachment are not ameliorated by a new, more nurturing attachment.

Family Level Factors

In a meta-analysis of 66 studies, researchers found that the family risk factors responsible for greatest increased risk of violent or serious delinquency are parental attitudes favorable to violence, poor family-management practices, parental criminality during the child's adolescence, family conflict, and residential mobility (Grinberg et. al., 2005; Hawkins et al., 2000). Other researchers found that parental psychopathology and parenting practices that are either harsh or lax increase the risk of delinquency, whereas parental behavior that is involved and accepting decreases the risk (McMahon & Kotler, 2006; Stuewig & McCloskey, 2005).

A history of maltreatment is a robust predictor of adolescent delinquency, whereas attachment to parents is found to lessen the risk for violent delinquency (Malmgren & Meisel, 2004; Perez, 2001; Salzinger, Rosario, & Feldman, 2007). In one study, physical abuse at an early age was found to be a risk factor for alienation and antisocial behavior in adolescence, mediated by a poor-quality parent–child relationship (Egeland et al., 2002). Sexual abuse also predicts adolescent delinquency, especially among girls, because of behavior or emotions associated with the abuse, and because girls' risk of delinquency increases as a result of having entered foster care (Ryan & Testa, 2005; Stuewig & McCloskey, 2005).

Warm, supportive relationships with parents or other caring adults serve as protective factors at the family level (Frick, 2001). Monitoring by parents or parent figures is also associated with reducing the risk of delinquency, as is parents' positive evaluation of peers (Shader, 2001).

School Factors

Low academic performance and behavioral problems at school predict delinquent and violent behavior, as does low commitment (attachment) to school (Fonagy et al., 1997; Grinberg et al., 2005; Hawkins et al., 2000; Malmgren & Meisel, 2004; Ryan, Testa, & Zhai, 2008). Low educational aspirations and multiple school transitions, both often a part of the foster care experience, also predict a significantly increased risk for violence at age 18 (Hawkins et al., 2000). Evidence of academic competence serves as a protective factor (Frick, 2001). Studies have found an inverse relationship between extracurricular activity and delinquency (Huebner & Betts, 2002).

Students who were involved in prosocial school activities had lower levels of serious delinquency, but in unexpected ways. For boys, involvement in nonsport school activities was a protective factor, whereas involvement in school sports was a protective factor for girls (Booth, Farrell, & Varano, 2008).

Peer Factors

Peers are a major proximal cause of antisocial behavior, beginning in early childhood, and association with deviant peers is the strongest predictor of escalating adolescent problem behavior (Dishion & Patterson, 2006; Frick, 2001; Grinberg et al., 2005; Hawkins et al., 2000). Gang membership at age 14 triples the risk for violent involvement at age 18, and membership at age 16 quadruples the risk (Dodge et al., 2006; Hawkins et al., 2000). On the other hand, friends who engage in conventional or prosocial behavior function as protective factors (Frick, 2001; Shader, 2001).

Juvenile court processing itself has adverse effects on subsequent criminal offending; labeling may trigger stigma and exclusion in school, thereby affecting educational attainment and prospects for employment. Labeling by the mainstream world may result in self-derogation and feelings of helplessness, and the adolescent may attempt to restore self-esteem and sense of control by engaging in further deviant behavior (Bernburg & Krohn, 2003; Dodge et al., 2006). In addition, intervention by the juvenile court greatly increases the likelihood of involvement with the penal system in adulthood (Gatti, Tremblay, & Vitaro, 2009).

> *Ericka's story depicts risk factors of child maltreatment, criminal or deviant behavior by family members, residential instability, sexual assault (abuse), lack of connection to school, low academic performance, deviant peers, traumatic and sudden moves from placement to placement, stigma associated with foster care status and with juvenile-offender labeling.*

Community and Neighborhood Factors

Neighborhood characteristics can increase an individual's likelihood of antisocial behavior when there is wide availability of drugs, presence of adults involved in criminal activities, or a culture that supports and encourages violence (Frick, 2001; Hawkins et al., 2000; Stewart & Simons, 2006). Disadvantaged neighborhoods where there are few legitimate opportunities for employment and social status may give rise to a street culture in which self-worth is dependent on respect commanded in public by being willing to use violence as a strategy (Frick, 2001; Stewart & Simons, 2006). One study found that aggressive children are especially likely to become even more aggressive adolescents when they live in dangerous neighborhoods and receive little parental monitoring, but that they could be saved from an aggressive adolescence if they lived in safe environments with close parental monitoring (Dodge, 2001). The stability of communities also affects delinquency; high rates of mobility in communities are linked to high crime rates (Fonagy et al., 1997; Stewart & Simons, 2006). When ties to the community, via institutions such as church and school, are weak, they increase the risk for delinquency (Grinberg et al., 2005).

Social Bonds and Gender

Research suggests that different bonds of social control can be protective (or risk) factors for males and females. Involvement bonds of social-control theory are evident for both genders, but attachment bonds generally appear to provide more protection for females than for males (Huebner & Betts, 2002). In another study, attachment to parents functioned as a protective factor for adolescent boys, significantly decreasing the severity of delinquent behavior, whereas for girls, attachment to school and to prosocial peers had a similar significant effect. Consistent with this finding, another study indicated that the most influential decision for boys in joining a gang was their need for a familial relationship (Anderson, Holmes, & Ostresh, 1999).

Trajectories of Delinquency

An understanding of the ways in which delinquent behaviors develop and escalate illuminates those points when intervention is especially important. Most researchers identify two basic pathways in the development of delinquent behaviors. Early-onset or early-starter delinquents engage in overt antisocial behaviors beginning in either the preschool or early school years, as a result of the interactional patterning in the caregiver–child relationship. The child lacks a wide array of social skills; engages in confrontations with school authorities and caregivers; is rejected by conventional peers; learns covert skills, often in the company of deviant peers; has problems acquiring basic academic skills, possibly due to preexisting neuropsychological deficits, which manifest as verbal deficits and self-control problems; is at risk for depression and substance use; is arrested before age 14, and has a high rate of adult arrests (Dishion & Patterson, 2006; Dodge et al., 2006; McMahon & Kotler, 2006). In a study of adjudicated youth, those who had a family member convicted of a felony were nearly twice as likely to be early-start delinquents as those who did not. Significantly, those who had previous foster care experience were more than four times more likely to be early starters than those with no foster care experience, and (Alltucker et al., 2006).

The late-starter pathway is less consistently described. It begins in adolescence and is thought to result in less serious forms of conduct problems, although there are considerable risks for property and drug offenses

(McMahon & Kotler, 2006). Late starters demonstrate average to low levels of overt antisocial behavior in childhood and marginal levels of social skills. They become involved with deviant peers in mid-adolescence, and overt forms of antisocial behavior increase. Most late starters desist offending as they reach early adulthood (Dishion & Patterson, 2006).

An alternative model posits three pathways based on the nature of the behaviors. An overt path begins in childhood with minor bullying and aggression and, over time, progresses to more extreme antisocial behaviors. A covert path begins in childhood with minor behaviors such as lying, truancy, vandalism, and possibly fire-setting. In adolescence, the individual engages in more extreme behaviors, including substance abuse, risky sexual behavior, and burglary. Finally, the third pathway begins with noncompliance and defiance of authority, escalating to running away and truancy and increased risk of moving along one of the other paths (Dishion & Patterson, 2006).

In one of the few studies that look at offending trajectories of male youth emerging from foster care, researchers found that 52% were non-offenders, 21% were desisters (ceased offending), and 27% were chronic offenders. Those not enrolled in school and who experienced placement instability were significantly more likely to engage in subsequent delinquency and crime. Long-term offenders reported that their initial involvement with the juvenile justice system occurred while they were in care and continued after emancipation (Ryan, Hernandez, & Herz, 2007). A study comparing offending of youth leaving care with their peers in the general population found that youth aging out of care had higher rates across a range of behaviors, and were over ten times more likely to report having been arrested since age 18 than their peers. For both groups of youth, offending decreased by age 19 (Cusick & Courtney, 2007).

Conduct Disorders

Psychiatrically diagnosable conduct problems include oppositional defiant disorder (ODD) and conduct disorder (CD). Diagnostic criteria for ODD include negative, defiant, disobedient, and hostile behavior toward authority figures for a period of at least six months, with various behaviors present at a high level and with impairment to functioning at home or at school (American Psychiatric Association, 2000). The behaviors in question are common to all children, but the frequency, severity, and associated impairment distinguish the child who is diagnosable. CD is diagnosed when a youth engages in a pattern of behavior in which the basic rights of others or major age-appropriate societal norms or rules are violated. Behaviors include aggressive acts, property destruction, deceptiveness or theft, and serious rule violation. Three of 15 behaviors must have been present in the preceding 12 months (American Psychiatric Association, 2000).

Conduct problems are among the most frequently occurring behavior disorders of childhood. Results of twenty population-based studies of youth eight to 16 years old reported rates of 2% to 10% for ODD and 1% to 9% for CD. The behaviors of younger children were found to be more oppositional and overt, and those of older children more covert. Boys were more likely to exhibit conduct problems at earlier ages and higher rates than girls (McMahon & Kotler, 2006). Gender differences in physical aggression emerge as early as age three and remain stable through childhood and adolescence, with research indicating a rate of CD in girls at approximately half that of boys (Dodge et al., 2006).

The most severe problems associated with overt antisocial behavior are in place before first grade, whereas forms of covert antisocial behavior begin to appear in middle childhood, and accelerate in early adolescence. Illegal antisocial behavior (delinquency) increases during adolescence and peaks between 16 and 18 years of age (Dishion & Patterson, 2006; Hoffman & Cerbone, 1999). Adolescence offers expanded exposure to and opportunities to engage in sexual activities and substance use, a greater number of stresses in daily life, and, potentially, increased contact with antisocial or deviant peers. Violent offending almost always begins during the adolescent years: 19% of males and 12% of females in an offender sample reported committing at least one serious violent offense at the peak age of 17 (Dodge et al., 2006).

Co-occurring Disorders

Research consistently reveals high levels of psychiatric disorders among detained youth, but rates vary widely by study, ranging from more than 50% to 100% (Tarolla et al., 2002; Vermeiren, Jespers, & Moffitt, 2006). The percentage of youthful offenders diagnosed with mental health disorders (including substance-use disorders) is rising, and research shows a possible correlation between mental health disorders, offending, and recidivism (Hunsicker, 2007). While most studies have focused on DSM-IV disorders, many youth have also been identified as seriously emotionally disturbed (SED) by school personnel. The SED label captures a range of educational, emotional, social, and psychological problems at a level that interferes with educational performance. Studies of SED among incarcerated juveniles indicate that these rates, like those of DSM diagnoses, are higher than those in the general adolescent population. In addition, most of these youth enter the special educational system after or only shortly before being incarcerated, suggesting that the mental health needs of these youth went undetected prior to juvenile court involvement for serious delinquent activities (Jonson-Reid, Williams, & Webster, 2001).

Results of a large-scale study of youth at a juvenile temporary detention center were extrapolated to suggest that, on the average day, as many as 47,000 detained youth may suffer from two or more types of psychiatric disorder, and that more than 12,000 of these have a substance-abuse disorder as well as a major mental disorder (Abram et al., 2003). In another large-scale study of detained youth with comorbidity, females and non-Hispanic whites had the highest rates, African Americans had the lowest rates, followed by other minorities, despite the fact that more than 60% of the youth in the juvenile justice system are youth of color (Abram et al., 2003; Holman & Ziedenberg, 2006; Karnik et al., 2006).

Substance and alcohol use are common among juvenile offenders, with estimates ranging from 27% to 63% (Tarolla et al., 2002), and are robust predictors of recidivism among both male and female youthful offenders (Stoolmiller & Bleckman, 2005). Recent studies have shown SUDs of any kind in one-third to one-half of detained youth, and more than one-fifth of these are abusing more than one substance. SUDs are also associated with increased instances of risk-taking behaviors, including those associated with sexual activity and risk of AIDS. SUDs complicate the diagnostic picture and are, therefore, of great clinical importance (Vermeiren et al., 2006).

Depressive disorder in incarcerated juveniles is reported at rates of 14% to 36% among females, and between 2% and 13% among males (Vermeiren et al., 2006). Depression may be either masked or expressed by aggressive symptoms in boys, however. Depressed delinquents were found to have higher levels of substance abuse than those who were not depressed (Vermeiren et al., 2006). It should be noted that the high co-occurrence of depression and antisocial behavior may be explained by common risk factors, such as traumatization and familial disadvantage, and that depression may also be precipitated by experiences associated with arrest and incarceration. Likewise, the high rates of anxiety disorders found in some studies (20% to 21% in males and 31% to 59% in females) may be a function of both incarceration and previous out-of-home placements that often precede incarceration (Vermeiren et al., 2006).

Detained youth are at high risk for developing antisocial personality disorder (APD) as they enter adulthood, particularly those with five or more symptoms of CD. Nearly 20% of those developed APD, as compared to only 1% to 4% of the general population. Alcohol use disorders, dysthymia, and male gender were found to increase the risk of developing APD (Washburn et al., 2007).

A critical disorder for many detained maltreated juveniles is PTSD. A significant relation between PTSD and arrest and incarceration has been documented, and studies report that 32% of incarcerated juvenile offenders meet full criteria for PTSD, with another 20% meeting partial criteria (Tarolla et al., 2002). Much higher rates of PTSD are found in girls, with current diagnosis of PTSD ranging from 33% to 55%, and a lifetime rate of 65% (Vermeiren et al., 2006). In addition, PTSD is associated with higher levels of depression and anxiety and reduced levels of impulse control and aggression suppression, suggesting an overlap between victimization and offending (Tarolla et al., 2002; Vermeiren et al., 2006).

The functioning of abused and traumatized delinquent youth is very likely to be further compromised by the experience of incarceration, especially in the absence of any attention to mental health needs. The kind of environment generated in detention centers and the conditions of confinement interact with pre-existing poor mental health to lead to higher rates of depression and suicidal ideation (Holman & Ziedenberg, 2006).

Assessment

Because antisocial and violent behavior have so many dimensions and reside "at the intersection of the individual and the culture interacting over time," assessment must address many domains (Dodge, 2001). The assessment process must be developmentally sensitive with regard to age and gender; it must be contextually sensitive with regard to home, school, neighborhood, and community; and it must be culturally sensitive (Dishion & Patterson, 2006; McMahon & Kotler, 2006). In addition, the delinquent behaviors and current stressors must be explored. The clinician should screen for history of trauma, substance use or abuse, and other possible co-occurring disorders.

Antisocial behavior cannot be understood apart from history and current context. History-taking should include prenatal and birth history, maternal substance abuse, problems with attachment, and the presence of physical or sexual abuse (Steiner & Dunne, 1997). The quality of peer relationships should be explored, along with problems with aggression and impulse control. Assessment ideally involves multiple informants from multiple settings: academic, home or foster-care placement, and medical, if indicated. The complexity of diagnosis of conduct problems requires graduate-level social workers in mental health and correctional settings who are trained in substance-use disorders, delinquency, and patterns of co-occurring problems among high-risk youth (Jenson & Potter, 2003; Jonson-Reid et al., 2001).

Treatment and Intervention Approaches

The treatment literature encompasses youth with conduct problems in the general population and those who enter the juvenile justice system. This section summarizes approaches that have received the greatest research attention. Intervention with delinquent or conduct-disordered youth is variously described as having little success to having some degree of effectiveness at reducing recidivism (McMahon & Kotler, 2006; Tarolla et al., 2002; Zhang & Zhang, 2005). Citing a large scale meta-analysis on the effectiveness of treatment with juvenile delinquents, Zhang & Zhang report that effective programs share the following features: intensive supervision that aims at providing positive reinforcement for prosocial behavior, the targeting of high-risk offenders, matching services with identified needs, and providing prosocial contexts that help offenders connect to more constructive lifestyles (Zhang & Zhang, 2005). McMahon and Kotler describe the shared attributes of successful programs as: empirically supported developmental approaches that include coercion theory and social-ecological perspectives of risk and protection, targeting risk and protective factors, and addressing multiple socialization and support systems (McMahon & Kotler, 2006).

It is generally recognized that treatments must be multimodal, encompassing individual, family (if possible), and community dimensions. For both institutionalized and noninstitutionalized youth, lower recidivism rates were associated with individuals who received the full number of intervention sessions prescribed by treatment authors and with program lengths greater than six months. Recidivism does not appear to be affected by gender, ethnicity, or age (McMahon & Kotler, 2006). Theoretical and risk factors described in preceding sections are implicated in varying degrees in the treatments and modalities discussed below.

Family and Systems Models

Family and systems therapy models are highly studied, and many have shown great effectiveness; they are often cited as an essential component of an intervention program (McMahon & Kotler, 2006). Parent-based approaches recognize the interactional, developmental aspects of conduct problems, and are meant to improve discipline strategies, the quality of parent–child relationships, monitoring, and supervision (Dodge et al., 2006). This presents a problem for youth in foster care, whether adjudicated or not, who are unlikely to have a family member available for this kind of therapy. Therefore, I mention only briefly family models with the most empirical support, and the discussion will focus instead on treatment approaches that are more applicable to youth in care. *Functional family therapy*, which decreases subsequent court contacts over other conditions, focuses on adolescent–parent communication and broader systemic influences. Another family approach that has shown promise is *multisystemic therapy*, which employs well-validated treatment strategies and addresses cognitive, familial, extrafamilial, and biological factors that have been implicated in delinquency (Henggeler & Sheidow, 2003; Tarolla et al., 2002).

A program utilizing a multisystemic ecological approach is the Juvenile Counseling and Assessment Program (JCAP), which provides comprehensive treatment to court-referred youth and their families through a collaborative model. Youth receive assessment; individual, group, and family counseling; problem-solving, social skills, and career decision training; anger management training, and community resource coordination (Tarolla et al., 2002). Examination of treatment effectiveness with juvenile offenders who received JCAP indicates that individual therapy is the most effective component for creation of long-term changes throughout the individual's life, and that the group counseling component may be especially important for girls due to their relational needs (Calhoun, Glaser, & Bartolomucci, 2001). Social skills training, a component of JCAP and other multisystemic approaches, has shown promise, but has usually been studied in the context of family interaction and parent training, rather than with adolescents without families.

Cognitive Behavioral Treatment

Based on the idea that antisocial behavior is mediated through the individual's expectations, appraisals, and experiences, CBT aims to increase positive behaviors and thoughts and decrease negative ones, improving anger management and interpersonal skills along the way. Specific programs may differ in emphases, with the Self-Instructional Training Program focusing on inhibition of impulsive responses, the Anger Coping Program focusing on changing perceptual biases of peer intent, and the Promoting Alternative Thinking Strategies Curriculum (PATHS) focusing on development of social skills and emotional awareness (Frick, 2001). While some CBT programs report positive changes while the youth remain in an institutional setting, the differences between treatment and control groups disappear at follow-up at 12 and 24 months later (Tarolla et al., 2002). In another study, however, aggressive adolescents showed greater social problem-solving skills and some reductions in beliefs associated with aggression (McMahon & Kotler, 2006).

Peer-Group Counseling

Peer programs are aimed at interpersonal problem-solving, are low-cost, and have gained popularity as less punitive and restrictive than other approaches. However, most studies evaluating these programs have been methodologically flawed, and some researchers have concluded that there is minimal support for their effectiveness (Tarolla et al., 2002). Researchers have pointed to the danger of negative iatrogenic effects in groups where antisocial individuals interact (Frick, 2001). In responding to an informal survey, a foster care alumna youth told me that the group therapy in one of her group home placements was problematic "because we contributed to each other's bad behavior; it was a prescription for disaster to have kids who are all having the same or worse problems together, rather than anyone who was doing better, who cared about school, or could be a role model" (Rodriguez, 2010).

Community-Based/Cross-System Collaboration

JCAP, described above, is an example of an effective multimodal, community-based intervention. Another is the Los Angeles County Repeat Offender Prevention Program (ROPP), a three-year pilot project designed to improve school performance and prevent re-offending through a combination of social services, including intensive supervision, self-esteem building, educational tutoring, individual and group counseling, mental health services, substance-abuse education and treatment, family preservation, gang prevention alternatives, career development planning, and employment services. Those who successfully completed the program showed improvements in school performance and decreased new criminal offenses in the first six months following program completion; however, no significant effects were found in additional six-month periods. The researchers pose many possible reasons for the absence of continuing effects, such as contextual community factors, implementation problems, and lack of study of the probation officers and community staff as compared with those working with the control group; data collection had good measures of quantity of supervision and services, but no measures of quality (Zhang & Zhang, 2005).

Multidimensional-treatment foster care, involving training and support for foster parents, family therapy, individual therapy, and adjunctive services, has been shown to be efficacious for seriously delinquent and aggressive youth (McMahon & Kotler, 2006). A collaborative, cross-system intervention aimed at reducing mental-health and substance-use problems of detained youth showed significant reductions in mental-health problems and in self-reported delinquency and substance use in the six months following release from detention. These researchers propose that mental health services offered within the structure of a juvenile correctional facility may be a promising form of cross-system collaboration (Jenson & Potter, 2003). Another study of collaborative community-based programs suggested that community-based care coordinated across child-serving agencies can reduce or delay entry into the juvenile justice system, as well as recidivism among those who have already been involved (Foster, Qaseem, & Connor, 2004).

Psychopharmacological Treatment

To date, there are mixed results and little evidence that stimulants reduce conduct problems in children and adolescents who do not have comorbid ADHD. There is some evidence that stimulants can reduce aggressive behavior and some covert problem behaviors of children who do have ADHD, but the use of psychotropic drugs with young people must always be considered with a view to potential (and unknown) long-term effects on the still-developing adolescent brain (Dodge et al., 2006; McMahon & Kotler, 2006).

Key Treatment Principles

1. Provide early identification of mental health problems and early intervention.
2. Ensure that social work and psychology staff in mental health and juvenile justice settings and schools are trained to identify and treat conduct and related disorders, substance-use disorders, suicidality, and trauma-related problems.
3. The one-to-one relationship and intensity of involvement are critical aspects of treatment.
4. Tailor intervention to the individual, considering gender, culture, and developmental status.
5. Provide opportunities to address and heal traumatic childhood experiences.
6. Provide a plan for aftercare and transition services that includes community supports.

The Institutional Context

Crossover Kids

Children in care who fall under the jurisdiction of both the child welfare and juvenile justice systems are sometimes referred to as "crossover kids." Actions and circumstances of their early caregiving contexts bring them into foster care; the combined effects of those original experiences and those in the child welfare system, both directly and indirectly, often lead to their entry into the juvenile justice system. In addition to the child welfare and juvenile justice systems, the mental health system also has a role to play in the lives of crossover kids. In the past, children with severe behavior problems were treated in psychiatric hospitals, often with lengthy stays and multifaceted treatment. Many of the same behavioral issues once addressed in clinical settings are now addressed in juvenile justice settings, due, among other things, to managed health care changes such as decreased lengths of stay and fragmented care that focuses on crisis intervention only (Watkins, 1999). Another situation that can result in entry of children with mental health problems into the juvenile justice system is placement in inappropriate foster homes where their mental health needs go unaddressed and problems escalate. In such circumstances, caregivers may turn to law enforcement to control the increased acting-out behavior.

There is a high rate and wide range of mental illness within the juvenile justice system; it is estimated that upwards of two-thirds of youth in detention centers could meet the criteria for psychiatric disorders, and one-third need ongoing clinical care, twice the rate in the general adolescent population (Holman & Ziedenberg, 2006). Although these young people need and would benefit from mental health placements, the probability of a given youth to receive one is about 4%, depending on race and gender. Caucasian females, for example, are as many as eight times more likely than African American males to receive a mental health placement and 2.5 times more likely to receive one than African American females or Caucasian males (Rawal et al., 2004).

Considerable research demonstrates that maltreated children are at increased risk of delinquency compared with non-maltreated children (Egeland et al., 2002; Goodkind, Ng, & Sarri, 2006; Stuewig & McCloskey, 2005). One study found that children nine to twelve years old who have been reported abused or neglected are 67% more likely to be arrested (Higgins & Ricketts, 2005; Scrivner, 2002), and another reports that the delinquency rates of maltreated children are 47% higher than those of non-maltreated children (Ryan & Testa, 2005). Children who are placed in out-of-home care, and male children who experience placement instability, are at increased risk. Combined effects of gender and ethnicity result in African American males being at even higher risk subsequent to maltreatment, whether or not they have been removed from their homes. If they do enter foster care, their odds of delinquency are twice those of Caucasian youth who are placed (Ryan & Testa, 2005).

Maltreated children tend to be younger at their first arrest, commit nearly twice as many offenses, and are arrested more frequently than those who have not been maltreated (North Carolina Division of Social Services, 2007). Children who are chronically maltreated and whose maltreatment peaks at the age of transition to secondary school are more likely to offend than other maltreated children (Steward, Livingston, & Dennison, 2008; Stewart & Simons, 2006). Approximately 16% of children in substitute care experience at least one delinquency petition, compared to 7% of maltreatment victims who are not removed from their families (Ryan & Testa, 2005). Further, another study found that abused or neglected children who experience a family separation and are removed from their homes are almost twice as likely to have an arrest in adulthood as those who experience a family separation and are not removed. Females, in particular, face a greater risk of adult incarceration as the number of placements rises (McMahon & Clay-Warner, 2002). All five crossover youth interviewed in a qualitative study described removal from their family homes as a significant rupture of attachment and a critical life-point (Finlay, 2003).

Within the foster care system, different placements can have dramatically different effects. Children placed in group homes are about two and a half times more likely to enter the juvenile justice system than similar children in foster home settings. The group-home effect on delinquency is fairly immediate, with the majority of first-time arrests occurring while the youth is under the supervision of the group home (Chamberlain, 2008).

Youth are more likely to be arrested in group homes as a result of incidents in placements because some facilities turn quickly to the police for assistance rather than using internal strategies to manage behaviors (Finlay, 2003).

Racial Disparity in the Juvenile Justice System

Just as there is disproportionate representation of youth of color, especially African Americans, in the child welfare system, there is comparable overrepresentation in the juvenile justice system. In 2006, African American youth were 52% of those arrested for juvenile violent crimes and 37% of the youth in detention, yet they are only 16% of the youth population (Bilchik, 2008; Dodge et al., 2006). Among female juveniles in custody, 55% are girls of color, as compared with 62% among males in custody (Snyder & Sickmund, 2006; Snyder & Rogers, 2002).

Overrepresentation of youth of color is found at all decision points in the system: arrest, referral to juvenile court, detention, adjudication, probation, and placement (Bilchik, 2008; Conward, 2001; Engen, Steen, & Bridges, 2002). Studies of the child welfare system suggest that race strongly influences the reporting of child maltreatment, the substantiation of those reports, placement in substitute care, and reentry into care following attempts at family reunification (Lau et al., 2003). Because both child maltreatment and foster care placement place youth at greater risk of delinquency, the institutional racism within the child welfare system also plays a role in the disproportional representation of African American youth in the juvenile justice system. Children whose delinquency cases originate in foster care are less likely to receive probation than children in the general population, and they are, therefore, more likely to be incarcerated (North Carolina Division of Social Services, 2007; Ryan et al., 2007).

Common explanations for racial disparities include: differences in seriousness and frequency of offenses, racial discrimination in decision-making, and the structure of the decision-making process itself. There is significant evidence that race affects the severity of dispositions (decisions about next steps for the youth), and that youth of color are subject to more formal and punitive social control than Caucasian youth. Youth of color, especially African American youth, are less likely to be involved in diversion (strategies other than probation or incarceration, such as drug treatment or other programs) than similarly situated whites (Leiber et al., 2007). Youth of color "enter [the juvenile justice system] at higher numbers, receive harsher sentences for comparable infractions, and are often incarcerated for longer periods of time" (Jones, 2006). Youth of color are twice as likely to be held in secure pretrial confinement (Conward, 2001). Some research suggests that the literature, in general, may underestimate the extent to which there are consistent findings that race affects disposition, and that divergent findings are largely due to methodological differences in studies (Engen et al., 2002). A study comparing youth processed in juvenile court to those processed in adult criminal court finds that youth processed in the adult court are also disproportionately male, African American or Hispanic, and have much greater prevalence rates of psychiatric disorder than adult detainees (Washburn et al., 2008).

Gender and Juvenile Justice

Between 1985 and 2002, the overall delinquency caseload for females increased 92%, compared with a 29% increase for males. The largest increases for girls were in person-related offenses, such as assault, but girls also make up a large percentage in the offense categories of theft, drug law violations, and disorderly conduct (Snyder & Sickmund, 2006). Though boys continue to be at elevated risk for violent offending, committing 84% of violent crime, girls represent the fastest growing segment of the juvenile justice system (Abram et al., 2003), with girls of color occupying 56.4% of space in public detention centers (Abram et al., 2003; Le, Arifuku, & Nunez, 2003).

Some evidence suggests that girls receive differential treatment at every stage of the process. They are disproportionately detained for status offenses (behaviors that are law violations only if committed by a person of juvenile status), and once in the system, are more likely than boys to be recommitted (sent back to detention) for technical probation or parole violations rather than for committing a new crime (American Bar Association & National Bar Association, 2001). Studies of the effects of gender in the juvenile justice system have reported mixed findings. Some researchers report that officials may treat females more harshly than males, perhaps in an attempt to enforce stereotypical notions of proper female behavior and to protect the sexuality of young women. Conversely, others report that male decision-makers may treat females more leniently due to stereotypes and may believe that female offenders are more susceptible to rehabilitation (Leiber et al., 2007).

Girls are often placed in facilities and programs that were designed for boys, emphasize security over intervention, and are ill-equipped to meet the specific needs of girls (Conward, 2001). At the same time that the female population (of which more than half are girls of color) in the juvenile justice system is increasing, the high teenage birth rates among Hispanic and African American girls in the United States mean that the number of pregnant or parenting girls in the system is also rising. Detained adolescents are also at high risk for sexually transmitted diseases; 25% of the 12 million new STD cases in the United States annually are among adolescents. Health needs of detained adolescent girls, and those of pregnant girls and infants born in correctional settings in particular, are seriously underserved in the juvenile justice system (Acoca, 2004).

Sexual Minority Youth and Juvenile Justice

Lesbian, gay, bisexual, and transgendered (LGBT) youth are believed to represent up to 13% of youth in the juvenile justice system (Majd, Marksamer, & Reyes, 2009) and to comprise up to half of the homeless teen population in major cities (Wardenski, 2005). Biased responses to minority sexual orientation or youth questioning their sexual orientation can lead to family rejection, school harassment, running away, entry into foster care, and harassment or abuse by staff or other youth (Sullivan, Sommer, & Moff, 2001; Wardenski, 2005). Running away from home, foster care, or group homes is the most frequent path to homelessness and to delinquent and criminal behaviors associated with survival strategies on the street (Wardenski, 2005). LGBT youth who feel they must hide their orientation may be more likely to participate in risky or dangerous sexual encounters.

Within the juvenile justice system, LGBT youth are more likely to encounter discrimination and mistreatment on the basis of their sexual orientation than are heterosexual peers (Wardenski, 2005). They are often not protected from the aggression of others, including sex offenders, or those who are homophobic or antigay (Sullivan et al., 2001; Wardenski, 2005). In addition, many judges are unaware that specific adolescents who come before them are LGBT, and lawyers representing them may be similarly unaware of their orientation or ignorant of their special needs for protection or services (Wardenski, 2005).

Mental Health and Juvenile Justice

When an abused child or adolescent is placed in corrections as a result of delinquency, the services received there may not be appropriate or adequate to address issues associated with abuse. Of the roughly 109,000 youth under 18 who are incarcerated on an average day, approximately 7,500 are housed in adult facilities that lack mental health services for youth (Campaign for Youth Justice, 2007). Even the adolescent who enters the juvenile justice system with identified mental health needs has a low likelihood of receiving a mental health placement. The "bad" aspect of his or her behavior has taken precedence in the eyes of society. While all youth in the juvenile justice system with mental health problems are probably inadequately served, youth of color youth are most seriously underserved (Rawal et al., 2004).

Parental involvement can be crucial to good outcomes in the juvenile justice system. If, as in the case of most crossover children, there is no parental involvement, the child is at a disadvantage. For example, at an initial hearing to determine whether a youth should be detained or released to home pending the outcome of the delinquency case, judges are more likely to choose detention for youth who have no parental support from biological or foster parents.

Crossover Kids and the Transition to Adulthood

As described earlier in this chapter, individuals whose antisocial behavior begins in early childhood are less likely to desist from antisocial behavior in early adulthood than those whose problematic behavior begins during adolescence (Dishion & Patterson, 2006). The biological vulnerabilities, psychological sequelae of family disruption and foster placement, and social factors such as school instability result in these children having fewer social skills and less successful interaction with prosocial peers. Through the reciprocal interactions between personal traits and environmental reactions and circumstances, antisocial behaviors can become automatic and entrenched responses to new situations (Davis et al., 2004; Dishion & Patterson, 2006). Youth emerging from group homes and juvenile justice settings that lack appropriate and sufficient mental health and rehabilitative services face the challenges of the transition period at a great disadvantage. Those who have been fortunate enough to participate in programs in which caring adults have provided meaningful services may not be ready or able to cope with the demands of life outside an institution without the structure and supports that have enabled them to build coping skills while in care (Todis et al., 2001).

The ages of peak probability of being charged are 18 to 20 years, and this is also the time when youth leave care and have decreased access to the mental health services that might be critically important in fostering desistance. Youth who are 18 or older are treated as adults by the courts and are therefore at risk of more serious consequences from their behavior (Davis et al., 2004). Research provides some suggestions about factors that can promote better outcomes for youth who have spent time in juvenile facilities, suggesting that higher rates of involvement in work and school in the community are associated with lower rates of returning to the correctional system (Bullis et al., 2002). Transition planning and adult support that is caring as well as limit-setting can also help promote resiliency in the transition period (Todis et al., 2001). The following box summarizes practice principles for foster youth emerging from the juvenile justice system.

Key Practice Principles

1. Advocate for adequate clinical resources (staff) to be attached to group care and correctional settings.
2. The one-to-one relationship is critical: provide youth with adult support and monitoring through consistent and frequent contact.
3. Assist youth with seeking and obtaining housing or a transitional living program.
4. Ensure a plan for completion of a high school diploma and post-secondary training or education.
5. Assist youth in developing employment skills, job-seeking skills, and job-maintaining skills.
6. Ensure access to appropriate mental health services, including substance-abuse treatment.
7. Use cross-system collaboration to facilitate youth engagement in prosocial activities and building anetwork of prosocial peer relationships.

PART IV

PROGRAM CONSIDERATIONS

This book argues that a biopsychosocial perspective, knowledge of development, attachment theory, and dynamic systems theory can help us design effective programs and services for youth in transition. Part IV presents groups with special needs within the foster care population, discussion of the transition itself, and a description of programs for transitioning youth.

Chapter 10 focuses on three specific groups: youth with disabilities, LGBT youth, and pregnant and parenting youth. The chapter offers an overview of outcomes and issues for each group, a discussion of the effects of maltreatment, and interaction between the particular issue and development. Services and practice recommendations are described for each group.

Chapter 11 takes up the developmental changes and tasks of emerging adulthood and the transition out of foster care. The topics of education, employment, and relationships are presented in detail, followed by a description of relevant services and practice recommendations.

Chapter 12 provides an overview of outcomes following the exit from care. The chapter includes explanation of independent living programs (ILPs), along with research on their effectiveness. The bulk of the chapter is devoted to transitional living programs, with detailed discussion of key elements, and concludes with recommendations for a developmental, relationship-based approach to programs and services.

10

POPULATIONS NEEDING
SPECIAL ATTENTION

Youth leaving care have widely recognized poor outcomes with regard to education, employment, homelessness, incarceration, substance use, and psychosocial well-being. Among these youth are a smaller number who face even greater challenges: youth with disabilities, LGBT (lesbian, gay, bisexual, transgendered) youth, and pregnant and parenting adolescents. These young people are further marginalized or separated from the main-stream of society; their smaller numbers lead to less representation and greater disenfranchisement. Their multiple diversities, especially for youth of color, can create unique disadvantages in transition planning (Gil-Kashiwabara et al., 2007). This chapter presents an overview of the outcomes and issues for transitioning youth with disabilities, LGBT youth, and pregnant and parenting youth.

Youth with Disabilities: Overview

There is a higher incidence of physical impairments and mental health disorder within the foster care population than in the general public (Anctil et al., 2007). Studies of youth leaving care often exclude those with developmental disabilities, and research on transitioning foster care alumni with disabilities is limited. The studies that do exist suggest that youth leaving foster care with disabilities are less likely to graduate from high school, have social support, be employed, and be self-sufficient than those without disabilities (Geenen & Powers, 2006; Hill, 2009). Estimates of the number of foster care alumni with disabilities range from 50% to 80%; the percentage of youth with disabilities in the juvenile corrections population is estimated at 32% to 50% (Hill, 2009).

While a large percentage of youth in care receive special-education services, the needs of those with disabilities are often ineffectively addressed in the educational and child welfare systems (Geenen & Powers, 2006). In a review comparing findings from the 1987 and 2003 cohorts of the National Longitudinal Transition Study, researchers reported that, in 2003, only 70% of youth with disabilities had completed high school, and disabled youth were only half as likely as youth in the general population to attend post-secondary school (Wagner et al. 2005). Other authors state that youth with disabilities are at higher risk of dropping out of high school, are more likely to have criminal justice system involvement, and are at higher risk for abusing substances and experiencing unplanned pregnancy (Heflinger & Hoffman, 2008; Hill, 2009). The employment rate for youth with disabilities lags significantly behind employment for those in the general population, and those who do work generally find only sporadic employment rather than financial security (Hill, 2009).

Disabilities may be physical, psychological, developmental, or cognitive. Outcomes in different disability categories have some variation. For example, youth with either hearing or visual impairments have the highest rates of high school completion, while those with both, or other multiple disabilities, are least likely of all disability categories to finish high school. Youth with emotional disturbances have the lowest percentage of school completion of any category, and only one in five pursues post-secondary education. By two years after high school, nearly nine of ten youth with emotional disturbances have been in trouble at school, been fired from a job, or been arrested, a dramatic increase between 1987 and 2003. Youth with health impairments other than those of sight or hearing also have very poor outcomes with regard to negative consequences for behavior. Those with multiple disabilities or emotional problems have the weakest affiliations with prosocial community groups (Wagner et al., 2005).

There are some differences in outcomes associated with gender and race. Boys in the 2003 cohort showed significant improvement in high school completion and enrollment in four-year colleges. Girls showed increased post–secondary school enrollment, but primarily at two-year schools. Boys and girls had large increases in receiving negative consequences (arrest, loss of job, trouble at school) for their behavior. White youth experienced significant increases in overall rates of post–secondary education, but youth of color with disabilities did not. African American youth more or less caught up to white youth in having worked for pay by the second cohort of the study (Wagner et al., 2005).

The findings from the two transition cohorts indicate that, in the 16 years between the studies, outcomes improved for youth with hearing or visual impairments only, but outcomes for youth with other disabilities improved very little, or, in some cases, worsened considerably (Wagner et al., 2005). Psychological problems appear to place young people at highest risk of negative outcomes. Forty to sixty percent of youth in foster care have at least one psychiatric disorder, and approximately 33% have three or more diagnosed psychiatric problems. Children with chronic illness and disability are more likely to have mental health and social adjustment problems (dosReis et al., 2001).

Emotional or psychological disorders are classified according to the DSM in mental health systems, whereas educational systems use the "seriously emotionally disturbed" (SED) category. These parallel but different classification systems lead to disparate identification criteria, processes, service usage, and service integration. Assessment and diagnosis processes are comparable across sites within the mental health system. The educational system, however, defines "emotional disturbance" as a condition that adversely affects school performance and involves an inability to learn, an inability to relate appropriately to peers or teachers, pervasive unhappiness, physical symptoms or fears, or other types of inappropriate behaviors (Anderson, 2000).

Identification of the problem in the educational system usually begins with a teacher referral, and an assessment follows. Community agencies are not a part of the process, and because there is no built-in linkage with a DSM diagnosis, a large percentage of students with mental health needs may not receive intervention outside the school setting. On the other hand, children diagnosed with conduct disorder may not receive services in schools because social maladjustment is not explicitly included in the SED criteria. These children may instead be defined as delinquent rather than troubled (Anderson, 2000). Both educational and mental health needs may go unnoticed or unaddressed prior to the age of emancipation, contributing to the poor outcomes described above.

Disability, Maltreatment, and Attachment

A large body of research suggests that children with disabilities are at increased risk of maltreatment compared to children who are not disabled, and another line of research has found an association between disability and insecure parent–infant attachment (Howe, 2006). When children feel frightened or stressed, the attachment system is activated to evoke care or protection from the attachment figure. Children with disabilities may require unusual amounts or types of attuned caregiving, but if their caregivers have unresolved trauma or attachment problems, they may become anxious, dysregulated, or unavailable. Caregivers who feel overwhelmed can become hostile or helpless, resulting in abuse or neglect (Howe, 2006).

The nature of a child's disability affects the caregiver's response and the rate of maltreatment. Child neglect is highest for children with speech and language impairments, followed by mental retardation and health impairment, and lowest for children with autism, visual impairment, or physical disability. Finally, children with speech and language difficulties also suffer the highest rates of physical, sexual, and emotional abuse compared with non-disabled youth. Emotional abuse occurs at rates much higher than all of the other maltreatment categories (Howe, 2006).

Children with disabilities are at heightened risk for disorganized attachment, yet almost half of them are securely attached. Parents who are frightened of or overwhelmed by their child's disability are more likely to experience problematic anxiety or anger in response to it. It is the interaction between the caregiver's internal state and the disabled child's needs that accounts for the quality of the attachment relationship (Howe, 2006). Parental mental illness, substance abuse, and parental history of trauma are important in shaping the parent's response to the child's needs.

Disability and Adolescent Development

Chronic illness or disability can affect biological and psychosocial development. The risk of psychological adjustment problems has been found to vary across disease groups, for example, and also to vary with gender. Girls who are chronically ill have a higher incidence of emotional problems than their healthy peers, but the same is not true for boys. Young adults with asthma often suffer from depression at higher rates than peers, but those with Type I diabetes look more like youth in the general population (Suris, Michaud, & Viner, 2004).

Youth whose conditions require a treatment regimen must also contend with disclosure issues relative to peers and to school or the workplace, and they may themselves struggle with adherence to treatment. They may need help in accepting the need for treatment or, in some cases, in accepting the chronic nature of a condition, illness, or disorder. The adolescent desire for autonomy may conflict with disability-related dependency or treatment.

Youth with disabilities experience the same rapid physical and emotional changes, including an increased interest in social and sexual interactions, as their peers. Issues surrounding sexual behavior may be complicated by physical or emotional disability, and by being treated as asexual or asocial by others (Alexander & Schrauben, 2006). The fact of having a disability may often have obscured other aspects of personality, talents, and sexuality, to others and to the disabled youth. For youth in foster care with disabilities, the adolescent task of exploring and consolidating an identity to take forward into adult life will have many layers.

Disability and Placement

Studies have examined the relationship between placement types and child disabilities. Children with physical health problems are slower to reunify with parents by nearly 40% than those without health problems.

The presence of emotional or behavioral problems, especially externalizing disorders, is associated with a decreased likelihood of reunification among children in both non-relative and kinship foster care. Another study concluded that cognitive, emotional, and physical disabilities are associated with later permanent placement in non-relative foster care compared to reunification (Romney et al.2006).

The presence of a disability has potential continuing effects on the child—on the caregiving environment and early attachments, on the likelihood of maltreatment, and on the likelihood of reunification. The risk of additional mental health problems is heightened as a result, giving rise to vulnerabilities and sobering challenges at the transition to adulthood. Four to ten percent of people with developmental disabilities in the general population display self-harming behaviors, and approximately 90% of individuals who self-harm have severe learning disabilities (Murray, 2003).

Services for Transition Age Youth with Disabilities

The poor transition outcomes of foster care alumni with disabilities prompted legislation to improve discharge planning. The Individuals with Disabilities Education Act (IDEA) was amended in 2004 to require that the Individual Education Plan (IEP) include a transition plan and a description of needed services beginning when the student turns sixteen (Geenen & Powers, 2006; Hill, 2009). The John H. Chafee Foster Care Independence Act gives support through independent living programs and requires that all youth in foster care who are sixteen and older have a written independent living plan describing the services and programs needed during transition. These policies explicitly call for collaboration, but in too many instances this is not occurring (Geenen & Powers, 2006; Hill, 2009).

Transition plans for youth with disabilities are poor in quality in absolute terms and in comparison to special-education youth who are not youth in foster care. Plans for youth in care are significantly less likely to have goals involving independent living skills and post-secondary education, and those goals tend to be vague. Geenen reports that 20% of youth in care with disabilities had no goals listed at all, and of those who had them, only 6.8% of the goals had specific target dates for completion (Geenen & Powers, 2006).

Youth in foster care were not present 29% of the time at meetings held to design IEP transition plans, even when they were identified as the individual responsible for attaining specific goals. Advocates (family members, foster parents, or educational surrogates) were also absent from the majority of IEP and transition plan meetings, and in 40% of cases where a caseworker was to be the person responsible for an action step, no child welfare professional had attended the meeting. In comparisons of IEP transition plans to child-welfare independent living plans, researchers found duplication of services, little overlap, and plans that went in very different directions (Geenen & Powers, 2006). Another researcher found exclusion of certain participants from IEP and other team meetings to be the greatest area of noncompliance with IDEA mandates (Palladino, 2006).

A study of predictors of adult quality of life for foster youth with disabilities found that transition services (employment training, independent living training, resources at exit from care) were a positive predictor of higher educational attainment and self-esteem, and early receipt of mental health services for emotional problems increased their resilience (Anctil et al., 2007). Research indicates that self-determination plays a role in improving outcomes; successful transitions require that adolescents assume more prominent roles in transition planning (Carter et al., 2006; Geenen et al., 2007). Self-determination involves a set of skills, such as goal-setting, choice-making, problem-solving, and expressing ideas; opportunities to practice these skills must be made available (Carter et al., 2006; Geenen et al., 2007). Youth in care with emotional disabilities may have difficulties in these areas stemming from dysregulated stress-response systems and propensities to perceive neutral stimuli as threatening. Their foster care placements may have offered only limited opportunities to develop and practice decision-making skills.

Youth with disabilities will need the assistance of child-welfare and special-education personnel in developing educational and independent living goals. A coordinated network of services should be established in which representatives of both systems participate fully and information is shared (Hill, 2009). Educators, foster parents, and social workers will all need training to assist these youth. Teachers will need to learn more about foster care issues, social workers will need to learn about the educational needs and challenges faced by youth with disabilities, and foster parents will need support and education about the special needs of the youth in their care, especially as they prepare to leave care (Palladino, 2006).

Youth in foster care and their social workers need help in understanding how disability can interact with ethnicity, culture, foster care, and gender (Gil-Kashiwabara et al., 2007), sometimes in problematic ways. For example, a learning-disabled African American male youth who was maltreated as a child may have been in multiple foster homes and schools, and may have experienced school failure, peer rejection, and discrimination based on his disability as well as racial discrimination. His ability to make sense of these negative experiences and to emerge with a sense of hope and self-determination will depend, in great part, on caregivers, social workers, and educators who have an understanding of the dynamic interaction of these factors. This understanding should inform transition plans and the services that follow. The box below summarizes these practice principles.

**Box 10.1 Key Practice Principles for Youth
with Disabilities**

The principles listed here apply to general but necessary service needs of
transitioning youth who carry both foster care and disability statuses.
(Specific interventions for learning and physical disabilities are not covered
here, and mental health treatments are covered in previous chapters.)

1. Support to youth with disabilities should include a caring, stable
   relationship with someone who can provide information and support.
2. Development of self-determination should be a focus; plans should
   include opportunities to try and fail at new activities; youth should
   participate in creating the transition plan.
3. Transition planning should include screening of health needs and
   education about health risks.
4. Youth with disabilities who have experienced a high rate of placement change should receive special services to address mental health
   symptoms and needs.
5. Transition plans should include educational *and* independent living
   goals.
6. Child-welfare and special-education personnel and programs should
   engage in cross-system collaboration in transition planning and
   services.
7. Cross-train educators, foster parents, and social workers.
8. Educate youth in care about their opportunities and supports and
   prepare them to advocate for themselves.

Lesbian, Gay, Bisexual, and Transgendered Youth: Overview

Definitions of terms used to identify sexual orientation are varied; for the
purposes of this chapter, the following definitions will be used. Gay or
lesbian sexual orientation refers to a primary physical and emotional
attraction to persons of the same sex, and bisexual orientation implies
attraction to both males and females. Gender is a more personal and culturally defined construct than one's biological sex and is based upon one's
inner sense of being male or female. Transgendered individuals are those
for whom gender identity differs from biologically defined sex; sexual
orientation among transgendered youth may be difficult to characterize
because sexual orientation varies with both gender and biological sex
(Garofalo et al., 2006).

The concept of sexual orientation is a Western psychological construct
not universally found in or necessarily stigmatized in other cultures. In an
anthropological study, 64% of the societies included viewed same-gender
sexual behavior as normal or socially acceptable for some or all members

of the community. In Western civilization, LGBT sexual orientations depart from gender role expectations and conflict with the Judeo-Christian imperative to procreate (Fukuyama & Ferguson, 2000). Adolescence is a time of questioning and consolidating aspects of one's identity, including sexual dimensions. Ideally, the environmental surround provides sources of validation and encouragement to the adolescent's emerging sense of self. However, despite increased knowledge and acceptance of minority sexual orientations, LGBT youth most often find themselves in a world that lacks the validating reflection, role models, and acceptance that all youth need (Saltzburg, 2005). Institutionalized heterosexuality exerts a constant influence on all aspects of the environmental context in the form of definitions of the family and stereotypes about LGBT individuals and families (Lind, 2004).

LGBT (and questioning) youth in the general population are at increased risk for physical health conditions and limitations, mental health disorders, substance abuse, and suicidal behavior (Cochran & Mays, 2007; Cochran et al., 2007; Grossman & D'Augelli, 2006; Jacobs & Freundlich, 2006). Gay, lesbian, and bisexual students are more than three times as likely as their peers to have attempted suicide in the previous year, are almost five times as likely to have missed school due to safety fears, more than nine times as likely to have used injectable drugs, and are more likely to have experienced sex against their will (Garofalo et al., 1998). One longitudinal study reported that LGBT youth have rates of psychiatric disorders and suicidal behavior 1.9 to 6.2 times higher than other cohort members, and that these risks are most strongly related to sexual orientation (Fergusson, Horwood, & Beautrais, 1999).

Sexual-minority youth experience greater exposure to stressors, particularly in interpersonal domains, than sexual-majority adolescents. The most visible stressor is victimization, which may run the gamut from name calling and jokes to vandalism or physical assault (Ueno, 2005). Forty-six percent of LGBT youth in a 1999 survey reported verbal harassment, 36.4% reported sexual harassment, and 12.1% reported physical assault in their school settings (Saltzburg, 2005). Tellingly, 25% to 40% of homeless youth in New York City identify as LGBT or questioning; research suggests that because these youth are now coming out in their teen years, greater numbers of them are becoming homeless (Nolan, 2006). Sexual-minority youth often experience social isolation because of overt rejection or fear of disclosure (Ueno, 2005).

Among sexual-minority youth, transgendered youth are even more stigmatized. Transgendered individuals exhibit gender-nonconforming identities and behaviors; they include transsexuals, cross-dressers, and gender benders/blenders. Most are heterosexual, but many may not be. Many social structures assume a binary classification of gender, and individuals are expected to assume, not only the gender of their biological sex, but also the expectations and roles that go with it. Inconsistency between biological sex and gender expression is usually not tolerated, and such individuals are marginalized. Biological males are most often targets of verbal and physical abuse (Grossman & D'Augelli, 2006).

It is sometimes assumed that the dual minority status of sexual-minority youth of color generates even greater vulnerability to adverse mental health consequences of discrimination. A recent study, however, found no evidence that the social adversity associated with dual statuses among a sample of Latino and Asian American LGB adults results in higher levels of disorders compared to white LGB individuals. In fact, the two ethnic minority groups appeared to be at similar or somewhat lower risk (Cochran et al., 2007). However, in a study of sexual-minority youth, researchers found that perceptions of homophobia, fear of rejection, and avoidance of disclosure are greater among sexual-minority youth of color compared with white peers (Dube & Savin-Williams, 1999).

Minority Sexual Orientation, Maltreatment, and Attachment

A growing body of research indicates that adult minority sexual orientation is a risk indicator for histories of parental maltreatment during childhood. While it is only one among many risk and protective factors that play a role in child abuse, researchers suggest a number of possible ways in which sexual orientation may contribute to risk. Direct disclosure by a child or adolescent may generate risk; youth with minority sexual orientations may be more likely to engage in other disruptive behaviors that lead to conflict with parents; or children may exhibit more gender-atypical behavior, which evokes a negative parental reaction (Corliss, Cochran, & Mays, 2002). In turn, childhood maltreatment gives rise to negative mental and physical health outcomes, including, especially for gay and bisexual male youth, risky sexual behaviors that can lead to HIV exposure.

As discussed in Chapter 4, maltreatment in childhood is related to the development of insecure attachment. A study that examined the relationships between attachment style and high-risk behaviors among young men who have sex with men (YMSM) found that a history of foster care and childhood abuse increases the chances of developing fearful (anxious) attachment. Those with fearful attachments are more likely to experience homelessness and involvement in sex work. YMSM who identify as heterosexual, and transgender and Latino YMSM who experience multiple sources of stigma, are at particular risk (Gwadz et al., 2004).

Minority Sexual Orientation and Adolescent Development

LGBT youth are self-identifying earlier in adolescence than in years past, with the result that they face the challenges of a stigmatized identity while their cognitive, emotional, and social development is still very much under way (D'Augelli, 2006). Achieving a positive identity, the primary developmental task of adolescence, is complicated by being outside the normative group. LGBT youth who are also in foster care are marginalized because of differences that they have not chosen but that affect them on a daily basis. Sexual-minority youth are subject to bullying, harassment, and physical violence in their neighborhoods, schools, and in foster care placements (Harper & Schneider, 2003). The need to fit in and the fear of stigma and discrimination may cause youth to delay openly self-identifying, with the result that the task of a positive identity formation is forestalled (Alexander & Schrauben, 2006; Price, 2003). Youth may react to the sense of being different by socially isolating themselves and many develop low self-esteem, which may lead to vulnerability to sexual exploitation and risky behaviors (Price, 2003). (A detailed discussion of sexual identity development appeared in Chapter 5.)

Sexual exploration is a normal part of adolescence; heterosexual youth learn about their form of sexuality in sex education classes in school. It is a more stressful process for LGBT youth, who must discover their sexual experiences in a context of distorted stereotypes, rejection, harassment, and fear (Morrow, 2004). Those who are fearful of disclosure to peers may seek out adults to express their sexuality, leading to the potential for exploitation (Price, 2003). Foster care placements, and particularly group home settings, may be especially problematic because of the anticipation of lack of support at best and rejection or removal at worst.

It is profoundly challenging to develop a sense of self free of stigma in a context of discrimination, institutionalized homophobia, rejection by peers or family members, harassment, and victimization related to one's sexual self. Internalized stigma causes delays in identity formation, poor self-esteem, and feelings of guilt, shame, and self-loathing. Self-identification at a younger age can bring greater stress, more negative social pressure, and a greater need for support. Youth in foster care must manage a stigmatized identity without support from parents or other family, who may in fact have been rejecting or abusive (Ryan & Futterman, 2001).

In communities of color, family support and the ethnic community are essential to constructing a positive ethnic identity; but for LGBT youth of color, there is rarely support for minority sexual identities (Ryan & Futterman, 2001). Perceptions of homophobia, fear of rejection, and avoidance of disclosure appear to be greater among sexual-minority youth of color. Sexual identity must be integrated with and accepted in the context of an ethnic identity (Dube & Savin-Williams, 1999), but among Asian Americans, where the traditional family unit is highly valued and hierarchical, the continuity of the family name is more important to identity than is sexuality. Latin American cultures also place high value on family unity, welfare, and honor. Gender role expectations are clear: lesbianism violates these, as does male homosexual behavior in which a man takes the passive role. In the African American community, homosexuality may be seen as jeopardizing community support (Fukuyama & Ferguson, 2000).

Undisclosed sexual minority orientation is an invisible stigma, requiring careful and constant monitoring of one's interactions and management of both fear of exposure and losses consequent to disclosure. Youth may turn to anonymous sex to protect themselves from being known homosexuals, increasing the risk of STDs and HIV. The stress of hiding sexual identity can be extreme, yet openness may lead to discrimination and abuse (Ryan & Futterman, 2001). The young person treads a perilous path. Sexual identity distress plays a role in shaping the health status of LGBT youth and is strongly related to general psychological distress (Wright & Perry, 2006). LGBT individuals have consistently been found to be at higher risk for suicidal behaviors than their heterosexual counterparts, and the majority of suicide attempts occur in adolescence or early adulthood (McDaniel, Purcell, & D'Augelli, 2001). On the other hand, and importantly, many homosexual and transgendered individuals do not report significant psychological suffering (PDM Task Force, 2006).

LGBT Youth in Foster Care

Approximately 5% to 10% of the general population is estimated to be LGBT. In a foster care population of 244,000 youth aged 11 or older, there may be 12,000 to 24,000 LGBT adolescents, yet most states fail to acknowledge or address the unique needs and hazards of these youth, and no states mandate training for foster care parents and professionals on nondiscrimination (Sullivan, Sommer, & Moff, 2001). Further, LGBT youth in the child welfare and juvenile justice systems are routinely left unprotected from violence and harassment, subjected to differential treatment, or denied appropriate services (Estrada & Marksamer, 2006).

LGBT youth may have been rejected by their families of origin due to their sexual orientation or gender identity, or they may disclose their sexual orientation or gender identity while in care. Often they are not reunited with their birth families, and they may lack permanent connections to their communities and families of origin. Many run away from group homes or are placed in psychiatric facilities. LGBT youth often experience multiple unstable placements and are sometimes ejected due to staff discomfort with their sexual orientation. Transgendered youth are unlikely to be placed with foster families, and are frequently placed in group care where they do not receive needed services, and physical and sexual abuse are a risk (Jacobs & Freundlich, 2006).

One study indicated that 100% of LGBT youth in New York City group homes reported verbal harassment by peers, staff, or other providers; 70% reported physical violence; and 56% reported living on the streets for a while because they felt safer there than in their group or foster homes (Jacobs & Freundlich, 2006). LGBT youth need support and advocacy, especially as agency policies and procedures themselves often communicate a lack of acceptance or may screen out gay and lesbian foster parents who might have provided support or mentorship (Ragg, Patrick, & Ziefert, 2006).

Services for LGBT Youth

Attention to the needs of LGBT youth should begin with changes in the foster care and mental health systems, including the enactment of legislation such as the California Foster Care Nondiscrimination Act (AB 458), which prohibits discrimination within the foster care system (Jacobs & Freundlich, 2006). Foster parents, group home staff, and child welfare professionals should receive mandatory training on minority sexual orientation (Jacobs & Freundlich, 2006; Sullivan et al., 2001). Attempts should be made to recruit LGBT foster parents, who have historically been excluded. Programs that match LGBT teens with foster parents who are able and willing to take them have shown some evidence of success (Gilliam, 2004). There is a need for mental health and health-related service providers who are knowledgeable about work with LGBT youth. Too often, they are ill prepared (Davis, Satzburg, & Locke, 2009), demonstrate lack of knowledge about LGBT issues, and display heterosexist and homophobic attitudes (Morrison & L'Heureux, 2001). The staff working with LGBT youth in foster care and transitional living programs must create safe, respectful, and affirming environments for them.

Sexual-minority youth, especially youth of color, need opportunities to resolve the fears, lack of trust, and sense of rejection associated with experiences of discrimination or internalized homophobia. LGBT youth need help in developing tools to cope with societal bias (Saltzburg, 2005); contact with other youth who share these experiences and concerns can provide support, decrease isolation, and instill hope. LGBT-focused youth centers have been found to be crucial sources of emotional and social support for participants (Davis et al., 2009). Transgendered youth, especially of color, however, may feel disconnected from the greater gay and lesbian community, which is often seen as largely white and not supportive of transgenders (Garofalo et al., 2006). It may be necessary to make stronger efforts at outreach to these youth.

LGBT youth attempt suicide at a considerably higher rate than their heterosexual peers, make up a disproportionate number of "successful" youth suicides, and are at increased risk for a number of other problems (D'Augelli, 2006; Morrison & L'Heureux, 2001). Screening and assessment are vital to providing appropriate services, and must take into account specific circumstances of the individual youth, as well as differences in gender, age, race, and ethnicity that may further define the incidence of risk behaviors. Gay males, for example, generally have more risks for STDs, suicide, and substance abuse than do lesbian youth, but there are also wide individual differences that moderate or influence risk level (Alexander & Schrauben, 2006). Inquiry about feelings of hopelessness, use of substances, and risky sexual behaviors should be part of the assessment, along with direct questions about harassment at school or at work (McDaniel et al., 2001; Walls, Freedenthal, & Wisneski, 2008). The safety of a client's living and work situation is a critical part of the assessment.

Only about 10% of gay youth report being offered a chance to discuss sexual-orientation issues in the clinical setting, yet a majority of these youth say they would have welcomed such conversations (Alexander & Schrauben, 2006). Clinicians need to provide the opportunity for this discussion to take place by including the topic of sexuality as a part of the initial engagement. The extent of positive LGBT identity development is critical to an overall sense of well-being, and clinicians should seek to determine the status of the client's self-acceptance. The level of disclosure is related to self-acceptance: the more comfortable youth are with their LGBT identities, the more likely they are to disclose their sexual orientation. Clinicians must respect clients' levels of "outness," and refrain from pushing them to disclose beyond their comfort levels (Morrow, 2004).

Interventions for LGBT youth should take into account the attachment issues that are often associated with histories of maltreatment and foster care, and which have been further complicated by experiences of discrimination, rejection, exploitation, and harassment. Fearful attachment styles and negative representations can be explored within a therapeutic relationship that offers safety, acceptance, and a secure base from which to explore identity, including sexual identity. The attachment perspective points to the potential power of positive therapeutic relationship experiences to build different representations of the self and the world in place of re-enacting devalued-self views through high-risk behaviors and relationships.

Box 10.2 Key Practice Principles for LGBT Youth

1. Address discrimination, safety issues, and lack of support within the foster care system, via recruitment of LGBT-friendly foster parents and staff and mandatory training of foster parents, group home staff, and child welfare professionals on minority sexual orientation and gender identity.
2. Staffs of agencies providing aftercare should be diverse in gender identity and sexual orientation to provide mentorship and role modeling.
3. Agency environments and clinicians must provide safe and respectful environments for disclosure. Clinicians must provide opportunities for safe discussion of sexual identity issues.
4. Assessment processes should include consideration of status of identity development, including LGBT identity.

Box 10.2 Key Practice Principles for LGBT Youth (*cont.*)

5. Risk assessment should include ascertaining feelings of hopelessness, substance use, safety, suicidality, exposure to harassment and discrimination, health conditions and practices, and risky sexual behaviors.
6. Agencies and professionals need to be knowledgeable about resources for health education, STDs and HIV, and treatment of physical and mental health problems. Transgendered youth need appropriate medical care.
7. Be mindful of anxious or avoidant attachment patterns, and internalized homophobia that may be influencing youths' risky behaviors.
8. Professionals should be knowledgeable about community groups and supports for LGBT youth.

Pregnant and Parenting Youth: Overview

Becoming a parent before age 25 represents a risk for poor developmental outcomes as individuals make the transition into adulthood (McMahon, 2010). Early childbearing, a history of child abuse or neglect, and the foster care experience itself combine to make adolescent mothers in foster care an especially vulnerable group (Budd, Holdsworth, & HoganBruen, 2006). While the United States has the highest rate of adolescent pregnancies among developed countries, foster care alumni are more likely than girls in the general population to have been pregnant and to have carried a pregnancy to term (Budd et al., 2006; Sieger & Renk, 2007). In a recent study, at least 30% of female alumni had been pregnant more than once, and nearly 25% of them had at least two children. On average, they gave birth to their first child when they were 17.8 years old, but close to one-third had given birth by age 16 (Dworsky & DeCoursey, 2009). One-third of females in the first wave of a three-state, longitudinal study of emancipated foster youth had been pregnant, compared with less than one-fifth of their peers in a national sample. Two-thirds of those pregnancies were described as unwanted (Courtney, Terao, & Bost, 2004). In the second wave of the same study, 32% of the females and 14% of the males had had at least one child by age 19, and fully one-half of the girls had been pregnant by age 19 (Budd et al., 2006).

Risk Factors

Factors that have been identified as placing girls at risk for early pregnancy include teen pregnancy of the girl's mother, poor academic performance or dropping out of school, low self-esteem, substance-abuse disorders, lack of family closeness, and a history of sexual abuse (Jampolskaya, Brown, & Greenbaum, 2002; Roosa et al., 1997; Saewyc, Magee, & Pettingell, 2004). Research offers mixed findings as to the relationship between adolescent motherhood and child abuse and neglect, with less support for a link with physical child abuse or neglect than with sexual abuse (de Paul & Domenech, 2000). In a study examining the relative contribution of childhood sexual abuse, Roosa et al. concluded that social class, ethnicity, age at first coitus, not using birth control at first coitus, and sexual abuse by a boyfriend were significant predictors of teen pregnancy. Of these, early coitus that is voluntary and non-use of birth control at first coitus were the most significant (Roosa et al., 1997). Experiencing sexual abuse by both a family member and a non-relative constitutes a profound risk factor for a number of poor outcomes, including teenage pregnancy, and sexually abused males appear to be at greater risk of fathering a child than their non-abused peers (Saewyc et al., 2004).

Estimates of the rate of teen pregnancy among sexual-minority youth are two to seven times higher than among their heterosexual peers. Lesbian, gay, and bisexual youth are more likely to report a history of sexual abuse and teen pregnancy involvement than heterosexual peers (Saewyc et al., 2004). The risk of pregnancy increases with an earlier sexual debut, more frequent intercourse, more sexual partners, substance use before sex, and ineffective or no method of contraception. Sexually abused adolescents or those who are homeless are more likely to engage in these risk behaviors and to be exposed to sexual exploitation. LGBT youth may avoid disclosure or engage in "camouflage" behaviors (heterosexual unprotected sex or pregnancy itself) to avoid identification and discrimination or harassment (Nair, 2008; Saewyc et al., 2008).

Community characteristics play a role in teen pregnancy rates, with low income being most significant. Race and ethnicity have a statistically significant but small effect on adolescent birthrates, after controlling for education, poverty, and employment. In a Chicago study of pregnant or parenting youth in foster care, 86% were African American (Dworsky & DeCoursey, 2009), and another study of youth in care reported that African-American girls were three times more likely to be pregnant or parenting than white girls (Haight et al., 2009). Among ethnic communities, the birth rate was lower in those that were more ethnically homogeneous (Kirby, Coyle, & Gould, 2001). In some ethnic groups, adolescent pregnancy may serve as a means to gain status, solidify kin networks, or become independent (Sieger & Renk, 2007). Earlier studies of the relationship between ethnicity and teen fatherhood suggested that educational disadvantage and problem behaviors are related to the lack of pathways to adult status for young, urban males of color (Thornberry, Smith, & Howard, 1997), but further investigation is needed.

Foster Care and Teen Pregnancy

Young mothers in foster care in a British study had high levels of family disruption, with long spells in care, lack of continuity in care, and placement in residential care. In residential (group) homes, young people often experienced high levels of sexual exploitation and pressure to engage in sex, possibly exacerbated by lack of boundaries and lack of guidance and information from social workers (Barn & Mantovani, 2007). Number of placements appears to make a difference: in a California study, those with five or more placements were more than twice as likely to become pregnant before emancipation as those with only one placement, and nearly one-third of those emancipated had had more than five placements (Children's Law Center of Los Angeles, 2004).

At age 21, 71% of the young women in the three-state longitudinal Midwest Study of foster care alumni outcomes report having been pregnant, in comparison to only one-third of their peers in a national sample. The majority of the youth who had been in care had repeat pregnancies, and the majority of the national sample did not. By age 21, 55% of female foster care alumni and 29% of males were parents (Courtney et al., 2007). Early parenthood and, in particular, having more than one child is a significant barrier to educational attainment among female foster care alumni, and each additional child further reduces the odds of graduating from high school or completing a General Educational Development diploma by 45% (Dworsky & DeCoursey, 2009).

Attachment and Early Parenting

Living in foster or kinship care is significantly associated with high-risk reproductive behaviors, and foster care is associated with early first conception and more than the median number of partners (Carpenter et al., 2001). Attachment-related issues, such as the desire for closeness and connection, are understudied dimensions of teen pregnancy. Most research focuses on characteristics of the subjects, giving little attention to underlying or motivating factors.

Research suggests that sex in teens' relationships is delayed when adolescents feel connected to and supported by their parent(s), and that teen pregnancy is associated with unmet intimacy and affectional needs (Pistole, 1999). In a romantic relationship, the adolescent may use sex to maintain proximity (prevent the boy from abandoning her). Physical closeness and touch may provide a feeling of being cared for and comforted. When the longing for connection is combined with a lack of investment in school and little knowledge about or access to methods of contraception, the risk of early pregnancy is likely to increase. Some adolescents see having a baby as having someone to love who will never leave.

Ericka, described in Chapter 9, had two pregnancies early in her life, at a time when she had little emotional support, no investment in school, and had sustained many losses. Being a single parent is challenging, but the relationships with her young sons provide love and lasting attachments.

The quality of early relationships with parents and exposure to psychosocial stress affect the onset of puberty, and evidence confirms the link between early caretaking, psychosocial stress, and acceleration of pubertal development in girls. Positive early relationships with parents are associated with delay in the onset of puberty, and negative parenting in early to middle childhood is associated with early menarche (McMahon, 2010). When puberty occurs early and in the context of unstable, adverse conditions (family disruption and foster care, for example), pair bonding and sexual intercourse often begin sooner, and relationships are not enduring.

The internalized working model of early attachment experiences is present during adolescence and forms the basis of caregiving and sexual expression in the romantic relationships of early adulthood. Adverse childhood experience and entry into foster care can generate and promote insecure attachment. Anxious attachment is associated with engaging in sex to affirm self-esteem and diminish emotional distress, as well as with having more partners, earlier sexual relationships, and more use of drugs or alcohol during sex (McMahon, 2010). The young person with an avoidant attachment may avoid comforting types of touch, but be able to tolerate sexual behavior (Pistole, 1999).

Psychosocial Issues

The risks and outcomes associated with teen parenthood are widely reported in the literature. Early parenting has consequences for both parent and child. Pregnant or parenting teens are more likely than their peers to drop out of school and have reduced educational achievement, are more likely to receive welfare or live in poverty, have a lower income, and have higher rates of behavioral and psychological problems (Jampolskaya et al., 2002; Letourneau, Steward, & Barnfather, 2004; Monahan, 2002). Teenage mothers have diminished employment success and an increased risk of single parenthood (Turner, Sorenson, & Turner, 2000). They are less likely to receive prenatal care (Carpenter et al., 2001), and their babies have lower birth weights and are at risk for prematurity and health problems (Jampolskaya et al., 2002).

Teen mothers may be less accessible and less sensitive to their toddlers, who are at higher risk for maltreatment and changes in primary caregiver (Carpenter et al., 2001). The children of DCFS wards are especially vulnerable; 22% of mothers in a teen-parenting service network for youth in care (Dworsky & DeCoursey, 2009) were investigated for child abuse or neglect, and 11% had a child placed in foster care (Dworsky & DeCoursey, 2009). It is also true, as in the case of Ericka, that early parenting benefits and strengthens a positive sense of oneself as someone who can provide love and care. The new role can serve as a catalyst, motivating the young person to return to school or engage in vocational training. The opportunity to provide for a child the kind of mothering one wished for but never had can function as a reparative experience.

The literature on consequences for young fathers is much more limited. There is some evidence that the psychosocial adjustment of young fathers is poorer than that of their peers in adulthood. They are less likely to live with their children, less likely to provide financial support to them, more likely to remain involved in illegal activity, more likely to be receiving public entitlements, less likely to see their children, and more likely to be living in a second family with children they did not conceive (McMahon, 2010).

Findings on self-esteem and mental health problems are mixed and difficult to disentangle, as some of the literature looks at teen pregnancy and parenting in the general population, with a much smaller body of research on the foster care population. A small, qualitative study of resilient African-American adolescent mothers in transition from foster care found that cultural beliefs that placed a positive value on children and motherhood, spirituality, and community support contributed to resiliency (Haight et al., 2009). Some evidence suggests that pregnant and parenting youth have higher rates of depression, externalizing problems (Sieger & Renk, 2007), substance-abuse and status-offending (Lanctot & Smith, 2001), lowered aspirations for the future, and difficulty forming and maintaining relationships (Barn & Mantovani, 2007).

Parenting and Development

Adolescent parents in foster care must deal with the tasks of adolescence as well as the tasks of pregnancy and parenthood, and they must navigate this larger number of roles while struggling with unresolved childhood adversity and an as-yet-undeveloped personal identity (de Paul & Domenech, 2000). Their own experiences as children have generally given them few models of effective parenting, and their unrealistic childrearing expectations appear to be a marker for later parenting stress (Budd et al., 2006).

The risks to children of adolescent mothers begin in utero. Pregnant adolescents are at greater risk for pregnancy-induced hypertension, preterm labor and delivery, low birthweight, and birth complications (Irvine et al., 1997). Their babies spend more time in female-headed households, experience more poverty, have less permanent relationships with their fathers, and are more likely to have multiple childcare figures (Sieger & Renk, 2007). Many female youth in foster care receive some prenatal care, but in 22% of pregnancies, prenatal care begins very late or not at all (Dworsky & DeCoursey, 2009).

About one-third of adolescent mothers in foster care report having some degree of problem with parenting (Children's Law Center of Los Angeles, 2004). Teen mothers, in general, are at risk for abusing their own children, during infancy and during childhood (de Paul & Domenech, 2000; Dworsky & DeCoursey, 2009). Maternal depression that may have resulted from childhood neglect or abuse can affect the quality of parenting (Gilson & Lancaster, 2008). In a study examining the role of social support, researchers report that 42% of the children of the teen parent sample were maltreated, 36% showed externalizing behavior problems, and 10.8% showed internalizing problems. They lagged in cognitive abilities and repeated a grade more often than their peers. The study demonstrated that children whose mothers receive family support, return to school, enter a stable marriage, or restrict further childbearing have better outcomes (Sieger & Renk, 2007). However, for most youth in foster care, social supports are slim if they are present at all.

Services for Pregnant and Parenting Youth

Strategies and services for pregnant and parenting foster care alumni and their children should address prevention; mental and physical health; and psychosocial dimensions, such as social support, educational goals and plans, and support specifically related to parenting. The economic and housing circumstances of teen parents should be explored as a routine part of service planning. Because teen mothers often experience their status as a stigmatized identity, they may avoid situations where they anticipate discomfort, including the very social service agencies, schools, and prenatal care clinics that they need, to protect themselves (Fessler, 2005). Services must be offered in an environment that is nonjudgmental and accepting if they are to succeed at all. Positive change in maternal self-esteem is a predictor of continued resiliency; providers must ensure that the needs of young parents are met in ways that enhance their feelings of self-efficacy (Weed, Keogh, & Borkowski, 2006).

"Prevention" most often refers to education about safe sex and contraception, but it should also attend to the underlying motivations that may be involved in early sexual activity. A key assumption in the conceptual models of many teen pregnancy prevention programs is that it is possible to modify aspects of a teen mother's life that predispose her to rapid repeat pregnancies by supporting her efforts to use contraception and to pursue a career in addition to motherhood. Results of a recent study indicate that increasing access to and promoting the use of contraception were ineffective in preventing pregnancy (Stevens-Simon, Kelly, & Kulick, 2001). Adolescents in foster care may need help in distinguishing between sex and the longing for connection, security, or comfort.

The mental and physical health of pregnant and parenting youth, and of their children, should be assessed early. Developmental status of mothers, fathers, and children along biological, psychological, and social dimensions should be conducted at the point of planning services for a given individual or family. Pregnant and parenting youth are negotiating the challenges of being simultaneously parents and adolescents, and may need help with sidelined tasks of identity development so that they can plan for and safeguard their own futures as they also try to meet the needs of their children.

For many pregnant adolescents, a history of sexual or physical abuse may have disrupted developmental processes and undermined their self-worth, and given rise to a range of mental health problems (Boyer & Fine, 1992). Assessment should include screening for substance use and trauma history, and programs should provide treatment for both pre-existing and acute mental health problems. Teen mothers have unique health needs and risks; medical care must be sensitive to and cognizant of risks associated with early childbearing, both to infants and to their mothers (Irvine et al., 1997).

Adolescent mothers are less likely than older mothers to complete high school or attend college (Letourneau et al., 2004), but if they are able to stay in school and complete high school or beyond, more positive outcomes are evident for their children and themselves (Sadler, Swartz, & Ryan-Krause, 2003). Educational interventions can help adolescents set educational goals, and improve their ability to attend school consistently by assisting them in arranging child care. Services that enable youth to be successful and invested in school, such as academic program planning, career counseling, and tutoring, should be offered. Pregnant adolescents may need help in overcoming their fears of negative or stigmatizing experiences in the school setting.

Group experiences can offer teen parents social support, social contact, and opportunities to learn about parenting. Groups for adolescent mothers in foster care, for example, were found to have considerable appeal to young mothers. Young fathers should also be included in services, whether as part of a couple or on their own. Adolescent couples can be sources of emotional and practical support for each other, and for other teen parents (Haight et al., 2009). Professionals can help adolescent mothers develop appropriate parenting skills and expectations of their children's development. They can observe and assess the youth's parenting beliefs, childrearing skills, and interactions with their children in order to identify those who are at high risk for parenting stress (Budd et al., 2006).

Box 10.3 Key Practice Principles for Pregnant and Parenting Youth

1. Prevention and intervention should include attention to underlying motivations involved in early sexual activity.
2. Early and continuous prenatal care during pregnancy should be part of work with pregnant youth. Cross-system collaboration should include postnatal care for mothers and well-baby care for infants.
3. Provide education on safe-sex education and prevention of repeat pregnancies.
4. Conduct thorough developmental, psychological, and health assessment, including trauma history.
5. Help male, and especially female, youth stay in school or return to school.
6. Attend to parenting knowledge and skills.
7. Help pregnant and parenting youth identify, establish, and better utilize informal and formal sources of support, including social services, community groups, family members and other concerned adults, school personnel, and self-help groups.
8. Help pregnant and parenting youth negotiate the challenges of being simultaneously parents and adolescents.
9. Attend to identity issues, including maltreatment history, stigmatized identities, self-esteem, and attachment.

Conclusion

Youth in foster care require special attention as they move toward adulthood, but within this population, smaller groups, such as the ones described in this chapter, require additional support to make successful transitions. Youth who are multiply stigmatized or marginalized by society have a more circuitous path to a positive sense of self, the foundation for adult life.

All youth need opportunities to develop their decision-making capacity, social competence, sexual and social relationships, educational and employment skills, and a set of values and philosophy of life that can guide their future choices and decisions. Our services, programs, and policies should be constructed with an eye to reducing the barriers and obstacles in their paths. In the next chapter, we will turn to the specific developmental challenges of the transition years.

11

TRANSITION TO ADULTHOOD: EDUCATION, EMPLOYMENT, AND RELATIONSHIPS

> *Because of the institutional environments I was raised in, I had never learned how to manage relationships with adults or peers, to learn progressive responsibility, or to feel or take responsibility. I was so unbelievably lonely, scared and depressed when I exited care. I felt like everyone else in the world was connected and I was just a free blowing leaf. The grief was pretty intense.*
>
> —Jessica

Turning 18 usually signals more beginnings than endings: the arrival of the age of majority in some states, voting rights, the freedom to make decisions in many important domains, the beginning of college. For youth in the foster care system, it often signals the end of life as they have known it. Most young people in the general population experience a gradual shift from the parental context into one that is more self-defined, but for youth leaving care, the change is abrupt and dramatic.

Development from infancy through middle adolescence was discussed in Chapters 3, 4, and 5; here we pick up the developmental thread at the age of transition from care, which coincides with the developmental phase of emerging adulthood. This chapter provides an overview of important biological, psychological, and social developments of this period, including the separation from foster care, decisions about education and career, and relationships with significant others. The chapter concludes with recommended principles of practice related to education, employment, and relationships, some of which will inform the discussion of programs in Chapter 12.

Overview of Emerging Adulthood

Before the increased interest in gerontology in the 1950s, child development experts assumed that development was largely complete by the end of adolescence (Levinson, 1986). Since then, the two ends of the life-course have received the lion's share of research interest, but adulthood and early adulthood have received greater attention in recent years. There is currently theoretical and empirical recognition of this transitional period as a distinct phase—emerging adulthood—during which there is greater separation and independence from parent figures, accompanied by relative independence from social roles and normative expectations (Arnett, 2000).

The young person begins to form a place as an adult in the adult world (Levinson, 1986), learning to take responsibility for himself or herself, make independent decisions, and become financially self-sufficient (Cronce & Corbin, 2010). The transitional period is not a universal life stage; in some cultures, adulthood is signified by entry into marriage, which often takes place at 16 to 18 for girls and 18 to 20 for boys, precluding an extended period of exploration (Arnett, 2000).

Emerging adults are no longer embedded within their families of origin (or foster families or the foster care system), but commitments to adult roles and responsibilities have not yet occurred. The dynamic relations between the individual and the sociocultural contexts of development are in flux as self-regulation replaces regulation by others (Tanner, 2006).

Biological Changes in Post-Adolescence

As noted in earlier chapters, brain development continues into adulthood. In a study comparing MRIs of young adults with those of adolescents, researchers found reductions in gray matter and increased white matter (myelination) in the peripheral regions of the cortex. Myelination makes possible more effective transfer of signals and information, and these changes facilitate improved cognitive processing. In addition, areas of the frontal lobes that are essential for response inhibition, emotional regulation, and planning and organization continue to develop between adolescence and young adulthood (Nelson et al., 2004; Sowell et al., 1999). The emerging adult is increasingly capable of managing behavior and feelings and of engaging in the cognitive processes that work and higher education entail.

Cognitive development during this period involves increases in the capacity to think abstractly, consider multiple dimensions of problems, and reflect on one's own behavior and experience. These changes enable the kind of planning necessary for achieving educational and occupational goals and allow for relationships in which mutuality, empathy, and consideration are possible (Zarrett & Eccles, 2006).

Psychological Development

Emerging adult development builds on previous development and influences all future development (Tanner, 2006). The individual's childhood and adolescent experiences of self, others, and the world are carried forward into interactions with new circumstances and the demands of leaving home or leaving care. School, family, and the caregiving surround have provided scaffolding to the developing child and adolescent; leaving these contexts thrusts the young person back on her or his own resources to a much greater degree.

An important issue is learning to balance dependency and self-determination. Ties with parents or caregivers must be renegotiated. Separation and individuation, once thought of as disengaging from dependent ties in the service of enhanced autonomy, are now more commonly viewed as a complex interplay between the need for self-determination and the need for interpersonal relatedness (Gnaulati & Heine, 2001). When youth age out of care, their ties with their caregivers are often completely severed, precluding potential benefits that might result from the give-and-take of gradual shifts in dependency.

In a study exploring gender and ethnic differences in the separation-individuation process, researchers report that men's and women's patterns look similar, with two exceptions: men are more likely to deny their needs for close attachments, and women are more inclined to maintain close interpersonal connections, but only in peer relationships. The authors describe some differences between white and non-white ethnic groups, but none among non-white groups. African American young people show heightened reliance on caregivers for direction, reduced investment in the attachment to teachers, an increased tendency to anticipate rejection, and greater difficulty negotiating comfortable levels of closeness. Asian Americans show greater propensity than whites to deny the value of dependency needs, greater tendency to experience intimacy as engulfing, and more reliance on caregiver support. White and Hispanic groups show the fewest differences, with Hispanic Americans showing a greater propensity to depend heavily on caregivers for nurturance and to be more prone to engulfment fears (Gnaulati & Heine, 2001).

Career development in late adolescence is a central challenge of identity formation; research suggests that progress in resolving career development tasks is an expression of the general identity-exploration process (Lucas, 1997). A systems perspective identifies family, school, workplace, peer group, and the larger contexts of ethnicity, culture, and socioeconomic status as contributors to the process of career development (Iglehart & Becerra, 2002; Young, 1983). Family members and significant others such as teachers and social workers influence the young person's aspirations by suggesting what kinds of futures might be possible. When working is necessary for financial reasons, higher education or vocational training may not be an option for foster care alumni, and career identity exploration must be put aside. Early parenthood, occurring in high numbers among foster care alumni, is another obstacle to thinking about the fulfillment and self-expression dimensions of work.

The sense of self is still very much a work in progress for the emerging adult. In addition to a work and career identity, the young person is exploring a relationship identity. Exploration of these aspects of the self is made possible by delaying the assumption of adult roles, such as marriage and parenthood (Booth, Rustenbach, & McHale, 2008). Internal capacities such as affect regulation, impulse control, and the sense of efficacy or agency undergird exploration and experimentation of emerging adulthood. Childhood maltreatment and disturbed or disrupted attachments with significant others can compromise the optimal development of these capacities and the sense of oneself as worthwhile. The ability to pursue an education, maintain employment, initiate and sustain friendships and romantic relationships, and to find meaning in new roles rests on the solid or shaky foundation of these ego strengths.

Ethnic Identity Development

Positive ethnic identity is associated with higher self-esteem and better outcomes in academic success and mental health (White et al., 2008). Development of the ethnic sense of self begins in infancy and continues into adulthood. Many emerging adults face new situations in which race, ethnicity, or culture is made salient, and a reexamination of these issues may ensue. Individuals have varying degrees of need to confront and deal with ethnic issues; the environment is a critical determinant of the timing, duration, and nature of ethnic identity exploration in the transitional years (Phinney, 2006).

For many youth of color, being seen as different and as a minority is a constant throughout life, and many have had numerous experiences of discrimination. Sensitivity to discrimination varies from one person to another. Those who perceive more discrimination are likely to engage in more identity exploration, and some believe that ethnic identity resolution is critical to decisions in other areas of life (Phinney, 2006).

Most studies of ethnic identity have not focused on youth in foster care; in one such study however, black and Hispanic youth in care show a stronger sense of ethnic identity than white youth. They have more desire to learn about their ethnicity and have learned more about it, despite the difficulties sometimes presented by frequent placement moves (White et al., 2008). A sense of personal efficacy is enhanced by proactive orientation and socialization conveyed by parents; the lack of such parental ethnic socialization may be a factor in the social maladaptation of some African American and Latino adolescents in foster care (Yancey, Aneshensel, & Driscoll, 2001).

Individuals who are bicultural or multicultural must sort out their identifications with the culture(s) of their parents, the larger society, and possibly the culture of other caregivers. Moving into the broader worlds of work or higher education can lead to questioning of traditional cultural values, and to questions about oneself. Those who are biracial or multi-racial sometimes struggle with racial identity, connected with appearance, as well as ethnic identity, relating to the sense of group belonging (Phinney, 2006). Again, removal from one's family complicates the process of identification, especially if the culture or race of substitute caregivers does not reflect aspects of one's own race or culture.

Leaving Foster Care

In 2008, Congress unanimously passed the Fostering Connections to Success and Increasing Adoptions Act of 2008, amending parts B and E of Title IV of the Social Security Act to improve outcomes for children in foster care, support relative caregivers, provide for tribal foster care, and for other purposes (U.S. Congressional Research Service, 2008). The Act enables states, at their option, to support foster youth until the age of 21 when they are either completing high school or an equivalency program, enrolled in post-secondary or vocational school, employed or participating in a program to move them into employment, or unable to do any of these things due to a medical condition. Legislative amendments over the past two decades have been aimed at providing additional support to transition-aged youth. In practice, few states have allowed them to remain in care beyond age 18 because federal reimbursement has been limited to those under 18, or 19 if high school graduation or completion was likely to occur before the nineteenth birthday (Courtney, Dworsky, & Peters, 2009). Much of the research on emancipation outcomes predates the cohort of youth affected by this legislation, and the majority of youth who are currently in the transition years have not had the advantage of remaining in care until age 21.

Outcomes

Research demonstrates that those who leave care at 18 have worse outcomes than those who remain in care longer (McCoy, McMillen, & Spitznagel, 2008). After one year, for example, only 38% of those who had found employment were still employed. Of those who were employed, 90% earned less than $10,000 per year; 50% experienced extreme financial hardship (Henig, 2009). A large national study of youth involved with the child welfare system found that transition-age youth were twice as likely to be experiencing economic hardship as their peers in the general population; 29% of them were living with at least one child, and 60% of these reported living in households at or below the poverty level (Southerland, Casanueva, & Ringeisen, 2009).

Youth with a foster care history are at greater risk for mental health problems, and those at risk are four times more likely to report a recent history of arrest (Southerland et al., 2009). Involvement with the criminal justice system is much higher among foster care alumni than the general population; Henig (2009) reports that 31% to 42% of foster care alumni had been arrested, and 18% to 26% had been incarcerated. Others report that the rate of arrest among youth aging out of care is 32% (Southerland et al., 2009); or, in another study, that males in this population have an arrest rate of 81%, compared with only 17% of their peers (Courtney et al., 2009).

Almost half of transition-age youth in a sample of youth involved with the child welfare system were found to be at risk for at least one mental health problem, and more than one quarter of them scored in the clinical range for major depression, a rate nearly three times that of the general population (Southerland et al., 2009). A study of foster care alumni following discharge reported that 14% suffered from depression and 21% from PTSD, and that both groups had high rates of comorbidity. Researchers speculated that youth who have been in care have increased vulnerability to mental health disorders related to unresolved early trauma that may surface in the difficult transitional period (Pecora et al., 2009).

Youth and professionals agree that housing is a serious issue, that there is not enough timely focus on housing plans, and that, in general, preparation for life after care is poor (Freundlich & Avery, 2006). Young people leaving care have too often been without sufficient help in the development of both the tangible skills of finding and keeping a job, finding a place to live, and handling money; and the intangible skills of problem-solving, decision-making, and managing emotions and relationships (Iglehart, 1995). Post-secondary education, which is associated with higher-paid employment, better health, and decreased participation in criminal activity (Hass & Graydon, 2009), is too rarely part of the transition plan or reality. Indeed, 24% of foster care alumni have no high school diploma, compared with 7% of their peers; and 44% have only a high school diploma, compared with 32% of their peers (Courtney et al., 2009).

The Exit from Care

Two recent studies explore why youth leave care before they must. In one study, despite officially listed reasons for exiting, the examination of case record information revealed that only 20% (not the 60% shown in administrative data) left because they had attained their independent living goals, and another 17% left for other positive reasons. As many as 63% left due to unplanned exits: 26% were discharged for refusal of additional services, 10% had unplanned reunifications, 4% left because of marriage, 1% were incarcerated, and 5% were discharged for reasons that were unclear (McCoy et al., 2008).

The second study describes a small sample of emancipated youth, some of whom returned to care. The author concludes that exits from care are often about control, in both positive and negative circumstances, and that returns to care are about survival and a change in the individual's future orientation. Three subgroups are described: those who left early cite a lack of connection due to placement problems and failures, interpersonal conflict, or being asked to leave. In these cases, the decision to leave is experienced as taking control of one's own life. Youth in a second group were discharged but continued to voluntarily receive services, often in an independent living program that focused on work and skill development rather than educational progress. The third group also left to have control over their own lives and greater freedom, but, in contrast to the other two groups, had a network of family or friends and experienced fewer crises following their exit from care (Ward, 2009).

Youth with the fewest resources tend to have great instability in housing and food and need help from the social service system. Because their exits are unplanned, future planning begins only after the exit from care. In the same way that youth in the general population turn to their families when they lose jobs or cannot manage independent living, these youth turn to the institution that has resources to help them. Often, the reconnection with families of origin is marked by the same problems that led to entry into care, or the families simply lack resources. Youth in foster care build very little social capital (durable network of relationships) while in care and have little to draw on during the transition (Ward, 2009).

Education

For most young people, the end of adolescence brings entry into post-secondary education, vocational training, or the work world. A percentage of youth (only 13% in the general population compared with nearly one-third of youth who have been in care in one large study) are neither employed nor in school (Pecora et al., 2006). A disproportionately high number of foster care alumni (28.5% versus 5% of their peers) complete high school with a GED rather than a diploma, and completion rates for post-secondary education are low. A diploma makes a difference: those who obtain GEDs are more than twice as likely not to be enrolled in post-secondary education and to have a lower income than those with diplomas (Pecora et al., 2006). Approximately 7% to 13% of youth leaving care enroll in higher education, but fewer than 4% of them go on to earn a college certificate or degree (Fried, 2008; Wells & Zunz, 2009). Only 6% of foster care alumni complete a degree from either a two- or a four-year college, compared with 29% of youth in the general population (Courtney et al., 2009).

Educational problems begin well before emancipation. Children in care are more likely than other children to have academic and behavioral problems in school, with higher rates of absenteeism and disciplinary referrals.

Some research suggests that as many as 75% perform below grade level, and more than 50% are retained at least one year in school (Zeitlin, Weinberg, & Kimm, 2004). Factors associated with poor educational outcomes of youth in care include maltreatment, multiple placements, school transfers, inconsistent social support, gaps in school enrollment, inadequate school programs at group homes, falling behind in skill areas, delay in transfer of school records, and difficulty being evaluated for special education placement (Mech & Fung, 1999; Zeitlin et al., 2004). A history of physical abuse, placement in an inpatient psychiatric facility, and lack of significant improvement in the youth's condition or poor treatment while in care are associated with school failure (Shin, 2003). Research has demonstrated a correlation between less restrictive placement settings, such as family-type living arrangements, and better educational progress (Mech & Fung, 1999). The education of youth emerging from group homes and residential or institutional settings may have been more seriously compromised by inadequate educational services, gaps in attendance, and mental health problems.

> *Jessica, whose early life was described in Chapter 7 and whose feelings about the exit from care are reflected in the quote that opens this chapter, had been placed in special-education classes during foster care because of her serious emotional disturbance. When she left care, it became clear to her that getting a good job would depend on having some college classes, and she enrolled in community college. She had always hated school, and decided to take whichever program would most quickly lead to a job; the nursing assistant program had the fewest requirements. Biology was a prerequisite, but she had never had a science class before, and she felt overwhelmed and completely unequipped to take the class.*
>
> *Because the teacher was so nice, Jessica went to speak with her and explain why she was dropping out, so the teacher wouldn't take it personally. The teacher began to inquire more closely about why she was dropping out, and Jessica told her about foster care. The teacher, who had been in foster care herself, took Jessica under her wing, encouraging her to stay in class and promising to withdraw her if she was failing. This teacher helped her in practical ways as well, giving her part-time work tutoring and grading. Jessica did well in the class, and her teacher kept raising the bar, helping her complete the nursing assistant course, suggesting she go on for the LVN certificate, then the RN, and then suggesting medical school. At this point Jessica thought, "If I can do that, I can do anything I want—what do I want? The answer was advocacy." Jessica went to law school and now works as an advocate for youth in foster care.*
>
> *This part of Jessica's story demonstrates the complex dilemma of youth in care who have not received educational preparation for post-secondary school, and whose lack of confidence and self-esteem present additional barriers. It also provides a powerful illustration of how the attention and belief of a caring adult can constitute a turning point that, combined with the youth's strengths and aspirations, can enable a young person to try and succeed at things that initially seemed impossible.*

A study of older youth in care found that more than half had failed a class in the previous year, most had been suspended at some point, and many had had physical fights with other students or verbal fights with teachers. These problems were equally common among males and females (McMillen et al., 2003). It is easy to see the negative dynamic interaction among factors of early maltreatment and attachment problems and their impact on affect regulation, disruptions in placement and school settings, cognitive development, academic and social skill development, and effects of failure experiences in school.

Academic performance can enhance a positive self-perception or reinforce a negative one; however, some research suggests that the association between academic identification (valuing academic success) and self-perception does not hold for some youth of color. Black and Hispanic students demonstrate lower levels of academic achievement than whites, yet they have levels of global self-esteem and self-concept equal to or exceeding those of whites (Griffin, 2002). Griffin suggests that stigmatized individuals who are faced with psychologically threatening situations employ protective mechanisms, such as devaluing or disengaging from potentially harmful domains. "Academic disidentification," the process of placing less importance on academics, serves to protect students' self-perceptions in the school setting; when students disidentify, their self-perceptions are not influenced by their performance at school (Griffin, 2002). Youth of color, disproportionately represented in the foster care system, may be struggling with discrimination and protective academic disidentification as well as other risk factors associated with foster care.

The mean annual income for individuals with a high school diploma in 2005 was $27,000, compared with $53,000 for those with a bachelor of arts degree (Wells & Zunz, 2009). Youth in care are less likely to be placed in college preparatory classes than non-foster youth with the same aptitude; in matched samples, only 15% of those in care were placed in college preparatory classes, compared to 32% of non-foster youth (Shin, 2003). Despite the low rate of entrance into post-secondary education, there is evidence that youth in care do have high academic aspirations, even those who have problems or poor academic skills (McMillen et al., 2003). Aspiration for higher education is one of the most important factors in improving the educational achievement of youth in care (Shin, 2003).

A study of foster care alumni attending four-year universities suggests some factors that contribute to better educational outcomes: stability in high school, challenging programs, extracurricular activities, college preparatory classes and advisement, and information about financial aid. The vast majority of these students support themselves through financial aid and/or employment, although nearly half feel their financial situation is worse than that of others their age. Importantly, nearly 87% report that they have a friend or family member they can ask for help or advice. Authors of this study also point to the impact of individual attributes, including assertiveness, goal orientation, persistence, flexibility, and the ability to make conscious changes. They suggest that these characteristics enable youth to take advantage of the available resources and to influence the quality and abundance of resources, where youth who are depressed or rigid in their coping styles may be unable to do so (Merdinger et al., 2005). The dynamic nature of the person-environment system is vividly demonstrated in findings that show how potential environmental resources combine with internal resources and the presence of an encouraging other to build toward better outcomes.

For some foster care alumni, experiences of childhood emotional maltreatment (which often accompanies other forms of maltreatment) become more salient in the context of the developmental transition that college represents, and behavior developed to cope with the effects of abuse (avoidance of contact, denial of needs for help, aggression, or withdrawal) may interfere with relationships with peers and teachers or with academic tasks (Wright, Crawford, & Del Castillo, 2009).

Practice Principles Related to Education

There are several ways that educational attainment can be better supported by child-serving professionals and agencies. During foster care, the collaboration between educational and child welfare systems should be increased. Upon entry into care, for example, each child should receive a comprehensive educational assessment, and an education specialist can be assigned and function as a liaison between the two systems (Kaplan, Skolnik, & Turnbull, 2009; Zeitlin et al., 2004). Stability of foster care placement and school has been shown to be related to both educational attainment and risk for delinquency (Chamberlain, 2008; Ryan & Testa, 2005); changes of placement and schools should be kept to a minimum. When a placement change is unavoidable, every effort should be made to retain the child in his or her home school. In all cases, school records should not only be accurately maintained, but they should accompany the child when a school transfer does occur so that the child's academic experience has continuity and integrity.

Schools and professionals play a major role in the long-term futures of children in care. Participation in extracurricular activities and aspiration for educational attainment build and support a young person's sense of self and of the future, and increase the likelihood of completing high school and attending college. A high school diploma has lifetime benefits in terms of income and employment; children in foster care should be encouraged and helped to complete high school with a diploma rather than a GED. Similarly, children in care should receive college preparatory planning during middle school and be enrolled in college preparatory classes during high school. Those around them need to see them as college-bound, and to reflect that vision in practice and in attitude. Mentorship may be especially important in the area of educational aspirations (Shin, 2003). Concrete assistance with learning needs may be

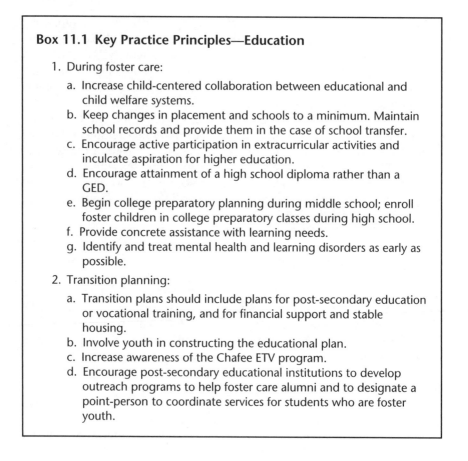

Box 11.1 Key Practice Principles—Education

1. During foster care:
    a. Increase child-centered collaboration between educational and child welfare systems.
    b. Keep changes in placement and schools to a minimum. Maintain school records and provide them in the case of school transfer.
    c. Encourage active participation in extracurricular activities and inculcate aspiration for higher education.
    d. Encourage attainment of a high school diploma rather than a GED.
    e. Begin college preparatory planning during middle school; enroll foster children in college preparatory classes during high school.
    f. Provide concrete assistance with learning needs.
    g. Identify and treat mental health and learning disorders as early as possible.

2. Transition planning:
    a. Transition plans should include plans for post-secondary education or vocational training, and for financial support and stable housing.
    b. Involve youth in constructing the educational plan.
    c. Increase awareness of the Chafee ETV program.
    d. Encourage post-secondary educational institutions to develop outreach programs to help foster care alumni and to designate a point-person to coordinate services for students who are foster youth.

necessary and can be provided in the form of tutoring, remedial classes, and study aids.

Mental health problems can and do interfere with learning and school performance. When children in care are struggling in school, assessment and identification of emotional or learning problems should be a first-line strategy. Appropriate treatment of these problems at an early stage can change a child's school experience dramatically.

Transition plans for adolescents in care should include explicit plans regarding post-secondary education or vocational training, and also for the financial support of post-secondary education. Youth involvement in construction of the educational plan is critical to youth follow-through; if the plan does not reflect their actual aspirations and capabilities, it is unlikely to be realized. Other threats to educational attainment are tenuous or unstable housing, which interferes with consistent school attendance; lack of financial resources; lack of child care and transportation; and untreated mental health problems. On the financial front, the Chafee Educational and Training Voucher Program, enacted in 2001, assists with financial needs of foster care alumni by providing up to $5000 per year up to age 23 for tuition and fees, room and board, transportation, and child-care expenses for both college and training programs (Wells & Zunz, 2009). Those who work with youth in foster care should work to increase awareness of this program, among youth and among caregivers and other concerned adults.

Post-secondary educational institutions can do more to reach out to students who are alumni of foster care. They can develop programs to assist with housing, financial aid, and mentoring. Secondary and post-secondary educational institutions can help these youth develop positive views of education and of themselves as individuals who can succeed in academic settings by treating them as valuable members of the academic community. Teachers and administrators can educate themselves to increase their own awareness and understanding of the needs of youth in care. Colleges and universities can designate a point-person who is responsible for coordinating services for students who are foster care alumni.

Employment and Career

Large-scale studies of foster care alumni paint a dismal picture of their financial well-being in the years following exit from care. Twelve to twenty percent of alumni experience homelessness for one or more days within a year of leaving care (Pecora et al., 2006). Current employment in one study was only 33.6% for males and 40.7% for females at the time of exit, climbing to 49.6% for males and 57.1% for females by age 21 (Courtney et al., 2007). At age 23 to 24, only 48% were employed (compared to 76% of their peers), and 85% of those had an income of $25,000 or less (Courtney et al., 2009). Sixteen to twenty-six percent of foster care alumni receive cash assistance from Temporary Aid to Needy Families, a rate five times higher than in the general population. Furthermore, one-third of alumni report a household income at or below the poverty level, and a similar number have no health insurance (Pecora et al., 2006). Five years post-discharge, 29% of youth were unable to pay their rent at least once in the previous year, 30% had had their phone service disconnected, and 68% of females had received food stamps (Courtney et al., 2009).

African American children, disproportionately removed from their birth families, are similarly disproportionately represented among youth aging out of care. A study of education and employment outcomes found that race and ethnicity are significant factors for three outcomes: white foster care alumni have better odds of having a household income at or above the poverty level, income at three times the poverty level, and home or apartment ownership than do African American alumni. The authors point out that while there are racial disparities, all youth exiting foster care are more likely to be unemployed and have poorer financial situations than youth in the general population (Harris et al., 2009).

Youth in foster care have higher than usual rates of mental illness, substance-abuse disorders, and overly reactive stress-response systems. A history of mental illness is associated with higher rates of unemployment, surpassed only by hypertension and heart disease as an economic burden to employers (Cronce & Corbin, 2010). These conditions have an impact on finding and sustaining employment—more work days missed or workplace conflict, for example—which, in turn, affect the ability to find or keep stable housing. Housing instability is a significant stressor, affecting psychological well-being and interpersonal functioning. Lack of financial, social, and educational resources at the threshold of adulthood can combine to further weaken the individual's internal and external coping, illustrating again the dynamic interaction of biological, psychological, and social factors.

Practice Principles Related to Employment

The preparation for employment, like education, should begin during foster care. Children should be exposed to a wide range of futures in which they can imagine themselves, by meeting adults who work in many different arenas, receiving career counseling, and attending job fairs (Kaplan et al., 2009). Opportunities for summer or after-school internships can extend their exposure to career possibilities.

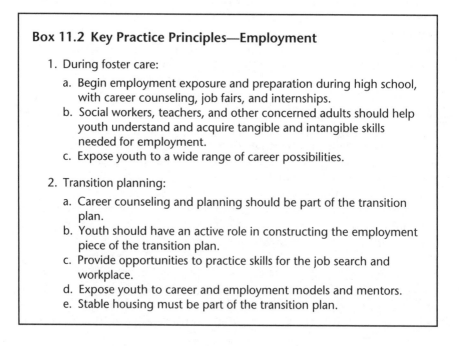

Box 11.2 Key Practice Principles—Employment

1. During foster care:
   a. Begin employment exposure and preparation during high school, with career counseling, job fairs, and internships.
   b. Social workers, teachers, and other concerned adults should help youth understand and acquire tangible and intangible skills needed for employment.
   c. Expose youth to a wide range of career possibilities.

2. Transition planning:
   a. Career counseling and planning should be part of the transition plan.
   b. Youth should have an active role in constructing the employment piece of the transition plan.
   c. Provide opportunities to practice skills for the job search and workplace.
   d. Expose youth to career and employment models and mentors.
   e. Stable housing must be part of the transition plan.

Youth need help in understanding and developing both tangible and intangible skills that are fundamental to seeking, obtaining, and maintaining employment. Youth need opportunities to learn and practice concrete skills, but they also need to develop confidence, decision-making, problem-solving, and interpersonal skills. Reassurance, advice, and role-playing experiences can increase their comfort in presenting themselves to potential employers.

The transition plan should incorporate career counseling and planning along with educational planning. Youth should play an active part in constructing this part of the plan as well, and this will be easier if they have been exposed to career and employment models and mentors. Youth cannot successfully engage in a job search if they cannot easily and reliably be reached, and they cannot sustain employment if they do not have housing stability. As with the educational piece of the transition plan, the employment piece depends on stable housing.

Relationships with Important Others

The transition to adulthood involves coming to terms with relationships of the past and establishing new relationships. As youth leave foster care, they may feel heightened uncertainty about which connections will endure, especially if there has been little or no contact with families of origin, or if their experiences in foster care were disappointing. Youth in the general population remain dependent on their families into their twenties, and there is increasing recognition that emotional (and financial) autonomy is a process rather than an event. Youth leaving care sometimes reconnect with their families of origin in the attempt to clarify what kind of relationship is possible for the future.

Birth Families

Researchers describe a range of patterns or trajectories of relationships with birth families: reunification, reconnection, or problematic reunification or reconnection (Collins, Paris, & Ward, 2008; Wade, 2008; Ward, 2009). Because different definitions of "family" are used in studies, the reported percentage of those who reunify after emancipation ranges from 17% to nearly 50% living with family members at discharge, with a significant number still living with family members several years later (Collins et al., 2008). Those who *reconnect* with their families in some way are less easy to identify and count and findings are sometimes contradictory. Five years after exit from care, almost all youth in a large study said they had maintained ties with biological family members, with 79%

reporting that they feel very close to at least one family member (Courtney et al., 2009). Another study found that youth had more contact with family than they had had in care, and that relationships with grandparents and siblings were stronger than those with parents (Collins et al., 2008; Wade, 2008). Another study reported that regular contact is more common with siblings and birth mothers than with birth fathers (Wade, 2008).

For many, the stressors and circumstances that led to disruption and removal are still present following discharge. While just over half of one sample felt they had a strong relationship with key family members one year after discharge, 54% of respondents in another study reported family conflict due to dysfunctional parental behavior, in some cases leading to youth homelessness (Collins et al., 2008; Wade, 2008). Relationships with family members can be fragile, and the youth's desire for connection may be painfully rebuffed or lead to a final rupture and loss. Social workers generally pay more attention to housing, education, life skills, and finances than to family-related issues, but youth value mediation and family counseling, even when it is not successful (Wade, 2008).

Caregivers

Youth who stay on with caregivers seem to benefit: they are more likely to be engaged in education and training, less likely to be unemployed one year later, and more likely to have connection with growth-promoting others (Wade, 2008; Ward, 2009). Continuing contact with caregivers after discharge can provide stability and continuity; 46% of youth in one study were still in contact with caregivers or social workers following their exit from care (Wade, 2008). During childhood, the attachment figure serves as a secure base from which to explore the world and provide safety or reassurance when stress or danger is present; the caring, interested adult serves a parallel function for the emerging adult.

Peers

Relationships with peers can be an important source of support, or, in some cases, can lead to an increased likelihood of delinquency and substance use (Shook et al., 2009). School and workplace environments introduce an individual to a different set of peers, thereby reshuffling or eliminating previous delinquent networks in favor of new, sometimes more positive, networks (Wright & Cullen, 2004). For youth who feel isolated and cut off as a result of placement moves and discharge from care, friends may acquire heightened importance and meaning. The social niches that are available to an individual strongly influence the nature of potential peer networks: an unemployed, homeless young person does not have the same opportunities to develop social capital among prosocial peers as one who is attending school or vocational training, or is employed in a meaningful, well-paid job.

Mentors

Naturally occurring or structured mentoring relationships can be life-changing. In one study of youth leaving care, two-thirds report having had a non-kin natural mentor at some point between ages 18 and 19, and one-third say the relationship lasted over time. Youth whose mentoring relationships last more than one year report fewer depression symptoms and greater satisfaction with life than those whose relationships are short-er-lived (Munson & McMillen, 2009). Some research suggests that formal mentoring programs have a positive, but modest effect on the participants (Hass & Graydon, 2009) and that natural mentoring may provide a better fit (Greeson & Bowen, 2008). Young people who receive guidance and advice from mentors are significantly more likely to be employed than those who do not; mentoring that occurs prior to adulthood tends to have a causal effect on employment opportunities later in life (McDonald et al., 2007).

Intimate Relationships

The ability to have high-quality intimate relationships is a critical element of adult well-being; it supports and is supported by the sense of personal identity (Montgomery, 2005). Internal resources influence the amount and quality of intimate relationships that an individual can establish and maintain. Early attachment experiences affect the developing adult's attachment style, in turn shaping intimate relationships. Young adults with secure attachment styles tend to have positive relationships, more happiness, and less loneliness in their romantic relationships, whereas those with anxious attachment styles seek and desire intimacy, but have trouble achieving it. Anxiously attached individuals tend to be dependent and jealous, take greater sexual risks, and have both a greater number of lifetime sexual partners and more infidelity. Those with avoidant styles fear intimacy and may be less interested in close, committed sexual rela-tionships. They may engage in sex more casually or use it more manipu-latively (Auslander & Rosenthal, 2010).

Maltreatment and Intimate Relationships

Problematic early attachment experiences and childhood maltreatment give rise to internal working models of rejecting others and a devalued self; these predispose individuals to expect their needs for acceptance and support to be rejected. Such individuals are likely to perceive ambiguous social cues as rejection or hostility, resulting in behaviors that can undermine relationships. People who are "rejection-sensitive" are prone to interpret their partners' negative behavior as motivated by hurtful intent, leading them to withdraw or become hostile and blaming (Downey & Feldman, 1996). Similar dynamics can become active in relationships with peers, co-workers, or employers, thus interfering with friendships and the ability to maintain employment.

The intimate relationships of those who have been maltreated in childhood differ from those of other adults, indicating long-term interpersonal effects of childhood abuse and neglect. The bulk of research addressing the impact of childhood maltreatment on adult intimate relationships has focused on child sexual abuse, but a large prospective study demonstrates that the impact on adult intimate relationships does not vary with type of child maltreatment. Abused males and females have significantly higher rates of relationship disruption (divorce and walking out) than adults who were not maltreated; maltreated females are less likely to see their partners as supportive and caring and are less likely to be sexually faithful to their partners and spouses than women who have not been maltreated. Maltreated adults are more likely to have cohabited with partners and are less likely to be involved in a committed romantic relationship (Colman & Widom, 2004)

Parental abuse during childhood negatively affects social bonding in general during young adulthood. Individuals who have been exposed to violence in their families of origin are less likely to make a successful transition to adulthood and are at increased risk for partner violence, but if they are able to develop stronger social bonds during young adulthood, they may reduce the risk. Increases in commitment to a partner or to work significantly mediate the effect of victimization by parents on later partner violence (Lackey, 2003). Twenty percent of foster care alumni in one study were cohabiting with a partner one year after discharge; however, stability in relationships is hard to achieve, and many young people need professional support to strengthen and improve relationships (Wade, 2008).

Practice Principles Regarding Relationships

Relationships constitute the network of social supports for young adults. Transition plans for youth leaving care must address the need for relationships, including families of origin, substitute caregivers, peer networks, and other significant adults. Beyond this, the plan should identify one or more specific adults who have committed themselves to maintaining an ongoing relationship with the youth (Bussiere, 2006). No transition plan should be considered complete without this element, and no young person should leave care without the certainty of a connection to a caring and available adult. (These principles are summarized in Box 11.3 below.)

Transition planning should include preparation concerning the youth's relationship with the family of origin. Because the history of these relationships is complex and problematic, youth need opportunities prior to their exit from care to explore their hopes and expectations, and preparation for possible disappointment. They may need help with setting boundaries and reality-testing. Unplanned reunifications sometimes lead to further rejection and ultimately, to homelessness; counseling with regard to family issues and identification of potential dangers and potential sources of support can be helpful in preventing painful outcomes (Collins et al., 2008; Ward, 2009).

Relationships with social workers and caregivers are often the most enduring that youth have had up to the point of leaving care. If these relationships are not going to continue during the transition period or beyond it, the termination must be done carefully and over time. Abrupt termination can be detrimental to psychological outcomes (Munson & McMillen, 2009), and this is especially the case for youth whose earlier attachments were characterized by loss and disruption, often of a sudden and absolute nature. Youth leaving care may feel disconnected from familiar sources of support; the transition plan can prevent an overwhelming sense of isolation or disconnection by ensuring that a network of support is in place prior to the conclusion of the placement relationships.

Box 11.3 Key Practice Principles—Relationships

1. The transition plan must address the need for relationships and social support, including families of origin, substitute caregivers, peer networks, and other significant adults.
2. The transition plan should identify one or more adults committed to maintaining an ongoing relationship with the youth.
3. The transition plan should include preparation for reconnection with the family of origin, addressing expectations, boundary setting, coping with loss, fostering empowerment, and identifying potential sources of support.
4. Termination of professional relationships must be done carefully and over time.
5. Transition planning must address the potential for feeling disconnected and isolated by including plans for connection with individuals, groups, and institutions.
6. Youth should have the opportunity to explore attachment issues and relationship patterns, preparatory to leaving care.

The transition period can be one of examining the nature and effects of past attachments and preparing for a future of meaningful and sustaining relationships. Youth need a complex network of relationships to help them regulate impulses and emotions, to meet basic needs, and to feel a sense of belonging to a community and to society (Kaplan et al., 2009). Their ability to develop relationships that will sustain them depends on having positive experiences with the adults who care for them and about them. It is through relationships with reliable, trustworthy, supportive others that they can build internal representations of self and others that will carry them into successful adulthoods. In Chapter 12, we will see how these ideas can be incorporated into transitional living programs and services.

12

TRANSITIONAL LIVING PROGRAMS: BEST PRACTICES

Until recently, foster care effectively ended when a young person reached the age of 18. Discussion and research on outcomes and services has historically been divided between youth under 18 and those 18 and over, as if the eighteenth birthday marked a substantial change in something more than the youth's status relative to funding and jurisdiction. Development, however, is continuous, and individuals do not change dramatically overnight.

Despite renewed efforts at addressing the challenges of aging out, "outcomes for most youth are still indicating heartbreaking results and it is still not clear what more is needed" (Scannapieco, Connell-Carrick, & Painter, 2007). Program design for transitioning youth must take into account all that has preceded emancipation (early adverse experience, foster care experience); the youth's current state in a number of domains ("outcomes" such as educational attainment, mental and physical health, social support network); individual characteristics (attachment patterns, strengths, and vulnerabilities); and the contextual features of the program environment (funding, policies, community resources). Planning and design must be youth-focused rather than service-focused and must be developmentally informed. The frameworks outlined in Chapter 2 (biopsychosocial perspective, attachment theory, developmental traumatology, dynamic systems theory, resiliency theory) can inform program design to address the needs of developing youth on the threshold of adulthood.

Key outcomes at exit from care were provided in Chapter 11. Chapter 12 begins with a brief overview of outcomes in the years following discharge, including the effects of independent-living services provided during foster care on later outcomes. Discussion of selected program components makes up the bulk of the chapter, followed by a summary of principles for developmentally informed, relationship-based practice in transitional living programs.

Overview of Outcomes

Understanding of the range and nature of important outcomes is evolving as it becomes increasingly difficult to ignore the complex influences of interacting domains and factors. Homelessness serves as an excellent example; it is inevitably cited by researchers as a serious problem for foster care alumni (Brandford & English, 2004; Casey Family Programs, 2008; Havalchak, White, & O'Brien, 2008; Naccarato & DeLorenzo, 2008; Pecora et al., 2010; Choca et al., 2004; Fowler, Toro, & Miles, 2009). Homelessness and housing instability, however, are integrally related to the lack of resources and, in turn, give rise to a progression of accumulating risks. Prevalence rates for mental and behavioral problems are much higher among homeless adolescents than their housed peers, and mental health problems, in turn, compromise their ability to obtain or maintain employment (Haber & Toro, 2004). Post-secondary educational achievement and employment earnings for foster care alumni are "unacceptably poor" (Pecora et al., 2010), making it difficult for them to sustain stable housing.

Outcomes such as employment, educational attainment, physical health problems, diagnosable mental health disorders, involvement with the criminal justice system, early pregnancy and parenthood, possession of personal documents, cash or savings, and dependence on public assistance are tracked in many studies. Other significant indicators of well-being or successful transition that may collectively be thought of as *social capital* are only now coming into the foreground. They include an enduring relationship with a caring adult, a network of social supports, community engagement or involvement, connections to health resources and employment resources, self-esteem, sense of purpose and hopefulness, romantic relationships, and relationships with biological or foster families. Of these, the establishment of lifelong connections may be most important to the overall well-being of former foster youth (Pecora et al., 2010). Former foster youth interviewed about their social networks most frequently cite emotional support as the support most needed and most lacking (Samuels, 2008).

Effects of Independent Living Programs

Independent living services target adolescents whose permanency plans are neither family reunification nor adoption, and they are meant to prepare youth for adult living on their own. ILPs provide financial and other assistance (often life-skills classes and training) to eligible youth to prepare for and make successful transitions to independence. They are administered by states and counties, using federal, state, local, and private funds (U.S. General Accounting Office, Health, Education, and Human Services Division, 1999 [hereafter, US GAO, HEHSD, 1999]). The Independent Living Program was initially enacted through Title IV-E of the Social Security Act of 1985 (PL 99-272) and was augmented through the Foster Care Independence Act (FCIA) of 1999, when it became known as the Chafee Foster Care Independent Living Program ("Chafee"). The FCIA made youth eligible for IL funding at 14 and gave states the option to provide Medicaid to foster care alumni up to age 21 (Naccarato & DeLorenzo, 2008). However, the U.S. government estimates that two-fifths of eligible youth do not receive IL services, and when they do, it is unlikely that they receive the full range of services described in the Chafee program (Courtney & Heuring, 2005).

Most ILPs offer life-skills training in the areas of employment, money management, community resources, and decision-making in a classroom setting, though some also offer subsidized independent living (SIL) in approved settings for youth 16 and older (Georgiades, 2005b). Research on the effectiveness of ILPs in improving outcomes of youth leaving care is mixed at best: in two national studies in the 1990s, the data were not encouraging. One reported that the youth who had received IL services looked more like those living below the poverty level than the general population in terms of high school completion, early pregnancy, and receipt of public assistance (Cook, 1994). The second found that ILPs were falling short in offering opportunities for real-life practice of skills, esteem-building experiences, assistance with potential employment, and super-vised transitional housing sites (US GAO, HEHSD, 1999). A 1995 study of the effects of a single ILP program concluded that ILP youth were more likely to complete high school and have employment at discharge, but that a significant percentage (87%) of eligible youth were not involved in ILP and did not complete high school at time of discharge, indicating that either access to or awareness of ILP services was sorely lacking (Scannapieco, Schagrin, & Scannapieco, 1995).

The number of programs and effectiveness studies has increased in the past decade. A review of eight studies that assessed the effectiveness of ILPs by comparing them to "usual care," "no intervention," or "another intervention" reports that some ILPs may improve educational, employ-ment, and housing outcomes for youth leaving care, but that the evidence cannot be considered robust because of weak evaluation methodology. The evidence does not allow identification of which elements of the ILPs are most effective or which youth may benefit most from ILPs. Finally, these authors state that, compared to the general population, ILP partici-pants still report extensively poorer outcomes (Montgomery, Donkoh, & Underhill, 2006).

A second review of effectiveness studies looked more specifically at the domains of housing, educational attainment, placement history, and employment, as these are frequently measured indicators of readiness for independent living (Naccarato & DeLorenzo, 2008). In the studies that compare youth who receive ILP services with those who do not, the ILP group compares favorably with the non-ILP group in earning high school diplomas and GEDs and in college enrollment. In the employment domain, 59% of the ILP group was employed compared with 44% of the non-ILP group. Eighty-one percent of non-ILP youth experienced unemployment for more than one month since discharge, compared with 63% of the ILP group. In 10 of the 19 studies reviewed, the ILP group's rate of employment was poorer than the national average, and their median weekly salary was lower than that of the general population. Homelessness was roughly comparable, with about 52% of both ILP and non-ILP groups having experienced one or more episodes of homelessness (Naccarato & DeLorenzo, 2008).

A rigorously designed study of the Life Skills Training Program (LST) in Los Angeles County reports few significant differences in outcomes between the LST group and control groups at the second follow-up. The results call into question the idea that classroom-based life skills training in and of itself is likely to have much impact on the well-being of foster care alumni in transition to adulthood (Courtney & Heuring, 2005). Similarly, Georgiades reports that findings of outcome evaluation studies on ILPs appear equivocal, though some suggest that IL participation may be related to better outcomes in education, employment, housing, early parenting–prevention, and self-evaluation. An evaluation of an IL program in Florida replicates those positive findings, but finds relatively high rates of criminal involvement and incarceration in both IL and non-IL groups (Georgiades, 2005b). Youth in care report general satisfaction with IL services, but mention gaps in parenting skills training and housing preparation. They recommend strong educational, employment, and housing components, and organizational and money-management skills training. Those no longer in care are less satisfied and feel services have been inadequate or nonexistent, and that planning for discharge did not begin early enough. In one study, the majority of youth who did not participate in IL had never heard about it, and in another, nearly half of the foster care alumni had not had an independent living coordinator. Life skills classes got mixed reviews from the participants (Georgiades, 2005a; Petr, 2008). In my own informal survey of foster care alumni, only four of 14 respondents included ILP classes as one of the things that helped them make the transition to independence.

The wide range of methodologies, outcome measures, and samples makes it difficult to draw conclusions about the effectiveness of ILPs and which program components are most helpful to which youth. Youth respondents in a qualitative study, for example, recall their participation in ILPs in terms of the people they met and report the relationship aspects of the programs as overshadowing skill development (Iglehart & Becerra, 2002). A national database with uniform measurements is needed to continue to shape and prioritize program and funding goals. Too often, sample sizes are small and there is excessive reliance on exit or "snapshot" data (Pecora et al., 2010). Studies should collect service data on the frequency, timing, and number of ILP sessions received; use control groups; standardize outcome measures; and collect post-discharge data

(Naccarato & DeLorenzo, 2008). In addition to the usual outcome domains (housing, employment, education, financial self-sufficiency), researchers should begin more routinely to look at how youth are doing in the emotional and interpersonal domains.

Transitional Living Programs

Youth transitioning into adulthood from foster care face the usual challenges of emerging adulthood, as well as the continuing impact of childhood trauma, problematic or disrupted attachments, and the effects of experiences in foster care. Their education may have been compromised and their social networks abruptly severed on more than one occasion, including that of exit from care. Programs that aim to prepare them for adult life must address these background factors in addition to providing them with tangible skills and services. The lack of social capital that characterizes the lives of most youth leaving care should also be a significant focus of transitional living services, as high levels of social capital have been linked to positive life outcomes such as occupational viability, individual health, and psychological well-being (Avery, 2010). Of greatest concern in this regard are youth of color, who must constantly negotiate their sense of self in relation to discriminatory attitudes and evidence of lower status and power in society (Avery & Freundlich, 2009). Reconnecting marginalized youth with a sense of power can and should be a part of their preparation for adulthood (Propp, Ortega, & NewHeart, 2003).

There is growing consensus among researchers and practitioners that an array of program components is important to effective preparation for adulthood. Many program designers and administrators look to the framework provided in the Child Welfare League of America's (CWLA) revised Standards of Excellence for Transition, Independent Living, and Self-sufficiency Services (TILSS), which is based on a positive youth-development philosophy (Child Welfare League of America, 2005). Positive youth development is a strength-based perspective that derives from developmental systems theory, taking into account the plasticity of human development, and emphasizing strengths and potential rather than problems or deficits (Crowe, 2007; Lerner et al., 2005). An operational definition of positive youth development describes the following components: it promotes bonding; fosters resilience; promotes social, emotional, cognitive, and behavioral competence; fosters self-determination; fosters spirituality; fosters clear and positive identity; fosters belief in the future; and provides opportunities for prosocial involvement (Catalano et al., 2004).

CWLA's TILSS standards emphasize individual strengths, youth participation in decision-making, learning by doing, promotion of healthy relationships, community involvement, and recognition that it takes time to become self-sufficient and that successful adult living is never truly independent (Child Welfare League of America, 2005). Additional core program components described by other authors include life skills, housing, youth engagement, education, employment, and identity development (including cultural identity), with a smaller number also mentioning emotional healing (Abney, Park, & Yamashiro, 2007; Casey Family Programs Integrated Transition Practice Framework Task Force, 2001; Choca et al., 2004; Colca & Colca, 1996; Delgado et al., 2007; Kroner, 2007; McMillen et al., 1997; Rashid, 2004; Reid, 2007). The continuous and interacting nature of the many factors influencing the transition to adulthood not only makes it difficult to discuss program components in isolation, but suggests (somewhat falsely) that they can be considered separately. The following sections nevertheless attempt to highlight selected individual program components, some of which have also have been addressed in previous chapters.

Housing

The high risk for homelessness and precarious housing among former foster youth has been described in previous chapters. Lack of educational achievement, joblessness, and lack of social capital generally are, of course, integrally related to housing problems, and programs that offer housing almost always provide other services as well. The two most frequently found housing models are congregate (50%) and scattered-site models (36%). While there is no evidence that one specific housing model is better than another in terms of outcomes (Abney et al., 2007), it is possible to note some advantages and disadvantages of each.

Scattered-site housing may be easier to obtain and can be located close to clients' schools, workplaces, or social networks. It most closely resembles after-program living, and may provide more opportunities for decision-making and problem-solving on one's own. In some programs, the apartments youth live in during the program are designed to be available on a long-term basis following their discharge from the program. First Place Fund for Youth in Northern California is an example of the scattered-site permanent model. The agency owns the unit or lease and provides a rent subsidy that decreases gradually over two years. Youth receive additional services (move-in assistance and stipend, food stipend, employment and educational counseling, and monthly community-building events), and participants are reported to be less likely to become incarcerated, homeless, or receive public assistance than the general population of foster care alumni 12 to 18 months after discharge from care (Abney et al., 2007; Packard et al., 2008).

Scattered-site models may present obstacles to frequent youth–staff contact and life skills or other classes, and opportunities for community- and network-building may be more difficult to arrange. Congregate model programs enable wraparound services and classes to be offered onsite, and youth are in daily contact, not only with staff, but also with one another, thereby potentially building long-term connections that can endure past the term of the program. United Friends of the Children's Pathways to Independence Program in Los Angeles is an example of the congregate model, with five sites of differing capacity, ranging from four to 36 beds. Residents pay rent, which increases gradually over 18 months and is set aside and returned to them upon graduation from the program. Life skills classes, career and educational counseling, community events, substance-abuse and mental health services are provided onsite, along with weekly meetings with advocacy counselors who continue with youth throughout their tenure in the program and beyond. Pathways provides an alumni-services component that includes help with finding and moving into post-program housing, alumni events centered on employment and emotional healing, emergency financial assistance, and holiday celebrations. Pathways reports rates of post-program employment (74%) and housing stability (87%) (United Friends of the Children, 2010) that exceed those of the broader population of foster care alumni, and both programs report particularly high rates of secondary education completion and post-secondary education participation (Abney et al., 2007).

There are drawbacks to the congregate model as well. For some youth, the congregate setting is too reminiscent of group homes, and they are anxious to be in a more independent setting with fewer restrictions and greater autonomy. Finding affordable congregate space can be difficult for agencies. Youth living in congregate sites will not have the option to transition into long-term tenancy of their living space.

Whether housing is apartment-based or congregate may ultimately matter less than whether the model incorporates a developmental perspective, recognizing that housing needs and capabilities change over time and circumstances. The Rediscovery House in Waltham, Massachusetts, is an example of a "graduated" range of options as youth move from the foster care system to independence. It offers three programs for youth aged 16 to 20: a 12-bed "pre-independent" group home, a scattered-site apartment program, and a program called Stepping Out that brings youth another step closer to full independence (Pitchal, 2008-2009). An ideal program might offer a continuum of options, from emergency housing to long-term housing that can be taken over by youth at the end of the program.

Transitional housing is subsidized through a number of funding sources, often in combination: up to 30% of Chafee funds can be used for room and board; the U.S. Department of Housing and Urban Development (HUD) has a supportive housing program; states and counties often have grants that can support housing for youth at risk for homelessness; and private funding is available through nonprofits and foundations. There is increasing recognition of the need to expand the housing inventory for foster care alumni, including transitional housing and affordable permanent housing (Naccarato & DeLorenzo, 2008). Local and regional collaborations that link developers, service providers, and state and local governments are coming together to create innovative programs with new partners. These collaborations also include other organizations, such as schools and foster youth organizations, which can play vital roles in strategic planning for the development of housing and related services (Choca et al., 2004).

There are few transitional living programs designed for mother–child cohabitation with comprehensive healthcare services in the United States. The Thresholds Mothers' Project, for pregnant and parenting foster care youth with severe mental illness, uses a congregate housing model where mothers live with their children for an average stay of 22½ months. The residents have access to a drop-in center; 24-hour staff support; employment, education, and mental health services; as well as child development classes and a therapeutic nursery school. Outcomes for the high-risk population in this program are mixed. The program is effective in keeping mothers in school via school and employment incentive programs, thereby reducing rates of rapid subsequent births, school dropout, and unemployment. However, mothers in the program have a high rate of unplanned departure, with about 40% having left at least once, and the majority of mothers were at or above the clinically relevant threshold on the Child Abuse Potential scale, indicating potential for child abuse (Vorhies et al., 2009).

Lighthouse Youth Services in Cincinnati, seen as a model program for youth in care, recognizes the need for early preparation and development of skills for apartment living while building in protections for youth whose independent living skills do not develop in a straight line. This scattered-site program serves an average of 65 youth ages 16 to –19 (and 15 of their children) at any given time, renting apartments in affordable neighborhoods close to clients' schools or jobs and providing security deposits, furnishings, and telephones. Clients who are doing well and have jobs at termination can take over their leases. The program additionally provides some financial support, life skills training in modules that can be completed at the client's pace, emotional support, and case management. The agency has a crisis shelter and boarding homes for youth who are not yet able to manage in supervised apartments. Youth in this program can move along a continuum of living arrangements, depending on their behavior and level of functioning; they can fail at one level, move to a level with greater support, and then move forward again (Kroner, 2007; Pitchal, 2008).

A study of four transitional living programs in California found support for a link between service-enriched transitional housing programs and improved outcomes for former foster youth, though it was difficult to determine which factors in the programs contributed to their success. These programs variously employed scattered-site and congregate housing models. The authors caution that screening during program application and admission may be a key factor in outcomes (Abney et al., 2007).

Emotional Healing

The discharge from foster care often brings with it a sense of isolation, lack of social support, and worries associated with having to rely on oneself (Iglehart, 1995). Underlying unresolved feelings connected to childhood experiences of abuse or neglect, separation from one's family, possible negative experiences while in care, and what is often an abrupt departure from care further complicate the transition. Depression rates are disproportionately high among alumni of foster care, relative to a matched sample of their peers (White et al., 2009), and rates of nine mental health disorders are significantly higher than in the general population (White et al., 2007). For older adolescents in care, attention is focused much more on the development of concrete independent living skills in preparation for aging out than on their psychological functioning, especially the management of affect and behavior during care or upon exit. Yet unresolved trauma can interfere with acquiring and using skills, just as it prevents younger youth in care from being able to engage fully in learning at school. Many of these youth have experienced uncertainty and fear, with relatively little opportunity to feel safe or comforted during their time in care (Duval & Vincent, 2009).

Youth who have diagnosed or diagnosable disorders may receive mental health treatment within transitional living programs, but these programs need to consider more generally the emotional well-being of all transitioning youth. Other cultural perspectives that are oriented toward wholeness and interrelatedness rather than individual autonomy can contribute to our thinking about how best to conceptualize a context that supports emotional healing.

The Japanese concept of *Ibasho* may offer useful insight in creating an atmosphere where healing can take place. *Ibasho* connotes a place where a person feels peace, security, acceptance, and belonging. It occurs through empathetic and mutually accepting interpersonal relationships, and opportunities to contribute to the well-being of others through the use of one's natural gifts and abilities and through performance of roles within groups. We might translate this as emphasizing attachment possibilities, giving back to the community, using a strengths-based approach, and building competence and self-esteem through participation. *Ibasho* is subjectively experienced: what makes an individual feel safe and peaceful changes with one's developmental stage or state (Bamba & Haight, 2007; Bamba & Haight, 2009). The youth perspective constitutes our reframing of what "subjectively experienced" means; we need to hear from youth in order to create an environment of safety and acceptance.

A healing environment enables optimal development and learning, including the skills and tasks necessary to negotiating the transition to adulthood. All program elements—relationships between staff and youth, relationships among youth, activities in groups (life skills classes, community groups, employment), and leisure activities—can be seen as related potential contributors to healing and growth. For example, in addition to the concrete and intangible supports that mentors typically provide to mentees, the benefits of mentoring relationships can be expanded to encompass the growth-enhancing possibilities that arise from being a mentee whose unique qualities bring something to the mentoring relationship and the mentor.

A wellness paradigm centers on aiming toward a state of being in which optimal health is achieved, including positive physical and psychological functioning, culture, and lifespan development. It attends to gender differences and the effects of external forces on well-being and, like the youth development model, sees individuals as having potential and strengths instead of weaknesses and deficits (Hartwig & Myers, 2003).

An Afrocentric perspective suggests that the incorporation of principles such as collective identity, interconnectedness, and spiritual aspects of human life into practice (programs) contributes to engagement and participation. This perspective assumes that affective knowledge is as valid as other forms of knowledge; subjective experience has a central place, as in the Japanese approach described above (Stewart, 2004). The First Voice curriculum for work with foster care alumni uses a Native American philosophy based on belonging, mastery, independence, and generosity. "Independence" in this approach refers to having the skills needed for decision-making and self-control, and the "spirit of belonging" points to the need for support from others (Reid & Ross, 2005). Through service to the community, performance of leadership roles, and the practice of social skills, youth can experience themselves and others in ways that contribute to identity and to healing.

Attachment

A *sine qua non* of healing (and resolution of trauma) is feeling safe. Anxiety about physical or emotional danger activates the stress-response system and defensive measures; self-protection becomes the first priority. The more complete the sense of safety, the more available the person is for learning, interacting, and working. While the housing component of transitional living programs goes a long way toward addressing physical safety, emotional safety rests on relationships with trustworthy others, both staff and peers. Individual differences in attachment history and traumatic interpersonal experiences appear to influence the degree to which young adults are able to garner and utilize social capital, including new attachment opportunities (Avery, 2010). Few programs explicitly attend to attachment issues and patterns (Schwartz, McRoy, & Downs, 2004) or the relational aspects of programs themselves, such as relationships among youth participants and youth–staff relationships, yet they may be critical to the effectiveness of other program elements.

New attachment experiences with staff and with peers can provide a foundation for the continuation of developmental tasks and additional scaffolding for the emerging young adult identity. The disappointments many youth have had in their primary attachment relationships will inform their style of relating to new individuals; qualified staff who are well-trained and who understand development, trauma, and attachment will be much more able to meet the challenges of building relationships with suspicious, wounded youth. A reasonable staff–client ratio, frequent and consistent contact, and a low turnover rate among staff will help facilitate richer personal and social development than is sometimes found in transitional living programs (Goyette, 2007). This is more likely to occur in programs that also provide support and attention to the needs of staff, whose work is demanding and can be emotionally draining (Pitchal, 2008).

Education and Employment

The interconnectedness and central roles of education and employment in moving toward a successful adulthood are not in dispute. Recommendations for transitional living programs almost universally include provision of educational supports and services, and stress the importance of completing high school with a diploma and enrolling in and completing post-secondary education or vocational training (Casey Family Programs Integrated Transition Practice Framework Task Force, 2001; Casey Family Programs, 2008; Child Welfare League of America, 2005; Frey, Greenblatt, & Brown, 2005; Shirk & Stangler, 2006).

Employment services and supports range from access to community resources and information to preparation for employment, internships, and career mentors (Avery & Freundlich, 2009; Child Welfare League of America, 2005; Naccarato & DeLorenzo, 2008; Nixon & Jones, 2000). The importance of relationships and social capital in career and career identity development cannot be overestimated (Avery & Freundlich, 2009). The particular strengths, affinities, and gifts of individual youth need to be determined so that they can be helped to locate jobs or careers that will provide income and satisfaction, and with which they will be likely to stay (Bach et al., 2001). Employment training is crucial, but not sufficient, and youth need actual employment opportunities. Programs may need to develop relationships with potential employers, as well as to equip youth to compete in the employment market (Naccarato & DeLorenzo, 2008).

Employability rests, not only on specific job skills and life skills related to the workplace, but also on housing, transportation, and possession of documents such as a driver's license and a Social Security card (Bussiere, 2006; Pecora et al., 2010). Youth whose preparation for leaving care has led to their having concrete resources at exit have better employment and finance outcomes, as do youth who have had early and positive engagement with employment (Casey Family Programs, 2008).

Identity Development

As discussed in Chapters 5 and 11, identity development is an ongoing process, continuously interacting with internal and external conditions and changes. Identity formation is one of the seven outcomes of interest listed in the CWLA Standards of Excellence for TILSS, yet it is rarely mentioned in the literature on transitional living programs (Child Welfare League of America, 2005). For many foster care alumni, childhood maltreatment and removal from their biological families and cultural origins have complicated the development of a positive sense of self. One study found that being in foster care two years or more had a negative impact on identity development, manifesting in devaluation of the self (Lopez & Allen, 2007). Youth may feel stigmatized by having been in care, and their positive identity may be tenuous.

The transitional living context presents opportunities for identity development via relationships, the learning of new skills, educational and work experiences, and exposure to new group and cultural experiences. Youth can see themselves differently in new settings and by playing new roles with greater responsibilities. Programs that allow youth to make mistakes may also allow them to become more forgiving of themselves, learning to see failure as a natural part of learning rather than as a reflection of something lacking in themselves.

Greater resolution of the relationship with the birth family can also contribute to identity formation, by reconnecting youth with their history and culture of origin, and by further clarifying that neglect or abuse is something that happened to them and may have had terrible consequences, but was not caused by them.

Health and Mental Health

A three-state study found that children in foster care have three to seven times as many acute and chronic health conditions and emotional adjustment problems as other mostly poor children receiving Medicaid (English, Morreale, & Larsen, 2003). Multiple placements disrupt health care, and children in care rely heavily on emergency rooms, resulting in health services during care that may not be appropriate to the level of medical need. Young people may exit care with serious or under-treated conditions.

Youth and children in care are 15 to 20 times more likely to use inpatient and outpatient mental health services compared to their peers in the general population, but service use falls off dramatically at exit from care.

Youth of color are less likely than white youth to receive outpatient specialty mental health services (Lopez & Allen, 2007; Ringeisen et al., 2009). Youth leaving foster care should have knowledge of their health and mental health conditions, their insurance coverage, and the names of providers who can serve them. Entrance into a transitional living program should include a comprehensive health screening and assistance with access to both insurance and care.

Mentoring

A connection to at least one caring adult who offers social support and connectedness has been identified as a protective factor across a variety of risk factors; mentoring is one way to provide such a connection (Greeson & Bowen, 2008). Mentoring relationships can be structured or naturally occurring, and can be life-changing (Munson & McMillen, 2009). Both natural and volunteer mentors can provide supportive relationships, serve as role models, and help youth acquire independent living skills (Osterling & Hines, 2006).

Most studies of mentoring outcomes have focused on programmatic mentoring relationships with assigned volunteers and report mixed results. Areas of improvement are educational attainment (with borderline significance), suicidal risk, physical aggression, and general health (Ahrens et al., 2008). In a review of 55 studies of mentoring program effectiveness, researchers found favorable effects across age, gender, race and ethnicity, and family structure, though typically the benefits are modest in magnitude. The authors find strong linkage with beneficial outcomes for quality and intensity of relationships; frequency of contact, emotional closeness, and longevity may each make important and distinctive contributions to positive outcomes. The review also supports the prevailing view that mentoring offers the greatest potential benefits to youth who are individually at-risk or who live in at-risk environments (DuBois et al., 2002). Foster care alumni who have had mentoring relationships during adolescence show more favorable outcomes in a number of domains than those who have not been mentored. However, at-risk youth seem vulnerable to negative outcomes when mentoring relationships are disrupted within the first six months (Ahrens et al., 2008).

Because youth in care have so often experienced disrupted relationships and attachments, natural mentoring may provide a better fit. The relationships can form gradually, the two individuals are already present in each other's environments, and the relationships may be more likely to endure over time. A qualitative study of mentoring relationships among female youth of color in foster care suggests that the mentoring pairs develop trusting relationships that both parties associate with positive psychological, health, academic, and career outcomes. Youth report feeling that they can count on their mentors for emotional, informational, and instrumental support (Greeson & Bowen, 2008). Youth of color may particularly benefit from exposure to positive role models of the same ethnicity (Yancey, 1998).

Natural mentoring relationships, before discharge and during transition, can play an important part in supporting youth leaving care. The relationship itself may provide encouragement, emotional support, advice, and information. The sustained interest of a caring adult contributes to identity- and confidence-building and may help youth persevere with educational or career aspirations. Mentoring relationships can connect youth with a social network, increasing their resources and contacts. In view of the potentially negative impacts of disrupted mentoring relationships, it is vital that those relationships receive support from programs and staffs.

Structured mentoring can have a particular focus (cultural empowerment, career or job placement, or mentoring for young parents), but informal mentors can serve the same or similar purposes. Program staff can and do function as mentors to youth, both in helping them with independent living skills and in demonstrating consistent interest and caring.

Life Skills

The CWLA Standards of Excellence for TILSS lists life skills (acquisition and practice of concrete and intangible skills needed for daily living) as a youth outcome, and most ILPs and TLPs have a life skills component (Child Welfare League of America, 2005). A 2000 review of literature on independent living reports that over 90% of programs studied directly deliver modules on employment skills, communication, money management, decision-making, locating and maintaining housing, socialization, and healthy relationships. Fewer than 30% of programs studied directly provide vocational training, computer classes, or driver's education (Sheehy et al., 2000).

Youth in care often lack real-world opportunities to develop and practice skills that children and youth in the general population learn gradually over time as parents allow them to try things and fail and try them again (Loman & Siegel, 2000). Life skills training for youth in care comes during late adolescence if at all, and usually in the form of time-limited classes rather than through opportunities to experiment with new responsibilities in daily life. Youth need to internalize and personalize what they have learned and develop confidence about using the skill in the future (Sheehy et al., 2000). Assessment of life skills does not routinely occur prior to or at discharge, although this may be increasing with the use of the Ansell-Casey Life Skills Assessment instrument, a strength-based tool that involves youth and caregiver in identifying existing strengths and needed skills (Casey Family Programs Integrated Transition Practice Framework Task Force, 2001; Nollan et al., 2000).

Foster care alumni who were interviewed about their preparation for independent living state that instruction in organizational and money-management skills, and skills associated with getting a good job, are very important to them, but they give classes a mixed review (Georgiades, 2005a; Petr, 2008). Classes can provide information and exposure on the cognitive level, but youth need the lived experience of managing money, preparing food, preparing for a job interview, making a dental or medical appointment, or opening a bank account to fully develop these skills. Also, as the CWLA Standards point out, the acquisition of life skills is not an event, but a lifelong process (Child Welfare League of America, 2005).

Community Connections

Youth need help in developing connections with community life, including biological families, spiritual or religious organizations, cultural events and organizations, recreational and civic organizations, and school-related groups (Casey Family Programs Integrated Transition Practice Framework Task Force, 2001). Investment in the community *by* youth leads to community investment *in* youth and contributes to youth's identity development and their network of social support or social capital. Greater exposure in the community may also lead to naturally occurring mentoring relationships for youth.

Interdependence

No young adult lives truly independently, nor can youth emerging from foster care. The most recent studies of outcomes five years post-discharge provide convincing evidence that, for all the reasons described in the preceding chapters, most of them simply cannot make it on their own (Avery, 2010; Frey et al., 2005; Pecora et al., 2010). It is increasingly clear that the goals of transition programs must align with our understanding of the necessity for connection to others and a network of support. Programs give youth the time to establish the beginnings of these connections, and to build the internal and external resources that can provide a foundation for life in the adult world. Goyette (2007) refers to the "constructive interdependence" that is necessary for autonomous adult functioning. Formal and informal enduring connections, with family members, foster parents, and other significant adults, are needed to help youth feel grounded in the community and to provide social capital and psychological support (Scannapieco et al., 2007). Those who experience life without support are prone to loneliness and mental health problems (Propp et al., 2003). Without a safety net of relationships with adults who care, foster care alumni are at risk for falling through the economic and social cracks.

Voices of Foster Care Alumni

In Chapter 11, the importance of youth participation in creating transition plans was highlighted; the youth perspective is no less central to the design of effective transitional living programs (Child Welfare League of America, 2005; Crowe, 2007; Mendes & Moslehuddin, 2006; Naccarato & DeLorenzo, 2008). A study that asked youth focus groups what is needed for successful transitions described three major themes: youth-focused practice by child welfare workers, the need for collaboration and better communication with youth, and unmet needs and permanent connections (Scannapieco et al., 2007). A study of youth perspectives on placement moves reported, among other findings, that children in care too often felt uninformed about moves and were not allowed to grieve separations and losses, making it hard to trust others (Unrau, Seita, & Putney, 2008).

With the help of California Youth Connection, an advocacy group run by and for foster care alumni, I undertook an informal written survey of youth currently or formerly in foster care, to which 14 youth responded. I asked them to identify three things that had been most difficult about transitioning out of care, three that had been most helpful, advice they would give to social workers, and what they felt youth leaving care need most. Their answers are not dissimilar to the studies mentioned above. The difficulties most frequently cited are feeling alone and disconnected, with no support from an individual or family members; fear and worry about making the right decisions (about school, work, money); housing and transportation; and money management. Resilience makes a poignant appearance: many youth report feeling most helped by their own resourcefulness or abilities. Next in helpful experiences is a person they could trust (foster parent, family member, social worker); probably all those who cite their own strength would have named a helpful person, if they had been lucky enough to have one. ILP workshops or assistance and college preparatory programs are also mentioned as having been helpful.

The advice to social workers is telling: well over two-thirds of the youth feel that social workers need to listen more, be more involved, be less judgmental, get to know their clients better ("even if you have a big case load"), be honest, and provide more access to resources and follow-up to make sure youth are following their plans and not having problems. When asked what youth need most, they state strongly that youth most need support, love, and guidance—someone who will be there for them and care about them. A somewhat distant second need is housing.

Though not explicitly included as a question in the survey, the matter of unresolved trauma and grief was raised by youth, most often in response to the question, "Is there anything else about your foster care experience you would like to tell me?" Here are some of their comments:

"People think you're put together, so they forget you've been through trauma and you don't get help with it."

"I have not dealt with my father's death, so I sometimes hide behind my smile."

"I was adopted and did not see my social worker again ... my adoption was not a good one ... it was like they locked me up and threw away the key ... no one checked on me ... she kicked me out one week after graduation and threw away my college acceptance packet."

"I'm 16 and I've been through trauma for almost five years ... it has caused a lot of depression and slowing my roller coaster down.... Sometimes I can't receive the help they give but sometimes it needs to heal itself so I can feel better."

"Overall, my experience has been a struggle. I have been in countless homes (at least 16) and in so many places."

These responses remind us that many youth age out of care into a bleak and frightening world in which they feel alone. In most of this (admittedly small) sample, there was no reliable, caring adult in the picture. The provision of connection and adult support should be at the heart of services to youth in transition, in the form of stronger relational dimensions before and after the exit from care. The reflection of the self as valuable and deserving of adult care allows youth to step forward to meet the challenges of adulthood. The themes of relationship, connection, development, resolution of traumatic experience, and resilience inform the practice principles described below.

A Developmental, Relationship-Based Approach: Practice Principles

1. *Begin preparation for adulthood for youth in foster care early in adolescence and continue into the mid-twenties.* During early and mid-adolescence, expose youth in care to college preparation and planning, begin teaching life skills and enabling youth to practice them, and begin building connections to caring adults that can endure into adulthood. Provide aftercare into the late twenties and alumni programs that have no time limit.

2. *Tailor planning and programming to the individual youth,* based on comprehensive knowledge of the youth's life before and during care. Assessment should include life skills, supportive relationships, community connections, attachment history, physical and mental health, educational history, and strengths and aspirations. Consider factors of gender, race/ethnicity, sexual orientation, identity issues, and experiences of discrimination. Diversity and cultural competence of staff are necessary to effective assessments.

3. *Employ a two-pronged developmental approach.* First, evaluate biological and psychosocial development relative to normative

development, including impacts of early trauma or disrupted attachments, and the status of identity development. Second, adapt individual programs and plans over time as young adult development and growth continue to occur. Youth will need a different menu of services and support at 18 than they do at 20, 22, or 24.

4. *Design programs to be comprehensive and dynamic.* Program components should be capable of influencing and building on other components and designed as part of a continuous effort toward a better person–environment fit. For example, community connections might intersect with and contribute to cultural identity or emotional healing, which might then lead to availability or motivation for higher education. Housing components can be on a continuum, with more supervision at the outset, followed by a range of levels of responsibility, and leading to permanent housing options. Alumni of a program can serve as peer mentors to new residents, or have periods of responsibility for alumni activities and communications, thereby building interpersonal skills as well as developing networks of social support.

5. *Incorporate attachment-related elements into program design.* Foster care alumni have experienced many "ambiguous losses," those in which a person may be physically absent but psychologically present, or physically present but psychologically absent. Their relationships have been marked by impermanence and lack of resolution in the past, including when they exit from care (Samuels, 2008).

    a. Develop staff knowledge and awareness of the impact of maltreatment and family disruption on development, attachment patterns, and affect regulation so that they can recognize and intervene appropriately with youth who have experienced trauma.

    b. Incentivize and cultivate long-term commitments to programs among staff, so that relationships with youth can be sustained throughout the term of their participation in the program, if at all possible.

    c. Nurture community within programs, through contact, activities, and service as well as ties to the community beyond programs. Youth need and benefit from relationships and sharing of experiences with other youth who have been in foster care (McMillen et al., 1997).

6. *Reconceptualize successful young adult life as interdependent.* An emphasis on self-sufficiency as a measure of success is unrealistic, for adolescents in general and for foster care alumni, as all young people need to feel and be connected as they move toward adulthood. *Interdependent living* is a goal that more accurately represents the process of emerging adult development,

with its uncertainties, steps forward and back, and gaps in ability to navigate the transition. Internal and external resources develop and grow from connectedness to significant others, organizations, and communities.

7. *Incorporate the voice of foster care alumni in program design.*
   As consumers of transitional living services, youth are able to provide a unique perspective on how existing services are or are not helpful and what changes could be useful.

8. *Include rigorous evaluation protocols.* Conceptualization of program components should incorporate a methodology for measuring outcomes, relating them to program elements where possible, and data collection over time.

PART **V**

FUTURE DIRECTIONS

13

POLICY IMPLICATIONS AND DIRECTIONS FOR FUTURE RESEARCH

We all need somebody to lean on.

—Bill Withers

Policy, research, and practice are continuously influenced by one another, along with other features of the social and political environment. The relations among these domains can be beneficial, with all parties acting as collaborators, resources, and advisors to one another, but this is not inevitably the case. Policy and practice can (and should more often) be shaped by research, which may identify gaps, failures, and successes. Practice may be both guided and constrained by policy requirements. Practice phenomena and policy interests may give rise to research, which, in turn, shapes ensuing practice and policy.

This chapter considers how the ideas and research presented throughout the book can be embodied in policy and future research contexts. We begin with a discussion of the philosophy underlying the most recent legislation affecting youth leaving care, PL 110-351, the Fostering Connections to Success and Increasing Adoptions Act of 2008. The next section looks at key provisions of the Act, as well as recommendations for policies affecting children in care and youth leaving care. The chapter then describes the current state of research, identifies understudied areas, and presents recommendations for future research.

Policy

The Social Construction of Youth Leaving Care

Social policies result when problems find their way onto the policy agenda through problem definitions that are compelling and persuasive enough to influence political processes. Elections, the national mood, the needs and values of local populations, community and judicial actions, the influence of interest groups, the social construction of the problem population, and the presence or absence of a solution all play roles in the status of a problem on the agenda (Collins & Clay, 2009; Webb & Harden, 2003).

Collins and Clay outline the dichotomies involved in the social construction of a problem population: worthy–unworthy, deserving–undeserving, familiar–strange, and sympathetic–threatening. The problem of youth leaving care has been defined in a number of ways that paint a sympathetic portrait: the system's inability to adequately address transition, lack of permanent relationships, history of trauma, lack of skills for adult life, and fewer resources. On the other hand, the politics of child welfare issues are that they are often marginalized within state policy agendas, or the focus is on the tragedies that affect the very young. As vulnerable, abused children become troubled adolescents with poor social outcomes, the social construction may lean more toward the negative (Collins & Clay, 2009).

The funding for child welfare reflects the low placement of child well-being generally on the national agenda of priorities: since 2001, entitlement spending (including child welfare) has accounted for only eight percent of new federal legislation contributing to the soaring federal deficit. By contrast, 85% goes to defense, homeland security, and tax cuts. The remaining seven percent of new legislation is other domestic discretionary funding (Laird & Michael, 2006).

The current construction of the problems of transition-age youth has begun to emphasize connection and interdependence, where previously self-sufficiency and independence were prominent (Courtney, 2009; Mendes & Moslehuddin, 2006; Propp, Ortega, & NewHeart, 2003). The title of the new legislation, Fostering Connections to Success and Increasing Adoptions Act, expressly recognizes the importance of connection and even lifelong connection. It supports youth in care and improves upon previous legislation by allowing states to claim federal funds for continuing foster care payments for older youth in care (and, in some cases, guardianship or adoption-assistance payments) up to age 21. To be eligible, youth must be engaged in work, school, or a program designed to eliminate barriers to or promote employment or be unable to engage in those activities due to a medical condition. In addition, states can claim funds to assist relatives who want to provide permanent guardianship to children in care, and Indian tribes can directly claim Title IV-E funds for eligible youth in care without state–tribal agreements. The Act further requires states to help children in foster care remain in their original schools or get a prompt transfer to a new school that is more appropriate for them (Children's Defense Fund, 2009). These provisions constitute tacit recognition of the fact that the state, via the courts and child welfare agencies, has taken on the role of "corporate parent," in which public institutions share responsibility to provide the kind of support that good parents would provide to their own children (Courtney, 2009).

The social construction of young adulthood and transitioning out of foster care is in flux: most parents do not stop supporting their children until their thirties, and most Americans do not consider a person to be an adult until about age 26 or when he or she has finished school, obtained a full-time job, and begun to raise a family. Furthermore, money is not the only form of support that parents provide during the transition to adulthood (Delgado et al., 2007). Advances in brain research demonstrating that development of the executive functions of the brain is still very much in progress into the twenties have informed the view that reaching adulthood is a process rather than an event. Greater general understanding of long-term consequences of trauma or maltreatment experienced during childhood have also deepened awareness of the ongoing needs of foster care alumni as they move into adulthood.

Two additional recent philosophical trends are reflected in the literature and legislation: the role of the voice of foster care alumni, and the need for collaboration among youth-serving agencies and individuals. Youth in the foster care system are increasingly seen by researchers and professionals in the field as necessary partners in creating their individual transition plans and in program design more generally (Child Welfare League of America, 2005; Mendes & Moslehuddin, 2006; Mosqueda & Rodriguez, 2006; Naccarato & DeLorenzo, 2008). Individual plans and program design involve an array of overlapping domains and services; the success of a plan or program depends upon the coordination and integration of constituent parts. Communication and collaboration are mentioned frequently as critical factors in policy recommendations (Casey Family Programs Integrated Transition Practice Framework Task Force, 2001; Casey Family Programs, 2008; Courtney, 2009; Mares, 2008).

Policy Issues Affecting Children While in Care

Research in recent years has identified a number of issues that may contribute to poor outcomes for alumni of foster care and are beginning to be addressed on both the policy and the practice levels.

Placement Stability

The first of these is the adverse effects of placement instability on a variety of outcomes, including educational achievement, identity development, and rates of entry into the juvenile justice system (Courtney & Heuring, 2005; Mosqueda & Rodriguez, 2006; Ryan & Testa, 2005; Samuels, 2008). There needs to be greater recognition by policy makers, but also by foster families, that many youth have lived in very troubled situations prior to entering care and that this has had an impact on their ability to adjust to any given substitute-care situation. Future policies should focus on greater stability and continuity in placement by means of effective intervention during placement problems. Policy directed toward this end calls for manageable caseloads, appropriately trained staff, and supports to foster families. The Fostering Connections Act of 2008 seeks to address the educational fallout of placement changes—disruptions to education, delays in transfer of school records—by requiring states to help foster children remain in their original schools.

Developmental Needs of Children

Policies need to support a focus on the child's developmental needs, including rapid and specialized assessments upon entry into the system, screening and treatment for mental health disorders, and training for foster caregivers on mental health disorders (Badeau et al., 2004; Casey Family Programs Integrated Transition Practice Framework Task Force, 2001). The quality of the caregiving surround makes a difference: high-quality foster homes that provide emotional support and cognitive stimulation lead to better outcomes in behavior problems, cognitive and language scores, and social skills (Harden et al., 2010).

A focus on development includes recognition of the fact that identity development is an ongoing process throughout childhood and adolescence. The potential of substitute-care experiences to affect that process can be influenced by the kinds of supports available to caregivers. Substitute-care relationships themselves should be supported through training and attention to the relational components of existing services (Duval & Vincent, 2009; Munson & McMillen, 2009).

Racial Disproportionality

The disproportionality in the child welfare system (and the juvenile justice system) calls for a policy response. Data from the National Survey of Child and Adolescent Well-Being show that "an overwhelming number of children of color are in the child welfare system," and African American children are the single most over-represented and disproportionate group in foster care (Ortega et al., 2010). The fact that every jurisdiction except the District of Columbia shows some level of disproportionate representation of children of color underscores the system-wide nature of the problem. There are many contributing factors: poverty, institutional racism, cultural insensitivity, substance abuse, racial disparities at each decision-point of the child welfare and juvenile justice systems, and the fact that most federal and state funding supports services and programs that are offered after entry into care (Jones, 2006; Webb & Harden, 2003). Research demonstrates that racial disproportionality exists within the child welfare and juvenile justice systems as it does in many other systems in our society; the question of how to intervene preventively prior to entry into the system is complex and requires broader changes in the sociopolitical surround.

Within-system change requires greater emphasis on culturally competent staff and programs, more inclusion of communities and families in developing solutions to strengthen family life, and increased education and training on institutional racism.

Policy Issues Affecting the Transition to Adulthood

Extending Care

The process of moving from adolescence to adulthood is longer, more complex, and more challenging for all youth, most of whom draw heavily on family resources as they make the transition. These challenges are multiplied many times for youth in foster care, whose support in many states ends at just this point. The age of biological maturity is demonstrably later than age 18, occurring sometime in the early or mid-twenties (Magyar, 2006).

The factor that most determines how youth experience the transition out of care is the way in which particular states implement federal legislation (Dworsky & Havlicek, 2008). The federal government provides funds to states, some of which directly administer and supervise their programs for transitioning youth, and about one-third of which supervise county-administered programs. States have discretion in determining eligibility and can allow youth to remain in care until age 21 under conditions described earlier in this chapter, yet in many states youth leave care at 18 or soon after. The minimum age for Chafee-funded services is 14, but despite calls to start preparation early, more than one-quarter of states do not begin serving youth until they are 15. The option to continue Medicaid coverage until age 21 is implemented in only two-thirds of states, and although not mandated to do so, many states still require youth to apply for extended coverage (Dworsky & Havlicek, 2008). Young adults aged 18 to 24 have the highest uninsured rate of all age groups; the Medicaid option could (and should) be converted into a national mandate so that all foster care alumni would have health insurance (Casey Family Programs, 2008; English & Grasso, 2000; Shirk & Stangler, 2006).

The Fostering Connections Act will begin reimbursing states for extending care in fiscal year 2010; funding for foster care alumni is a primary capacity–building need for states and counties (Courtney, Dworsky, & Peters, 2009). Legislators and the public consider the costs of extending care and not the benefits, but the improved potential outcomes of additional support to foster care alumni affect society as well as the individual youth. In a cost-benefit analysis of extending care to age 21 for the State of California, Courtney et al. estimate the average cost per youth at approximately $37,948 overall, to be shared by federal ($13,282), state ($9,866), and county ($14,800) governments. Extending care is associated with increased post-secondary educational attainment, delayed pregnancy, higher earnings, less likelihood of incarceration, and reduced dependency on public assistance (Courtney et al., 2009; Magyar, 2006). The benefits even when youth do not complete college are estimated at $84,000 overall, and they are higher for those who complete college (Courtney et al., 2009). A second cost-benefit analysis in California adds savings in incarceration costs and recidivism, and assumes cost-avoidance in mental health services, substance abuse, homelessness, and second-generation foster care as long-term potential benefits to society of extending care (Packard et al., 2008).

Option to Return

Youth who can remain in care but choose not to should be able to opt back in if, like adolescents in the general population who leave home and then return because they cannot yet manage independence, they find themselves in need of services. Federal policy should permit any youth who has spent time in care after age 16, including those who have returned to their (often troubled) families or have run away, to return through age 21(Courtney, 2009; Delgado et al., 2007).

Family Relationships and Permanent Connections

The arena of family relationships is another poorly addressed but important domain in the lives of foster care alumni, many of whom have considerable ongoing contact with their families of origin, well into young adulthood (Courtney, 2009). Birth families and foster families constitute potential resources during early adulthood, but youth and their families may need additional help or supports to build constructive relationships going forward. Relationships between youth and other caring or committed adults may need ongoing or occasional support from professionals. Child welfare agencies could add services that focus on family dynamics as a component of transitional living or aftercare services.

Aftercare

Even with the extension of transitional living services to age 21, there is a need for aftercare: helping youth get into and stay in college, assisting with long-term housing and jobs, facilitating alumni relationships and networking, and ongoing mentoring. As described in Chapters 6 through 9, many youth struggle with substance abuse and other mental health disorders and will continue to need access to treatment. The importance of having professional staff with training and knowledge of development and trauma cannot be overstated, and it underscores the need for public

> **Box 13.1 Key Policy Recommendations**
>
> 1. Interdependence and connection should (continue to) be defining constructs within which policies for youth leaving care are considered.
> 2. The individual, developmental, and ethnocultural needs of youth should shape transition planning and services, with the active participation of youth.
> 3. Stability of placement should be prioritized and supported.
> 4. Federal legislation should mandate (rather than merely allow) an early beginning to transition planning and services and extended care, including Medicaid, for all youth who have been in foster care after the age of 16.
> 5. Youth who were in care after age 16 and who exit care before age 21 should have an opportunity to opt back in up to age 21.
> 6. Funding for aftercare services should include mental health services, and family- and relationship-focused interventions.
> 7. The recognition of the importance of permanent, caring relationships should be supported by relationship-centered services. Child welfare, juvenile justice, and transitional-living workers should receive training in development, trauma, and attachment.

investment in the clinical infrastructure of youth-serving agencies and systems (Frey, Greenblatt, & Brown, 2005; Nissen, 2006).

Research

The Current State of Research

The research literature on the transition to adulthood for youth leaving foster care is itself in transition. Most studies have focused on foster care outcomes or independent living program evaluation. There have been large-scale studies that demonstrate generally sobering outcomes in the areas of educational attainment, mental health problems, incarceration, early pregnancy and parenthood, and unemployment (Courtney, 2009).

Many early studies used retrospective follow-up designs, obtaining primarily descriptive information from samples of former foster youth sometime after discharge (Mech, 2001). Subsequent and more-current studies look at outcomes beginning at the time of discharge and then in successive waves for the first few years after exit from care (Courtney et al., 2007; Havalchak, White, & O'Brien, 2008; Pecora et al., 2010). Georgiades points out that many studies have been largely theoretically uninformed in design and interpretation, although the Northwest Foster Care Alumni Study is an outstanding exception (Georgiades, 2005b; Pecora et al., 2010). Studies of independent living services have typically not analyzed relationships between well-defined service patterns and operational outcomes, and there is a need for a widely accepted core set of performance measures or outcome indicators (Courtney et al., 2008; Mech, 2001). Rigorously designed evaluation of programs is just now beginning; one such evaluation of life skills training occurred in Los Angeles and failed to detect a significant impact on any concrete indicators of successful transition (Courtney et al., 2008; Nixon & Jones, 2000).

There is a great need to know what helps youth who have been in foster care become successful as adults, but we must first be able to define and measure "success." Historically, success has been defined as the ability to maintain oneself without outside assistance, but, as discussed, this is not a realistic goal for individuals in their early twenties, even in the general population (Samuels & Pryce, 2008). Because tangible skills and outcomes are more easily measured, research is often designed to gauge concrete outcomes; intangibles, such as a sense of purpose, connection, and belonging, have not been yet operationalized in measurable ways (Propp et al., 2003). But it is the connections to others and a well-developed sense of self that enable young people to persevere with their education, maintain positive workplace relationships, and engage in prosocial community activities. A small, but growing, number of authors are focusing on more qualitative, theory-driven analyses with youth perspectives in the foreground (Avery, 2010; Scannapieco, Schagrin, & Scannapieco, 1995; Scannapieco, Connell-Carrick, & Painter, 2007; Unrau, 2007; Unrau, Seita, & Putney, 2008).

Under-Studied Areas

Despite the disproportionate representation of youth of color in the foster care system, there is little research that focuses on the specific ways the system serves or fails to serve diverse ethnic populations (Badeau et al., 2004). Emotional well-being, relationships with biological and foster families, and relationships with professionals in the child welfare and juvenile justice systems are under-studied, but they could provide important guidance for policy and practice. Examination of mental health status at entry into care, prior to leaving care, and after discharge could tell us more about the effects of the emancipation process on mental health (Rashid, 2004; White et al., 2009).

Placement stability may be critical to building positive attachments during foster care; research is needed to clarify the contributors to that process (Pecora et al., 2010; Schwartz, McRoy, & Downs, 2004). We know little about the later attachments of foster care alumni, or about the long-term effects of trauma, especially unresolved trauma, among these youth. There are few data about the relationships between gender, ethnicity, or sexual orientation and particular outcomes.

Future Directions for Research

Program evaluation that is rigorous and connects specific outcomes (housing stability, educational attainment, career satisfaction, networks of social support) to specific program components (education, employment, housing, or relational interventions, for example) is essential to ensuring that policies support effective services and discontinue those that have little benefit. Qualitative, longitudinal research could delineate the reasons why some youth choose not to participate in independent living services (Georgiades, 2005a). Along with evaluation of programs, we need to learn more about the risk and protective factors that contribute to different outcomes and, importantly, whether extending care to age 21 does improve outcomes for foster youth (Courtney et al., 2007).

Studies of LGBT youth in care and after exit could provide documentation of their experiences and point the way to interventions that can support them more effectively. Studies of specific racial/ethnic youth in care could examine their unique needs and problems and clarify issues of institutional racism or discrimination (Mendes & Moslehuddin, 2006; White et al., 2007). Identity development in the foster care population,

---

Box 13.2 Key Research Recommendations

1. Convene stakeholders (researchers, providers, former foster youth) to arrive at nationally agreed-upon outcome indicators for rigorous evaluations of independent living services and programs.
2. Move developmental and relational issues to share center stage with concrete indicators in designing longitudinal research.
3. Bring gender, ethnicity, and sexual orientation more centrally onto the research agenda.
4. Study the impact of extending care to age 21, and the impact of aftercare services and social networks.
5. Use research to identify risk and protective factors that have a bearing on outcomes and resiliency.

including ethnic identity, is another area for longitudinal, large-scale study. Finally, though mentorship has been studied among youth in care, attachment relationships of adolescence and adulthood, such as those with other adults, foster parents, program staff, young adult peers, and partners, have not been examined.

Concluding Thoughts

Society's stakes are always high in child welfare services.

(Berrick et al., 1998)

The generally poor outcomes of foster care alumni show us just how high those stakes can be. Despite increased attention, legislation more supportive of youth aging out of care, and a greater range and number of transition-related services, foster care alumni continue to face greater psychosocial and economic hardships and generally fare more poorly than young adults in the general population. The purpose of this book has been to broaden and deepen our understanding of factors that contribute to these poor outcomes in order to improve the effectiveness of the child welfare community's efforts to assist the youth who have been in its care. We have argued that the ongoing interaction of early childhood adversity, infant and child development, individual and family characteristics and relationships, the foster care system, and the larger social context exerts a continuous influence on the emerging adult.

From the earliest moments of life, infant brain development is being shaped by experience; physiological or psychological trauma, neglect, and separation from primary attachment figures can set the stage for subsequent developmental problems, dysregulated stress-response systems, academic difficulty, and disturbed future attachments. These problems can preclude adjustment to foster placement and relationships with peers and potentially helpful adults, and heighten the risk of mental-health and substance-use disorders. Any of these difficulties, in turn, can lead to disruption of foster placement, placement instability, school instability, and an accumulation of losses that may go unresolved and unassuaged. If, in addition, youth are members of ethnic or sexual minority groups, have disabilities, or have juvenile justice involvement, the sense of self bears the weight of multiple stigmatized identities. For many youth, the internal sequelae of childhood maltreatment may be hidden beneath visible and concrete problems like homelessness, substance abuse, or criminal involvement.

Central themes of this book, and central to policy and practice with youth leaving care, are knowledge of development from infancy through emerging adulthood and opportunities for positive attachments. Recent advances in the understanding of young adult development make it clear that the areas of the brain involved in judgment and decision-making continue to develop well into one's twenties (Blakemore & Choudhury, 2006), and that psychosocial readiness to be self-sufficient progresses gradually (Arnett, 2000; Avery, 2010). Yet society asks foster care alumni, whose development may already have been compromised by adverse experience and who may have a stunted network of support, to be ready to take on adulthood overnight at age 18.

The importance of relationships with significant, caring, and consistent adults during the transitional period cannot be overstated. All of the young people described in the book, and nearly all of the youth who responded to my survey, mentioned the need for people who care about them, believe in them, or are models of something they can admire and wish to emulate. Current policies call for the identification of a committed adult in every youth's transition plan; this is necessary, but not sufficient. Greater attention must be given to attachment and relational dimensions of foster placement, whether in foster family settings or group homes, mental health interventions, transitional living programs, and community involvement. It is within these dimensions that the greatest power and the most painful disappointments, but also the greatest hopes, reside. We see ourselves in the eyes of those we care about and who care about us: when those eyes are attentive, engaged, and loving, the construction of self-worth, competence, and optimism begins. A sturdy, positive sense of self nested in a social network is what youth leaving the foster care system need to face the challenges of life after care.

REFERENCES

AACAP (1998). Practice parameters for the assessment and treatment of children and adolescents with depressive disorder. *Journal of the American Academy of Child and Adolescent Psychiatry, 37*(10), 63S.

AACAP (2000). Practice parameters for the assessment and treatment of children and adolescents with suicidal behavior. *Journal of the American Academy of Child and Adolescent Psychiatry,39* 1–53.

AACAP (2007). Practice parameter for the assessment and treatment of children and adolescents with bipolar disorder. *Journal of the American Academy of Child and Adolescent Psychiatry, 46*(1), 107.

Abney, M., Park, M., & Yamashiro, N. (2007). *Model practices study of transitional housing programs for emancipated foster youth.* Unpublished Master of Arts thesis. University of Southern California, Los Angeles, CA. :May 9, 2007.

Abram, K., Teplin, L., McClelland, G., & Dulcan, M. (2003). Comorbid psychiatric disorders in youth in juvenile detention. *Archives of General Psychiatry, 60,* 1097–1108.

Acoca, L. (2004). Are those cookies for me or my baby? Understanding detained and incarcerated teen mothers and their children. *Juvenile and Family Court Journal, 55*(2), 65–80.

Aglan, A., Kerfoot, M., & Pickles, A. (2008). Pathways from adolescent deliberate self-poisoning to early adult outcomes: A six-year follow up. *Journal of Child Psychology and Psychiatry, 49*(5), 508–515.

Ahrens, K., DuBois, D., Richardson, L., Fan, M., & Lozano, P. (2008). Youth in foster care with adult mentors during adolescence have improved outcomes. *Pediatrics, 121*(2), e246–52.

Ainsworth, M., Blehar, M., Waters, E., & Wall, S. (1978). *Patterns of attachment.* Hillsdale, NJ: Lawrence Erlbaum Associates.

Alderson, K. (2003). The ecological model of gay male identity. *The Canadian Journal of Human Sexuality, 12*(2), 75–85.

Alegría, M., Canino, G., Shrout, P. E., Woo, M., Duan, N., Vila, D., Torres, M., Chen, C., & Meng, X. (2008). Prevalence of mental illness in immigrant and non-immigrant U.S. Latino groups. *The American Journal of Psychiatry, 165*(3), 359–70.

Alegria, M., Chatterji, P., Wells, K., Cao, Z., Chen, C., Takeuchi, D., Jackson, J., & Meng, X. (2008). Disparity in depression treatment among racial and ethnic minority populations in the United States. *Psychiatric Services, 59*(11), 1264–72.

Alexander, B., & Schrauben, S. (2006). Outside the margins: Youth who are different and their special health care needs. *Primary Care: Clinics in Office Practice, 33*(2), 285–303.

Allen, J., & Land, D. (1999). Attachment in adolescence. In J. Cassidy & P. Shaver (Eds.), *Handbook of attachment: Theory, research, and clinical applications* (pp. 319–34). New York: The Guilford Press.

Allen, M., & Bissell, M. (2004). Safety and stability for foster children: The policy context. *The Future of Children, 14*(1), 48–73.

Alltucker, K., Bullis, M., Close, D., & Yovanoff, P. (2006). Different pathways to juvenile delinquency: Characteristics of early and late starters in a sample of previously incarcerated youth. *Journal of Child and Family Studies, 15*(4), 479–92.

Amaro, H., Chernoff, M., Brown, V., Arevalo, S., & Gatz, M. (2007). Does integrated trauma-informed substance abuse treatment increase treatment retention? *Journal of Community Psychology, 35*(7), 845–62.

American Bar Association, & National Bar Association (2001). *Justice by gender: The lack of appropriate prevention, diversion and treatment alternatives for girls in the justice system.* Chicago: American Bar Association and National Bar Association.

American Psychiatric Association (2000). *Diagnostic and statistical manual of mental disorders, 4th edition, text revision.* Arlington, VA: American Psychiatric Association.

Anctil, T., McCubbin, L., O'Brien, K., & Pecora, P. (2007). An evaluation of recovery factors for foster care alumni with physical or psychiatric impairments: Predictors of psychological outcomes. *Children and Youth Services Review, 29*, 1021–34.

Anctil, T., McCubbin, L., O'Brien, K., Pecora, P., & Anderson-Harumi, C. (2007). Predictors of adult quality of life for foster care alumni with physical and/or psychiatric disabilities. *Child Abuse & Neglect, 31*, 1087–1100.

Anda, R., Felitti, V., Bremner, J., Walker, J., Whitfield, C., Perry, B., Dube, S., & Giles, W. (2006). The enduring effects of abuse and related adverse experiences in childhood. *European Archives of Psychiatry and Clinical Neuroscience, 256*, 174–86.

Andersen, S., & Teicher, M. (2008). Stress, sensitive periods and maturational events in adolescent depression. *Trends in Neuroscience, 31*(4), 183–91.

Anderson, B., Holmes, M., & Ostresh, E. (1999). Male and female delinquents' attachments and effects of attachments on severity of self-reported delinquency. *Criminal Justice and Behavior, 26*(4), 435–52.

Anderson, J. (2000). The need for interagency collaboration for children with emotional and behavioral disabilities and their families. *Families in Society, 81*(5), 484–93.

Applegate, J., & Shapiro, J. (2005). *Neurobiology for clinical social work: Theory and practice.* New York: W. W. Norton & Company.

Archer, J. (2001). Broad and narrow perspectives in grief theory: Comment on Bonanno and Kaltman. *Psychological Bulletin, 127*(4), 554–60.

Ards, S., Myers, S., Malkis, A., Sugrue, E., & Zhou, L. (2003). Racial disproportionality in reported and substantiated child abuse and neglect: An examination of systematic bias. *Children and Youth Services Review, 25*(5/6), 375–89.

Arnett, J. (2000). Emerging adulthood: A theory of development from the late teens through the twenties. *American Psychologist, 55*(5), 469–80.

Ashby, L. (1997). *Endangered children: Dependency, neglect, and abuse in American history.* New York: Twayne Publishers.

Auslander, B., & Rosenthal, S. (2010). Intimate romantic relationships in young adulthood: A biodevelopmental perspective. In J. Grant & M. Potenza (Eds.), *Young adult mental health* (pp. 158–68). New York: Oxford University Press.

Auslander, B., Rosenthal, S., & Blythe, M. (2005). Sexual development and behaviors of adolescents. *Pediatric Annals, 34*(10), 785–93.

Avery, R. (2010). An examination of theory and promising practice for achieving permanency for teens before they age out of foster care. *Children and Youth Services Review, 32,* 399–408.

Avery, R., & Freundlich, M. (2009). You're all grown up now: Termination of foster care support at age 18. *Journal of Adolescence, 32,* 247–57.

Bach, C., Downs, A., Friend, R., Patz, C., & Topkins, R. (2001). Preparation of youth for employment (PYE): Description and evaluation of a competency-based approach to economic independence. In K. Nollan & A. Downs (Eds.), *Preparing youth for long-term success: Proceedings from the Casey family program national independent living forum* (pp. 61–72). Washington, DC: Child Welfare League of America.

Badeau, S., Perez, A., Lightbourne, W., Gray, E., & Gonzalez, L. (2004). Five commentaries: Looking to the future. *The Future of Children, 14*(1), 174–89.

Baer, J., & Martinez, C. (2006). Child maltreatment and insecure attachment: A meta-analysis. *Journal of Reproductive and Infant Psychology, 24*(3), 187–97.

Bamba, S., & Haight, W. (2007). Helping maltreated children to find their *ibasho*: Japanese perspectives on supporting the well-being of children in state care. *Children and Youth Services Review, 29,* 405–27.

Bamba, S., & Haight, W. (2009). The developmental-ecological approach of Japanese child welfare professionals to supporting children's social and emotional well-being: The practice of *mimamori. Children and Youth Services Review, 31,* 429–39.

Barn, R., & Mantovani, N. (2007). Young mothers and the care system: Contextualizing risk and vulnerability. *British Journal of Social Work, 37,* 225–43.

Bass, S., Shields, M., & Behrman, R. (2004). Children, families, and foster care: Analysis and recommendations. *The Future of Children, 14*(1), 4–29.

Battjes, R. J., Gordon, M. S., O'Grady, K. E., Kinlock, T. W., & Carswell, M. (2003). Factors that predict adolescent motivation for substance abuse treatment. *Journal of Substance Abuse Treatment, 24*(3), 221–32.

Beck, A. T. (2008). The evolution of the cognitive model of depression and its neurobiological correlates. *The American Journal of Psychiatry, 165*(8), 969–77.

Beeman, S., Kim, H., & Bullerdick, S. (2000). Factors affecting placement of children in kinship and nonkinship foster care. *Children and Youth Services Review, 22*(1), 37–54.

Bender, K., Springer, D. W., & Kim, J. S. (2006). Treatment effectiveness with dually diagnosed adolescents: A systematic review. *Brief Treatment and Crisis Intervention: Special Issue on Evidence-Based Brief Treatment and Crisis, 6*(3), 177–205.

Bennett, M. D., Jr. (2006). Culture and context: A study of neighborhood effects on racial socialization and ethnic identity content in a sample of African American adolescents. *Journal of Black Psychology, 32*(4), 479–500.

Bernburg, J., & Krohn, M. (2003). Labeling, life chances, and adult crime: The direct and indirect effects of official intervention in adolescence on crime in early adulthood. *Criminology, 41*(4), 1287–1318.

Bernier, A., & Meins, E. (2008). A threshold approach to understanding the origins of attachment disorganization. *Developmental Psychology, 44*(4), 969–82.

Berrick, J. (1998). When children cannot remain home: Foster family care and kinship care. *The Future of Children, 8*(1), 72–87.

Berrick, J., Needell, B., Barth, R., & Jonson-Reid, M. (1998). *The tender years: Toward developmentally sensitive child welfare services for very young children.* New York: Oxford University Press.

Bettmann, J., & Jasperson, R. (2010). Anxiety in adolescence: The integration of attachment and neurobiological research into clinical practice. *Clinical Social Work Journal, 38*, 98–106.

Bifulco, A., Kwon, J., Jacobs, C., Moran, P., Bunn, A., & Beer, N. (2006). Adult attachment style as mediator between childhood neglect/abuse and adult depression and anxiety. *Social Psychiatry and Psychiatric Epidemiology, 41*, 796–805.

Bilchik, S. (2008). Is racial and ethnic equity possible in juvenile justice? *Reclaiming Children and Youth, 17*(2), 19–23.

Birmaher, B., Axelson, D., Monk, K., Kalas, C., Clark, D., Ehmann, M., Bridge, J., Heo, J., & Brent, D. (2003). Fluoxetine for the treatment of childhood anxiety disorders. *Journal of the American Academy of Child and Adolescent Psychiatry, 42*(4), 415–23.

Blair, C. (2006). How similar are fluid cognition and general intelligence? A developmental neuroscience perspective on fluid cognition as an aspect of human cognitive ability. *Behavioral and Brain Sciences, 29*, 109–60.

Blakemore, S., & Choudhury, S. (2006). Development of the adolescent brain: Implications for executive function and social cognition. *Journal of Child Psychology, 47*(3), 296–312.

Boden, J. M., Fergusson, D. M., & Horwood, L. J. (2007). Anxiety disorders and suicidal behaviors in adolescence and young adulthood: Findings from a longitudinal study. *Psychological Medicine, 37*(3), 431–40.

Bolen, R. (2000). Validity of attachment theory. *Trauma, Violence, & Abuse, 1*(2), 128–53.

Bolen, R. (2002). Child sexual abuse and attachment theory: Are we rushing headlong into another controversy? *Journal of Child Sexual Abuse, 11*(1), 95–124.

Bolland, J., Bryant, C., Lian, B., McCallum, D., Vazsonyi, A., & Barth, J. (2007). Development and risk behavior among African American, Caucasian, and mixed-race adolescents living in high poverty inner-city neighborhoods. *American Journal of Community Psychology, 40*, 230–49.

Booth, A., Rustenbach, E., & McHale, S. (2008). Early family transitions and depressive symptom changes from adolescence to early adulthood. *Journal of Marriage and Family, 70*, 3–14.

Booth, J., Farrell, A., & Varano, S. (2008). Social control, serious delinquency, and risky behavior: A gendered analysis. *Crime & Delinquency, 54*(3), 423–56.

Boss, P. (2007). Ambiguous loss theory: Challenges for scholars and practitioners. *Family Relations, 56*, 105–111.

Bowlby, J. (1988). *A secure base.* New York: Basic Books.

Boyer, D., & Fine, D. (1992). Sexual abuse as a factor in adolescent pregnancy and child maltreatment. *Family Planning Perspectives, 24*(1), 4–19.

Bracey, J., Bamaca, M., & Umana-Taylor, A. (2004). Examining ethnic identity and self-esteem among biracial and monoracial adolescents. *Journal of Youth and Adolescence, 33*(2), 123–32.

Brady, K., & Sinha, R. (2005). Co-occurring mental and substance use disorders: The neurobiological effects of chronic stress. *American Journal of Psychiatry, 162*(8), 1483–93.

Branch, C. (2001). The many faces of self: Ego and ethnic identities. *The Journal of Genetic Psychology, 162*(4), 412–29.

Brandford, C., & English, D. (2004). *Foster youth transition to independence study: Final report.* Seattle, WA: Office of Children's Administration Research.

Brannigan, R., Schackman, B., Falco, M., & Millman, R. (2004). The quality of highly regarded adolescent substance abuse treatment programs: Results of an in-depth national survey. *Archives of Pediatric and Adolescent Medicine, 158*, 904–909.

Breda, C. S., & Heflinger, C. A. (2007). The impact of motivation to change on substance used among adolescents in treatment. *Journal of Child & Adolescent Substance Abuse, 16*(3), 109–24.

Breland-Noble, A., Elbogen, E., Farmer, E., Dubs, M., Wagner, H., & Burns, B. (2004). Use of psychotropic medications by youths in therapeutic foster care and group homes. *Psychiatric Services, 55*(6), 706–708.

Bretherton, I., & Munholland, K. (1999). Internal working models in attachment relationships. In J. Cassidy & P. Shaver (Eds.), *Handbook of attachment: Theory, research, and clinical applications* (pp. 89–111). New York: The Guilford Press.

Brook, J., Brook, D., & Pahl, K. (2006). The developmental context for adolescent substance abuse intervention. In H. Liddle & C. Rowe (Eds.), *Adolescent substance abuse: Research and clinical advances* (pp. 25–51). Cambridge, UK: Cambridge University Press.

Brook, J. S., Brook, D. W., & Whiteman, M. (2003). Maternal correlates of toddler insecure and dependent behavior. *The Journal of Genetic Psychology, 164*(1), 72–87.

Brown, E. (2005). Psychosocial and psychiatric correlates and treatment of posttraumatic stress disorder in children and adolescents. *Psychiatric Annals, 35*(9), 759–65.

Brown, J., Cohen, P., Johnson, J., & Smailes, E. (1999). Childhood abuse and neglect: Specificity of effects on adolescent and young adult depression and suicidality. *Journal of the American Academy of Child and Adolescent Psychiatry, 38*(12), 1490–96.

Brown, S., & Abrantes, A. (2006). Substance use disorders. In D. Wolfe & E. Mash (Eds.), *Behavioral and emotional disorders in adolescents: Nature, assessment, and treatment* (pp. 226–56). New York: The Guilford Press.

Brown, S., Myers, M., Mott, M., & Vik, P. (1994). Correlates of success following treatment for adolescent substance abuse. *Applied and Preventive Psychology, 3*, 61–73.

Brown, S., & Ramo, D. (2006). Clinical course of youth following treatment for alcohol and drug problems. In H. Liddle & C. Rowe (Eds.), *Adolescent substance abuse: Research and clinical advances* (pp. 79–103). Cambridge, UK: Cambridge University Press.

Brown, S. A., McGue, M., Maggs, J., Schulenberg, J., Hingson, R., Swartzelder, S., Martin, C., Chung, T., Tapert, S. F., Sher, K., Winters, K. C., Lowman, C., & Murphy, S. (2008). A developmental perspective on alcohol and youths 16 to 20 years of age. *Pediatrics, 121*(Supplement 4), S290–S310.

Buckley, T., & Carter, R. (2005). Black adolescent girls: Do gender role and racial identity impact their self-esteem? *Sex Roles, 53*(9), 647–61.

Budd, K., Holdsworth, M., & HoganBruen, K. (2006). Antecedents and concomitants of parenting stress in adolescent mothers in foster care. *Child Abuse & Neglect, 30,* 557–74.

Bullis, M., Yovanoff, P., Mueller, G., & Havel, E. (2002). Life on the "outs"— examination of the facility-to-community transition of incarcerated youth. *Exceptional Children, 69*(1), 7–22.

Bussiere, A. (2006). Permanence for older foster youth. *Family Court Review, 44*(2), 231–43.

Buzi, R. S., Weinman, M. L., & Smith, P. B. (2007). The relationship between adolescent depression and a history of sexual abuse. *Adolescence, 42*(168), 679–88.

Cahn, N. (2002). Race, poverty, history, adoption, and child abuse: Connections. *Law & Society Review, 36*(2), 461–88.

Calhoun, G., Glaser, B., & Bartolomucci, C. (2001). The juvenile counseling and assessment model and program: A conceptualization and intervention for juvenile delinquency. *Journal of Counseling & Development, 79,* 131–41.

Calvin, E. (2010) *My so-called emancipation: From foster care to homelessness in California.* New York: Human Rights Watch.

Campaign for Youth Justice (2007). *Jailing juveniles fact sheet.* Washington, DC: Campaign for Youth Justice.

Cardemil, E., & Battle, C. (2003). Guess who's coming to therapy? Getting comfortable with conversations about race and ethnicity in psychotherapy. *Professional Psychology: Research and Practice, 34*(3), 278–86.

Carpenter, S., Clyman, R., Davidson, A., & Steiner, J. (2001). The association of foster care or kinship care with adolescent sexual behavior and first pregnancy. *Pediatrics, 108*(3), 1–6.

Carroll, K. M., & Onken, L. S. (2005). Behavioral therapies for drug abuse. *The American Journal of Psychiatry, 162*(8), 1452–60.

Carter, E., Lane, K., Pierson, M., & Glaeser, B. (2006). Self-determination skills and opportunities of transition-age youth with emotional disturbance and learning disabilities. *Exceptional Children, 72*(3), 333–46.

Casey Family Programs (2008). *Improving outcomes for older youth in foster care.* Seattle, WA: Casey Family Programs, 1-14.

Casey Family Programs Integrated Transition Practice Framework Task Force (2001). *It's my life: A framework for youth transitioning from foster care to successful adulthood.* Seattle, WA: Casey Family Programs, 1-99.

Cassidy, J. (1999). The nature of the child's ties. In J. Cassidy & P. Shaver (Eds.), *Handbook of attachment: Theory, research, and clinical applications* (pp. 3–20). New York: The Guilford Press.

Castro, F. G., & Alarcon, E. H. (2002). Integrating cultural variables into drug abuse prevention and treatment with racial/ethnic minorities. *Journal of Drug Issues, 32*(3), 783–810.

Catalano, R., Berglund, M., Ryan, J., Lonczak, H., & Hawkins, J. (2004). Positive youth development in the United States: Research findings on evaluations of positive youth development programs. *The Annals of the American Academy of Political and Social Science, 591*, 98–124.

Cauce, A., Paradise, M., Domenech-Rodriguez, M., Cochran, B., Shea, J., Srebnik, D., & Baydar, N. (2002). Cultural and contextual influences in mental health help seeking: A focus on ethnic minority youth. *Journal of Consulting and Clinical Psychology, 70*(1), 44–55.

Cellini, H. (2004). Child abuse, neglect, and delinquency: The neurological link. *Juvenile and Family Court Journal, 55 Fall, 2004*, 1–14.

Cernkovich, S., Lanctot, N., & Giordano, P. (2008). Predicting adolescent and adult antisocial behavior among adjudicated delinquent females. *Crime & Delinquency, 54*(1), 3–30.

Chamberlain, C. (February 28, 2008). Group homes appear to double delinquency risks for foster kids, study says. *U.S. Federal News Service.*

Chambers, R., Taylor, J., & Potenza, M. (2003). Developmental neurocircuitry of motivation in adolescence: A critical period of addiction vulnerability. *American Journal of Psychiatry, 160*(6), 1041–52.

Chambliss, D., & Ollendick, T. (2001). Empirically supported psychological interventions: Controversies and evidence. *Annual Review of Psychology, 52*, 685–716.

Chapman, D., Dube, S., & Anda, R. (2007). Adverse childhood events as risk factors for negative mental health outcomes. *Psychiatric Annals, 37*(5), 359–64.

Chapman, D. P., Dube, S. R., & Anda, R. F. (2007). Adverse childhood events as risk factors for negative mental health outcomes. *Psychiatric Annals, 37*(5), 359–64.

Chapple, C. L., Tyler, K. A., & Bersani, B. E. (2005). Child neglect and adolescent violence: Examining the effects of self-control and peer rejection. *Violence and Victims, 20*(1), 39–53.

Child Welfare League of America (2005). *CWLA standards of excellence for transition, independent living, and self-sufficiency services* (Revised ed.). Washington, DC: Child Welfare League of America.

Children's Defense Fund (2009). *Overview of the Fostering Connections to Success and Increasing Adoptions Act of 2008.* Washington, D. C.: Children's Defense Fund and Center for Law and Social Policy.

Children's Law Center of Los Angeles (2004). *Fostering the bond: Dependent teens and their babies.* Los Angeles: Children's Law Center of Los Angeles.

Chipungu, S., & Bent-Goodley, T. (2004). Meeting the challenges of contemporary foster care. *The Future of Children, 14*(1), 74–93.

Choca, M., Minoff, J., Angene, L., Byrnes, M., Kenneally, L., Norris, D., Pearn, D., & Rivers, M. (2004). Can't do it alone: Housing collaborations to improve foster youth outcomes. *Child Welfare, 83*(5), 469–92.

Chu, J. A., Frey, L. M., Ganzel, B. L., & Matthews, J. A. (1999). Memories of childhood abuse: Dissociation, amnesia, and corroboration. *American Journal of Psychiatry, 156*(5), 749–55.

Chung, T. (2008). Adolescent substance use, abuse, and dependence: Prevalence, course, and outcomes. In Y. Kaminer & O. Bukstein (Eds.), *Adolescent substance abuse: Psychiatric comorbidity and high-risk behaviors* (pp. 29–52). New York: Routledge.

Cicchetti, D., & Valentino, K. (2006). An ecological-transactional perspective on child maltreatment: Failure of the average expectable environment and its influence on child development. In D. Cicchetti & D. Cohen (Eds.), *Developmental psychopathology* (2nd ed., pp. 129–201). Hoboken, NJ: John Wiley & Sons.

Clark, D. B. (2004). The natural history of adolescent alcohol use disorders. *Addiction, 99*(Supplement 2), 5–22.

Clausen, J., Landsverk, J., Ganger, W., Chadwick, D., & Litrownik, A. (1998). Mental health problems of children in foster care. *Journal of Child and Family Studies, 7*(3), 283–96.

Cochran, S., & Mays, V. (2007). Physical health complaints among lesbians, gay men, and bisexual and homosexually experienced heterosexual individuals: Results from the California Quality of Life Survey. *American Journal of Public Health, 97*(11), 2048–55.

Cochran, S., Mays, V., Alegria, M., Ortega, A., & Takeuchi, D. (2007). Mental health and substance use disorders among Latino and Asian American lesbian, gay, and bisexual adults. *Journal of Consulting and Clinical Psychology, 75*(5), 785–94.

Cohen, J. A., Mannarino, A. P., Zhitova, A. C., & Capone, M. E. (2003). Treating child abuse-related posttraumatic stress and comorbid substance abuse in adolescents. *Child Abuse & Neglect, 27*(12), 1345–65.

Cohler, B., & Hammack, P. (2007). The psychological world of the gay teenager: Social change, narrative, and "normality." *Journal of Youth and Adolescence, 36,* 47–59.

Colca, L., & Colca, C. (1996). Transitional independent living foster homes: A step toward independence. *Children Today, 24*(1), 7–11.

Coleman, P., & Watson, A. (2000). Infant attachment as a dynamic system. *Human Development, 43,* 295–313.

Collins, M. (2001). Transition to adulthood for vulnerable youths: A review of research and implications for policy. *Social Service Review, 75*(2), 271–91.

Collins, M., & Clay, C. (2009). Influencing policy for youth transitioning from care: Defining problems, crafting solutions, and assessing politics. *Children and Youth Services Review, 31,* 743–51.

Collins, M., Paris, R., & Ward, R. (2008). The permanence of family ties: Implications for youth transitioning from foster care. *American Journal of Orthopsychiatry, 78*(1), 54–62.

Collins, W., & Steinberg, L. (2006). Adolescent development in interpersonal context. In N. Eisenberg (Ed.), *Handbook of child psychology* (pp. 1003–67). Hoboken, NJ: John Wiley & Sons.

Collishaw, S., Pickles, A., Messer, J., Rutter, M., Shearer, C., & Maughan, B. (2007). Resilience to adult psychopathology following childhood maltreatment: Evidence from a community sample. *Child Abuse & Neglect, 31,* 211–29.

Colman, R., & Widom, C. (2004). Childhood abuse and neglect and adult intimate relationships: A prospective study. *Child Abuse & Neglect, 28,* 1133–51.

Colucci, E., & Martin, G. (2007). Ethnocultural aspects of suicide in young people: A systematic literature review. Part I: Rates and methods of youth suicide. *Suicide & Life-Threatening Behavior, 37*(2), 197.

Comas-Diaz, L. (2006). Latino healing: The integration of ethnic psychology into psychotherapy. *Psychotherapy: Theory, Research, Practice, Training, 43*(4), 436–53.

Committee on Early Childhood, Adoption, and Dependent Care, American Academy of Pediatrics (2000). Developmental issues for young children in foster care. *Pediatrics, 106*(5), 1145–50.

Compton, S., Kratochvil, C., & March, J. (2007). Pharmacotherapy for anxiety disorders in children and adolescents: An evidence-based medicine review. *Psychiatric Annals, 37*(7), 504–517.

Consoli, A., Deniau, E., Huynh, C., Purper, D., & Cohen, D. (2007). Treatments in child and adolescent bipolar disorders. *European Child & Adolescent Psychiatry, 16*(3), 187.

Conward, C. (2001). Where have all the children gone? A look at incarcerated youth in America. *William Mitchell Law Review, 27*(4), 435–64.

Cook, A., Spinazzola, J., Ford, J., Lanktree, C., Blaustein, M., Cloitre, M., DeRosa, R., Hubbard, R., Kagan, R., Liautaud, J., Mallah, K., Olafson, E., & Van der Kolk, B. (2005). Complex trauma in children and adolescents. *Psychiatric Annals, 35*(5), 390–98.

Cook, R. (1994). Are we helping foster care youth prepare for their future? *Children and Youth Services Review, 16*(3/4), 213–29.

Corbin, J. (2007). Reactive attachment disorder: A biopsychosocial disturbance of attachment. *Child and Adolescent Social Work Journal, 24*, 539–52.

Corliss, H., Cochran, S., & Mays, V. (2002). Reports of parental maltreatment during childhood in a United States population-based survey of homosexual, bisexual, and heterosexual adults. *Child Abuse & Neglect, 26*, 1165–78.

Courtney, M. (2005). *Youth aging out of foster care* (Policy Brief Issue 19). Philadelphia, PA: MacArthur Foundation Research Network on Transitions to Adulthood and Public Policy.

Courtney, M. (2009). The difficult transition to adulthood for foster youth in the U.S.: Implications for the state as corporate parent. *Social Policy Report, 23*(1), 3–19.

Courtney, M., Barth, R., Berrick, J., Brooks, D., Needell, B., & Park, L. (1997). Race and child welfare services: Myths, realities, and next steps. *Family Resource Coalition of America Report, 16*(1 & 2), 5.

Courtney, M., Dworsky, A., Cusick, G., Havlicek, J., Perez, A., & Keller, T. (2007). *Midwest Evaluation of the Adult Functioning of Former Foster Youth: Outcomes at age 21.* Chicago: Chapin Hall at the University of Chicago.1-94.

Courtney, M., Dworsky, A., Lee, J., & Raap, M. (2009). *Midwest Evaluation of the Adult Functioning of Former Foster Youth: Outcomes at age 23 and 24.* Chicago: Chapin Hall at the University of Chicago, 1-116.

Courtney, M., Dworsky, A., & Peters, C. (2009). *California's Fostering Connections to Success Act and the costs and benefits of extending foster care to 21.* Seattle, WA: Partners for Our Children.

Courtney, M., Dworsky, A., Piliavin, I., & McMurtry, S. (2008). Comparing welfare and child welfare populations: An argument for rethinking the safety net. In D. Lindsey & A. Shlonsky (Eds.), *Child welfare research: Advances for practice and policy* (pp. 271–90). New York: Oxford University Press.

Courtney, M., & Heuring, D. (2005). The transition to adulthood for youth "aging out" of the foster care system. In D. Osgood, E. Foster, C. Flanagan, & G. Ruth (Eds.), *On your own without a net* (pp. 27–67). Chicago: University of Chicago Press.

Courtney, M., Piliavin, I., Grogan-Kaylor, A., & Nesmith, A. (2001). Foster youth transitions to adulthood: A longitudinal view of youth leaving care. *Child Welfare, 80*(6), 685–717.

Courtney, M., Terao, S., & Bost, N. (2004). *Midwest Evaluation of the Adult Functioning of Former Foster Youth: Conditions of youth preparing to leave state care.* Chicago: Chapin Hall Center for Children at the University of Chicago.

Courtney, M., Zinn, A., Zielewski, E., Bess, R., & Malm, K. (2008). *Evaluation of the Life Skills Training Program, Los Angeles County.* Washington, DC: U.S. Department of Health and Human Services, Administration for Children and Families, 1-128.

Cozolino, L. (2006). *The neuroscience of human relationships: Attachment and the developing social brain* (pp. 10–20). New York: W. W. Norton & Company.

Cozolino, L. (2006). *The neuroscience of human relationships: Attachment and the developing social brain. Chap. 3: The developing brain* (pp. 37–49). New York: W.W. Norton & Company.

Cozolino, L. (2006). *The neuroscience of human relationships: Attachment and the developing social brain. Chapter 6: Experience-dependent plasticity* (pp. 81–96). New York: W.W. Norton & Company.

Crawford, T., Cohen, P., Johnson, J., Sneed, J., & Brook, J. (2004). The course and psychosocial correlates of personality disorder symptoms in adolescence: Erikson's developmental theory revisited. *Journal of Youth and Adolescence, 33*(5), 373–87.

Creed, T., & Kendall, P. (2005). Therapist alliance-building behavior within a cognitive-behavioral treatment for anxiety in youth. *Journal of Consulting and Clinical Psychology, 73*(3), 498–505.

Crenshaw, D. (2006-2007). An interpersonal neurobiological-informed treatment model for childhood traumatic grief. *Omega, 54*(4), 319–35.

Crits-Christoph, P., Gibbons, M. B. C., Losardo, D., Narducci, J., Schamberger, M., & Gallop, R. (2004). Who benefits from brief psychodynamic therapy for generalized anxiety disorder? *Canadian Journal of Psychoanalysis, 12*(2), 301.

Crittenden, P. (1999). Danger and development: The organization of self-protective strategies. *Monographs of the Society for Research in Child Development, 64*(3), 145.

Crittenden, P. (2000). A dynamic-maturational approach to continuity and change in pattern of attachment. In P. Crittenden & A. Claussen (Eds.), *The organization of attachment relationships: Maturation, culture, and context* (pp. 343–57). New York: Cambridge University Press.

Crittenden, P. (2001). Organization, alternative organizations, and disorganization: Competing perspectives on the development of attachment among endangered children. *Contemporary Psychology APA Review of Books, 46*(6), 593–96.

Cronce, J., & Corbin, W. (2010). College and career. In J. Grant & M. Potenza (Eds.), *Young adult mental health* (pp. 80–95). New York: Oxford University Press.

Crowe, K. (2007). Using youth expertise at all levels: The essential resource for effective child welfare practice. *New Directions for Youth Development, 113*, 139–49.

Curtis, M., & Denby, R. (2004). Impact of the Adoption and Safe Families Act (1997) on families of color: Workers share their thoughts. *Families in Society, 85*(1), 71–79.

Cusick, G., & Courtney, M. (2007). *Offending during late adolescence: How do youth aging out of care compare with their peers?* (Issue Brief #111). Chicago: Chapin Hall Center for Children.

Cyranowski, J. M., Frank, E., Young, E., & Shear, M. K. (2000). Adolescent onset of the gender difference in lifetime rates of major depression: A theoretical model. Archives of General Psychiatry, *57*(1), 21.

Dadds, M. R., & Barrett, P. M. (2001). Practitioner review: Psychological management of anxiety disorders in childhood. *Journal of Child Psychology and Psychiatry and Allied Disciplines, 42*(8), 999.

D'Augelli, A. (2006). Developmental and contextual factors and mental health among lesbian, gay, and bisexual youths. In A. Omoto & H. Kurtzman (Eds.), *Recent research on sexual orientation.* Washington, DC: APA Books.

Davies, P. T., & Cicchetti, D. (2004). Toward an integration of family systems and developmental psychopathology approaches. *Development and Psychopathology, 16*, 477.

Davis, M., Banks, S., Fisher, W., & Grudzinskas, A. (2004). Longitudinal patterns of offending during the transition to adulthood in youth from the mental health system. *The Journal of Behavioral Health Services & Research, 31*(4), 351–60.

Davis, M., & Vander Stoep, A. (1997). The transition to adulthood for youth who have serious emotional disturbance: Developmental transition and young adult outcomes. *Journal of Mental Health Administration, 24*(4), 400–27.

Davis, T., Satzburg, S., & Locke, C. (2009). Supporting the emotional and psychological well being of sexual minority youth: Youth ideas for action. *Children and Youth Services Review, 31*, 1030–41.

De Bellis, M. (2001). Developmental traumatology: The psychobiological development of maltreated children and its implications for research, treatment, and policy. *Development and Psychopathology, 13*, 539–64.

De Bellis, M. (2002). Developmental traumatology: A contributory mechanism for alcohol and substance use disorders. *Psychoneuroendocrinology, 27*, 155–70.

De Bellis, M. (2005). The psychobiology of neglect. *Child Maltreatment, 10*(2), 150–72.

De Bellis, M., Clark, D., Beers, S., Soloff, P., Boring, A., Hall, J., Kersh, A., & Keshavan, M. (2000). Hippocampal volume in adolescent-onset alcohol use disorders. *American Journal of Psychiatry, 157*(5), 737–44.

de Paul, J., & Domenech, L. (2000). Childhood history of abuse and child abuse potential in adolescent mothers: A longitudinal study. *Child Abuse & Neglect, 24*(5), 701–713.

Delgado, M., Fellmeth, R., Packard, T., Prosek, K., & Weichel, E. (2007). *Expanding transitional services for emancipated foster youth: An investment in California's tomorrow.* San Diego: Children's Advocacy Institute, University of San Diego School of Law. doi:January 2007.

Derezotes, D., & Poetner, J. (2005). Factors contributing to the overrepresentation of African American children in the child welfare system. In D. Derezotes, J. Poetner, & M. Testa (Eds.), *Race matters in child welfare* (1st ed., pp. 1). Washington, DC: Child Welfare League of America.

Dhooper, S. J., & Moore, S. E. (2001). *Social work practice with culturally diverse people.* Thousand Oaks, CA: Sage Publications.

DiClemente, R., Wingood, G., Crosby, R., Sionean, C., Brown, L., Rothbaum, B., Zimand, E., Cobb, B., Harrington, K., & Davies, S. (2001). A prospective study of psychological distress and sexual risk behavior among black adolescent females. *Pediatrics, 108*(5), 1–6.

Dillon, D., Holmes, A., Birk, J., Brooks, N., Lyons-Ruth, K., & Pizzagalli, D. (2009). Childhood adversity is associated with left basal ganglia dysfunction during reward anticipation in adulthood. *Biological Psychiatry, 66,* 206–213.

Dishion, T., & Patterson, G. (2006). The development and ecology of antisocial behavior in children and adolescents. In D. Cicchetti & D. Cohen (Eds.), *Developmental psychopathology (Vol. 3): Risk, disorder, and adaptation* (2nd ed., pp. 503–41). Hoboken, NJ: John Wiley & Sons.

Dodge, K. (2001). The science of youth violence prevention: Progressing from developmental epidemiology to efficacy to effectiveness to public policy. *American Journal of Preventive Medicine, 20*(1S), 63–70.

Dodge, K., Coie, J., & Lynam, D. (2006). Aggression and antisocial behavior in youth. In N. Eisenberg (Ed.), *Handbook of child psychology (Vol. 3): Social, emotional, and personality development* (6th ed., pp. 719–88). Hoboken, NJ: John Wiley & Sons, Inc.

Doka, K. (1999). Disenfranchised grief. *Bereavement Care, 18*(3), 37–39.

Domalanta, D., Risser, W., Roberts, R., & Risser, J. (2003). Prevalence of depression and other psychiatric disorders among incarcerated youths. *Journal of the Academy of Child and Adolescent Psychiatry, 42*(4), 477–84.

Donaldson, D., Spirito, A., & Esposito-Smythers, C. (2005). Treatment for adolescents following a suicide attempt: Results of a pilot trial. *Journal of the American Academy of Child and Adolescent Psychiatry, 44*(2), 113.

Dore, M., Aseltine, R., Franks, R., & Schultz, E. (2006). *Endangered youth: A report on suicide among adolescents involved with the child welfare and juvenile justice system.* Hartford, CONN: Connecticut Center for Effective Practice of the Child Health and Development Institute of Connecticut, 1-56.

dosReis, S., Zito, J., Safer, D., & Soeken, K. (2001). Mental health services for youths in foster care and disabled youths. *American Journal of Public Health, 91*(7), 1094–99.

Downey, G., & Feldman, S. (1996). Implications of rejection sensitivity for intimate relationships. *Journal of Personality and Social Psychology, 70*(6), 1327–43.

Dozier, M., Albus, K., Fisher, P., & Sepulveda, S. (2002). Interventions for foster parents: Implications for developmental theory. *Development and Psychopathology, 14,* 843–60.

Draijer, N., & Langeland, W. (1999). Childhood trauma and perceived parental dysfunction in the etiology of dissociative symptoms in psychiatric inpatients. *American Journal of Psychiatry, 156*(3), 379–85.

Dube, E., & Savin-Williams, R. (1999). Sexual identity development among ethnic sexual-minority male youths. *Developmental Psychology, 35*(6), 1389–98.

DuBois, D., Holloway, B., Valentine, J., & Cooper, H. (2002). Effectiveness of mentoring programs for youth: A meta-analytic review. *American Journal of Community Psychology, 30*(2), 157–97.

Dutra, L., Stathopoulu, G., Basden, S. L., Leyro, T. M., Powers, M. B., & Otto, M. W. (2008). A meta-analytic review of psychosocial interventions for substance use disorders. *American Journal of Psychiatry, 165*(2), 179–87.

Duval, D., & Vincent, N. (2009). Affect regulation of homeless youth once in the child welfare system. *Child and Adolescent Social Work Journal, 26,* 155–73.

Dworsky, A. (2008). The transition to adulthood among youth "aging out" of care: What have we learned? In D. Lindsey & A. Shlonsky (Eds.), *Child welfare research: Advances for practice and policy* (pp. 125–44). New York: Oxford University Press.

Dworsky, A., & Courtney, M. (2009). Addressing the mental health service needs of foster youth during the transition to adulthood: How big is the problem and what can states do? *Journal of Adolescent Health, 44,* 1–2.

Dworsky, A., & DeCoursey, J. (2009). *Pregnant and parenting foster youth: Their needs, their experiences.* Chicago: Chapin Hall at the University of Chicago, 1-51.

Dworsky, A., & Havlicek, J. (2008). *Review of state policies and programs to support young people transitioning out of foster care* (No. 08-12-3903). Olympia, WA: Washington State Institute for Public Policy.

Egeland, B., Yates, T., Appleyard, K., & van Dulmen, M. (2002). The long-term consequences of maltreatment in the early years: A developmental pathway model to antisocial behavior. *Children's Services: Social Policy, Research, and Practice, 5*(4), 249–60.

Elwood, L., Hahn, K., Olatunji, B., & Williams, N. (2009). Cognitive vulnerabilities to the development of PTSD: A review of four vulnerabilities and the proposal of an integrative vulnerability model. *Clinical Psychology Review, 29,* 87–100.

Elwood, L. S., & Williams, N. L. (2007). PTSD-related cognitions and romantic attachment style as moderators of psychological symptoms in victims of interpersonal trauma. *Journal of Social and Clinical Psychology, 26*(10), 1189.

Emslie, G. J. (2008). Pediatric anxiety—underrecognized and undertreated. *The New England Journal of Medicine, 359*(26), 2835.

Engen, R., Steen, S., & Bridges, G. (2002). Racial disparities in the punishment of youth: A theoretical and empirical assessment of the literature. *Social Problems, 49*(2), 194–20.

English, A., & Grasso, K. (2000). The Foster Care Independence Act of 1999: Enhancing youth access to health care. *Journal of Poverty Law and Policy, July-August,* 217–32.

English, A., Morreale, M., & Larsen, J. (2003). Access to health care for youth leaving foster care: Medicaid and SCHIP. *Journal of Adolescent Health, 32S*(6S), 53–69.

English, D., Thompson, R., Graham, J., & Briggs, E. (2005). Toward a definition of neglect in young children. *Child Maltreatment, 10*(2), 190–206.

Epstein, S. (1994). Integration of the cognitive and the psychodynamic unconscious. *American Psychologist, 49*(8), 709–24.

Erikson, E. (1968). *Identity: Youth and crisis.*,p.165 New York: W. W. Norton & Company.

Ersche, K. D., & Sahakian, B. J. (2007). The neuropsychology of amphetamine and opiate dependence: Implications for treatment. *Neuropsychology Review, 17*(3), 317–36.

Esposito, C. L., & Clum, G. A. (2003). The relative contribution of diagnostic and psychosocial factors in the prediction of adolescent suicidal ideation. *Journal of Clinical Child and Adolescent Psychology, 32*(3), 386.

Estrada, R., & Marksamer, J. (2006). The legal rights of LGBT youth in state custody: What child welfare and juvenile justice professionals need to know. *Child Welfare, 85*(2), 171–94.

Fairchild, S. (2006). Understanding attachment: Reliability and validity of selected attachment measures for preschoolers and children. *Child and Adolescent Social Work Journal, 23*(2), 235–61.

Fass, S., & Cauthen, N. (2008). *Who are America's poor children: The official story,*1-4. New York: National Center for Children in Poverty, Mailman School of Public Health, Columbia University.

Feldstein, S. W., & Miller, W. R. (2006). Substance use and risk-taking among adolescents. *Journal of Mental Health, 15*(6), 633–43.

Fellitti, V. (2002). The relationship of adverse childhood experiences to adult health: Turning gold into lead [*Belastungen in der Kindheit und Gesundheit im Erwachsenenalter: die Verwandlung von Gold in Blei*]. *Z Psychsom Med Psychother, 48*(4), 359–69.

Fergusson, D., Horwood, J., & Beautrais, A. (1999). Is sexual orientation related to mental health problems and suicidality in young people? *Archives of General Psychiatry, 56,* 876–80.

Fessler, K. (2005). Adolescent mothers' perceptions and management of stigma. *Journal of Adolescent Health (Abstracts), 36,* 104.

Fiellin, D. A. (2008). Treatment of adolescent opioid dependence: No quick fix. *Journal of the American Medical Association, 300*(17), 2057–59.

Finlay, J. (2003). *Crossover kids: Care to custody.* Toronto, Ontario, Canada: Office of Child and Family Service Advocacy, 1-28.

Finzi, R., Ram, A., Har-Even, D., Shnit, D., & Weizman, A. (2001). Attachment styles and aggression in physically abused and neglected children. *Journal of Youth and Adolescence, 30*(6), 769–86.

Fishman, M. (2008). Treatment planning, matching, and placement for adolescents with substance use disorders. In Y. Kaminer & O. Bukstein (Eds.), *Adolescent substance abuse: Psychiatric comorbidity and high-risk behaviors* (pp. 87–110). New York: Routledge.

Fogel, A. (2000). Systems, attachment, and relationships. *Human Development, 43,* 314.

Fonagy, P., Target, M., Steele, M., Steele, H., Leigh, T., Levinson, A., & Kennedy, R. (1997). Morality, disruptive behavior, borderline personality disorder, crime, and their relationships to security of attachment. In L. Atkinson & K. Zucker (Eds.), *Attachment and psychopathology* (pp. 223–74). New York: The Guilford Press.

Fong, M., & Silien, K. (1999). Assessment and diagnosis of DSM-IV anxiety disorders. *Journal of Counseling and Development, 77*(2), 209–217.

Ford, J. (2005). Treatment implications of altered affect regulation and information processing following child maltreatment. *Psychiatric Annals, 35*(5), 410–419.

Ford, J., & Russo, E. M. (2006). Trauma-focused, present-centered, emotional self-regulation approach to integrated treatment for posttraumatic stress and addiction: Trauma adaptive recovery group education and therapy (TARGET). *American Journal of Psychotherapy, 60*(4), 335–55.

Foster, E., Qaseem, A., & Connor, T. (2004). Can better mental health services reduce the risk of juvenile justice system involvement? *American Journal of Public Health, 94*(5), 859–64.

Foster, L. (2001). *Foster care fundamentals: An overview of California's foster care system*. Sacramento: Assembly Judiciary Committee, State of California, 1-62.

Fowler, P., Toro, P., & Miles, B. (2009). Pathways to and from homelessness and associated psychosocial outcomes among adolescents leaving the foster care system. *American Journal of Public Health, 99*(8), 1453–58.

French, S., Seidman, E., Allen, L., & Aber, J. (2006). The development of ethnic identity during adolescence. *Developmental Psychology, 42*(1), 1–10.

Freundlich, M., & Avery, R. (2006). Transitioning from congregate care: Preparation and outcomes. *Journal of Child and Family Studies, 15*, 507–518.

Frey, L., Greenblatt, S., & Brown, J. (2005). *A call to action: An integrated approach to youth permanency and preparation for adulthood*. Baltimore, MD: Casey Family Services.

Frick, P. (2001). Effective interventions for children and adolescents with conduct disorder. *Canadian Journal of Psychiatry, 46*, 597–608.

Fried, T. (2008). Community colleges step up to support foster care students. *Community College Journal, 78*(4), 38–39.

Fukuyama, M., & Ferguson, A. (2000). Lesbian, gay, and bisexual people of color: Understanding cultural complexity and managing multiple oppressions. In R. Perez, K. DeBord, & K. Bieschke (Eds.), *Handbook of counseling and psychotherapy with lesbian, gay, and bisexual clients* (pp. 81–105). Washington, DC: American Psychological Association.

Gabbard, G. O. (2005). Mind, brain, and personality disorders. *The American Journal of Psychiatry, 162*(4), 648–55.

Garakani, A., Mathew, S., & Charney, D. (2006). Neurobiology of anxiety disorders and implications for treatment. *The Mount Sinai Journal of Medicine, 73*(7), 941–49.

Garland, A., Hough, R., McCabe, K., Yeh, M., Wood, P., & Aarons, G. (2001). Prevalence of psychiatric disorders across five sectors of care. *Journal of the American Academy of Child and Adolescent Psychiatry, 40*(4), 409–418.

Garofalo, R., Deleon, J., Osmer, E., Doll, M., & Harper, G. (2006). Overlooked, misunderstood and at-risk: Exploring the lives and HIV risk of ethnic minority male-to-female transgender youth. *Journal of Adolescent Health, 38*, 230–36.

Garofalo, R., Wolf, R., Kessel, S., Palfrey, J., & DuRant, R. (1998). The association between health risk behaviors and sexual orientation among a school-based sample of adolescents (youth risk behavior survey). *Pediatrics, 101*(5), 895–903.

Gatti, U., Tremblay, R., & Vitaro, F. (2009). Iatrogenic effect of juvenile justice. *The Journal of Child Psychology and Psychiatry, 50*(8), 991–98.

Geenen, S., & Powers, L. (2006). Are we ignoring youth with disabilities in foster care?: An examination of their school performance. *Social Work, 51*(3), 233–41.

Geenen, S., & Powers, L. (2006). Transition planning for foster youth. *The Journal for Vocational Special Needs Education, 28*(2), 4–15.

Geenen, S., & Powers, L. (2007). "Tomorrow is another problem": The experiences of youth in foster care during their transition into adulthood. *Children and Youth Services Review, 29*, 1085–1101.

Geenen, S., Powers, L., Hogansen, J., & Pittman, J. (2007). Youth with disabilities in foster care: Developing self-determination within a context of struggle and disempowerment. *Exceptionality, 15*(1), 17–30.

Gelman, C. R. (2004). Toward a better understanding of the use of psychodynamically informed treatment with Latinos: Findings from clinician experience. *Clinical Social Work Journal, 32*(1), 61.

Gemelli, R. (1996). *Normal child and adolescent development*. Washington, DC: American Psychiatric Press, Inc.

Georgiades, S. (2005). Emancipated young adults' perspectives on independent living programs. *Families in Society, 86*(4), 503–510.

Georgiades, S. (2005). A multi-outcome evaluation of an independent living program. *Child and Adolescent Social Work Journal, 22*(5-6), 417–38.

Gibbons, F., Yeh, H., Gerrard, M., Cleveland, M., Cutrona, C., Simons, R., & Brody, G. (2007). Early experience with racial discrimination and conduct disorder as predictors of subsequent drug use: A critical period hypothesis. *Drug and Alcohol Dependence, 88S*, S27–37.

Gil-Kashiwabara, E., Hogansen, J., Geenen, S., Powers, K., & Powers, L. (2007). Improving transition outcomes for marginalized youth. *Career Development for Exceptional Individuals, 30*(2), 80–91.

Gilliam, J. (2004). Toward providing a welcoming home for all: Enacting a new approach to address the longstanding problems lesbian, gay, bisexual, and transgender youth face in the foster care system. *Loyola of Los Angeles Law Review, 37*, 1037–63.

Gilson, K., & Lancaster, S. (2008). Childhood sexual abuse in pregnant and parenting adolescents. *Child Abuse & Neglect, 32*, 869–77.

Ginsburg, G. S., Riddle, M. A., & Davies, M. (2006). Somatic symptoms in children and adolescents with anxiety disorders. *Journal of the American Academy of Child and Adolescent Psychiatry, 45*(10), 1179.

Glassman, L. H., Weierich, M. R., Hooley, J. M., Deliberto, T. L., & Nock, M. K. (2007). Child maltreatment, non-suicidal self-injury, and the mediating role of self-esteem. *Behaviour Research and Therapy, 45*(10), 2483.

Glicken, M. (2004). *Using the strengths perspective in social work practice: A positive approach for the helping professions. Chap. 6: Resilience and the strengths perspective*. Boston: Pearson, Allyn & Bacon.

Gnaulati, E., & Heine, B. (2001). Separation-individuation in late adolescence: An investigation of gender and ethnic differences. *The Journal of Psychology, 135*(1), 59–70.

Goldberg, S., Muir, R., & Kerr, J. (1995). *Attachment theory: Social, developmental, and clinical perspectives*. Hillsdale, NJ: The Analytic Press.

Goldsmith, D., Oppenheim, D., & Wanlass, J. (2004). Separation and reunification: Using attachment theory and research to inform decisions affecting the placements of children in foster care. *Juvenile and Family Court Journal, 55*(2), 1–13.

Goldston, D., Daniel, S., & Arnold, E. (2006). Suicidal and nonsuicidal self-harm behaviors. In D. Wolfe & E. Mash (Eds.), *Behavioral and emotional disorders in adolescents: Nature, assessment, and treatment* (pp. 343). New York: The Guilford Press.

Goldston, D., Daniel, S., Mathias, C., & Dougherty, D. (2008). Suicidal and nonsuicidal self-harm behaviors in adolescent substance use disorders. In Y. Kaminer & O. Bukstein (Eds.), *Adolescent substance abuse: Psychiatric comorbidity and high-risk behaviors* (pp. 323–54). New York: Routledge.

Goodkind, S., Ng, I., & Sarri, R. (2006). The impact of sexual abuse in the lives of young women involved or at risk of involvement with the juvenile justice system. *Violence Against Women, 12*(5), 456–77.

Goyette, M. (2007). Promoting autonomous functioning among youth in care: A program evaluation. *New Directions for Youth Development, 113*, 89–105.

Greeson, J., & Bowen, N. (2008). "She holds my hand": The experiences of foster youth with their natural mentors. *Children and Youth Services Review, 230,* 1178–88.

Grella, C. (2006). The drug abuse treatment outcomes studies: Outcomes with adolescent substance abusers. In H. Liddle & C. Rowe (Eds.), *Adolescent substance abuse: Research and clinical advances* (pp. 148–73). New York: Cambridge University Press.

Griffin, B. (2002). Academic disidentification, race, and high school dropouts. *The High School Journal, 85*(4), 71–81.

Grinberg, I., Dawkins, M., Dawkins, M., & Fullilove, C. (2005). Adolescents at risk for violence: An initial validation of the life challenges questionnaire and risk assessment index. *Adolescence, 40*(159), 573–99.

Grossman, A., & D'Augelli, A. (2006). Transgender youth: Invisible and vulnerable. *Journal of Homosexuality, 51*(1), 111–28.

Grossman, A. H., & D'Augelli, A. R. (2007). Transgender youth and life-threatening behavior. *Suicide & Life-Threatening Behavior, 37*(5), 527.

Gutman, L. M., & Sameroff, A. J. (2004). Continuities in depression from adolescence to young adulthood: Contrasting ecological influences. *Development and Psychopathology, 16*(4), 967.

Gwadz, M., Clatts, M., Leonard, N., & Goldsamt, L. (2004). Attachment style, childhood diversity, and behavioral risk among young men who have sex with men. *Journal of Adolescent Health, 34,* 402–413.

Haber, M., & Toro, P. (2004). Homelessness among families, children, and adolescents: An ecological-developmental perspective. *Clinical Child and Family Psychology Review, 7*(3), 123–64.

Hacsi, F. (1995). From indenture to family foster care: A brief history of child placing. *Child Welfare, 74*(1), 162.

Haglund, M., Nestadt, P., Cooper, N., Southwick, S., & Charney, D. (2007). Psychobiological mechanisms of resilience: Relevance to prevention and treatment of stress-related psychopathology. *Development and Psychopathology, 19,* 889–920.

Haight, W., Finet, D., Bamba, S., & Helton, J. (2009). The beliefs of resilient African-American adolescent mothers transitioning from foster care to independent living: A case-based analysis. *Children and Youth Services Review, 31,* 53–62.

Hall, G. C. (2001). Psychotherapy research with ethnic minorities: Empirical, ethical, and conceptual issues. *Journal of Counseling and Clinical Psychology, 69*(3), 502.

Hamburger, M. E., Leeb, R. T., & Swahn, M. H. (2008). Childhood maltreatment and early alcohol use among high-risk adolescents. *Journal of Studies on Alcohol and Drugs, 69*(2), 291–95.

Harden, B., Whittaker, J., Hancock, G., & Wang, K. (2010). Quality of the early caregiving environment and preschool well-being: Child welfare system during infancy. In M. Webb, K. Dowd, B. Harden, J. Landsverk, & M. Testa (Eds.), *Child welfare & child well-being: New perspectives from the national survey of child and adolescent well-being* (pp. 55–82). New York: Oxford University Press.

Harden, B. J. (2004). Safety and stability for foster children: A developmental perspective. *The Future of Children, 14*(1), 30–46.

Harper, G., & Schneider, M. (2003). Oppression and discrimination among lesbian, gay, bisexual, and transgendered people and communities: A challenge for community psychology. *American Journal of Community Psychology, 31*(3/4), 243–52.

Harris, K., Duncan, G., & Boisjoly, J. (2002). Evaluating the role of "nothing to lose" attitudes on risky behavior in adolescence. *Social Forces, 80*(3), 1005–39.

Harris, M., Jackson, L., O'Brien, K., & Pecora, P. (2009). Disproportionality in education and employment outcomes of adult foster care alumni. *Children and Youth Services Review, 31*, 1150–59.

Harris, M., & Skyles, A. (2008). Kinship care for African American children: Disproportionate and disadvantageous. *Journal of Family Issues, 29*(8), 1013–30.

Hartwig, H., & Myers, J. (2003). A different approach: Applying a wellness paradigm to adolescent female delinquents and offenders. *Journal of Mental Health Counseling, 25*(1), 57–75.

Hasin, D., Hatzenbuehler, M., & Waxman, R. (2006). Genetics of substance use disorders. In W. Miller & K. Carroll (Eds.), *Rethinking substance abuse: What the science shows and what we should do about it* (pp. 61–80). New York: The Guilford Press.

Hass, M., & Graydon, K. (2009). Sources of resiliency among successful foster youth. *Children and Youth Services Review, 31*, 457–63.

Hauenstein, E. J. (2003). Depression in adolescence. *Journal of Obstetric, Gynecologic, and Neonatal Nursing, 32*(2), 239.

Havalchak, A., White, C., & O'Brien, K. (2008). *The Casey Young Adult Survey: Findings over three years* (No. 336-3030-08, 1-16). Seattle, WA: Casey Family Programs.

Hawke, J., Albert, D., & Ford, J. (2008). Trauma and post-traumatic stress disorder in adolescent substance use disorders. In Y. Kaminer & O. Bukstein (Eds.), *Adolescent substance abuse: Psychiatric comorbidity and high-risk behaviors* (pp. 291–322). New York: Routledge.

Hawkins, E. (2009). A tale of two systems: Co-occurring mental health and substance abuse disorders treatment for adolescents. *Annual Review of Psychology, 60*, 197–227.

Hawkins, J., Herrenkohl, R., Farrington, D., Brewer, D., Catalano, R., Harachi, T., & Cothern, L. (2000). *Predictors of youth violence.* Washington, DC: U.S. Department of Justice, Office of Juvenile Justice and Delinquency Prevention.

Haynie, D. L., South, S. J., & Bose, S. (2006). Residential mobility and attempted suicide among adolescents: An individual-level analysis. *Sociological Quarterly, 47*(4), 693.

Heflinger, C., Chatman, J., & Saunders, R. (2006). Racial and gender differences in utilization of Medicaid substance abuse services among adolescents. *Psychiatric Services, 57*(4), 504–511.

Heflinger, C., & Hoffman, C. (2008). Transition age youth in publicly funded systems: Identifying high-risk youth for policy planning and improved service delivery. *The Journal of Behavioral Health Services & Research, 35*(4), 390–401.

Heim, C., Meinlschmidt, G., & Nemeroff, C. (2003). Neurobiology of early-life stress. *Psychiatric Annals, 33*(1), 18–26.

Heim, C., & Nemeroff, C. (2001). The role of childhood trauma in the neurobiology of mood and anxiety disorders: Preclinical and clinical studies. *Biological Psychiatry, 49*, 1023–39.

Henggeler, S., & Sheidow, A. (2003). Conduct disorder and delinquency. *Journal of Marital and Family Therapy, 29*(4), 505–22.

Henig, A. (2009). Employment aid for youth aging out of foster care: Extending one-stop-career centers to include a division for foster care youth. *Family Court Review, 47*, 570.

Herrenkohl, T., Catalano, R., Hemphill, S., & Toumbourou, J. (2009). Longitudinal examination of physical and relational aggression as precursors to later problem behaviors in adolescents. *Violence and Victims, 24*(1), 3–19.

Higgins, G., & Ricketts, M. (2005). Self-control theory, race, and delinquency. *Journal of Ethnicity in Criminal Justice, 3*(3), 5–22.

Hill, K. (2009). Individuals with Disabilities Act of 2004 and The John H. Chafee Foster Care Independence Act of 1999: What are the policy implications for youth with disabilities transitioning from foster care? *Child Welfare, 88*(2), 5–23.

Hoffman, J., & Cerbone, F. (1999). Stressful life events and delinquency escalation in early adolescence. *Criminology, 37*(2), 343–73.

Hoffman, R. (2004). Conceptualizing heterosexual identity development: Issues and challenges. *Journal of Counseling and Development, 82*, 375–80.

Hohman, M., Oliver, R., & Wright, W. (2004). Methamphetamine abuse and manufacture: The child welfare response. *Social Work, 49*(3), 373.

Holman, B., & Ziedenberg, J. (2006). *The dangers of detention: The impact of incarcerating youth in detention and other secure facilities.* Washington, DC: Justice Policy Institute.

Holtan, A., Ronning, J., Handegard, B., & Sourander, A. (2005). A comparison of mental health problems in kinship and nonkinship foster care. *European Child and Adolescent Psychiatry, 14*, 200–207.

Hood, S., & Carter, M. (2008). A preliminary examination of trauma history, locus of control, and PTSD symptom severity in African American women. *Journal of Black Psychology, 34*(2), 179.

Horowitz, J., & Newcomb, M. (2001). A multidimensional approach to homosexual identity. *Journal of Homosexuality, 42*(2), 1–19.

Howe, D. (2006). Disabled children, maltreatment and attachment. *British Journal of Social Work, 36*, 743–60.

Huebner, A., & Betts, S. (2002). Exploring the utility of social control theory for youth development: Issues of attachment, involvement, and gender. *Youth & Society, 34*(2), 123–45.

Hukkanen, R., Sourander, A., & Bergroth, L. (2003). Suicidal ideation and behavior in children's homes. *Nordic Journal of Psychiatry, 57*(2), 131–37.

Hunsicker, L. (2007). Mental illness among juvenile offenders: Identification and treatment. *Corrections Today, 69*(5), 60–62.

Hunsley, J. (2007). Addressing key challenges in evidence-based practice in psychology. *Professional Psychology: Research and Practice, 38*(2), 113–21.

Iglehart, A. (1995). Readiness for independence: Comparison of foster care, kinship care, and non-foster care adolescents. *Children and Youth Services Review, 17*(3), 417–32.

Iglehart, A. P., & Becerra, R. M. (2002). Hispanic and African American youth: Life after foster care emancipation. *Journal of Ethnic & Cultural Diversity in Social Work, 11*(1), 79–107.

Irvine, H., Bradley, T., Cupples, M., & Boohan, M. (1997). The implications of teenage pregnancy and motherhood for primary health care: Unresolved issues. *British Journal of General Practice, 47*, 323–26.

Jacobs, J., & Freundlich, M. (2006). Achieving permanency for LGBTQ youth in care. *Child Welfare, 85*(2), 299–316.

Jacobson, C. M., Muehlenkamp, J. J., Miller, A. L., & Turner, J. B. (2008). Psychiatric impairment among adolescents engaging in different types of deliberate self-harm. *Journal of Clinical Child and Adolescent Psychology, 37*(2), 363.

James, S., Landsverk, J., & Slymen, D. (2004). Placement movement in out-of-home care: Patterns and predictors. *Children and Youth Services Review, 26,* 185–206.

Jampolskaya, S., Brown, E., & Greenbaum, P. (2002). Early pregnancy among adolescent females with serious emotional disturbances: Risk factors and outcomes. *Journal of Emotional and Behavioral Disorders, 10*(2), 108–115.

Jenson, J., & Potter, C. (2003). The effects of cross-system collaboration on mental health and substance abuse problems of detained youth. *Research on Social Work Practice, 13*(5), 588–607.

Joe, G., Simpson, D., & Broome, K. (1998). Effects of readiness for drug abuse treatment on client retention and assessment of process. *Addiction, 93*(8), 1177–90.

Joe, G., Simpson, D., Dansereau, D., & Rowan-Szal, G. (2001). Relationships between counseling rapport and drug abuse treatment outcomes. *Psychiatric Services, 52*(9), 1223–29.

Johnson, E., & Waldfogel, J. (2002). Parental incarceration: Recent trends and implications for child welfare. *Social Service Review, 76*(3), 460–79.

Johnson, R., Rew, L., & Sternglanz, R. (2006). The relationship between childhood sexual abuse and sexual health practices of homeless adolescents. *Adolescence, 41*(162), 221–34.

Johnston, L. D., O'Malley, P. M., Bachman, J. G., & Schulenberg, J. E. (2009). *Monitoring the future national results on adolescent drug use: Overview of key findings 2008* (NIH Publication No. 09-7401, 1-74). Bethesda, MD: National Institute on Drug Abuse.

Jones, E. (2006). *Public policies and practices in child welfare systems that affect life options for children of color.* Washington, DC: Joint Center for Political and Economic Studies.

Jonson-Reid, M., & Bivens, L. (1999). Foster youth and dating violence. *Journal of Interpersonal Violence, 14*(12), 1249–62.

Jonson-Reid, M., Williams, J., & Webster, D. (2001). Severe emotional disturbance and violent offending among incarcerated adolescents. *Social Work Research, 25*(4), 213–22.

Kaminer, Y. (2002). Adolescent substance abuse treatment: Evidence-based practice in outpatient services. *Current Psychiatry Reports, 4,* 397–401.

Kaminer, Y., & Napolitano, C. (2004). Dial for therapy: Aftercare for adolescent substance use disorders. *Journal of the American Academy of Child and Adolescent Psychiatry, 43*(9), 1171–74.

Kaplan, S., Skolnik, L., & Turnbull, A. (2009). Enhancing the empowerment of youth in foster care: Supportive services. *Child Welfare, 88*(1), 133–61.

Kaplan, S. J., Pelcovitz, D., Salzinger, S., Weiner, M., Mandel, F. S., Lesser, M. L., & Labruna, V. E. (1998). Adolescent physical abuse: Risk for adolescent psychiatric disorders. *The American Journal of Psychiatry, 155*(7), 954.

Kaplow, J., Saxe, G., Putnam, F., Pynoos, R., & Lieberman, A. (2006). The long-term consequences of early childhood trauma: A case study and discussion. *Psychiatry, 69*(4), 362–75.

Karnik, N., Jones, P., Campanaro, A., Haapanen, R., & Steiner, H. (2006). Ethnic variation of self-reported psychopathology among incarcerated youth. *Community Mental Health Journal, 42*(5), 477–86.

Karr-Morse, R., & Wiley, M. (1997). *Ghosts from the nursery: Tracing the roots of violence.* New York: Atlantic Monthly Press.

Kaufman, J., Yang, B., Douglas-Palumbieri, H., Houshyar, S., Lipschitz, D., Krystal, J., & Gelernter, J. (2004). Social supports and serotonin transporter gene moderate depression in maltreated children. *Proceedings of the National Academy of Sciences, 101*(49), 17316–21.

Keeton, C., & Ginsburg, G. (2008). Combining and sequencing medication and cognitive-behaviour therapy for childhood anxiety disorders. *International Review of Psychiatry, 20*(2), 159–64.

Keller, T., Cusick, G., & Courney, M. (2007). Approaching the transition to adulthood: Distinctive profiles of adolescents aging out of the child welfare system. *Social Service Review, 81*(3), 453–84.

Keller, T., Salazar, A., & Courtney, M. (2010). Prevalence and timing of diagnosable mental health, alcohol, and substance use problems among older adolescents in the child welfare system. *Children and Youth Services Review, 32*, 626–34.

Kempe, C. H., Silverman, F., Steele, B., Droegemueller, W., & Silver, H. (1985). The battered child syndrome. *Child Abuse & Neglect, 9*, 143–54.

Kendall, P., Hedtke, K., & Aschenbrand, S. (2006). Chap. 7: Anxiety disorders. In D. Wolfe & E. Mash (Eds.), *Behavioral and emotional disorders in adolescents: Nature, assessment, and treatment* (pp. 259–99). New York: The Guilford Press.

Kennard, B. D., Emslie, G. J., Mayes, T. L., Nightingale-Teresi, J., Nakonezny, P. A., Hughes, J. L., Jones, J. M., Tao, R., Stewart, S. M., & Jarrett, R. B. (2008). Cognitive-behavioral therapy to prevent relapse in pediatric responders to pharmacotherapy for major depressive disorder. *Journal of the American Academy of Child and Adolescent Psychiatry, 47*(12), 1395.

Kennard, B. D., Silva, S. G., Tonev, S., Rohde, P., Hughes, J. L., Vitiello, B., Kratochvil, C. J., Curry, J. F., Emslie, G. J., Reinecke, M., & March, J. (2009). Remission and recovery in the treatment for adolescents with depression study (TADS): Acute and long-term outcomes. *Journal of the American Academy of Child and Adolescent Psychiatry, 48*(2), 186.

Kerker, B., & Dore, M. (2006). Mental health needs and treatment of foster youth: Barriers and opportunities. *American Journal of Orthopsychiatry, 76*(1), 138–47.

Kessler, M., Gira, E., & Poertner, J. (2005). Moving best practice to evidence-based practice in child welfare. *Families in Society, 86*(2), 244–50.

Kessler, R., Avenevoli, S., & Merikangas, K. (2001). Mood disorders in children and adolescents: An epidemiologic perspective. *Biological Psychiatry, 49*, 1002–1014.

Kilpatrick, D., Acierno, R., Saunders, B., Resnick, H., Best, C., & Schnurr, P. (2000). Risk factors for adolescent substance abuse and dependence: Data from a national sample. *Journal of Consulting and Clinical Psychology, 68*(1), 19–30.

Kingery, J. N. (2007). Somatic symptoms and anxiety among African American adolescents. *Journal of Black Psychology, 33*(4), 363.

Kirby, D., Coyle, K., & Gould, J. (2001). Manifestations of poverty and birthrates among young teenagers in California Zip code areas. *Family Planning Perspectives, 33*(2), 63–69.

Kliewer, W., Lepore, S., Oskin, D., & Johnson, P. (1998). The role of social and cognitive processes in children's adjustment to community violence. *Journal of Consulting and Clinical Psychology, 66*(1), 199–209.

Klonsky, E. D., & Muehlenkamp, J. J. (2007). Self-injury: A research review for the practitioner. *Journal of Clinical Psychology, 63*(11), 1045.

Knudsen, H. K. (2009). Adolescent-only substance abuse treatment: Availability and adoption of components of quality. *Journal of Substance Abuse Treatment, 36*(2), 195–205.

Kools, S. (1997). Adolescent identity development in foster care. *Family Relations, 46*(3), 263–71.

Kools, S. (1999). Self-protection in adolescents in foster care. *Journal of Child and Adolescent Psychiatric Nursing, 12*(4), 139–52.

Kozlowska, K., & Hanney, L. (2002). The network perspective: An integration of attachment and family systems theories. *Family Process, 41*(3), 285–312.

Kroner, M. (2007). The role of housing in the transition process of youth and young adults: A twenty-year perspective. *New Directions for Youth Development, 113,* 51–75.

Kupinsel, M. M., & Dubsky, D. D. (1999). Behaviorally impaired children in out-of-home care. *Child Welfare League of America, 78*(2), 297.

Lackey, C. (2003). Violent family heritage, the transition to adulthood, and later partner violence. *Journal of Family Issues, 24*(1), 74–98.

Laird, D., & Michael, J. (2006). Budgeting child welfare. *Children's Voice, 15*(4), 32–35.

Lakhan, S. (2006). *The biopsychosocial model of health and illness.* Retrieved January 26, 2010, from http://cnx.org/content/m13589/1.2/.

Lanctot, N., & Smith, C. (2001). Sexual activity, pregnancy, and deviance in a representative urban sample of African American girls. *Journal of Youth and Adolescence, 30*(3), 349–72.

Lau, A., McCabe, K., Yeh, M., Garland, A., Hough, R., & Landsverk, J. (2003). Race/ethnicity and rates of self-reported maltreatment among high-risk youth in public sectors of care. *Child Maltreatment, 8*(3), 183–94.

Lawrence, C., Carlson, E., & Egeland, B. (2006). The impact of foster care on development. *Development and Psychopathology, 18,* 57–76.

Le, T., Arifuku, I., & Nunez, M. (2003). Girls and culture in delinquency intervention: A case study of RYSE. *Juvenile and Family Court Journal, 54,* 25–34.

Leathers, S., & Testa, M. (2006). Foster youth emancipating from care: Caseworkers' reports on needs and services. *Child Welfare, 85*(3), 463–98.

Lee, B. R., Munson, M. R., Ware, N. C., Ollie, M. T., Scott, J., Lionel D., & McMillen, J. C. (2006). Experiences of and attitudes toward mental health services among older youths in foster care. *Psychiatric Services, 57*(4), 487–92.

Lee, V., & Hoaken, P. (2007). Cognition, emotion, and neurobiological development: Mediating the relation between maltreatment and aggression. *Child Maltreatment, 12*(3), 281–98.

Leiber, M., Johnson, J., Fox, K., & Lacks, R. (2007). Differentiating among racial/ethnic groups and its implications for understanding juvenile justice decision making. *Journal of Criminal Justice, 35*(5), 471–84.

Lemstra, M., Neudorf, C., D'Arcy, C., Kunst, A., Warren, L. M., & Bennett, N. R. (2008). A systematic review of depressed mood and anxiety by SES in youth aged 10-15 years. *Canadian Journal of Public Health, 99*(2), 125.

Lerner, R., Almerigi, J., Theokas, C., & Lerner, J. (2005). Positive youth development: A view of the issues. *Journal of Early Adolescence, 25*(1), 10–16.

Letourneau, N., Steward, M., & Barnfather, A. (2004). Adolescent mothers: Support needs, resources, and support-education interventions. *Journal of Adolescent Health, 35,* 509–25.

Leverich, G. S., & Post, R. M. (2006). Course of bipolar illness after history of childhood treatment. *Lancet, 367*(9516), 1040.

Levinson, D. (1986). A conception of adult development. *American Psychologist, 41*(1), 3–13.

Lewinsohn, P., Rohde, P., & Seeley, J. (1998). Major depressive disorder in older adolescents: Prevalence, risk factors, and clinical implications. *Clinical Psychology Review, 18*(7), 765–94.

Lewinsohn, P. M., Clarke, G. N., Seeley, J. R., & Rohde, P. (1994). Major depression in community adolescents: Age at onset, episode duration, and time to recurrence. *Academy of Child and Adolescent Psychiatry, 33*(6), 809.

Lin, H. (2002). Theories of organizational and social systems. *Futurics, 26*(1), 1–10.

Lind, A. (2004). Legislating the family: Heterosexist bias in social welfare policy frameworks. *Journal of Sociology and Social Welfare, 31*(4), 21–35.

Lindsey, D. (1994). *The welfare of children*. New York: Oxford University Press.

Lindsey, D. (2004). *The welfare of children* (2nd ed.). New York: Oxford University Press.

Linning, L. M., & Kearney, C. A. (2004). Post-traumatic stress disorder in maltreated youth: A study of diagnostic comorbidity and child factors. *Journal of Interpersonal Violence, 19*(10), 1087–1101.

Liotti, G. (2004). Trauma, dissociation, and disorganized attachment: Three strands of a single braid. *Psychotherapy: Theory, Research, Practice, Training, 41*(4), 472–486.

Lipschitz, D., Rasmusson, A., & Southwick, S. (1998). Childhood posttraumatic stress disorder: A review of neurobiologic sequelae. *Psychiatric Annals, 28*(8), 452.

Lloyd-Richardson, E. E. (2008). Adolescent nonsuicidal self-injury: Who is doing it and why? *Journal of Developmental and Behavioral Pediatrics, 29*(3), 216.

Logan, D., & Marlatt, G. (2010). Harm reduction therapy: A practice-friendly review of research. *Journal of Clinical Psychology: In Session, 66*(2), 201–214.

Loman, L., & Siegel, G. (2000). *A review of literature on independent living of youths in foster and residential care*. St. Louis, MO: Institute of Applied Research.

Lopez, P., & Allen, P. (2007). Addressing the health needs of adolescents transitioning out of foster care. *Pediatric Nursing, 33*(4), 345–55.

Lucas, M. (1997). Identity development, career development, and psychological separation from parents: Similarities and differences between men and women. *Journal of Counseling Psychology, 44*(2), 123–32.

Luthar, S., & Brown, P. (2007). Maximizing resilience through diverse levels of inquiry: Prevailing paradigms, possibilities, and priorities for the future. *Development and Psychopathology, 19*, 931–55.

Lyman, S., & Bird, G. (1996). A closer look at self-image in male foster care adolescents. *Social Work, 41*(1), 85–96.

Lyons-Ruth, K., & Jacobvitz, D. (1999). Attachment disorganization: Unresolved loss, relational violence, and lapses in behavioral and attentional strategies. In J. Cassidy & P. Shaver (Eds.), *Handbook of attachment: Theory, research, and clinical applications* (pp. 520–54). New York: The Guilford Press.

Macgowan, M. J. (2004). Psychosocial treatment of youth suicide: A systematic review of the research. *Research on Social Work Practice, 14*(3), 147.

Maciejewski, P., Zhang, B., Block, S., & Prigerson, H. (2007). An empirical examination of the stage theory of grief. *Journal of the American Medical Association, 297*(7), 716–24.

MacMillan, H., Georgiades, K., Duku, E., Shea, A., Steiner, M., Niec, A., Tanalka, M., Gensey, S., Spree, S., Vella, E., Walsh, C., De Bellis, M., Van der Meulen, J., Boyle, M., & Schmidt, L. (2009). Cortisol response to stress in female youths exposed to childhood maltreatment: Results of the youth mood project. *Biological Psychiatry, 66*, 62–68.

Magyar, K. (2006). Betwixt and between but being booted nonetheless: A developmental perspective on aging out of foster care. *Temple Law Review, 79*(2), 557–605.

Main, M. (1995). Recent studies in attachment. In S. Goldberg, R. Muir, & J. Kerr (Eds.), *Attachment theory: Social, developmental, and clinical perspectives* (pp. 407–74). Hillsdale, NJ: The Analytic Press.

Main, M., & Hesse, E. (1992). Disorganized/disoriented infant behavior in the strange situation, lapses in the monitoring of reasoning and discourse during the parent's adult attachment interview, and dissociative states. In M. Ammanti & D. Stern (Eds.), *Attachment and psychoanalysis.* (86–140). Rome, Italy: Gius, Laterza and Figli.

Main, M., & Solomon, J. (1986). Discovery of an insecure-disorganized/disoriented attachment pattern. In T. Brazelton & M. Yogman (Eds.), *Affective development in infancy* (pp. 95–124). Norwood, NJ: Ablex.

Majd, K., Marksamer, J., & Reyes, C. (2009). *Hidden injustice: Lesbian, gay, bisexual, and transgender youth in juvenile courts.* San Francisco, CA: The Equity Project.

Malmgren, K., & Meisel, S. (2004). Examining the link between child maltreatment and delinquency for youth with emotional and behavioral disorders. *Child Welfare, 83*(2), 175–88.

Manly, J., Kim, J., Rogosch, F., & Cicchetti, D. (2001). Dimensions of child maltreatment and children's adjustment: Contributions of developmental timing and subtype. *Development and Psychopathology, 13*, 759–82.

Mares, A. (2008). *Needs assessment of emancipating foster youth in Lucas County, Ohio.* Toledo, OH: Toledo Community Foundation. doi:October 28, 2008.

Massinga, R., & Pecora, P. (2004). Providing better opportunities for older children in the child welfare system. *The Future of Children, 14*(1), 151–73.

Masten, A. (2001). Ordinary magic: Resilience processes in development. *American Psychologist, 56*(3), 227.

Masten, A. (2007). Resilience in developing systems: Progress and promise as the fourth wave rises. *Development and Psychopathology, 19*, 921–30.

Masterman, P. W., & Kelly, A. B. (2003). Reaching adolescents who drink harmfully: Fitting intervention to developmental reality. *Journal of Substance Abuse Treatment, 24*(4), 347–55.

Maxmen, J., & Ward, N. (1995). Anxiety disorders. In J. Maxmen & N. Ward (Eds.), *Essential psychopathology and its treatment* (2nd ed., pp. 244–83). New York: W. W. Norton & Company.

McClure, E., & Pine, D. (2006). Social anxiety and emotion regulation: A model for developmental psychopathology perspectives on anxiety disorders. In D. Cicchetti & D. Cohen (Eds.), *Developmental psychopathology, vol. 3* (2nd ed., pp. 470). Hoboken, NJ: John Wiley & Sons.

McCoy, H., McMillen, J., & Spitznagel, E. (2008). Older youth leaving the foster care system: Who, what, when, where, and why? *Children and Youth Services Review, 30*, 735–45.

McCutcheon, V. V. (2006). Toward an integration of social and biological research. *The Social Service Review, 80*(1), 159–214.

McDaniel, J., Purcell, D., & D'Augelli, A. (2001). The relationship between sexual orientation and risk for suicide: Research findings and future directions for research and prevention. *Suicide and Life-Threatening Behavior, 31*(supplement), 84–105.

McDonald, S., Erickson, L., Johnson, M., & Elder, G. (2007). Informal mentoring and young adult employment. *Social Science Research, 36,* 1328–47.

McElwee, N., O'Connor, M., & McKenna, S. (2007). Juvenile offenders and independent living: An Irish perspective on program development with St. Xavier's. *New Directions for Youth Development, 113,* 107–117.

McGowan, B., & Walsh, E. (2000). Policy challenges for child welfare in the new century. *Child Welfare, 79*(1), 11–27.

McGuire, W. (2005). Beyond EBM: New directions for evidence-based public health. *Perspectives in Biology and Medicine, 48*(4), 557–69.

McLaughlin, K. A., Hilt, L. M., & Nolen-Hoeksema, S. (2007). Racial/ethnic differences in internalizing and externalizing symptoms in adolescents. *Journal of Abnormal Child Psychology, 35*(5), 801.

McLean, L., & Gallop, R. (2003). Implications of childhood sexual abuse for adult borderline personality disorder and complex posttraumatic stress disorder. *The American Journal of Psychiatry, 160*(2), 369–71.

McLellan, A. T. (2006). Foreword. In H. Liddle & C. Rowe (Eds.), *Adolescent substance abuse: Research and clinical advances* (p. xii). Cambridge, UK: Cambridge University Press.

McLewin, L., & Muller, R. (2006). Attachment and social support in the prediction of psychopathology among young adults with and without a history of physical maltreatment. *Child Abuse and Neglect, 30,* 171–91.

McMahon, J., & Clay-Warner, J. (2002). Child abuse and future criminality: The role of social service placement, family disorganization, and gender. *Journal of Interpersonal Violence, 17*(9), 1002–1019.

McMahon, R., & Kotler, J. (2006). Conduct problems. In D. Wolfe & E. Mash (Eds.), *Behavioral and emotional disorders in adolescents: Nature, assessment, and treatment* (pp. 153–225). New York: The Guilford Press.

McMahon, T. (2010). Developmental pathways to parenting. In J. Grant & M. Potenza (Eds.), *Young adult mental health* (pp. 181–94). New York: Oxford University Press.

McMillen, C., Auslander, W., Elze, D., White, T., & Thompson, R. (2003). Educational experiences and aspirations of older youth in foster care. *Child Welfare, 82*(4), 475–95.

McMillen, J. C., & Raghavan, R. (2009). Pediatric to adult mental health service use of young people leaving the foster care system. *Journal of Adolescent Health, 44,* 7–13.

McMillen, J. C., Scott, L. D., Zima, B. T., Ollie, M. T., Munson, M. R., & Spitznagel, E. (2004). Use of mental health services among older youths in foster care. *Psychiatric Services, 55*(7), 811.

McMillen, J., Rideout, G., Fisher, R., & Tucker, J. (1997). Independent-living services: The views of former foster youth. *Families in Society: The Journal of Contemporary Human Services, 78*(5), 471–79.

McMillen, J., & Tucker, J. (1999). The status of older adolescents at exit from out-of-home care. *Child Welfare, 78*(3), 339–60.

McRoy, R. (2005). Overrepresentation of children and youth of color in foster care. In G. Mallon & P. McCartt (Eds.), *Child welfare for the 21st century* (1st ed., pp. 623–34). New York: Columbia University Press.

McWey, L. (2004). Predictors of attachment styles of children in foster care: An attachment theory model for working with families. *Journal of Marital and Family Therapy, 30*(4), 439-52.

Mech, E. (1994). Foster youths in transition: Research perspectives on preparation for independent living. *Child Welfare, 73*(5), 603–s.

Mech, E. (2001). Where are we going tomorrow?: Independent living research. In K. Nollan & C. Downs (Eds.), *Preparing youth for long-term success: Proceedings from the Casey Family Program National Independent Living Forum* (pp. 27–43). Washington, DC: Child Welfare League of America Press.

Mech, E., & Fung, C. (1999). Placement restrictiveness and educational achievement among emancipated foster youth. *Research on Social Work Practice, 9*(2), 213–28.

Mendes, P., & Moslehuddin, B. (2006). From dependence to interdependence: Towards better outcomes for young people leaving state care. *Child Abuse Review, 15,* 110–26.

Merdinger, J., Hines, A., Osterling, K., & Wyatt, P. (2005). Pathways to college for former foster youth: Understanding factors that contribute to educational success. *Child Welfare, 84*(6), 867–96.

Messer, S. (2004). Evidence-based practice: Beyond empirically supported treatments. *Professional Psychology: Research and Practice, 35*(6), 580–88.

Michael, K., & Crowley, S. (2002). How effective are treatments for child and adolescent depression? A meta-analytic review. *Clinical Psychology Review, 22,* 247–69.

Miklowitz, D. J., & Chang, K. D. (2008). Prevention of bipolar disorder in at-risk children: Theoretical assumptions and empirical foundations. *Development and Psychopathology, 20*(3), 881.

Miley, K., O'Melia, M., & DuBois, B. (2004). *Generalist social work practice: An empowering approach.* Boston, MA: Pearson, Allyn & Bacon.

Miller, A. (2007). Social neuroscience of child and adolescent depression. *Brain and Cognition, 65,* 47–68.

Miller, P., Gorski, P., Borchers, D., Jenista, J., Johnson, C., Kaufman, N., Levitzky, S., Palmer, S., & Poole, J. (2000). Developmental issues for young children in foster care. *Pediatrics, 106*(5), 1145–50.

Miller, W. (2000). Motivational interviewing: IV. Some parallels with horse whispering. *Behavioural and Cognitive Psychotherapy, 28,* 285–92.

Mineka, S., & Zinbarg, R. (2006). A contemporary learning theory perspective on the etiology of anxiety disorders: It's not what you thought it was. *American Psychologist, 61*(1), 10–26.

Miranda, J., Bernal, G., Lau, A., Kohn, L., Hwang, W., & LaFromboise, T. (2005). State of the science on psychosocial interventions for ethnic minorities. *Annual Review of Clinical Psychology, 1,* 113–42.

Monahan, D. (2002). Teen pregnancy prevention outcomes: Implications for social work practice. *Families in Society, 83*(4), 431–39.

Monroe, S., Rohde, P., Seeley, J., & Lewinsohn, P. (1999). Life events and depression in adolescence: Relationship loss as a prospective risk factor for first onset of major depressive disorder. *Journal of Abnormal Psychology, 108*(4), 606–614.

Montgomery, M. (2005). Psychosocial intimacy and identity: From early adolescence to emerging adulthood. *Journal of Adolescent Research, 20,* 346–74.

Montgomery, P., Donkoh, C., & Underhill, K. (2006). Independent living programs for young people leaving the care system: The state of the evidence. *Children and Youth Services Review, 28,* 1435–48.

Moore, S. E., Madison-Colmore, O., & Moore, J. L. (2003). An Afrocentric approach to substance abuse treatment with adolescent African American males: Two case examples. *Western Journal of Black Studies, 27*(4), 219.

Morrison, L., & L'Heureux, J. (2001). Suicide and gay/lesbian/bisexual youth: Implications for clinicians. *Journal of Adolescence, 24,* 39–49.

Morrow, D. (2004). Social work practice with gay, lesbian, bisexual, and transgender adolescents. *Families in Society, 85*(1), 91–99.

Mosqueda, J., & Rodriguez, J. (2006). *Change begins with action: California Youth Connection 2006 Policy Conference Report.* San Francisco: California Youth Connection.

Muck, R., Zempolich, K. A., Titus, J. C., Fishman, M., Godley, M. D., & Schwebel, R. (2001). An overview of the effectiveness of adolescent substance abuse treatment models. *Youth & Society, 33*(2), 143–68.

Mueser, K. T., & Taub, J. (2008). Trauma and PTSD among adolescents with severe emotional disorders involved in multiple service systems. *Psychiatric Services, 59*(6), 627.

Muller, R. T., Sicoli, L. A., & Lemieux, K. E. (2000). Relationship between attachment style and posttraumatic stress symptomatology among adults who report the experience of childhood abuse. *Journal of Traumatic Stress, 13*(2), 321.

Munoz-Solomando, A., Kendall, T., & Whittington, C. J. (2008). Cognitive behavioural therapy for children and adolescents. *Current Opinions in Psychiatry, 21*(4), 332.

Munson, M., & McMillen, J. (2009). Natural mentoring and psychosocial outcomes among older youth transitioning from foster care. *Children and Youth Services Review, 31,* 104–111.

Muratori, F., Picchi, L., Bruni, G., Patarnello, M., & Romagnoli, G. (2003). A two-year follow-up of psychodynamic psychotherapy for internalizing disorders in children. *Journal of the American Academy of Child and Adolescent Psychiatry, 42*(3), 331–39.

Murray, L. (2003). Self-harm among adolescents with developmental disabilities: What are they trying to tell us? *Journal of Psychosocial Nursing & Mental Health Services, 41*(11), 36–45.

Naccarato, T., & DeLorenzo, E. (2008). Transitional youth services: Practice implications from a systematic review. *Child and Adolescent Social Work Journal, 25,* 287–308.

Nair, Y. (2008). High pregnancy rate for LGB teens. *Windy City Times* (Dec. 27, pp. 1–7).

Narendorf, S., & McMillen, J. (2010). Substance use and substance use disorders as foster youth transition to adulthood. *Children and Youth Services Review, 32,* 113–119.

National Council on Disability (2008). *Youth with disabilities in the foster care system: Barriers to success and proposed policy solutions.* Washington, DC: National Council on Disability.

Nelson, C., Bloom, F., Cameron, J., Amaral, D., Dahl, R., & Pine, D. (2002). An integrative, multidisciplinary approach to the study of brain-behavior relations in the context of typical and atypical development. *Development and Psychopathology, 14,* 499–520.

Nelson, E., Leibentuft, E., McClure, E., & Pine, D. (2004). The social reorientation of adolescence: A neuroscience perspective on the process and its relation to psychopathology. *Psychological Medicine, 35,* 163–74.

Nissen, L. (2006). Effective adolescent substance abuse treatment in juvenile justice settings: Practice and policy recommendations. *Child and Adolescent Social Work Journal, 23*(3), 298–315.

Nixon, R., & Jones, M. (2000). *Improving transitions to adulthood for youth served by the foster care system: A report on the strengths and needs of existing aftercare services.* Washington, DC: Child Welfare League of America.

Noam, G., & Hermann, C. (2002). Where education and mental health meet: Developmental prevention and early intervention in schools. *Development and Psychopathology, 14,* 861–75.

Nock, M. K., Teper, R., & Hollander, M. (2007). Psychological treatment of self-injury among adolescents. *Journal of Clinical Psychology, 63*(11), 1081.

Nolan, T. (2006). Outcomes for a transitional living program serving LGBTQ youth in New York City. *Child Welfare, 85*(2), 384–406.

Nollan, K., Wolf, M., Ansell, D., Burns, J., Barr, L., Copeland, W., & Paddock, G. (2000). Ready or not: Assessing youths' preparedness for independent living. *Child Welfare, 79*(2), 159–76.

North Carolina Division of Social Services (2007). Child welfare, juvenile justice, and the courts. *North Carolina Division of Social Services Practice Notes, 12*(4), 1-8.

Olfson, M., Gameroff, M., Marcus, S., & Waslick, B. (2003). Outpatient treatment of child and adolescent depression in the United States. *Archives of General Psychiatry, 60,* 1236–42.

Ompad, D., Ikeda, R. M., Shah, N., Fuller, C. M., Bailey, S., Morse, E., Kerndt, P., Maslow, C., Wu, Y., Vlahov, D., Garfein, R., & Strathdee, S. (2005). Childhood sexual abuse and age at initiation of injection drug use. *American Journal of Public Health, 95*(4), 703–709.

Ortega, R., Grogan-Kaylor, A., Ruffolo, M., Clarke, J., & Karb, R. (2010). Racial and ethnic diversity in the initial child welfare experience: Exploring areas of convergence and divergence. In M. Webb, K. Dowd, B. Harden, J. Landsverk & M. Testa (Eds.), *Child welfare & child well-being: New perspectives from the National Survey of Child and Adolescent Well-Being* (pp. 236–71). New York: Oxford University Press.

Osterling, K., & Hines, A. (2006). Mentoring adolescent foster youth: Promoting resilience during developmental transitions. *Child and Family Social Work, 11,* 242–53.

Packard, T., Delgado, M., Fellmeth, R., & McCready, K. (2008). A cost-benefit analysis of transitional living services for emancipating foster youth. *Children and Youth Services Review, 30,* 1267–78.

Pagani, L. S., Japel, C., Vaillancourt, T., Cote, S., & Tremblay, R. E. (2008). Links between life course trajectories of family dysfunction and anxiety during middle childhood. *Journal of Abnormal Child Psychology, 36*(1), 41.

Palladino, J. (2006). "Don't sell them dreams without the foundations": Collaboration for the transitional needs of foster care adolescents with disabilities. *High School Journal, 90*(1), 22–32.

Paniagua, F. (1998). *Assessing and treating culturally diverse clients: A practical guide* (2nd ed.). Thousand Oaks, CA: Sage Publications.

Park, J., Metraux, S., Brodbar, G., & Culhane, D. (2004). Public shelter admission among young adults with child welfare histories by type of service and type of exit. *Social Service Review, 78*(2), 284–303.

Parvizi, J., & Damasio, A. (2001). Consciousness and the brainstem. *Cognition, 29*(1-2), 135–60.

Patel, N. C., DelBello, M. P., Keck, P. E., & Strakowski, S. M. (2005). Ethnic differences in maintenance antipsychotic prescription among adolescents with bipolar. *Journal of Child and Adolescent Psychopharmacology, 15*(6), 938.

Patton, G. C., Coffey, C., Posterino, M., Carlin, J. B., & Bowes, G. (2003). Life events and early onset depression: Cause or consequence? *Psychological Medicine, 33*(7), 1203.

Patton, G. C., McMorris, B. J., Toumbourou, J. W., Hemphill, S., Donath, S., & Catalano, R. (2004). Puberty and the onset of substance use and abuse. *Pediatrics, 114*(3), e300–e305.

Paxson, C., & Waldfogel, J. (2002). Work, welfare, and child maltreatment. *Journal of Labor Economics, 20*(3), 435–74.

PDM Task Force (2006). *Psychodynamic diagnostic manual.* Silver Spring, MD: Alliance of Psychoanalytic Organizations.

Pearlman, L. A., & Courtois, C. A. (2005). Clinical applications of the attachment framework: Relational treatment of complex trauma. *Journal of Traumatic Stress, 18*(5), 449–59.

Pecora, P. (2007). *Why should the child welfare field focus on minimizing placement change as part of permanency planning for children?* Presentation for the California Permanency Conference. Seattle, WA: Casey Family Programs.

Pecora, P. (2010). Why current and former recipients of foster care need high quality mental health services. *Administration and Policy in Mental Health, 37,* 185–90.

Pecora, P., Kessler, R., O'Brien, K., White, C., Williams, J., Hiripi, E., English, D., White, J., & Herrick, M. (2006). Educational and employment outcomes of adults formerly placed in foster care: Results from the Northwest Foster Care Alumni Study. *Children and Youth Services Review, 28,* 1459–81.

Pecora, P., Kessler, R., Williams, J., Downs, A., English, D., White, J., & O'Brien, K. (2010). *What works in foster care? Key components of success from the Northwest Foster Care Alumni Study.*p.10 New York: Oxford University Press.

Pecora, P., White, C., Jackson, L., & Wiggins, T. (2009). Mental health of current and former recipients of foster care: A review of recent studies in the USA. *Child and Family Social Work, 14,* 132–46.

Penza, K. M., Heim, C., & Nemeroff, C. B. (2003). Neurobiological effects of childhood abuse: Implications for the pathophysiology of depression and anxiety. *Archives of Women's Mental Health, 6,* 15–22.

Penzerro, R., & Lein, L. (1995). Burning their bridges: Disordered attachment and foster care discharge. *Child Welfare, 74*(2), 351.

Pepin, E. N., & Banyard, V. L. (2006). Social support: A mediator between child maltreatment and developmental outcomes. *Journal of Youth and Adolescence, 35*(4), 617–30.

Perepletchikova, F., Krystal, J. H., & Kaufman, J. (2008). Practitioner review: Adolescent alcohol use disorders: Assessment and treatment issues. *Journal of Child Psychology and Psychiatry, 49*(11), 1131–54.

Perez, D. (2001). Ethnic differences in property, violent, and sex offending for abused and nonabused adolescents. *Journal of Criminal Justice, 29,* 407–417.

Petr, C. (2008). Foster care independent living services: Youth perspectives. *Families in Society, 89*(1), 100–108.

Phinney, J. (2006). Ethnic identity exploration in emerging adulthood. In J. Arnett & J. Tanner (Eds.), *Emerging adults in America: Coming of age in the 21st century* (pp. 117–34). Washington, DC: American Psychological Association.

Pilowsky, D. J., Keyes, K. K., & Hasin, D. S. (2009). Adverse childhood events and lifetime alcohol dependence. *American Journal of Public Health, 99*(2), 258–63.

Pine, D. S. (2002). Treating children and adolescents with selective serotonin reuptake inhibitors: How long is appropriate? *Journal of Child and Adolescent Psychopharmacology, 12*(3), 189.

Pistole, M. (1999). Preventing teenage pregnancy: Contributions from attachment theory. *Journal of Mental Health Counseling, 21*(2), 93–112.

Pitchal, E. (2008-2009). Thickening the safety net: Key elements to successful independent living programs for young adults aging out of care. *St. John's Legal Comment, 23*, 447–75.

Pizarro, M., & Vera, E. (2001). Chicana/o ethnic identity research: Lessons for researchers and counselors. *Counseling Psychologist, 29*(1), 91–117.

Pleasants, R. (2007). Teaching young men in correctional education: Issues and interventions in male identity development. *Journal of Correctional Education, 58*(3), 249–61.

Plomin, R., DeFries, J., McClearn, G., & McGuffin, P. (2001). *Behavioral genetics* (4th ed.). New York: Worth Publishers.

Pottick, K. J., Bilder, S., Stoep, A. V., Warner, L. A., & Alvarez, M. F. (2008). U.S. patterns of mental health service utilization for transition-age youth and young adults. *Journal of Behavioral Health & Services Research, 35*(4), 373–89.

Price, D. (2003). A developmental perspective of treatment for sexually vulnerable youth. *Sexual Addiction and Compulsivity, 10*(4), 225–45.

Propp, J., Ortega, D., & NewHeart, F. (2003). Independence or interdependence: Rethinking the transition from "ward of the court" to adulthood. *Families in Society, 84*(2), 259–66.

Quintana, S. (2007). Racial and ethnic identity: Developmental perspectives and research. *Journal of Counseling Psychology, 54*(3), 259–70.

Racusin, R., Maerlender, A., Sengupta, A., Isquith, P., & Straus, M. (2005). Psychosocial treatment of children in foster care: A review. *Community Mental Health Journal, 41*(2), 199.

Ragg, D., Patrick, D., & Ziefert, M. (2006). Slamming the closet door: Working with gay and lesbian youth in care. *Child Welfare, 85*(2), 243–64.

Raghavan, R., & McMillen, J. C. (2008). Use of multiple psychotropic medications among adolescents aging out of foster care. *Psychiatric Services, 59*(9), 1052.

Raine, A. (2002). Biosocial studies of antisocial and violent behavior in children and adults: A review. *Journal of Abnormal child Psychology, 30*(4), 311–326.

Ramchandani, P. (2004). Treatment of major depressive disorder in children and adolescents. *British Medical Journal (International Edition), 328*(7430), 3.

Rashid, S. (2004). Evaluating a transitional living program for homeless, former foster care youth. *Research on Social Work Practice, 14*(4), 240–48.

Rawal, P., Romansky, J., Jenuwine, M., & Lyons, J. (2004). Racial differences in the mental health needs and service utilization of youth in the juvenile justice system. *Journal of Behavioral Health Services & Research, 31*(3), 242–54.

Rawson, R. A., Gonzales, R., Obert, J. L., McCann, M. J., & Brethen, P. (2005). Methamphetamine use among treatment-seeking adolescents in Southern

California: Participant characteristics and treatment response. *Journal of Substance Abuse Treatment, 29*(2), 67–74.

Reid, C. (2007). The transition from state care to adulthood: International examples of best practices. *New Directions for Youth Development, 113,* 33–49.

Reid, J., & Ross, J. (2005). First Voice: The circle of courage and independent living. *Reclaiming Children and Youth, 14*(3), 164–68.

Reilly, T. (2003). Transition from care: Status and outcomes of youth who age out of foster care. *Child Welfare, 82*(6), 727–46.

Reinherz, H. Z., Paradis, A. D., Giaconia, R. M., Stashwick, C. K., & Fitzmaurice, G. (2003). Childhood and adolescent predictors of major depression in the transition to adulthood. *American Journal of Psychiatry, 160*(12), 2141.

Research Units on Pediatric Psychopharmacology Anxiety Study Group (2003). Searching for moderators and mediators of pharmacological treatment effects in children and adolescents with anxiety disorders. *Journal of the American Academy of Child and Adolescent Psychiatry, 42*(1), 13–21.

Richardson, L. P., DiGiuseppe, D., Garrison, M., & Christakis, D. A. (2003). Depression in Medicaid-covered youth. *Archives of Pediatrics & Adolescent Medicine, 157*(10), 984.

Rick, S., & Douglas, D. (2007). Neurobiological effects of childhood abuse. *Journal of Psychosocial Nursing, 45*(4), 47.

Ringeisen, H., Casanueva, C., Urato, M., & Stambaugh, L. (2009). Mental health service use during the transition to adulthood for adolescents reported to the child welfare system. *Psychiatric Services, 60*(8), 1084–91.

Ritakallio, M., Riittakerttu, K., Kivivuori, J., & Rimpela, M. (2005). Brief report: Delinquent behaviour and depression in middle adolescence: A Finnish community sample. *Journal of Adolescence, 28,* 155–59.

Roberts, D. (2002). *Shattered bonds: The color of child welfare.*1-99. New York: Basic Civitas Books.

Roberts, D. (2003). Child welfare and civil rights. *University of Illinois Law Review, 2003*(1), 171.

Roberts, R., Phinney, J., Masse, L., Chen, Y., Roberts, C., & Romero, A. (1999). The structure of ethnic identity of young adolescents from diverse ethnocultural groups. *Journal of Early Adolescence, 19*(3), 301–22.

Rodriguez, J. (2010). Personal communication with author.

Rohde, P., Clarke, G. N., Mace, D. E., Jorgensen, J. S., & Seeley, J. R. (2004). An efficacy/effectiveness study of cognitive-behavioral treatment for adolescents with comorbid major depression and conduct disorder. *Journal of the American Academy of Child and Adolescent Psychiatry, 43*(6), 660.

Rohde, P., Seeley, J. R., Kaufman, N. K., Clarke, G. N., & Stice, E. (2006). Predicting time to recovery among depressed adolescents treated in two psychosocial group interventions. *Journal of Consulting and Clinical Psychology, 74*(1), 80.

Romney, S., Litrownik, A., Newton, R., & Lau, A. (2006). The relationship between child disability and living arrangement in child welfare. *Child Welfare, 85*(6), 965–84.

Roosa, M., Tein, J., Reinholtz, C., & Angelini, P. (1997). The relationship of childhood sexual abuse to teenage pregnancy. *Journal of Marriage and Family, 59*(1), 119–30.

Rosen, C. S., Ouimette, P. C., Sheikh, J. I., Gregg, J. A., & Moos, R. H. (2002). Physical and sexual abuse history and addiction treatment outcomes. *Journal of Studies on Alcohol, 63*(6), 683–87.

Rosenberg, D. R. (2003). Psychopharmacology of child and adolescent anxiety disorders. *Psychiatric Annals, 33*(4), 273.

Rotheram-Borus, M., Lightfoot, M., Moraes, A., Dopkins, S., & LaCour, J. (1998). Developmental, ethnic, and gender differences in ethnic identity among adolescents. *Journal of Adolescent Research, 13*(4), 487.

Rothman, E. F., Edwards, E. M., Heeren, T., & Hingson, R. (2008). Adverse childhood experiences predict earlier age of drinking onset: Results from a representative U.S. sample of current or former drinkers. *Pediatrics, 122*(2), e298–e304.

Rounds-Bryant, J. L., Kristiansen, P. L., & Hubbard, R. L. (1999). Drug abuse treatment outcome study of adolescents: A comparison of client characteristics and pretreatment behaviors in three treatment modalities. *American Journal of Drug and Alcohol Abuse, 25*(4), 573–91.

Ruble, D., Martin, C., & Berenbaum, S. (2006). Gender development. In N. Eisenberg (Ed.), *Handbook of child psychology: Social, emotional, and personality development* (pp. 858–932). Hoboken, NJ: John Wiley & Sons.

Rudolph, K., Hammen, C., & Daley, S. (2006). Mood disorders. In D. Wolfe & E. Mash (Eds.), *Behavioral and emotional disorders in adolescents: Nature, assessment, and treatment* (pp. 300). New York: The Guilford Press.

Rutter, M. (1999). Resilience concepts and findings: Implications for family therapy. *Journal of Family Therapy, 21*, 119–44.

Rutter, M. (2002). The interplay of nature, nurture, and developmental influences. *Archives of General Psychiatry, 59*, 996–203.

Rutter, M. (2006). Psychopathological development across adolescence. *Journal of Youth and Adolescence, 36*, 101–110.

Rutter, M. (2008). Developing concepts in developmental psychopathology. In J. Hudziak (Ed.), *Developmental psychopathology and wellness* (pp. 3–22). Washington, DC: American Psychiatric Publishing, Inc.

Ryan, C., & Futterman, D. (2001). Social and developmental challenges for lesbian, gay, and bisexual youth. *SIECUS Report, 29*(4), 5–18.

Ryan, J., Hernandez, P., & Herz, D. (2007). Developmental trajectories of offending for male adolescents leaving foster care. *Social Work Research, 31*(2), 83–93.

Ryan, J., & Testa, M. (2005). Child maltreatment and juvenile delinquency: Investigating the role of placement and placement instability. *Children and Youth Services Review, 27*, 227–49.

Ryan, J., Testa, M., & Zhai, F. (2008). African American males in foster care and the risk of delinquency: The value of social bonds and permanence. *Child Welfare, 87*(1), 115–40.

Sadler, L., Swartz, M., & Ryan-Krause, P. (2003). Supporting adolescent mothers and their children through a high school-based child care center and parent support program. *Journal of Pediatric Health Care, 17*(3), 109–117.

Saewyc, E., Magee, L., & Pettingell, S. (2004). Teenage pregnancy and associated risk behaviors among sexually abused adolescents. *Perspectives of Sexual and Reproductive Health, 36*(3), 98–105.

Saewyc, E., Poon, C., Homma, Y., & Skay, C. (2008). Stigma management? The links between enacted stigma and teen pregnancy trends among gay, lesbian, and bisexual students in British Columbia. *The Canadian Journal of Human Sexuality, 17*(3), 123–38.

Safren, S. A., Gonzalez, R. E., Horner, K. J., Leung, A. W., & et al. (2000). Anxiety in ethnic minority youth. *Behavior Modification, 24*(2), 147.

Saltzburg, S. (2005). Co-constructing adolescence for gay and lesbian youth and their families. In G. Mallon & P. Hess (Eds.), *Child welfare for the 21st century: A handbook of practices, policies, and programs* (pp. 212–27). New York: Columbia University Press.

Salzinger, S., Rosario, M., & Feldman, R. (2007). Physical child abuse and adolescent violent delinquency: The mediating and moderating roles of personal relationships. *Child Maltreatment, 12*(3), 208–129.

Salzinger, S., Rosario, M., Feldman, R., & Ng-Mak, D. (2007). Adolescent suicidal behavior: Associations with preadolescent physical abuse and selected risk and protective factors. *Journal of the American Academy of Child and Adolescent Psychiatry, 46*(7), 859–66.

Samuels, G. (2008). *A reason, a season, or a lifetime: Relational permanence among young adults with foster care backgrounds.* Chicago: Chapin Hall Center for Children at the University of Chicago.

Samuels, G. (2009). Ambiguous loss of home: The experience of familial (im) permanence among young adults with foster care backgrounds. *Children and Youth Services Review, 31*, 1229–39.

Samuels, G., & Pryce, J. (2008). "What doesn't kill you makes you stronger": Survivalist self-reliance as resilience and risk among young adults aging out of foster care. *Children and Youth Services Review, 30*, 1198–1210.

Sanders, D. (2003). Toward creating a policy of permanence for America's disposable children: The evolution of federal funding statutes for foster care from 1961 to the present. *International Journal of Law, Policy, and the Family, 17*(2), 211–243.

Scannapieco, M., Connell-Carrick, K., & Painter, K. (2007). In their own words: Challenges facing youth aging out of foster care. *Child and Adolescent Social Work Journal, 24*, 423–35.

Scannapieco, M., Schagrin, J., & Scannapieco, T. (1995). Independent living programs: Do they make a difference? *Child and Adolescent Social Work Journal, 12*(5), 381–89.

Schneider, R., Baumrind, N., & Kimerling, R. (2007). Exposure to child abuse and risk for mental health problems in women. *Violence and Victims, 22*(5), 620.

Schneider, R., Burnette, M. L., & Timko, C. (2008). History of physical or sexual abuse and participation in 12-step self-help groups. *American Journal of Drug and Alcohol Abuse, 34*(5), 617–25.

Schofield, G., & Beek, M. (2005). Risk and resilience in long-term foster-care. *British Journal of Social Work, 35*, 1283.

Schore, A. (2003). *Affect regulation and the repair of the self.* New York: W. W. Norton & Company.

Schore, A. (2003). Early relational trauma, disorganized attachment, and the development of a predisposition to violence. In M. Solomon & D. Siegel (Eds.), *Healing trauma: Attachment, mind, body, and brain* (pp. 107–67). New York: W. W. Norton & Company.

Schore, J., & Schore, A. (2008). Modern attachment theory: The central role of affect regulation in development and treatment. *Clinical Social Work Journal, 36*(9), 9–20.

Schorr, A. (2000). The bleak prospect for public child welfare. *Social Service Review, March 2000*, 124–36.

Schwartz, A. (2008). Connective complexity: African American adolescents and the relational context of kinship foster care. *Child Welfare, 87*(2), 77–97.

Schwartz, A., McRoy, R., & Downs, A. (2004). Adolescent mothers in a transitional living facility: An exploratory study of support networks and attachment patterns. *Journal of Adolescent Research, 19*(1), 85–111.

Schwartz, R. H. (1998). Adolescent heroin use: A review. *Pediatrics, 102*(6), 1461–66.

Scrivner, K. (2002). Crossover kids: The dilemma of the abused delinquent. *Family Court Review, 40*, 135–54.

Sellers, R., Caldwell, C., Schmeelk-Cone, K., & Zimmerman, M. (2003). Racial identity, racial discrimination, perceived stress, and psychological distress among African American young adults. *Journal of Health and Social Behavior, 43*, 302–317.

Sewitch, M. J., Blais, R., Rahme, E., Bexton, B., & Galarneau, S. (2005). Pharmacological response to depressive disorders among adolescents. *Psychiatric Services, 56*(9), 1089.

Shader, M. (2001). *Risk factors for delinquency: An overview.* Washington, DC: U.S. Department of Justice, Office of Juvenile Justice and Delinquency Prevention.

Shea, A., Walsh, C., MacMillan, H., & Steiner, M. (2004). Child maltreatment and HPA axis dysregulation: Relationship to major depressive disorder and posttraumatic stress disorder in females. *Psychoneuroendocrinology, 30*, 162–78.

Shedler, J. (2010). The efficacy of psychodynamic psychotherapy. *American Psychologist, 65*(2), 98–109.

Sheehy, A., Oldham, E., Zanghi, M., Ansell, D., Correia, P., & Copeland, R. (2000). *Promising practices: Supporting the transition of youth served by the foster care system.* Baltimore, MD: Annie E. Casey Foundation.

Sher, L. (2004). Recognizing post-traumatic stress disorder. *Quarterly Journal of Medicine, 97*, 1–5.

Shin, S. (2003). Building evidence to promote educational competence of youth in foster care. *Child Welfare, 82*(5), 615–32.

Shin, S. H. (2005). Need for actual use of mental health service by adolescents in the child welfare system. *Children and Youth Services Review, 27*, 1071.

Shirk, M., & Stangler, G. (2006). *On their own: What happens to kids when they age out of the foster care system?* 245-287. New York: Basic Books.

Shirk, S., & Karver, M. (2003). Prediction of treatment outcome from relationship variables in child and adolescent therapy: A meta-analytic review. *Journal of Consulting and Clinical Psychology, 71*(3), 452–64.

Shirk, S. R., Gudmundsen, G., Kaplinski, H. C., & McMakin, D. L. (2008). Alliance and outcome in cognitive-behavioral therapy for adolescent depression. *Journal of Clinical Child and Adolescent Psychology, 37*(3), 631.

Shook, J., Vaughn, M., Litschge, C., Kolivoski, K., & Schelbe, L. (2009). The importance of friends among foster youth aging out of care: Cluster profiles of deviant peer affiliations. *Children and Youth Services Review, 31*, 284–91.

Siegel, D. (2003). An interpersonal neurobiology of psychotherapy: The developing mind and the resolution of trauma. In M. Solomon & D. Siegel (Eds.), *Healing trauma: Attachment, mind, body, and brain* (pp. 1–56). New York: W. W. Norton & Company.

Sieger, K., & Renk, K. (2007). Pregnant and parenting adolescents: A study of ethnic identity, emotional and behavioral functioning, child characteristics, and social support. *Journal of Youth and Adolescence, 36,* 567–81.

Sihvola, E., Rose, R., Dick, D., Pulkkinen, L., Marttunen, M., & Kaprio, J. (2008). Early-onset depressive disorders predict the use of addictive substances in adolescence: A prospective study of adolescent Finnish twins. *Addiction, 103,* 2045–53.

Silenzio, V. M. B., Pena, J. B., Duberstein, P. R., Cerel, J., & Knox, K. L. (2007). Sexual orientation and risk factors for suicidal ideation and suicide attempts among adolescents and young adults. *American Journal of Public Health, 97*(11), 2017.

Silverman, W., Pina, A., & Viswesvaran, C. (2008). Evidence-based psychosocial treatments for phobic and anxiety disorders in children and adolescents. *Journal of Clinical Child and Adolescent Psychology, 37*(1), 105–30.

Simon, G. E., Savarino, J., Operskalski, B., & Wang, P. S. (2006). Suicide risk during antidepressant treatment. *American Journal of Psychiatry, 163*(1), 41.

Simon, V., & Feiring, C. (2008). Sexual anxiety and eroticism predict the development of sexual problems in youth with a history of sexual abuse. *Child Maltreatment, 13*(2), 167–81.

Slesnick, N., Kaminer, Y., & Kelly, J. (2008). Most common psychosocial interventions for substance use disorders. In Y. Kaminer & O. Bukstein (Eds.), *Adolescent substance abuse: Psychiatric comorbidity and high-risk behaviors* (pp. 111–44). New York: Routledge.

Smetana, J., Campione-Barr, N., & Metzger, A. (2006). Adolescent development in interpersonal and societal contexts. *Annual Review of Psychology, 57,* 255–84.

Snyder, H., & Sickmund, M. (2006). *Juvenile offenders and victims: 2006 National Report.* Washington, DC: U.S. Department of Justice, Office of Justice Programs, Office of Juvenile Justice and Delinquency Prevention.

Snyder, J., & Rogers, K. (2002). The violent adolescent: The urge to destroy versus the urge to feel alive. *The American Journal of Psychoanalysis, 62*(3), 237–53.

Society for Neuroscience (2008). *Mirror neurons.* (Nov.) Retrieved January 29, 2010, from http://www.sfn.org/index.aspx?pagename=brainBriefings_MirrorNeurons.

Solomon, J., & George, C. (1999). The measurement of attachment security in infancy and childhood. In J. Cassidy & P. Shaver (Eds.), *Handbook of attachment: Theory, research, and clinical applications* (pp. 287–316). New York: The Guilford Press.

Solomon, J., & George, C. (1999). The place of disorganization in attachment theory: Linking classic observations with contemporary findings. In J. Solomon & C. George (Eds.), *Attachment disorganization* (pp. 3–32). New York: The Guilford Press.

Southam-Gerow, M., & Kendall, P. (2002). Emotion regulation and understanding: Implications for child psychopathology and therapy. *Clinical Psychology Review, 22*(2), 189–222.

Southerland, D., Casanueva, C., & Ringeisen, H. (2009). Young adult outcomes and mental health problems among transition age youth investigated for maltreatment during adolescence. *Children and Youth Services Review, 31,* 947–56.

Sowell, E., Thompson, P., Homes, C., Jernigan, T., & Toga, A. (1999). In vivo evidence for post-adolescent brain maturation in frontal and striatal regions. *Nature Neuroscience, 2*(10), 859–61.

Soydan, H. (2006). Improving the teaching of evidence-based practice—challenges and priorities. Symposium at University of Texas, Austin, October 2006.

Sroufe, L. A., Egeland, B., Carlson, E. A., & Collins, W. A. (2005). *The development of the person: The Minnesota Study of Risk and Adaptation from Birth to Adulthood.* New York: The Guilford Press.

Sroufe, L., & Fleeson, J. (1986). Attachment and the construction of relationships. In W. Hartup & Z. Rubin (Eds.), *Relationships and development* (pp. 51–72). Hillsdale, NJ: Lawrence Erlbaum Associates.

Stein, B., Zima, B., Elliott, M., Burnam, M., Shahinfar, A., Fox, N., & Leavitt, L. (2001). Violence exposure among school-age children in foster care: Relationship to distress symptoms. *Journal of the American Academy of Child and Adolescent Psychiatry, 40*(5), 588–94.

Stein, M. (2006). Research review: Young people leaving care. *Child and Family Social Work, 11,* 273–79.

Stein, M. B., Fuetsch, M., Muller, N., Hofler, M., Lieb, R., & Wittchen, H. (2001). Social anxiety disorder and the risk of depression: A prospective community study of adolescents and young adults. *Archives of General Psychiatry, 58*(3), 251.

Steiner, H., & Dunne, J. (1997). Summary of the practice parameters for the assessment and treatment of children and adolescents with conduct disorder. *Journal of the American Academy of Child and Adolescent Psychiatry, 36*(10), 1482–85.

Stevens-Simon, C., Kelly, L., & Kulick, R. (2001). A village would be nice but…it takes a long-acting contraceptive to prevent repeat adolescent pregnancies. *American Journal of Preventive Medicine, 21*(1), 60–65.

Steward, A., Livingston, M., & Dennison, S. (2008). Transitions and turning points: Examining the links between child maltreatment and juvenile offending. *Child Abuse & Neglect, 32,* 51–66.

Stewart, E., & Simons, R. (2006). Structure and culture in African American adolescent violence: A partial test of the "code of the street" thesis. *Justice Quarterly, 1,* 1–33.

Stewart, P. (2004). Afrocentric approaches to working with African American families. *Families in Society: The Journal of Contemporary Social Services, 85*(2), 221–28.

Stoltzfus, E. (2008). *Child welfare: The Fostering Connections to Success and Increasing Adoptions Act of 2008* (No. RL34704). Washington, DC: Congressional Research Service.

Stoolmiller, M., & Bleckman, E. (2005). Substance use is a robust predictor of adolescent recidivism. *Criminal Justice and Behavior, 32*(3), 302–28.

Stovall-McClough, K. C., & Cloitre, M. (2006). Unresolved attachment, PTSD, and dissociation in women with childhood abuse histories. *Journal of Consulting and Clinical Psychology, 74*(2), 219.

Stuewig, J., & McCloskey, L. (2005). The relation of child maltreatment to shame and guilt among adolescents: Psychological routes to depression and delinquency. *Child Maltreatment, 10*(4), 324–36.

Sullivan, C., Sommer, S., & Moff, J. (2001). *Youth in the margins: A report on the unmet needs of lesbian, gay, bisexual, and transgender adolescents in foster care.* New York: Lambda Legal Defense & Education Fund.

Sullivan, M., Bennett, D., Carpenter, K., & Lewis, M. (2008). Emotion knowledge in young neglected children. *Child Maltreatment, 13*(3), 301–306.

Suris, J., Michaud, P., & Viner, R. (2004). The adolescent with a chronic condition. Part I: Developmental issues. *Archives of Disease in Childhood, 89*, 938–42.

Swann, C., & Sylvester, M. (2006). The foster care crisis: What caused caseloads to grow? *Demography, 43*(2), 309–35.

Tanner, J. (2006). Recentering during emerging adulthood: A critical turning point in life span human development. In J. Arnett & J. Tanner (Eds.), *Emerging adults in America: Coming of age in the 21st century* (pp. 21–55). Washington, DC: American Psychological Association.

Tarolla, S., Wagner, E., Rabinowitz, J., & Tubman, J. (2002). Understanding and treating juvenile offenders: A review of current knowledge and future directions. *Aggression and Violent Behavior, 7*(2), 125–43.

Tarren-Sweeney, M. (2008). The mental health of children in out-of-home care. *Current Opinion in Psychiatry, 21*(4), 345.

Tarullo, A., & Gunnar, M. (2006). Child maltreatment and the developing HPA axis. *Hormones and Behavior, 50*, 632–39.

Taussig, H., Clyman, R., & Landsverk, J. (2001). Children who return home from foster care: A 6 year prospective study of behavioral health outcomes in adolescence. *Pediatrics, 108*(1), 1-7.

Taussig, H. N. (2002). Risk behaviors in maltreated youth placed in foster care: A longitudinal study of protective and vulnerability factors. *Child Abuse & Neglect, 26*, 1179–99.

Teicher, M., Andersen, S., Polcari, A., Anderson, C., Navalta, C., & Kim, D. (2003). The neurobiological consequences of early stress and childhood maltreatment. *Neuroscience & Biobehavioral Reviews, 27*(1–2), 33–44.

Teicher, M., Samson, J., Polcari, A., & McGreenery, C. (2006). Sticks, stones, and hurtful words: Relative effects of various forms of maltreatment. *American Journal of Psychiatry, 163*(6), 993–1000.

Teisl, M., & Cicchetti, D. (2008). Physical abuse, cognitive and emotional processes, and aggressive/disruptive behavior problems. *Social Development, 17*(1), 1–23.

Testa, M. (2005). The quality of permanence—lasting or binding? Subsidized guardianship and kinship foster care as alternatives to adoption. *Virginia Journal of Social Policy & the Law, 12*(3), 499–534.

Texas Health and Human Services Commission & Department of Family and Protective Services (2006). *Disproportionality in Child Protective Services—Policy Evaluation and Remediation Plan.* Midland, Texas: Texas Health and Human Services Commission.

Thelen, E. (2005). Dynamic systems theory and the complexity of change. *Psychoanalytic Dialogues, 15*(2), 255.

Thomas, W., Stubbe, D., & Pearson, G. (1999). Race, juvenile justice, and mental health: New dimensions in measuring pervasive bias. *Journal of Criminal Law & Criminology, 89*(2), 615–69.

Thombs, D. L. (1994). *Introduction to addictive behaviors.*49-138. New York: The Guilford Press.

Thompson Jr., R. G., & Auslander, W. F. (2007). Risk factors for alcohol and marijuana use among adolescents in foster care. *Journal of Substance Abuse Treatment, 32*(1), 61–69.

Thompson, V., Bazile, A., & Akbar, M. (2004). African Americans' perceptions of psychotherapy and psychotherapists. *Professional Psychology: Research and Practice, 35*(1), 19.

Thornberry, R., Smith, C., & Howard, G. (1997). Risk factors for teenage fatherhood. *Journal of Marriage and the Family, 59*, 505–22.

Tiet, Q. Q., Bird, H. R., Hoven, C. W., & Moore, R. (2001). Relationship between specific adverse life events and psychiatric disorders. *Journal of Abnormal Child Psychology, 29*(2), 153.

Todis, B., Bullis, M., Waintrup, M., Schultz, R., & D'Ambrosio, R. (2001). Overcoming the odds: Qualitative examination of resilience among formerly incarcerated adolescents. *Exceptional Children, 68*(1), 119–39.

Tolin, D., & Foa, E. (2006). Sex differences in trauma and posttraumatic stress disorder: A quantitative review of 25 years of research. *Psychological Bulletin, 132*(6), 959–92.

Troiden, R. (1988). Homosexual identity development. *Journal of Adolescent Health, 9*, 105–113.

Trowell, J., Joffe, I., Campbell, J., Clemente, C., Almqvist, F., Soininen, M., Koskenranta-Aalto, U., Weintraub, S., Kolaitis, G., Tomaras, V., Anastasopoulos, D., Grayson, K., Barnes, J., & Tsiantis, J. (2007). Childhood depression: A place for psychotherapy: An outcome study comparing individual psychodynamic psychotherapy and family therapy. *European Child & Adolescent Psychiatry, 16*(3), 157.

Tubman, J., Montgomery, M., Gil, A., & Wagner, E. (2004). Abuse experiences in a community sample of young adults: Relations with psychiatric disorders, sexual risk behaviors, and sexually transmitted diseases. *American Journal of Community Psychology, 34*(1), 147–62.

Tubman, J., Wagner, E., Gil, A., & Pate, K. (2002). Brief motivational intervention for substance-abusing delinquent adolescents: Guided self-change as a social work practice innovation. *Health & Social Work, 27*(3), 208–212.

Tucker, J. S., Ellickson, P. L., Orlando, M., Martino, S. C., & Klein, D. J. (2005). Substance use trajectories from early adolescence to emerging adulthood: A comparison of smoking, binge drinking, and marijuana use. *Journal of Drug Issues, 35*(2), 307–31.

Turner, R., Sorenson, A., & Turner, J. (2000). Social contingencies in mental health: A seven-year follow-up study of teenage mothers. *Journal of Marriage and the Family, 62*, 777–91.

Tyler, K., Johnson, K., & Brownridge, D. (2008). A longitudinal study of the effects of child maltreatment on later outcomes among high-risk adolescents. *Journal of Youth and Adolescence, 37*, 506–21.

Tyler, K., & Johnson, K. (2006). A longitudinal study of the effects of early abuse on later victimization among high-risk adolescents. *Violence and Victims, 21*(3), 287–306.

Tyler, K. A., Stone, R. T., & Bersani, B. (2006). Examining the changing influence of predictors on adolescent alcohol misuse. *Journal of Child & Adolescent Substance Abuse, 16*(2), 95–114.

U.S. Census Bureau (2010). *State and county QuickFacts*. Retrieved January 18, 2010, from http://www.census.gov.libproxy.usc.edu/qfd/states/00000.html.

U.S. Congressional Research Service (2008). *H.R. 6893: Fostering Connections to Success and Increasing Adoptions Act of 2008: summary*. Washington, DC: U.S. Library of Congress.

U.S. Department of Health and Human Services, Administration for Children and Families (2000). *Report to the Congress on kinship foster care*. Washington, DC: U.S. Department of Health and Human Services, p. vii. Retrieved from http://aspe.hhs.gov/hsp/kinr2c00/full.pdf.

U.S. Department of Health and Human Services, Administration for Children and Families (2006). *The AFCARS Report* (No. 13). Washington, DC: U.S. Department of Health and Human Services. Retrieved from http://www.acf. hhs.gov/programs/cb/stats_research/afcars/tar/report13.htm.

U.S. Department of Health and Human Services, Administration for Children and Families, Administration on Children Youth and Families Children's Bureau (2008). *Child maltreatment and fatality statistics 2006*. Washington, DC: U.S. Department of Health and Human Services, Administration for Children & Families, p.3.

U.S. Department of Health and Human Services, Administration for Children and Families, Administration on Children, Youth, Families, Children's Bureau (2009). *The AFCARS Report FY 2008 estimates* (No. 16). Washington, DC: U.S. Department of Health and Human Services, Administration for Children & Families Retrieved from http://www.acf.hhs.gov/programs/cb/stats_ research/afcars/tar/report16.htm.

U.S. Department of Health and Human Services, Health Resources and Services Administration, Maternal and Child Health Bureau (2004). *Child health USA 2004*. Rockville, MD: U.S. Department of Health and Human Services. Retrieved from http://mchb.hrsa.gov/mchirc/chusa_04/pages/0301pc.htm.

U.S. General Accounting Office, Health, Education, and Human Services Division (1999). *Foster care: Effectiveness of independent living services unknown* (No. GAO/HEHS-00-13). Washington, DC: U.S. General Accounting Office.

Ueno, K. (2005). Sexual orientation and psychological distress in adolescence: Examining interpersonal stressors and social support processes. *Social Psychology Quarterly, 68*(3), 258–77.

Umana-Taylor, A., Diversi, M., & Fine, M. (2002). Ethnic identity and self-esteem of Latino adolescents: Distinctions among the Latino populations. *Journal of Adolescent Research, 17*(3), 303–27.

Unger, J., Kipke, M., Simon, T., Montgomery, S., & Johnson, C. (1997). Homeless youths and young adults in Los Angeles: Prevalence of mental health problems and the relationship between mental health and substance abuse disorders. *American Journal of Community Psychology, 25*(3), 371.

United Friends of the Children (2010). Retrieved February 19, 2010, from www. unitedfriends.org/about-ufc/faq.

Unrau, Y. (2007). Research on placement moves: Seeking the perspective of foster children. *Children and Youth Services Review, 29*, 122–37.

Unrau, Y., & Grinnell, R. (2005). Exploring out-of-home placement as a moderator of help-seeking behavior among adolescents who are at high risk. *Research on Social Work Practice, 15*(6), 516–30.

Unrau, Y., Seita, J., & Putney, K. (2008). Former foster youth remember multiple placement moves: A journey of loss and hope. *Children and Youth Services Review, 30*, 1256–66.

Vaddiparti, K., Bogetto, J., Callahan, C., Abdallah, A., Spitznagel, E., & Cottler, L. (2006). The effects of childhood trauma on sex trading in substance-using women. *Archives of Sexual Behavior, 35,* 451–59.

van der Kolk, B. (1996). The complexity of adaptation to trauma: Self-regulation, stimulus discrimination, and characterological development. In B. van der Kolk, A. McFarlane, & L. Wiesaeth (Eds.), *Traumatic stress: The effects of overwhelming experience on mind, body, and society* (pp. 182). New York: The Guilford Press.

Varela, R. E., Weems, C. F., Berman, S. L., Hensley, L., & de Bernal, M. C. R. (2007). Internalizing symptoms in Latinos: The role of anxiety sensitivity. *Journal of Youth Adolescence, 36,* 429.

Vaughn, M. G., Ollie, M. T., McMillen, J. C., Scott Jr., L., & Munson, M. (2007). Substance use and abuse among older youth in foster care. *Addictive Behaviors, 32,* 1929–35.

Velting, O. N., Setzer, N. J., & Albano, A. M. (2004). Update on and advances in assessment and cognitive-behavioral treatment of anxiety disorders in children and adolescents. *Professional Psychology: Research and Practice, 35*(1), 42.

Venet, M., Bureau, J., Gosselin, C., & Capuano, F. (2008). Attachment representations in a sample of neglected preschool-age children. *School Psychology International, 28*(3), 264–93.

Verdejo-Garcia, A., Lopez-Torrecillas, F., Gimenez, C. O., & Perez-Garcia, M. (2004). Clinical implications and methodological challenges in the study of the neuropsychological correlates of cannabis, stimulant, and opioid abuse. *Neuropsychology Review, 14*(1), 1–41.

Vermeiren, R., Jespers, I., & Moffitt, T. (2006). Mental health problems in juvenile justice populations. *Child and Adolescent Psychiatric Clinics of North America, 15,* 333–51.

Vinnerljung, B., Hjern, A., & Lindblad, F. (2006). Suicide attempts and severe psychiatric morbidity among former child welfare clients—a national cohort study. *Journal of Child Psychology and Psychiatry, 47*(7), 723–33.

Vorhies, V., Glover, C., Davis, K., Hardin, T., Krzyzanowski, A., Harris, M., Fagan, M., & Wilkniss, S. (2009). Improving outcomes for pregnant and parenting foster care youth with severe mental illness: An evaluation of a transitional living program. *Psychiatric Rehabilitation Journal, 33*(2), 115–24.

Wade, J. (2008). The ties that bind: Support from birth families and substitute families for young people leaving care. *British Journal of Social Work, 38,* 39–54.

Wagner, M., Newman, L., Cameto, R., & Levine, P. (2005). *Changes over time in the early post-school outcomes of youth with disabilities: A report of findings from the National Longitudinal Transition Study (NLTS) and the National Longitudinal Transition Study 2 (NLTS2)* (No. SRI Project P11182). Menlo Park, CA: SRI International.

Waldron, H. B., & Turner, C. W. (2008). Evidence-based psychosocial treatments for adolescent substance abuse. *Journal of Clinical Child and Adolescent Psychology, 37*(1), 238–61.

Wallis, P., & Steele, H. (2001). Attachment representations in adolescence: Further evidence from psychiatric settings. *Attachment and Human Development, 3*(3), 259–68.

Walls, N., Freedenthal, S., & Wisneski, H. (2008). Suicidal ideation and attempts among sexual minority youths receiving social services. *Social Work*, 53(1), 21–29.

Ward, R. (2009). *"I took a break, but now I'm back": Foster youths' perspectives on leaving and returning*. (Unpublished Ph.D. dissertation). Boston, MA: Boston University. (UMI number 3363651).

Wardenski, J. (2005). A minor exception?: The impact of *Lawrence v. Texas* on LGBT youth. *Journal of Criminal Law & Criminology*, 95(4), 1363–1410.

Warren, S., Huston, L., Egeland, B., & Sroufe, A. (1997). Child and adolescent anxiety disorders and early attachment. *Journal of the American Academy of Child and Adolescent Psychiatry*, 36(5), 637–44.

Washburn, J., Romero, E., Welty, L., Abram, K., Teplin, L., McClelland, G., & Paskar, L. (2007). Development of antisocial personality disorder in detained youths: The predictive value of mental disorders. *Journal of Consulting and Clinical Psychology*, 75(2), 221–31.

Washburn, J., Teplin, L., Voss, L., Simon, C., Abram, K., & McClelland, G. (2008). Psychiatric disorders among detained youths: A comparison of youths processed in juvenile court and adult criminal court. *Psychiatric Services*, 59(9), 965–73.

Watkins, J. (1999). Commitment to care: Managed care and child incarceration. *Journal of Psychosocial Nursing & Mental Health Services*, 37(2), 24–29.

Watt, T. T., & Sharp, S. F. (2002). Race differences in strains associated with suicidal behavior among adolescents. *Youth and Society*, 34(2), 232.

Webb, M., & Harden, B. (2003). Beyond child protection: Promoting mental health for children and families in the child welfare system. *Journal of Emotional and Behavioral Disorders*, 11(1), 49–58.

Weed, K., Keogh, D., & Borkowski, J. (2006). Stability of resilience in children of adolescent mothers. *Applied Developmental Psychology*, 27, 60–77.

Weinberg, L. (2007). *The systematic mistreatment of children in the foster care system: Through the cracks*. New York: The Haworth Press.

Weiss, S. R. B., Kung, H., & Pearson, J. L. (2003). Emerging issues in gender and ethnic differences in substance abuse and treatment. *Current Women's Health Reports*, 3(245), 253.

Wells, M., & Zunz, S. (2009). Chafee educational and training voucher programs: System coordination in rural New England. *Child and Adolescent Social Work Journal*, 26, 103–20.

Welte, C. (1997). *Detailed summary of the Adoption and Safe Families Act*. Retrieved May 29, 2009, from http://www.casanet.org/reference/asfa-summary.htm.

Wertheimer, R. (2002). *Youth who "age out" of foster care: Troubled lives, troubling prospects* (No. 2002-59). Washington, DC: Child Trends.

Westen, D., Nakash, O., Cannon, T., & Bradley, R. (2006). Clinical assessment of attachment patterns and personality disorder in adolescents and adults. *Journal of Consulting and Clinical Psychology*, 74(6), 1065–85.

Westen, D., Novotny, C., & Thompson-Brenner, H. (2004). The empirical status of empirically supported psychotherapies: Assumptions, findings, and reporting in controlled clinical trials. *Psychological Bulletin*, 130(4), 631–33.

Whaley, A. (1997). Ethnicity/race, paranoia, and psychiatric diagnoses: Clinician bias versus sociocultural differences. *Journal of Psychopathology and Behavioral Assessment*, 19(1), 1–20.

Whaley, A., & Davis, K. (2007). Cultural competence and evidence-based practice in mental health services: A complementary perspective. *American Psychologist, 62*(6), 563–74.

Wheeler, K. (2007). Psychotherapeutic strategies for healing trauma. *Perspectives in Psychiatric Care, 43*(3), 132–41.

White, C., Havalchak, A., Jackson, L., O'Brien, K., & Pecora, P. (2007). *Executive summary: Mental health, ethnicity, sexuality, and spirituality among youth in foster care* (No. 311.1-3030-07). Seattle, WA: Research Services at Casey Family Programs.

White, C., O'Brien, K., Jackson, L., Havalchak, A., Phillips, C., Thomas, P., & Cabrera, J. (2008). Ethnic identity development among adolescents in foster care. *Child and Adolescent Social Work Journal, 25*, 497–515.

White, C., O'Brien, K., Pecora, P., English, D., Williams, J., & Phillips, C. (2009). Depression among alumni of foster care: Decreasing rates through improvement of experiences in care. *Journal of Emotional and Behavioral Disorders, 17*(1), 38–48.

Whitmore, E., & Riggs, P. (2006). Developmentally informed diagnostic and treatment considerations in comorbid conditions. In H. Liddle & C. Rowe (Eds.), *Adolescent substance abuse: Research and clinical advances* (pp. 264–83). Cambridge, UK: Cambridge University Press.

Wilcox, H. C., Storr, C. L., & Breslau, N. (2009). Posttraumatic stress disorder and suicide attempts in a community sample of urban American young adults. *Archives of General Psychiatry, 66*(3), 305.

Wilkinson, G. B., Taylor, P., & Holt, J. R. (2002). Bipolar disorder in adolescence: Diagnosis and treatment. *Journal of Mental Health Counseling, 24*(4), 348.

Williams, T., Connolly, J., Pepler, D., & Craig, W. (2005). Peer victimization, social support, and psychosocial adjustment of sexual minority adolescents. *Journal of Youth and Adolescence, 34*(5), 471–82.

Windle, M., & Wiesner, M. (2004). Trajectories of marijuana use from adolescence to young adulthood: Predictors and outcomes. *Development and Psychopathology, 16*(4), 1007–27.

Winters, K., Stinchfield, R., & Bukstein, O. (2008). Assessing adolescent substance use and abuse. In Y. Kaminer & O. Bukstein (Eds.), *Adolescent substance abuse: Psychiatric comorbidity and high-risk behaviors* (pp. 53–86). New York: Routledge.

Wise, L. A., Zierier, S., Krieger, N., & Harlow, B. L. (2001). Adult onset of major depressive disorder in relation to early life violent victimisation: A case-control study. *The Lancet, 358*(9285), 881.

Wolfe, D., & Mash, E. (2006). Behavioral and emotional problems in adolescence: Overview and issues. In D. Wolfe & E. Mash (Eds.), *Behavioral and emotional disorders in adolescents: Nature, assessment, and treatment* (p. 3). New York: The Guilford Press.

Woodward, L. J., & Fergusson, D. M. (2001). Life course outcomes of young people with anxiety disorders in adolescence. *Journal of the American Academy of Child and Adolescent Psychiatry, 40*(9), 1086.

Wrenn, L. J. (2003). Trauma: Conscious and unconscious meaning. *Clinical Social Work Journal, 31*(2), 123–37.

Wright, E., & Perry, B. (2006). Sexual identity distress, social support, and the health of gay, lesbian, and bisexual youth. *Journal of Homosexuality, 51*(1), 81–110.

Wright, J., & Cullen, F. (2004). Employment, peers, and life-course transitions. *Justice Quarterly, 21*(1), 183–205.

Wright, M., Crawford, E., & Del Castillo, D. (2009). Childhood emotional maltreatment and later psychological distress among college students: The mediating role of maladaptive schemas. *Child Abuse & Neglect, 33*, 59–68.

Wu, P., Hoven, C. W., Okezie, N., Fuller, C. J., & Cohen, P. (2007). Alcohol abuse and depression in children and adults. *Journal of Child & Adolescent Substance Abuse, 17*(2), 51–69.

Wulczyn, F., Kogan, J., & Harden, B. (2003). Placement stability and movement trajectories. *Social Service Review, 77*(12), 212–36.

Yancey, A. (1998). Building positive self-image in adolescents in foster care: The use of role models in an interactive group approach. *Adolescence, 33*(130), 253–67.

Yancey, A., Aneshensel, C., & Driscoll, A. (2001). The assessment of ethnic identity in a diverse urban youth population. *Journal of Black Psychology, 27*(2), 190–208.

Yates, T. (2009). Developmental pathways from child maltreatment to nonsuicidal self-injury. In M. Nock (Ed.), *Understanding nonsuicidal self-injury: Origins, assessment, and treatment* (pp. 117–37). Washington, DC: American Psychological Association.

Yeh, C., & Hwang, M. (2000). Interdependence in ethnic identity and self: Implications for theory and practice. *Journal of Counseling and Development, 78*, 420–29.

Young, R. (1983). Career development of adolescents: An ecological perspective. *Journal of Youth and Adolescence, 12*(5), 401–417.

Zarrett, N., & Eccles, J. (2006). The passage to adulthood: Challenges of late adolescence. *New Directions for Youth Development, 111*, 13–28.

Zeanah, C., Mammen, O., & Lieberman, A. (1993). Disorders of attachment. In C. Zeanah Jr. (Ed.), *Handbook of infant mental health* (pp. 332–49). New York: The Guilford Press.

Zeitlin, A., Weinberg, L., & Kimm, C. (2004). Improving education outcomes for children in foster care: Intervention by an education liaison. *Journal of Education for Students Placed at Risk, 9*(4), 421–29.

Zhang, S., & Zhang, L. (2005). An experimental study of the Los Angeles County Repeat Offender Prevention Program: Its implementation and evaluation. *Criminology & Public Policy, 4*(2), 205–36.

Zima, B., Bussing, R., Crecelius, G., Kaufman, A., & Belin, T. (1999). Psychotropic medication use among children in foster care: Relationship to severe psychiatric disorders. *American Journal of Public Health, 89*(11), 1732–35.

Zimmerman, P., Wittchen, H. -., Hofler, M., Pfister, H., Kessler, R. C., & Lieb, R. (2003). Primary anxiety disorders and the development of subsequent alcohol use disorders: A 4-year community study of adolescents and young adults. *Psychological Medicine, 33*(7), 1211.

Zito, J., Safer, D., Devadatta, S., Gardner, J., Thomas, D., Coombes, P., Dubowski, M., & Mendez-Lewis, M. (2008). Psychotropic medication patterns among youth in foster care. *Pediatrics, 121*(1), e157–63.

INDEX